Advance Praise for
DYNAMIC URBAN DESIGN

Michael von Hausen has given us a clear and hopeful path to the creation of a sustainable urbanism, one that will be inspiring and instructive to practitioners, students, and all those who are focused on the most fundamental issue of our time.
  —Jim Adams, architect and principal, McCann Adams Studio, Austin, Texas

Dynamic Urban Design establishes Michael von Hausen as a sustainable urban design authority. Sharing insights taken from six millennia … von Hausen articulates a clearly understandable and masterfully illustrated process. The ideologies presented are universal to the human condition, while balancing public and private agendas.
                    —Kevin Harris, architect and principal, Kevin Harris Architect,
                                                              Baton Rouge, Louisiana

Michael von Hausen dissects the problems we face and concludes with a positive outlook that *design still matters. Dynamic Urban Design* is an inspired synthesis of theory and practice that proposes a tangible, viable approach to urban design and community development on a worldwide scale. As a practitioner and teacher I fully endorse the book's humanistic approach, visual clarity, and rich content.
                    —Mina Marefat, principal, Design Research, Washington, DC;
                                                        Faculty, Georgetown University

Dynamic Urban Design is an impressive effort to pull it all together as compactly as possible. We don't have time for longer tracts these days. Good for him.
                    —Andrés Duany, founding member, Congress for the New Urbanism,
                          and author of *The Smart Growth Manual* and *Suburban Nation*

Michael von Hausen contributes something valuable to the growing shelf of books on sustainable urban design—the perspective of an experienced practitioner who is also a teacher. His book is generous in sharing the lessons of a productive career for both students and experienced designers.
                              —Hank Dittmar, chief executive, Prince's Foundation for
                                                          Building Community, London, UK

This new book addresses the essential task of making sustainable urbanism the rule rather than the exception. Michael's wide experience as a practitioner and educator informs this manual-like publication, which is a worthy contribution to the ongoing campaign to influence the agenda at every level, from students and concepts to developers and implementation.
                        —Noel Isherwood, architect, urban designer, and consultant to
                          the Prince's Foundation for Building Community, London, UK

Finally, in one book a complete guide to the theory, practice, and potential of urban design by one of Canada's preeminent urban designers. Michael von Hausen has crafted a deep, rich, and compelling book that provides emerging urban designers and seasoned veterans with a carefully interwoven fabric of theory and practice.

—David R. Witty, vice president academic and provost, Vancouver Island University, former dean, School of Architecture, University of Manitoba, and former president, Canadian Institute of Planners

Michael puts forward a model, which is sustainable but endeavors to meet the aspirations and cultural needs of people everywhere. It is an ambitious book, very well researched, written, and illustrated—a welcome and truly invaluable resource for our time.

—Mark Harris, architect and principal, John R. Harris & Partners, Architects & Urban Designers, London, UK

Michael von Hausen's new book takes us far back through the history of urban design, reaching into a worldwide treasure chest of examples. This makes it both an excellent resource for European architects, as well as an interesting read. Especially noteworthy is its qualified and highly professional attention to "public space"—an all-too-often neglected segment of city design. Michael von Hausen's book has certainly earned its place as a standard in any architect's library.

—Michael Frank, president, frankundfeil, Architects & Urban Designers, Bad Kreuznach, Germany

Sustainable urban design is not an alternative but the only way to the future. Michael von Hausen's book intelligently combines urban design and sustainable planning as powerful allies in this transformative process for cities around the world. His book is invaluable to architects and planners in Brazil, where I practice, as hundreds of communities, towns, and cities struggle with the issues of rapid growth.

—Roberto Aflalo, architect and principal, Alfalo & Gasperini Arquitetos, São Paulo, Brazil

Michael von Hausen's book draws the world much closer, as principles espoused are applicable across cultural and geopolitical divides. Through his personal experiences and field observations, we get to share in the practice of sustainable urban design at the grassroots level and gain from the practical and philosophical discussions.

—Peter Poon, architect and principal, Peter F. Poon Architect PC, New York

Through this book, Michael von Hausen has presented a universal strategy for synthesizing urban design with sustainable urban development that can be applied anywhere in the world ... I not only wholeheartedly endorse this book but actively promote his concepts and ideas in India, a country where rapid urban development requirements have the potential of leading to the addition of the equivalent of one Chicago every year for the next two decades.

—Taranjot K. Gadhok, executive director, Human Settlement Management Institute, Housing and Urban Development Corporation, New Delhi, India

This richly illustrated book offers a wealth of information related to urban design methods, typologies, and contemporary practice that will be equally appreciated by the beginner and by the seasoned practitioner. With great erudition and clarity, Michael synthesizes theory and practice of urban design into a coherent and inspirational place-making guide.

—Sonny Tomic, manager, Centre City Planning & Implementation, Calgary, Alberta, Canada

As an elected official, I am very aware that in planning for the future of our communities we need to combine solid articulated theory with sound realistic application. Michael's book is a road map to doing it right!

—Peter Fassbender, mayor, Langley, British Columbia, Canada

Michael von Hausen's compelling new book makes us aware of the challenges of urbanization worldwide by revealing general design principles and providing tips for responsible professional practice of a universal nature, while being equally aware of the singularities of place and culture. His work calls for creative cross-disciplinary efforts capable of understanding complex environmental, socioeconomic, cultural, and physical conditions in order to provide frameworks to envision and sustain high-quality urban scenarios.

—David Gouverneur, former national director of urban planning in Venezuela; associate professor at the Department of Landscape Architecture, University of Pennsylvania

—Oscar Grauer, Planning Division of Petróleos de Venezuela SA; Robert F. Kennedy Visiting Professor at Harvard University, Spring 2011 (Gouverneur and Grauer are cofounders of the Urban Design Program at Universidad Metropolitana in Caracas, Venezuela)

Von Hausen's … examples of real-world experience provide a comprehensive approach to designing cities that retain long-term economic and human value. The suggested process elevates design above the often "cookbook" … zoning techniques into solution sets that are a "good fit" within the nuances, challenges, and subtleties of real living communities. Although there have been many books written on the subject, Michael captures where we are today and the current emerging challenges and potential solutions and methodologies to deal with them.

—Steven Kellenberg, vice president/principal, AECOM Design + Planning, Irvine, California

Thank you, Michael, for your commitment to transforming community vision into sustainable action plans. This amazing resource book is destined to become a valued reference guide in every planner's library. Your passion for excellence in design and sustainability principles is your legacy.

—Gerald Minchuk, director of development services and economic development, Langley, British Columbia, Canada

DYNAMIC
URBAN DESIGN

A HANDBOOK FOR CREATING SUSTAINABLE COMMUNITIES WORLDWIDE

MICHAEL A. VON HAUSEN

iUniverse, Inc.
Bloomington

Dynamic Urban Design
A Handbook for Creating Sustainable Communities Worldwide

iUniverse books may be ordered through booksellers or by contacting:

iUniverse
1663 Liberty Drive
Bloomington, IN 47403
www.iuniverse.com
1-800-Authors (1-800-288-4677)

ISBN: 978-1-4759-4989-6 (sc)
ISBN: 978-1-4759-4987-2 (hc)
ISBN: 978-1-4759-4988-9 (e)

Printed in the United States of America

iUniverse rev. date: 12/21/2012

To my family, Laura and Athena, who support me, help edit my work, and inspire me to reach higher. My love and deep gratitude go out to my parents, Bill and Clare, and my uncle Henning, who planted the seeds for my endless curiosity, pointing out the wealth of knowledge that sits at our fingertips

CONTENTS

FOREWORD

Michael von Hausen is upping his game. The goal: to take urban design to a higher level. His vision: a universal strategy that unites urban design and sustainability in a practical, measured way. By being rooted in the local community through his research and practice, Michael has developed a process he believes can be applied anywhere in the world.

Michael uniquely combines teaching and decades of experience in both private and public practice, and he knows from experience and observation that urban design can become isolated, unable to overcome those disciplinary enclaves that our specialized, technologically complex world requires. Often missing from the process are the people directly affected by change, particularly those with generations of understanding of a place and its social structure.

To address this lack of local input, Michael von Hausen always brings the personal and the local into his urban design process, to which he then applies a rigor that takes the process out of the fanciful and impractical—without ever losing the inspirational. As a teacher, that is his strength: he inspires. As a consultant and designer, he knows the difference between recognized limits and being unnecessarily limited.

He also appreciates that "theory has no meaning for those who can't comprehend it"—and consumers certainly will not pay a premium to live in something branded "sustainable" if they do not understand or appreciate it. This book builds the bridge between theory and a layperson's (or developer's) understanding of a more sustainable world.

This book is actually radical in its implications: it fundamentally questions the way we view the world. But the results are worth the effort if plans and designs successfully integrate the social aspects with the economic, the sustainable with the new, producing results that are, in Michael von Hausen's own words, "flexible, diverse, and enduring."

Gordon Price
Director, City Program
Simon Fraser University

PREFACE

My mission is plain and simple—to serve and teach worldwide. Colin Powell, former US secretary of state, recently said that there is no greater calling than serving your country. I want to spread my wings to serve the world. I say this sincerely and humbly, because it is a great honor to work on projects or share insights on a world scale. And more than ever, a global vision is sorely needed—especially in urban design and sustainable community development—as many nations face mounting issues, such as climate change, financial instability, and political turmoil.

My teaching, design and planning practice, and writing have expanded in recent years to include areas outside North America, among them Russia, China, Italy, and India. In the summer of 2011, I was invited by Taranjot Gadhok—now executive director, Human Settlement Management Institute—as a keynote speaker to the National Seminar on Design and Planning for Sustainable Habitat in New Delhi, India. As it turned out, I could not attend, but the seminar sponsors still published an excerpt on Vancouver from this book as part of the proceedings. More recently, the Canada Mortgage and Housing Corporation invited me to speak on the topic of sustainable communities planning and design in Russia at the international conference of the Canada Eurasia Russia Business Association (CERBA) in Toronto, Canada. In September 2012, I participated as part of the Canadian delegation in the sixth session of the World Urban Forum, in Naples, Italy, convened by UN-Habitat. These experiences reinforced and further informed my views on sustainable urbanism in a global context.

There exists an almost insatiable appetite for Western ideas on sustainable urban design that somehow can be molded to fit far-removed cultures, politics, and economic growth challenges. The North American dream of a big house, a big yard, and a fancy automobile is something nearly everyone shares, but they do not realize the dream's shortcomings in many cases or else tend to ignore them. This is understandable, as the North American dream often represents progress and achievement. Yet, as many have discovered on closer examination, this dream is environmentally wasteful and irresponsible, socially and culturally deficient, and economically unsustainable.

My travels in Russia, China, Korea, Panama, and, most recently, Vietnam have reinforced for me the fact that we are all connected. What happens in New Delhi, India, affects the Silicon Valley in California in some way—economically, socially, and/or environmentally. Microsoft Corporation now hires computer engineers from India to do its programming. When you call to make a Holiday Inn reservation in the United States, your call ends up somewhere in the Philippines, where labor is cheaper and location does not matter. Our worldwide e-mail network and use of social networking is accelerating cyber-adoption of "Western" designs and sustainable community concepts by Eastern cultures. The results have been spotty at best—attempting to create a sustainable community or designing a "Western" city while wiping out the historical culture of an entire area.

This book outlines a process to find appropriate sustainable urban design solutions worldwide—in different cultures and in different geographic locations. To paraphrase Albert Einstein, you can't solve a problem with the same process, or you will end up with the same results every time. I have tested my process in Canada and the United States, as well as most recently in Russia. Good things take time, and I hope my results will stand the test of time in terms of social, economic, and ecological integrity. I want to share these ideas with you to inspire your own practice or contribution to designing your own great community.

What this book does not do is propose solutions to poverty and social inequity worldwide through urban design and sustainable community planning. At most, it sets out a process that can be used to begin to address these needs, for to do more is a huge challenge and one beyond the scope of this book.

Jimmy Carter, former president of the United States, wrote to me recently to raise funds for his world-renowned Carter Center. He and his wife, Rosalyn, are taking on the world and making great progress in advancing peace and reducing world suffering. President Carter finished his letter with the statement, "We will all benefit from a world filled with peaceful, healthy, hope-filled, and productive people." My mission is simply part of that inspired challenge—to bring sustainable urban form to people around the world.

ACKNOWLEDGMENTS

This book is the result of many dedicated individuals lending their ideas and experience to a collective volume of work. I wish to extend my sincere appreciation to the Simon Fraser University City Program and the Urban Studies Program, as well as to the Real Estate Foundation of British Columbia for their support in developing this book. Specifically, my colleagues at Simon Fraser University—especially Gordon Price, Judy Oberlander, and Frank Pacella—spent countless hours with me, developing individual courses and an overall philosophy for the unique midcareer Urban Design Certificate Program at the university.

David Witty helped me develop and refine urban design ideas. I also thank Gordon Price for his great photographic images. My sincere appreciation goes to Judy Oberlander, Ken Cameron, and Randy Fasan for their editorial reviews and also to Joshua Randall for his help in obtaining permission for using photos and other images. My dear sister, Sasha Detre, provided extensive professional editing and content advice. In addition, the dedicated editorial staff at iUniverse deserve credit for the refinement of the manuscript and shaping it into a well-crafted book. Finally, I would like to thank Naomi Pauls, my editor in Vancouver, who added the final polish to the book.

Anthony Perl, professor of urban studies and former director of the Urban Studies Program at Simon Fraser University, has been part of the supporting cast in ongoing discussions on urban design and on training graduate students in this field. I sincerely acknowledge my key architects, landscape architects, designers, planners, engineers, and innovators in my consulting work—Don Wuori, Calum Srigley, Al Endall, Dolores Altin, and Paul Turje—who provide the necessary rigor to develop and test design and planning ideas in the field. Finally, a sincere thank-you goes out to my students. I learn as much from them as they do from me.

INTRODUCTION

First, we need more accurate models, metaphors, and measures to describe the human enterprise relative to the biosphere. We need a compass that defines true north for a civilization long on means and short on direction.

—David W. Orr, *The Last Refuge: Patriotism, Politics, and the Environment in the Age of Terror*

The urgency for more sustainable urban design has never been greater. More than one-half of the world population now lives in urban areas, and the quality of life in many of these environments continues its steep decline. Witness the poor air quality and extreme congestion in cities such as Shanghai and Mexico City. As the world population approaches 7 billion people, cities such as Mumbai, São Paulo, Seoul, and Moscow join the increasing number of megacities, with more than 10 million people. Even smaller cities with less concentrated populations, such as Los Angeles and Atlanta, face debilitating traffic congestion and increasing air pollution.

As urban areas have grown over the past half century, tree cover and green areas have significantly decreased. Parking areas and roads, meanwhile, have expanded—dead space exchanged for natural space— and now consume 30 to 40 percent of cities in North America. On a world scale, urbanization and industrialization have shifted back to Asia. China's transformation is happening at 100 times the scale and 10 times the speed of the first country in the world to urbanize—the United Kingdom. It is estimated that the top 600 world cities will generate 65 percent of the world's gross domestic product by 2025.[1] As humans we continue to devour valuable farmland and environmental areas for development at an ever faster rate. In the United States, for example, two-thirds of the development on the ground in 2050 will be built between now and then.[2] In addition, personal automobile use around the world accounts for roughly one-third of greenhouse gas emissions.[3] These and other conditions are elevating health problems; side effects such as cancer, respiratory disorders, diabetes, and obesity continue to erode the quality and length of human life in cities.

The need for enduring solutions

The "Sustainability Revolution," as Andrés Edwards refers to this movement, is here—an alternative paradigm that supports economic viability and healthy ecosystems by modifying our consumption patterns and implementing a more equitable social framework.[4] As Edwards and countless others recognize, existing consumption patterns cannot be retained in the long term. The trend toward sustainability is here to stay. However, time, perseverance, and progressive thinking all will be required to both create the frameworks for change and adapt to the new normal.

Fundamental change in how we design cities is a necessity at this time, and the good news is that a paradigm shift is happening worldwide. Sociopolitical forces of democracy, environmental responsibility, social equity, and economic accountability are under way that cannot easily be turned back, as witnessed in the Occupy Wall Street movement and the Arab Spring. As climate and weather pattern changes worldwide exacerbate our abuse of Mother Earth, these sociopolitical forces must be directed to create positive transformations in urban form and sustainable development around the globe. This may be a momentous task, but the timing may never be better.

The emerging new normal is far from normal. The background of rapid economic, social, and environmental change presents a host of challenges for urban designers. Even as the global population is growing, some cities are shrinking at the core. Alarming trends can be seen in the United States, where for every two urban cores that are growing, three are shrinking. In America, fifty-nine cities with a population of 100,000 or more have lost at least 10 percent of their population since 1950. Detroit has lost one-half of its inhabitants during the same period.[5] This trend could be changing according to July 2011 population estimates released by the US Census Bureau in June 2012. The nation's largest cities—thirty-one with a population over 500,000—grew faster than the country as a whole. There could be several factors at play, including the higher cost of commuting, smaller households, and the attraction of urban amenities.[6]

At the same time, significant government policy changes and progressive design responses worldwide are creating a momentum of positive changes that could eventually alter our lives in every way. These transformations include more compact new communities, higher transit orientation, less waste, more jobs closer to home, healthier and more energy-efficient buildings, increasing housing diversity, and more participatory design processes. Inner-city parking tolls in Stockholm, Sweden, or compensation for collecting garbage off the streets in Curitiba, Brazil, are sample initiatives improving transportation and human health in these cities.

The twenty-first century presents a unique opportunity to take urban design to a higher level, aligned with sustainable community development, as part of a new urban agenda. Theory and practice need to align so we achieve more built sustainable communities and a higher *quality* of life—not just a higher *quantity* of life. As noted earlier, Curitiba, Brazil, has transformed its urban form and function by progressive social, environmental, and economic policies and practices. Unfortunately, this shining example is not yet the norm. In many cities, a disjunction still exists between the approved plan and the final result. Many communities are becoming disillusioned by unfilled promises or "status quo" projects that are presented as sustainable developments. Often the theory behind sustainable private housing developments has no real meaning to ordinary citizens, and they certainly will not pay a premium for what they do not value or comprehend. "Greenwashing" was coined to describe empty promises of environmental friendliness; real estate developers have been known to use the same PR technique in efforts to garner political and community support for project approvals.

To create truly sustainable or resilient communities, urban designers, architects, planners, landscape architects, engineers, real estate developers, and governments must consider not only the physical but also the political, economic, social, and technological aspects of an urban design project. Sustainable planning on its own is not enough. Economic rationalization is not enough either, but it is a basis of measuring progress. We just have to start measuring the right things to change what we value. Cities are still the economic engines of North America. As pioneering urban economist Edward Glaeser points out, Americans who live in cities with more than 1 million residents, on average, are more than 50 percent more productive than Americans who live in smaller metropolitan areas.[7]

We have to start building more truly sustainable communities through what I call a comprehensive urban design approach (the dynamic urban design model), as defined later in this book. Collectively, these considerations create the framework for sustainable urban design. Yet, besides the broad challenges mentioned earlier, constraints include short-term political vision and self-interest, limited budgets, traditional land use regulations, and differing professional perspectives.

In any professional process, challenges are the norm. As urban designers, we need to analyze both challenges and opportunities and then come up with a strategy to work creatively with both to produce a comprehensive plan that can and will be implemented. Instead, frequently, a noninclusive planning process leads to splintered urban design plans that have few implementation "legs" to stand on. Such a plan is fragmentary; it consists of pieces of visions that are not woven together, leading to dubious results and questions, such as "How did that building get there?" or "Why does this road lead nowhere?" In other instances, a beautifully illustrated plan collects dust on a shelf. In each of these instances, there is a lack of follow-through, accountability, and responsibility, and little if any substantial public and political support backed by financial resources to realize the plans. We need to heal this disconnect between good intentions and bad results. A broad and concerted effort, grounded in the community, needs to be initiated early in the urban design process. This effort will ignite excitement and a common vision that is embraced as a priority and acted on at the government, private, and community levels.

Whether we are practicing urban designers or interested citizens, virtually all of us want to live in communities that are safe, attractive, and healthy. Yet our good intentions face conflicting goals. How are we going to improve community health, reduce crime, and improve mobility in cities while at the same time expanding our cities to accommodate growth? How are we going to do all this with seemingly limited financial resources? How do we do more with less, live within our means, and still create a higher quality of life? The list of challenges is almost endless. Urban design is emerging as a critical interface that brings various professions together to address these challenges and improve our communities.

To reiterate, for future human survival and quality of life, the world needs a more inclusive, rigorous, socially inspired, and comprehensive urban design model integrated with sustainable development. This approach considers not only objects and interspatial context but also the cultural meaning, beliefs, and traditions that these objects and spaces hold. As many unsuccessful urban design projects have shown, the previous mostly deterministic approach—design with little or no meaningful public input—works poorly in the emerging highly interactive, community-based environment where people demand and deserve to be heard. This separation of the public from the challenge of designing urban spaces is not the only separation that plagues contemporary urban design.

Lessons from a taxi driver and a prince

As humans we tend to separate things in our lives into compartments or areas. This convenient and frequently necessary analytic separation extends to our education, jobs, and the way we view our urban environments. Yet this compartmentalization does not reflect the real world, which is complex and intricately connected. In urban planning, we also have conveniently separated urban design and sustainable community development, yet the two are fundamentally connected. To achieve better long-term results, we need a new approach that better aligns urban design and sustainable community planning. Urban design, after all, can be a catalyst to realize sustainable development. However, as design professionals, government officials, politicians, or real estate developers, we often suffer from short-term motivations of private gain and from political shortsightedness, both of which skew results away from longer-term community interests. As this book makes clear, designing for the local culture and physical location is fundamental to creating resilient communities.

Two recent experiences inspired me to search the world in earnest for enlightened urban design and sustainable planning solutions. The first experience happened a few years ago. I flew into Calgary, Canada, as I often do, early in the morning on a crisp December day on the way to a business meeting. I hustled down the escalator and jumped into one of the taxis standing in front of the terminal. Preoccupied by my early morning e-mail messages, I struck up the normal small talk with the driver to get the latest news on what was happening in the former Winter Olympics city, also home to the exciting annual Calgary Stampede. What happened next was a game-changer for me.

I noticed that the taxi driver had a distinct African accent. I could not pinpoint the exact origin, which is a challenge I always set for myself when I meet someone new. As we got past the pleasantries, I asked, "Where are you from?"

"I am from Sudan," he said proudly. He then asked me what I do, and I said, "I design cities around the world." Without hesitation the driver blurted out, "Can you redesign our cities in southern Sudan? We have been devastated by civil war for over twenty years, and our cities are in ruins!" Then the statement came that I was not expecting. "Can you design the cities here and send the plans over to our country?"

I try never to export Western ideas into countries without understanding the specifics of the locale and its important attributes. I replied, "I have to understand the place before I can design for it. I have to go there; otherwise, the design will not fit the place." As I left the taxi, the driver had a big smile. I had encouraged him to help his country back from ruin. I also left the taxi with a mission—I wanted to help design world communities that are resilient and fit local needs. To accomplish this mission, I needed to understand more about my urban design specialty, the process of creating a plan, and two misunderstood terms: urban design and sustainable communities.

The second pivotal experience happened more recently. Since meeting that taxi driver, I had been doing research and working internationally in the field of urban design and sustainable community planning. I had developed processes, guidelines, and plans for various communities that emphasized the importance of "place-making" and, maybe more importantly, "place-keeping." In 2011, a partnership between the Prince's Foundation for Building Community[8] in the United Kingdom and Simon Fraser University in Vancouver, Canada, reinforced for me that "place-keeping" is crucial to urban design and sustainable community planning. Working with Hank Dittmar, chief executive of the Prince's Foundation, and Noel Isherwood, architect with the foundation, I came to appreciate firsthand their mandate to improve the quality of people's lives by teaching and practicing timeless and ecological ways of planning, designing, and building.

Traditional building for local climate using local materials is evident in the history of our communities worldwide. Whether it is the new Zähringer towns of twelfth-century southern Germany or the twentieth-century redevelopment example of Poundbury in England, rich local histories should inform future design decisions. In many cases, the traditional urban forms were built to last thousands of years, not to be demolished after fifty years or less like most recent buildings, especially in North America.

These two experiences brought me to two important conclusions: first, that we need a new or improved urban design process; and second, that we need to connect sustainable community planning with urban design to get desired results on the ground. How can we satisfy these needs? First, we need to understand the meanings of urban design and sustainable community planning separately and then to see if there is a potential for integration. We know our destination, and our journey has only begun.

About this book

This book is divided into four parts. Part 1 outlines the background and history of urban design and sustainable community development. It also sets out, in chapter 4, a framework of elements and principles for sustainable urban design. Part 2 examines the comprehensive plan-making process, including the critical analysis and synthesis components. Part 3 describes the urban design evaluation process and then highlights innovative downtown as well as suburban development projects. Part 4, the final portion of the book, discusses the pitfalls of urban design implementation and what conditions are required to create sustainable urban design plans. The core content of this book is supplemented by two appendices that provide templates to customize economic and sustainability measurement, extensive print and online resources, as well as a glossary.

Dynamic Urban Design brings theory and practice together in a tapestry of explanations, illustrations, and case studies. It provides a strategic framework and a tool kit to redesign existing suburbs, enhance rural towns, retrofit downtowns, and design new, sustainable communities worldwide. Although the case studies center on North America, the intent is to present a strategy and process that can be applied to urban design projects anywhere in the world.

I

A SUSTAINABLE FRAMEWORK

1
BUILDING BLOCKS

Urban design has always had no clear role, territory, and authority. In the last 100 years, the design and planning professions have increasingly formed distinct disciplinary enclaves. In this context, perhaps urban design's unique value stems from its vagueness or rather from its provision of an overarching framework that can bridge more specialized design efforts.
—Richard Marshall, *The Elusiveness of Urban Design*

The practice of urban design is relatively young and varies widely. Most practitioners agree, however, on what it means. Urban design is the art and science of making places for people—traditionally cities, towns, or new communities. The term "urban design" became formalized in education only in the late 1960s with Harvard University's Urban Design Program. Its earlier manifestation in the late nineteenth century and early twentieth century was "civic design" in the United Kingdom, which mainly dealt with the larger streets and municipal buildings, such as courthouses, fire halls, city halls, and other government structures. Collectively, this "civic design" direction was reflected in part in the Garden City and new town movements initiated in the United Kingdom and the City Beautiful movement that swept through North America after the Chicago World's Fair in 1893. Urban design encompassed the design of the greater city.

Many professional designers see urban design not as a separate discipline but as an interdisciplinary practice of architects, landscape architects, urban planners, and civil engineers. The different knowledge, skills, and abilities of these practitioners—along with their biases—can bring breadth and depth or fragmentation and dysfunction to a project. Unfortunately, the separate disciplines can often isolate themselves rather than use urban design as a forum for interdependence and further depth. The architects are concerned with the buildings, the landscape architects with the landscape, the civil engineers with the supporting infrastructure of roads, water, and sanitary sewer, and the urban planners with the land use and building regulations.

In a perfect world, urban design should unite these professions to create a coherent, practical, and unified plan. Instead, professional barriers, distinct roles, and lack of design integration can result in less than optimal urban design plans. The size and complexity of many current projects adds to these professional divisions. Multiple private, public, and political interests further skew good intentions. Finally, unbalanced private property interests of land use rights and cost considerations can outweigh community and government needs, creating the wrong solution in the wrong place. As a result, in many cases, an unimaginative and unfitting urban design plan is approved and built.

The nature of urban design

Effective urban design is much more than the sum of its parts. It is more than a building and a site; it is much more than a block and a street. Effective urban design is the seamless fit of design and context that pleases the eye and satisfies the soul. One design element seems to flow effortlessly into another, creating an integrated, cohesive whole, where form and function meet. Successful neighborhood designs of this caliber include the layout, architecture, and formality of Beacon Hill in Boston, heritage conservation projects in Mount Pleasant in Vancouver, Canada, and the timeless architecture of the residential and commercial community surrounding the Pantheon in Rome. Also noteworthy are iconic pieces of urban design such as the Guggenheim Museum Bilbao, by Frank Gehry, and Montreal's Habitat 67, by Moshe Safdie. Each of these projects leaves an indelible impression and has achieved special stature, because each is sensitively designed for a specific purpose and respects or contrasts its urban context in a measured and purposeful way.

Urban design, to be comprehensive, entails more than simply the physical design of an urban area. It is the process by which new communities are planned, designed, and built. It varies in scale and is affected by many private- and public-sector professionals, as well as community members. By nature it is complex and interdisciplinary. It needs to be collaborative. Urban design requires understanding of the interplay between the ecological, physical, economic, and social factors and the physical form of a particular site or area. It also requires an understanding of the following three scales:

- *Region:* greater surrounding area and city
- *Community:* surrounding neighborhoods, districts, or corridors, including residents, businesses, and the sociocultural profile
- *Site:* specific block, street, and buildings

These three scales are collectively known as "designing in context."

Context is so important yet often ignored in urban design. All the three scales need to be considered, for both regional and community designs are key to achieving sustainable site development. Regional design of suburban and rural settlements aims to make them enduring, self-sufficient, and resilient, as well as to weave them into a synergistic network around the larger city. In practical terms this means that if the urban design fits within its regional context, the resulting land uses and associated activities contribute a building block to making the region function better or more efficiently. The contribution could be appropriate land uses, such as needed multiple-family housing that is more attainable for young families and seniors, and commercial office and retail space that provides services and employment close by. The new development can also provide the necessary intensity of people to make bus transit or some other forms of rapid transit feasible. For instance, as a rule of thumb, an average density of ten housing units per acre (twenty-five units/ha) is required to support rapid transit like Light Rail Transit (LRT). Too often urban design focuses solely on downtown "city" design. Urban design has traditionally neglected suburban and rural areas that need attention in order to convert urban and rural sprawl into viable, responsibly designed communities.

During the past fifty years, urban design has extended urban sprawl while failing to recognize emerging challenges of rural sprawl. In simple terms, urban sprawl is low-density housing developments that have no commercial services or jobs nearby. The result is an auto-oriented community that is designed around the car rather than the person. Wide, lifeless streets, garage-dominated housefronts, disconnected neighborhoods, and lack of neighbor interaction are some of the outcomes. The houses have larger yards and fenced enclosures, and residents tend to "cocoon," interacting less with neighbors than in urban neighborhoods. Emerging health problems such as obesity, lung ailments, and psychological disorders from isolation are by-products of this car orientation and inward-oriented urban sprawl communities. Rural sprawl takes suburban sprawl one step further. It creates even lower densities on larger lots, normally eroding valuable regional farmland or natural space, and creating even greater commuting distances that only exacerbate traffic and associated pollution challenges.

Both urban and rural sprawl need to be reconfigured to become part of an interdependent, regionally designed system. Progressive urban design over the next few decades will entail recognizing the synergistic and complementary powers of urban, suburban, and rural areas, and respecting their unique characters while building community networks. Urban design is also transformative from the region or surrounding larger city to the site in a local residential neighborhood. As you move from the region to the city center and site, there is normally a scale change in the form of narrower streets, increased frequency of streets, higher buildings, and reduced setbacks of buildings, and in the type of land uses. On this journey from the larger regional context to the city center or the urban local residential neighborhood, the grander, less personal, auto-oriented scale evolves to the more personal, pedestrian-scale place, especially in historic cities.

Place is both a physical location, defined by buildings, public spaces, and landmarks, and a product of social interaction with the space, defined by people who use it. Place is much more than "urban decoration" or the design of individual buildings. As Jonathan Barnett astutely points out, urban design is about designing cities without designing buildings.[1] It is the process by which a whole set of elements should come together to form a coherent and attractive place. Urban design thus requires a set of tools or tool kit that can respond to different places and address requirements at the most fundamental level or at the most complex level.

People and place are intricately connected in urban design. The cities, towns, and villages we remember have distinct elements that remain fixed in our minds, etched in our memories. These elements might include a vibrant marketplace, a magnificent church, or simply a stately tree-lined street. Taken together or alone, they create a distinct sense of place. Listening to the people who live or work in a particular place and finding out what makes it unique in their experience is fundamental to developing a successful urban design plan. Involving people protects what is important by ensuring that their values and visions are reflected in the plan as it evolves. The end result is a vibrant, enduring place.

Place-keeping and place-making are essential processes of effective and sustainable urban design. Place-keeping is a process that keeps what is essential to defining that place. Place-keeping elements are those that require retention or enhancement and essentially create the essence of the place. These elements may include a historic church, public square, or significant collection of trees. They may be as small as particular brick paving materials, architectural facade details, or a distinctive fountain feature. All of these elements collectively shape the "signature" of a place or unique identifiers.

Place-making is the process of adding new physical elements and activity programming that will make the place more complete or simply enhance it. Place-making elements include new or altered structures or public spaces to complement or contrast with the current place, with the intention of creating or improving the place. These elements may include a new landmark building, additional specific trees, a new or expanded community gathering lawn, or a new statue that commemorates history or culture.

The most significant space for place-making or place-keeping is the space between buildings—streets, lanes, plazas, and parks—normally referred to as the "public realm." The public realm, where the community comes together, is where we can gain the most appreciation for urban design and its components. This eclectic mix of public, semiprivate, and private spaces, in addition to the buildings themselves, gives our communities their fundamental character. The public realm also embraces urban design's roots in civic design, the historic tradition of building grand civic structures and boulevards to be filled in by the private sector (consider Washington, Paris, and Rome). The resilience of some of these great world cities and their designs provides clues that sustainability has a fundamental role in the evolution and health of our cities.

Origins of sustainable community development

> A sustainable community is one that allows its inhabitants to live in a way that does not damage the environment or consume nonrenewable resources. At the same time, a sustainable community supports the realization of human potential.
>
> —Judy and Michael Corbett, *Designing Sustainable Communities*

The term "sustainable community development" is quite young and suffers from similar misunderstandings and misapplications to urban design. It originates from the term "sustainable development." Born in what is commonly known as the Brundtland Report, *Our Common Future*, in 1987, the term has now been in use for twenty-five years. The global trends revealed in this report caught the attention of politicians and citizens on a scale not seen before. For instance, the fact that one-quarter of the world's population consumes three-quarters of its resources should be a particular concern to developed countries. Imagine the implications of bringing the underdeveloped regions up to North American living standards by making a five- to tenfold increase in world industrial production! To address such challenges, the Brundtland Commission coined the term "sustainable development," which it defined "as meeting the needs of the present without compromising the ability of future generations to meet their own needs."[2]

The Brundtland Report created a groundswell of support for starting to think differently and to do things differently to get different results. Yet subsequent reports did not show promising trends. North Americans have twice the ecological footprint of Europeans and seven times the average footprint of Asians and Africans. This means that North Americans require double the amount of land and natural capital as Europeans and seven times as much as Asians and Africans to support their lifestyles, including housing, industrial/commercial development, water, food, and fossil fuels.[3]

The challenge of this unsustainable world condition is to define a sustainable community development model in which humans live by consuming or using less yet experience at the same time a higher quality of life. One theory can be illustrated by a six-legged stool. Six forms of social capital, or assets of a community, form the six legs that support the stool—social, cultural, human, economic, physical, and natural capital. These forms of capital require that citizens of the world, especially North Americans, to find ways of living more lightly on the planet and learn to live more on our "natural income" rather than deplete our natural capital. Our natural income refers to developing those resources that are renewable rather than extracting nonrenewable resources. In the theory behind sustainable development, each of these forms of capital can be applied to a community differently depending on its individual needs, and these needs change over time.[4] Sustainable development calls into question the fundamental economic measurement of gross domestic product, seeing it as a flawed measurement of national progress and wealth. As an alternative, the World Bank recently introduced the measurement of natural capital as a gauge for progress and national healthy development.[5]

Significant cultural barriers hamper the acceptance of sustainable community development. Many businesses and real estate developers see sustainable community development as an unrealistic and unattainable goal. Others view it as a convenient corporate term used to justify continued economic growth. In fact, current zoning and associated development policies reinforce the status quo and make sustainable community development largely illegal. For example, many regional and city regulations do not permit or require sustainable elements, such as mixed uses, narrower (more livable) streets, live/work residential areas, secondary suites, mixed-income neighborhoods, smaller lots, or reduced parking requirements. Furthermore, some building codes or design standards disallow or limit sustainable initiatives, such as green roofs, innovative construction, and environmentally sensitive materials and applications. And developers building innovative infrastructure such as reconstructed wetlands are required to build duplicate systems to ensure that if the infrastructure fails, the conventional backup system compensates for the failure.[6]

At the same time, the terms "sustainability" and "sustainable development" have undeniably come of age and entered the mainstream. Sustainability is catching fire as a major change agent in our world on the personal, community, and corporate levels. Its greatest strength may be as a catalyst for major shifts in the way we view and interact with our environment. An important business transformation movement is placing environmental, social, and physical sustainability at the center of many corporate boardroom discussions. The new sustainable triple bottom-line (social, economic, and environmental) measurement of corporate gains creates a new, broader performance platform for many corporations. Sustainability and sustainable community development may start with alternative personal choices, but these choices herald changes in our corporate and community culture.

The new triple bottom-line performance criteria for many progressive businesses can be illustrated clearly by an e-mail from a former classmate who heads a real estate development firm in Dhaka, Bangladesh. A line at the bottom of the e-mail instructed me not to print this page unless essential with the heading "Save paper, for good." This phrase had two meanings for me—save paper to do good for the earth, and save paper permanently. In other words, sustainability is not one act but a permanent personal change in habits that has wider implications.

As I explored my colleague's corporate website, I noticed that sustainability had further dimensions for his firm, beyond the environment. For instance, corporate social responsibility is a dominant theme, with the intention of helping unskilled and semiskilled workers in the firm to break the cycle of poverty through increasing the "market wage" to a "living wage." The goal is to help the workers live a longer and more productive life. Bay Developments' sustainable approach means not only attending to its corporate well-being by generating profits. The company also espouses a greater mission of contributing to the welfare of its community.

So we find sustainable community development in a different or similar form is also taking center stage in the corporate boardrooms around the world. How then do we link this incredible opportunity with the practice of urban design to create the next generation of the world's greater cities and regions around them?

Linking disciplines across boundaries

This brings us to the challenge of how we can link sustainable community development with urban design. Current processes in these two areas are undertaken by professions that normally do not align. As previously outlined, the architects, landscape architects, planners, and civil engineers focus on the design aspects of the project, often driven by cost concerns and the delivery of the project from a private-sector development perspective of maximum profit with least expenditures. For these professions, the sustainability aspects of a project are confined to technical building, landscape, regulation, or infrastructure terms. Social planners or community advocates, meanwhile, are often isolated from the design process, attending only the token first meeting or marginalized until the end. Their concerns are not really heard, acknowledged, or addressed in any equitable manner. In some cases, granted, a joint public-private partnership (PPP or P3) brings public interest more to the foreground, but this is not always the case.

The standard urban design process fails to adequately address aspects such as social equity, cultural programming, and economic diversity. Rather, private interests tend to dominate the process. Somewhat understandably, commensurate with private ownership rights and the risks associated with project funding, the focus of a project is on the site itself rather than the broader spectrum of community and government needs. Experience would argue for a new, enlightened self-interest viewpoint that understands that working together at the community level can create benefits that far exceed the potential of individual efforts. After all, mutual benefit was the reason humans moved to urban settlements in the first place. We saw the merit of working together rather than separately. I am hopeful that the typical isolated professional silos can be bridged based on recent progress in technical and process innovations.

Significant progress has taken place on the technical side of sustainable urban design, advancing standards such LEED-ND (Leadership in Energy and Environmental Design for Neighborhood Development), created by the US Green Building Council (USGBC) in the 1990s.[7] At the same time, the Congress for the New Urbanism (CNU) has made great strides to create alternatives to urban sprawl by advancing a different approach for designing communities. The CNU's Charter begins:

> The Congress for the New Urbanism views disinvestment in central cities, the spread of placeless sprawl, increasing separation by race and income, environmental deterioration, loss of agricultural lands and wilderness, and the erosion of society's built heritage as one interrelated community-building challenge.[8]

The Charter, originating at the Charleston, South Carolina, CNU IV conference in 1996, launched a new way of looking at community design. Maybe most importantly, the CNU movement captured the attention of the media and politicians as an alternative to placeless sprawl and its attendant problems.

What the New Urbanism movement does best is embrace the timeless principles of traditional neighborhoods of the early twentieth century. These principles include the following:

- various access and exit options, supported by transit
- a more compact neighborhood with increased density and a diversity and mix of land uses
- a pedestrian orientation, encouraging convenience and safety
- respect for environmentally sensitive areas
- conservation of significant buildings and landscapes
- celebration and integration of public and community places
- active, citizen-based participation in planning and design

Important precedents for looking at and implementing urban plans differently include Seaside (east of Pensacola, Florida); Kentlands, Maryland (outside Washington, DC); Laguna West (in Sacramento, California); and Disney's Celebration (on the south edge of Orlando, Florida). These precedents are not without their detractors or weaknesses. For more discussion of New Urbanism, see chapters 3 and 11.

New Urbanism has shortcomings, which include decreased housing affordability, auto dependency because of these communities' suburban locations, and relatively low densities. As the majority of these new communities are greenfield developments—or, in other words, new developments set in suburban locations—continuing dependence on the automobile does not solve the urban sprawl problem. More fundamentally, the regional growth plans affecting transportation, land use, and the location of New Urbanism communities are part of the larger problem—not specifically the community's urban design. As mentioned earlier, there should be a link between new community location decisions and proximity to services and transportation at the local and regional planning level.[9] Most importantly, New Urbanism has made us reexamine the fundamental design of our communities. In his book *Sustainable Urbanism,* Douglas Farr provides a technical exploration of walkable and transit-served urbanism, with high-performance buildings and high-performance infrastructure.[10] Even with all this effort, significant work remains to be done in aligning the principles of New Urbanism with the process side of the equation. Only when principles and process come together will we realize the full breadth and potential of sustainable community development.

A dynamic urban design model

Our world calls for a more dynamic urban design model combined with a sustainable community development model that is inclusive, responsive, and positive in its approach to overcome the shortcomings of New Urbanism and the ills of isolated urban design. Such a process follows the history of a place and its people, reflects its ecological integrity, and builds a prosperous community that is enduring and vibrant. It integrates social, ecological, and economic components, anchored by targets (quantifiable goals) that ensure better success.

This new model provides a consistent process for urban design analysis, synthesis, and implementation. The result is a "family" of urban design plans that work together. These urban design plans span land use, urban form and massing, mobility, green infrastructure, parks and recreation, and economic and sociocultural strategies. And they include an implementation action plan that can be measured for success by specific targets. Urban design in this form is comprehensive—it goes well beyond physical form, leading us to create truly sustainable communities.

An effective and enlightened sustainable urban design approach has at its heart place, process, and plans. This model recognizes people and their interaction with the place where they live or work. It entails a process that includes the people who live and work there, and it results in plans that reflect the place and local values brought to the place. A comprehensive and inclusive process helps define the different plans—from transportation to urban form—that collectively determine a healthy and responsive urban fabric. The final plans are flexible yet appropriate to the time in history and resources, dynamic in their very nature and responsiveness. This model also requires a multidisciplinary urban design strategy that includes architects, landscape architects, planners, engineers, developers, and economists, among others, in both the public and private sectors. An important aim of this model is to blend and balance multiple public and private objectives in a series of plans to achieve the desired result.

The dynamic urban design model is what this book is about. The model dissects the requirements for a truly comprehensive urban design plan that is enduring and effective. It is comprised of the three building blocks of framework, components, and measurement (fig. 1.1).

- *Framework:* place, process, and plans, including acknowledgment of the importance of the physical *place,* the *process* required to recognize important local values, and the *plans* required to actualize the vision and requirements of the community, including land use, mobility, and urban form

- *Components:* social, ecological, and economic areas that examine the sociocultural aspects of the community, its interrelationship and synergies with nature, and the important means of livelihood or economic prosperity in the area
- *Measurement:* all the elements of urban design are included or considered; the principles set the guiding rules for the community and the targets set quantifiable goals

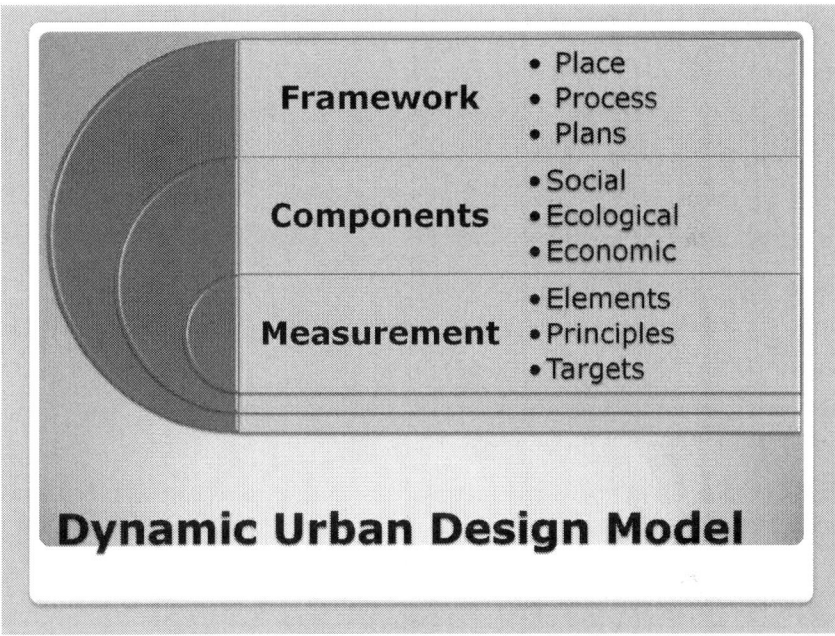

Figure 1.1. Dynamic Urban Design Model. This model combines a framework of place, process, and plans with social, ecological, and economic analytic components. This dynamic approach is then measured by elements, principles, and targets, as an urban design plan is developed and evolves over time.

Together the framework, components, and measurement of the dynamic urban design model shape an accountable and complete urban design plan integrated with sustainable community planning. The model uses both a substantive and procedural approach. The substantive portion includes the understanding of place through careful observation and description/illustration; measuring the interaction of people with their environment (both natural and man-made); and classifying urban elements such as buildings, spaces, and streets based on uniform characteristics.[11] Empiricism carefully measures particular positive and negative responses to design alternatives, such as various housing types or streetscape design. Community involvement informs design choices.

This "dynamic" urban design model uses time as an element in the transformation of a place. It recognizes what I refer to as the 3 Ps of urban design as the past (heritage of *place*), the present (in a collaborative *process* with the community), and the future in the form of *plans* (e.g., land use, mobility, recreation/open space, building form and massing, social and cultural programming), which collectively form the urban design family of plans.

This urban design process, like any other, requires time, people, and financial resources. Although similar to constructing a building, this process can be infinitely more complex, involving multiple stakeholders and often-conflicting public and private agendas. Change is likely to be seen as a threat to the status quo and, therefore, perceived as risky. Yet the same people who are threatened continue to complain about the effects of urban sprawl and undesirable development patterns. Understanding this paradox and addressing the perspectives of stakeholders is crucial to creating a plan that will lead to a sustainable community.

As much as possible, all stakeholders need to see their concerns resolved in the plan. Obviously, this is a tall order. It requires an urban design strategy that unfolds from a detailed analysis of political, economic, ecological, sociocultural, and technological factors. Realistic implementation frameworks, based on the analysis, are important to ensure the design translates into reality.

In the end, shared ownership of the urban design vision creates the most successful enduring communities. Ownership—in the form of formal or informal partnerships—creates enduring support to get buildings, streets, and pathways built in the ways they should be. Ownership also ensures safety, because most residents and businesses cherish their homes and commercial enterprises and also take pride in their streets, open spaces, and parks. As current or potential urban designers, we need to foster ownership, involving people in the creation of their own spaces in which to live, work, and play. Communities are organic, as varied as the people who live there. Whatever templates we generate must be flexible, diverse, and enduring, not only to address the needs of people, which will grow and change, but also to accommodate climate change. Achieving the kind of urban designs that are sensitive to today's needs while anticipating those of the future is a huge challenge but one that cannot be ignored. Meeting this challenge requires a dynamic, strategic approach to urban design and sustainable community development. That is the subject of this book.

2
FROM ANCIENT ROME TO CITY BEAUTIFUL

They chose a flat but sloping site (to ensure good drainage) that was high enough to avoid future floods. A Roman priest examined the livers of a rabbit and a pheasant from the area to find out if it would be a healthy place in which to live. When the animals were found to be without fault and an investigation of the land turned up no stagnant pools, the gods were thanked and the choice of the site was officially confirmed.

—David Macaulay, *City: A Story of Roman Planning and Construction*

It was a life-altering experience. As I walked in front of the Pantheon building in Rome in 2006, I was struck by an overwhelming realization—the building in front of me was nearly two thousand years old! This realization was compounded by the building itself, which not only physically overshadowed me but also psychologically pushed me backward (fig. 2.1). I cautiously stepped back a few paces, for I was literally shaken. The Pantheon is circular with an immense portico of large granite Corinthian columns at the entrance. It is the world's largest unreinforced concrete dome, standing at 142 feet (43.3 meters) and the same dimension at the base of the dome. I turned to look behind me and was then struck by the presence of an Egyptian obelisk. It was *hundreds* of years older!

Caught between two timeless landmarks, I had to sit down on the steps at the obelisk's base to comprehend what was happening. At that moment I finally realized the true meaning of "spirit of place," or what the Romans referred to as "genius loci." I could feel the immense physical and spiritual presence of each of these structures and their surrounding spaces. In fact, their spiritual auras were much greater than their physical footprints. That day I learned a valuable historical and cultural lesson. Where a place has authentic form and purpose, there is reason to conserve and enhance that place, for it represents our cultural roots.

Figure 2.1. The Pantheon, Rome. Rebuilt in AD 126 by Emperor Hadrian, the Pantheon is nearly two thousand years old.

Discovering the spirit of place

Dynamic urban design starts with understanding the evolution of our urban form and cultural importance. The past informs our future. Most of the cities, towns, and villages of today are products of years of building, replacement, and expansion. Many villages grew into towns, and towns into cities, simply because of their strategic location for defense and trade. Many individuals influenced the thinking and forms of urban design. This chapter and the next highlight historical and theoretical developments in the evolution of a city, town, and village, providing a rich context for the chapters that follow.

The formative years

It is difficult to develop a historic typology for cities around the world, especially from a sustainable urbanism perspective. The world's cities not only had different cultural and spiritual references but also evolved over thousands of years. Cities like Rome, Mexico City, and Babylon grew from rustic ancient settlements to fortified walled cities, and eventually to the more open and contemporary cities of the twenty-first century. As we will see in this chapter, the car orientation in the twentieth century eroded and eventually destroyed the pedestrian roots in many cities. This car dominance is most readily seen in North American cities' four hundred years of history. These cities were at first largely shaped by European precedents, but most of these cities fell victim to car dominance, freeways, and the accompanying destruction of many neighborhoods.

Kevin Lynch classified historic city design into three categories—organic, practical, and cosmic.[1] He somehow missed or consciously ignored the contemporary car city that currently dominates many of our landscapes.[2] The organic city is shaped by the buildings, with streets responding to building form in historic cities like Rome and London. The second, cosmic city combines spiritualism and government dominance, shaping a hierarchy of building size and formal spatial geometry, as seen in the Orient in cities like Beijing and Seoul or in ancient India. The third, practical city may be best characterized by the Roman garrison towns that were "new towns" in the Roman Empire and also some Greek cities. These Roman "new towns" have an orthogonal street grid pattern for access efficiency and easy expansion. The fourth, contemporary car-oriented city is dominated and shaped by the car; freeways and streets determine urban form and separate land uses, as seen in Houston, Phoenix, Los Angeles, and Atlanta (fig. 2.2).

The evolution of early urban design had as much to do with defense requirements and essentials to sustain life as it did with the aesthetics of form and experience. People assembled in urban settlements for protection, culture, and commerce. At the same time, freshwater sources and access to food and materials were important. From massive external walls for self-defense to glorious cathedrals and castles, early forms of urban design met the needs of pedestrian inhabitants. The narrow streets of Rome, Venice, Nice, and Cairo are reflective of this human scale and orientation. Early urban materials and building form also responded to local climate and culture.

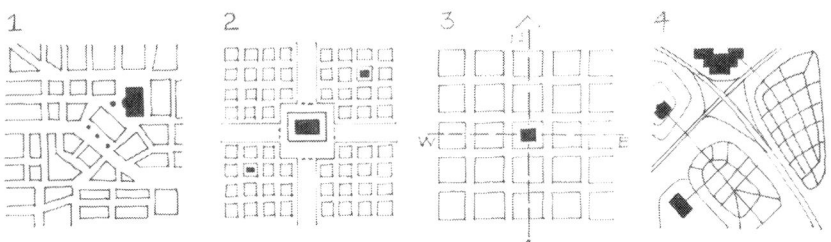

Figure 2.2. Four conceptual models of urban design. The four diagrams illustrate four patterns of urban development—(left to right) 1. Organic; 2. Cosmic; 3. Practical; and 4. Car-oriented.

As we will see in the discussion that follows, early cities had a much more "sustainable footprint" than modern-day cities, as size and land uses were dictated by walking distances. Primary resources such as food and materials were local. Most residents worked and shopped locally. The central marketplace provided for local food distribution, and the settlement was surrounded by agriculture. Mixed uses in a tightly knit layout of buildings were the norm.

The tightly knit organic street system of some ancient European cities evolved slowly, in contrast to the larger organized town planning that came later in the Renaissance of the sixteenth century, as seen in Rome and later in Paris. Narrow early streets responded to the built form with jagged turns and varied widths. The resulting street and building patterns were diverse and ever-changing. With the evolution of the city, especially during the Renaissance period, the design of streets followed a more formal geometry for efficient movement of goods to and from town centers. The adjacent buildings had to respond in a disciplined manner. Wider streets lost some of the wonderful pedestrian scale and local expressions of earlier forms. Examples of this transformation can easily be seen in Nice, France, and Bilbao, Spain (figs. 2.3 and 2.4).

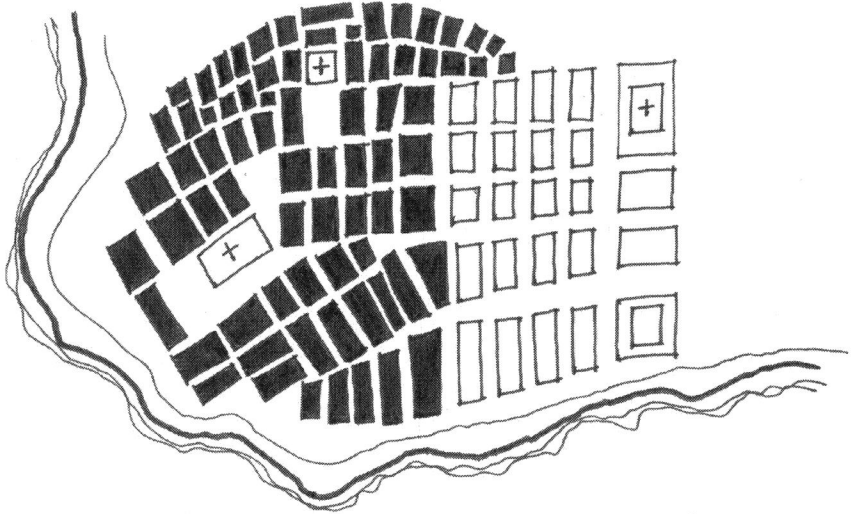

Figure 2.3. Historic sketch plan of Nice, France. The plan illustrates the organic-to-practical pattern evolution of the city's street and block system. The black blocks represent the original organic "Old City" settlement, evolving to the more practical geometric grid layout expressed in the white blocks of later centuries.

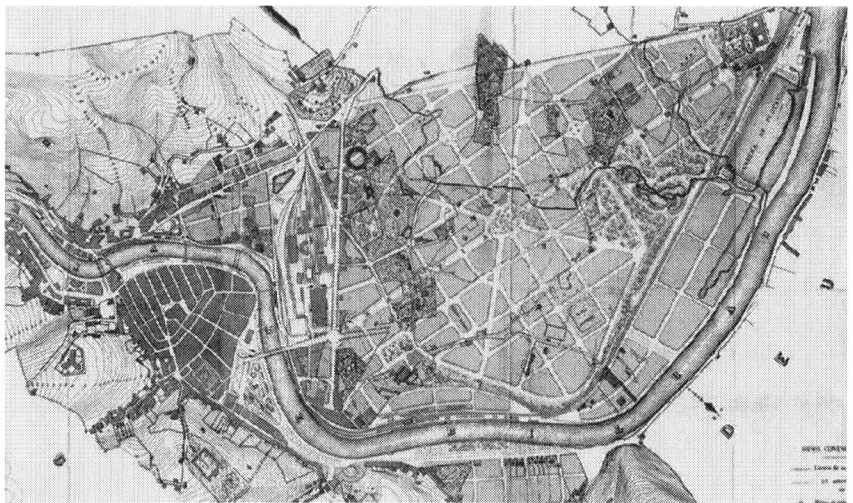

Figure 2.4. The *ensanche* project, as proposed by Alzola, Achucarro, and Hoffermeyer in Bilbao, Spain, 1876. This plan illustrates the contrasts between the more organic evolution of the original townsite on the left side of the river and the more practical, larger street grid and bisecting street geometry proposed on the right side of the river.

In contrast to those in Europe, other early cities from Babylon to Peking had distinctly rectilinear forms shaped by a few major roads and public areas or squares with undifferentiated residential areas within a city wall. Many of the ancient Chinese settlements followed cosmic forms and principles of feng shui, such as "wind and water," which sought to find balance and harmony within a geographic framework related to the sun. In Chinese capital cities, the settlement was set out in a perfect square. Each of the four sides had three gates, for a total of twelve gates, representing the twelve months of the year. In these settlements, the east-west and north-south grid orientation of major roads and the city wall created a basic structure for attaching other elements, such as temples and ceremonial gathering areas.

The classic city of the ancient Greeks set the pattern of many settlements around the Mediterranean Sea, from the north coast of Africa to Asia Minor. The Greeks used a disciplined orthogonal street grid pattern, allowing all dwellings to orient to the southerly sun and providing easy access to the main community spaces and buildings, including the agora or marketplace, theater, and stadium. These straight lines, main accesses, southerly orientation, and easy access to public facilities became standard for many cities over time. The uniform street grid served as an adaptable framework for growing cities, yet also created a familiar pattern for newcomers. This grid street pattern in Greek cities, the birthplace of democracy, shaped a "democratic" street grid that maximized freedom of choice—in direction and orientation. The Roman garrison towns constructed throughout the Roman Empire from England to North Africa in the early centuries display this same pattern. This "democratic" grid street pattern would reemerge in North American city design in such cities as Philadelphia and Savannah.

Growth in a Roman settlement was limited by the city's walls. Sometimes a radial pattern of streets evolved to access gates, main buildings, and the market. The importance of the block (building area between streets) versus the street was obvious in these early settlements, and early radial streets were precursors to the radial-centric form of later cities. The grid symmetry within fortified walls followed through the Middle Ages. Cities such as London, Cologne, and Paris continued to grow organically out of former Roman towns or feudal villages through the Middle Ages.

The standard grid street symmetry and organization shaped Londonderry in Ireland and Zurich in Switzerland.[3]

Varied street patterns evolved from the somewhat organic street system in ancient Rome (fig. 2.5) to the more rigid geometric forms first embraced in the Renaissance and Baroque periods and further articulated in the eighteenth and nineteenth centuries by such planners as Thomas Adams and Walter Baumgartner (fig. 2.6). Landmarks and public spaces such as the Piazza San Marco in Venice (which originated in the 800s and evolved until today) were important elements in urban design. The Pope Sixtus V Plan for Rome of 1590 took two hundred years to build (fig. 2.7). This far-reaching plan established major landmarks and transportation routes. Rome, with key government involvement, combined the grandeur of public buildings with conscious placement of landmark obelisks to define spatial orientation and importance, as well as gain quicker access to important parts of the city.

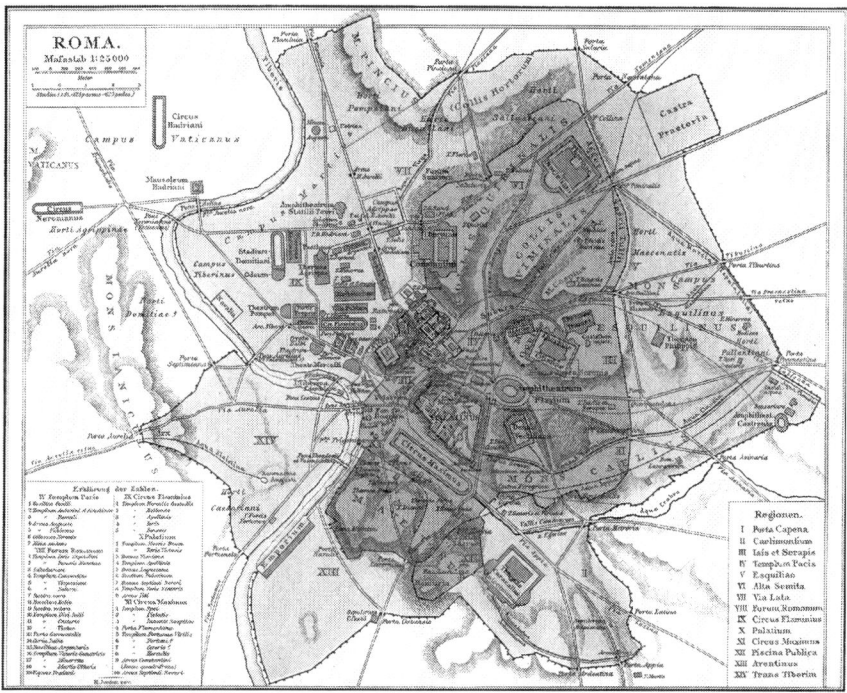

Figure 2.5. Map of Rome during antiquity. The traditional aspects of the ancient walled city located on high ground along a river are evident, with the organic form of streets shaped by buildings. Rome was the largest city in the world during the reign of Emperor Augustus (63 BC to AD 14), when its population approximated 1 million people.

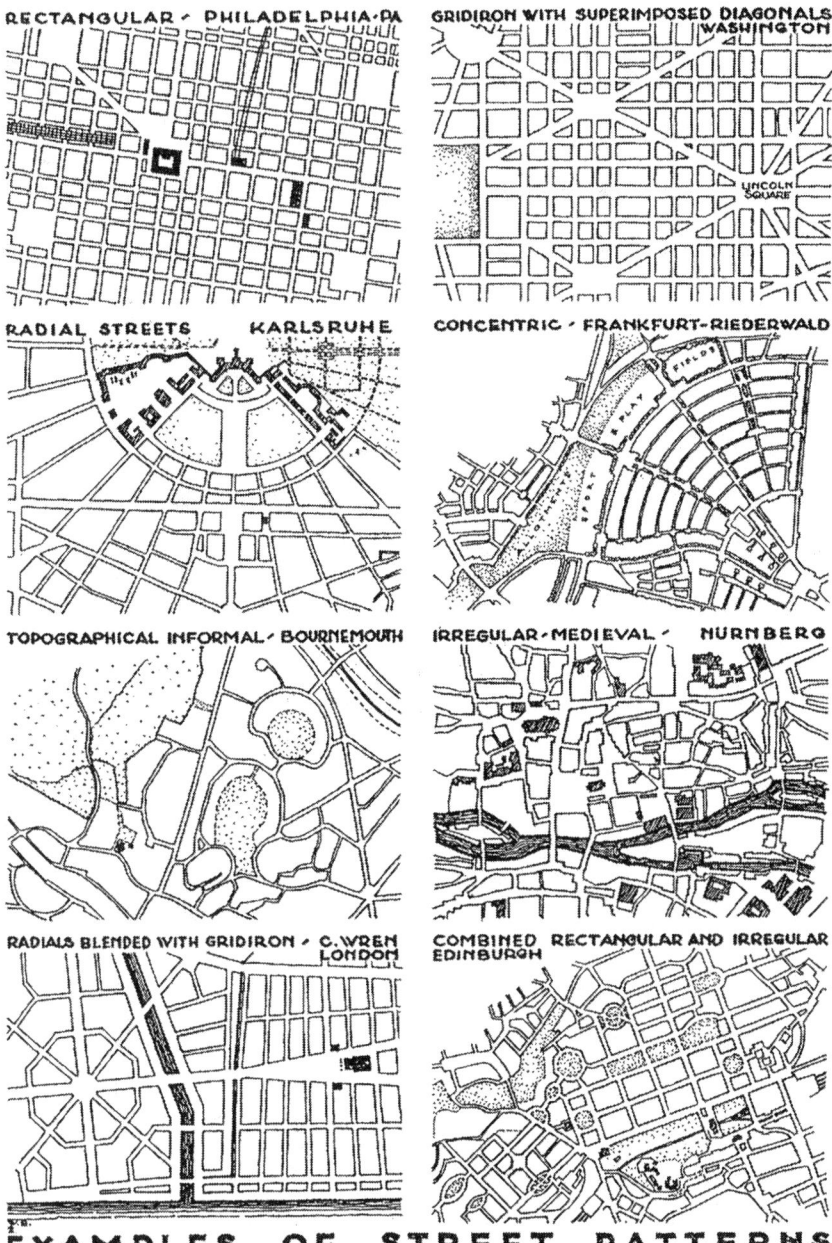

EXAMPLES OF STREET PATTERNS

Figure 2.6. Adams and Baumgartner street patterns and blocks (1934). These drawings create a basis for street and block typologies that can be differentiated by function, geographical location, geometric forms, incremental design, and democratic/civic doctrine, from Philadelphia and Washington in North America to Nuremburg and Edinburgh in Europe.

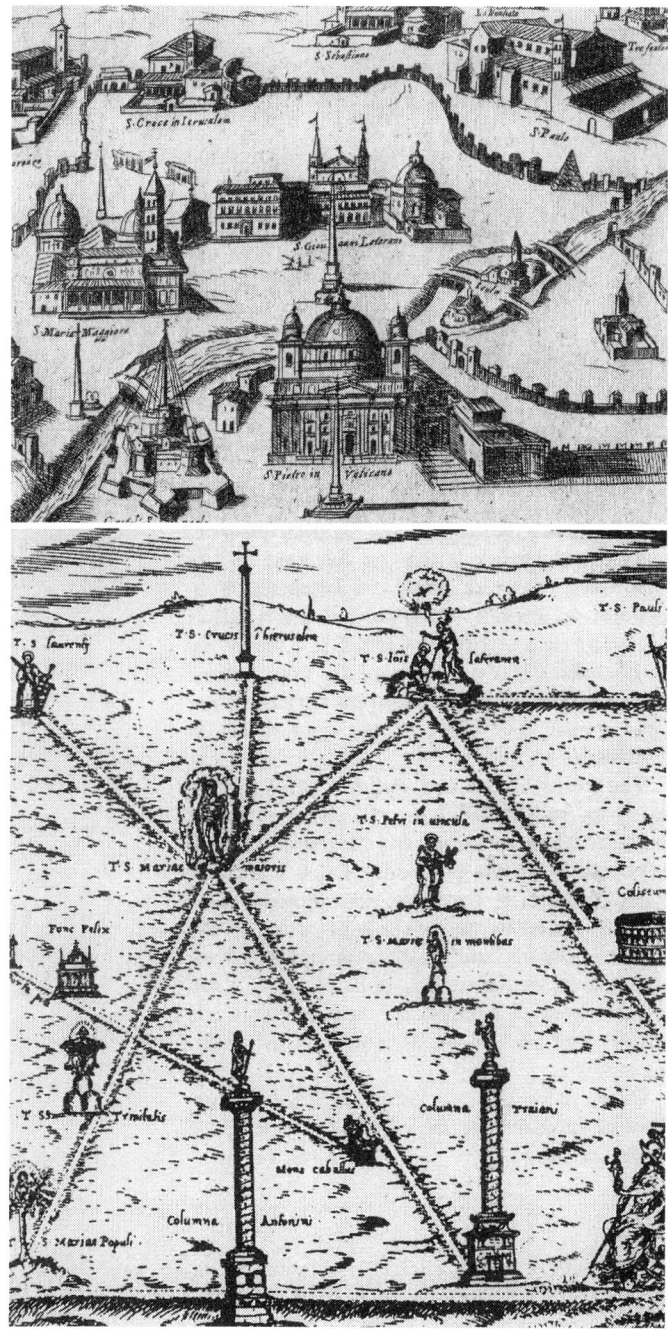

Figure 2.7. Pope Sixtus V Plan for Rome (1590). This plan features the importance of monumental civic buildings and carefully placed monuments in alignment with roads at strategic points in the city.

35

Industrial new towns, grand city plans, and livability

As cities, towns, and villages expanded over time in Europe and the Mediterranean area, city size was sometimes limited by local and regional mobility. This affected even the biggest cities of Babylon, Rome, and Alexandria.[4] Defense became less of a preoccupation as time progressed. Water and sanitary aspects of urban infrastructures varied from sophisticated Roman piping systems to open sewers in parts of England. The use of horses for transport caused a huge waste problem in denser urban centers. In fact, the city of New York in the late 1800s discontinued a city planning exercise on the grounds that horse excrement would overwhelm the city's waste management capacity. Little did the city planners know that Henry Ford's idea for the automobile would emerge in just a few years.

Mixed-use and compact layout of buildings represented the standard for urban design of the 1800s, and only royalty could occupy larger homes. The Industrial Revolution of the mid-nineteenth century prompted the search for better living conditions and ultimately better worker productivity. This search led to the development of Saltaire, a new village designed by Sir Titus Salt in Yorkshire, England, in 1853, and Bournville, a new community built by the Cadbury brothers of chocolate fame just outside Birmingham in 1879. The concept was simple: better living conditions, better health, and better production from the workers.

Grand plans for urban design were created during the same era, including Major Pierre Charles L'Enfant's plan for Washington, DC, in 1791 (fig. 2.8), and the Haussmann plan for Paris, developed from 1853 to 1869. Both plans featured grand avenues, site lines, and landmarks in a formal geometry. L'Enfant's plan for Washington combined the major axial design for larger boulevards with the democratic grid pattern for local streets; everyone had equal access to the same size of street blocks. High ground for important sites and river views were features of this plan. The Haussmann plan required massive removal of housing to make room for the grand boulevards of the Champs-Élysées, public parks, and the grand houses along the routes. Such aesthetic considerations presaged the next trend in urban design, whose key goal was to make cities more beautiful.

Figure 2.8. Major Pierre Charles L'Enfant's plan for Washington, DC (1791). The famous L'Enfant Plan combined a street grid pattern with grand axial boulevards that bisected the grid at various strategic locations—connecting important landmarks such as the Capitol with the White House and allowing views of the Potomac River. (Source: Library of Congress.)

City Beautiful movement

> Men are becoming convinced that the formless growth of the city is neither economic nor satisfactory.
>
> —Daniel Burnham and Edward Bennett, *The Plan for Chicago*

The City Beautiful movement aimed to uplift urban residents' spirit and health by creating inspiring surroundings. The movement originated in the 1800s to alleviate the drab and unsanitary conditions of most cities created by the Industrial Revolution. Frederick Law Olmsted, widely seen as the father of American landscape architecture, teamed up with the architect and urban planner Daniel Burnham to illustrate the power of the City Beautiful movement in the plan for Chicago's World's Fair of

1893. The fair occupied more than one square mile and filled more than two hundred buildings. About 27.5 million people attended the exposition over six months—this at a time when the country's entire population was 65 million. Because the fair's neoclassical buildings were all painted white, the site became known as the "White City." This dream city captured the public's imagination, representing a grand urban landscape never before created in one place. People even wept at its beauty.[5] Interestingly enough, Walt Disney's father was one of the construction workers on the site and could easily have inspired his son to create Disneyland. Critiques of the City Beautiful movement in the 1890s are echoed in those of Disneyland and Disney World today. These critiques focused on the artificial and almost irresponsible fantasyland that the fair created.

Critics and many architects saw the City Beautiful movement as decorative, classical, and monumental urban design with little relevance to contemporary architectural expression, as exemplified by neoclassical architecture in the Court of Honor (fig. 2.9). Countering these critiques were inspired visions of grand civic plans like the former Baroque city of Rome (late sixteenth century), with axial avenues terminating in focal points and landmarks, grand squares and plazas, wide boulevards, and large-scale classical buildings enclosing spaces and streets. Although the City Beautiful design principles have never been implemented for a city as a whole, efforts were made in Canberra, Australia, and imperial New Delhi, India, although both have Garden City overlays. Nevertheless, the City Beautiful movement created significant efforts to improve the health, look, and civic nature of cities, especially during the heavily industrial nineteenth century.

As the City Beautiful movement spread, grand boulevards and city parks became ways to escape the dark corners of unhealthy cities degraded by industrial pollution and overcrowding. During the latter part of the nineteenth century, Frederick Law Olmsted gave form to Central Park in New York City and Mount Royal Park in Montreal. Design of the former reflected his ability to think long term. He stated, "In laying out Central Park, we determined to think of no result to be realized in less than forty years."[6] Olmsted even combined storm water management with a linear park system design in Boston, which became known as the "emerald necklace." Parks were seen as the lungs of the city and a place to escape from the pollution.

Figure 2.9. Court of Honor, World's Columbian Exposition, Chicago (1893). The City Beautiful movement was criticized by some as being superficial and did not reflect contemporary architectural design expression. (Source: Paul Gavin Library, Illinois Institute of Technology.)

The Plan of Chicago, developed by Daniel Burnham in 1909, created a comprehensive and definitive vision for the city. This plan—a rich tapestry of parks, streets, and physical form—was farsighted and still stands as an exemplary achievement and a timeless guide for urban planning in Chicago. The Chicago plan created a whole series of continuous public waterfront parks along Lake Michigan and an organized hierarchy of streets with civic landmarks and buildings. The plan brought a long-term logic and elegance to the elements of street, building, and public domain, connecting Chicago to its region with a prominent network of streets and landmarks. (For more on the Chicago of today, see chapter 12.)

Farther north, Thomas Mawson developed a plan for the city of Calgary, Canada, before World War I that exemplified many elements of the City Beautiful movement (fig. 2.10). As a landscape architect from England, he recognized the importance of streets and parks as overall form-makers for the city. Mawson developed a series of grand boulevards, the Bow River Valley park system, and Stampede Park with Centre Street as a major north-south axis. Much of his work and vision was lost with the advent of the Great War and the redirection of resources and priorities (fig. 2.11). Remnants remain. In fact, and fortunately, the last copy of the Mawson Plan was discovered in the wallboards of a Calgary garage and deposited in the Calgary Archives apparently in the 1960s. The plan featured insightful ideas, including the use of civic buildings and landmarks as orientation points and an interlinked park and boulevard system that connected to and followed the river systems.

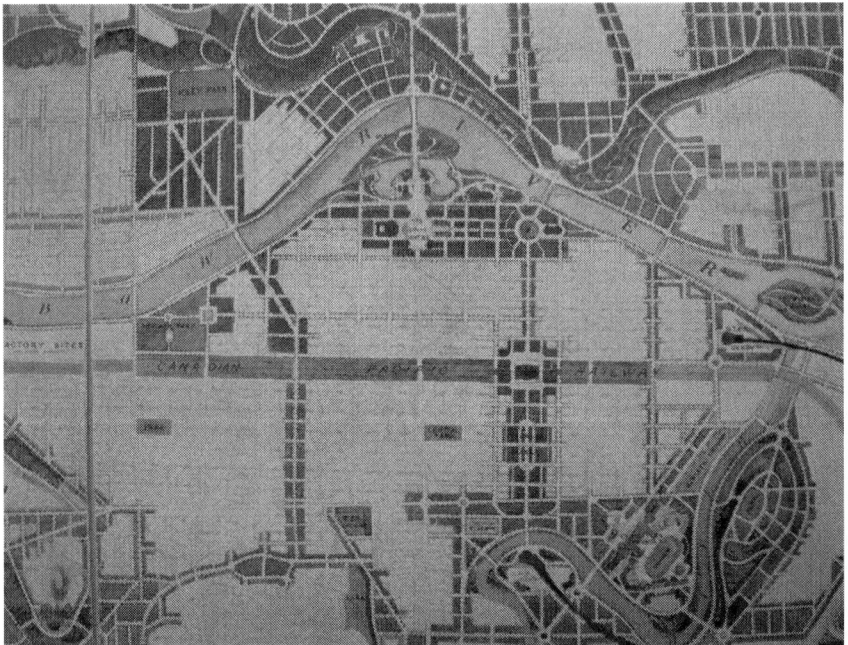

Figure 2.10. Mawson Plan for Calgary, Alberta (1914). This plan captured many elements of the City Beautiful movement, including grand boulevards, axial street design, focal landmarks, elegant civic buildings, and a connected network of public parks and spaces. (Source: City of Calgary.)

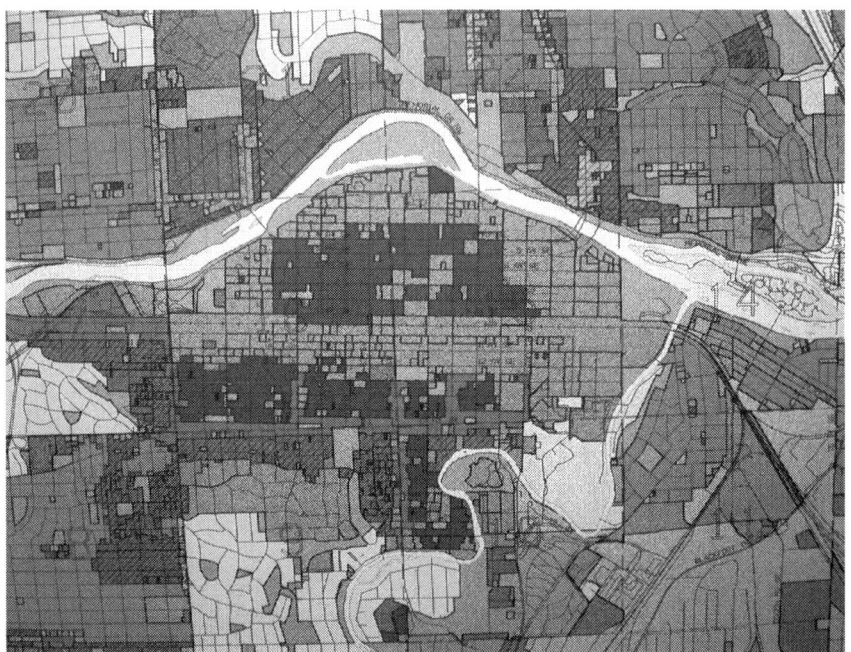

Figure 2.11. Calgary land use districts (zoning) today. Only some of the remnants of the Mawson Plan can be seen in the Bow River park network and Stampede Park. (Source: City of Calgary.)

Alexandre Gustave Eiffel's grand Eiffel Tower in Paris rose out of the ground in 1889—the tallest structure in the world at 1,000 feet (305 m) (fig. 2.12 A.). Associated with another world's fair, the tower marked the entrance to the Exposition Universelle. It was not a skyscraper per se, but other tall steel-frame office buildings were soon known by that term. The birth of the skyscraper in North America occurred in 1884 with the creation of a ten-story building by William Le Baron Jenney in Chicago. The innovative steel skeletal structure carries the entire load of the walls instead of load-bearing walls carrying the entire weight of the building. From the 22-storey Flatiron Building in New York (Daniel Burnham, 1902) to the 102-story Empire State Building (Shreve, Lamb, and Harmon, 1930), these skyscrapers housed the elite businesses of the day, because they stood for capitalism and progress (figs. 2.12 B. and C.). They also made more economic sense as land values skyrocketed in

Figure 2.12 (from left to right) A. Eiffel Tower (1889), B. Flatiron Building (1902), C. Empire State Building (1930). Although not a skyscraper per se, the ten-story Eiffel Tower was soon followed by multistory steel-frame office buildings in cities such as Chicago and New York (Flatiron Building and Empire State Building).

downtown cores. The geographic limits imposed by water bodies in both Chicago and New York also pressed buildings higher. These higher forms of urban architecture began to detach the occupant from the street, but the race for the sky had only begun.

Just after the Eiffel Tower was built in France, a humble reporter and parliamentary recorder, Ebenezer Howard, developed the groundwork for the Garden City movement in England (fig. 2.13). In Howard's utopian model, country, city, and industry were blended to find the best of all worlds in a city of 1,000 acres (405 ha) surrounded by 5,000 acres (2,023 ha) of agricultural land for a population of 32,000 inhabitants, which surrounded a central garden city of 58,000 residents interconnected by railway links. Letchworth, north of London, and Welwyn, in Hertfordshire, were experiments in this direction. The Garden City movement intended to reverse the ill effects of the Industrial Revolution, which had left England suffering socially, physically, and culturally. This Garden City movement blended with the City Beautiful movement to shape cities in the early twentieth century.

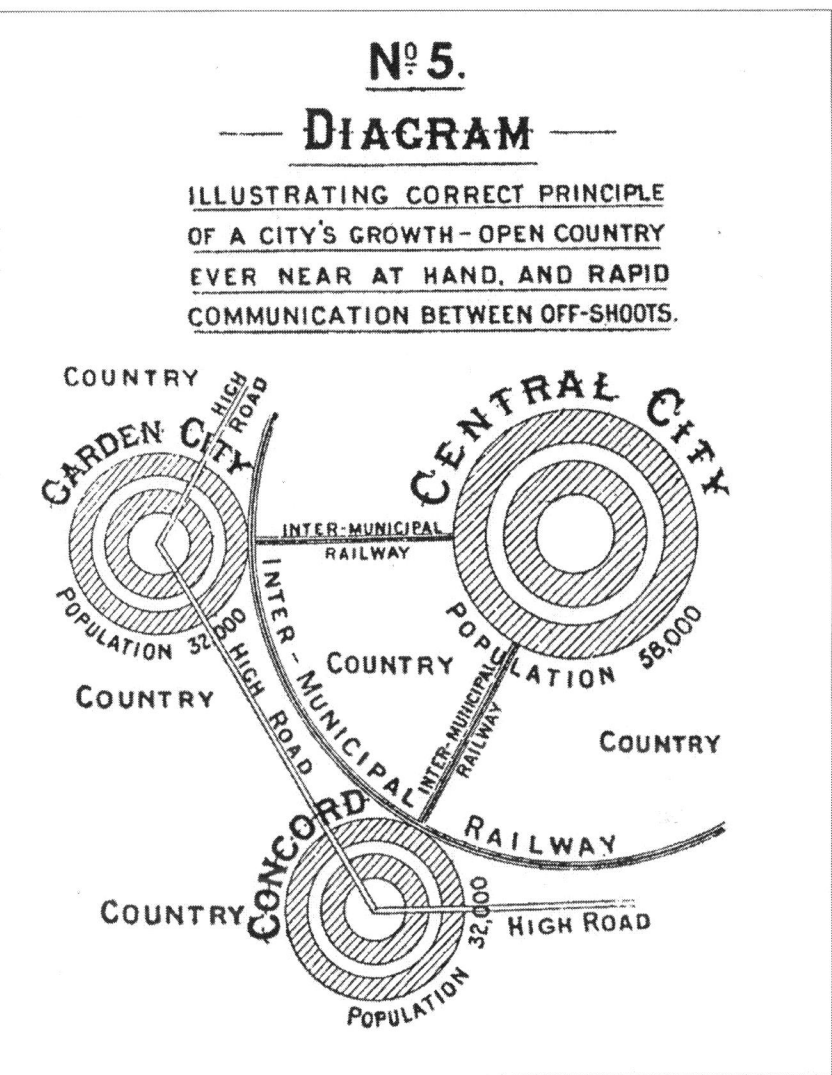

Figure 2.13. Ebenezer Howard's Garden City model (1898). His ideal city had 32,000 residents on 1,000 acres (405 ha) surrounded by 5,000 acres (2,023 ha) of farmland connected by railway to a central garden city of 58,000 residents—the ideal blending of the urban and the rural in the countryside that he referred to as the "group of slumless, smokeless cities."

In 1889, the Austrian art historian and architect Camillo Sitte wrote his seminal work, *City Planning According to Artistic Principles*, which significantly influenced Austrian and German city planning and urban design. Sitte's criticism of the pragmatic, sterile, and symmetrical approach to urban design in the nineteenth century foreshadowed the modernist movement of the early twentieth century. Similar criticisms reemerged in different forms in the late 1960s as part of the postmodernist movement.

Sitte's theories focused on the formation of less formal and rather irregular urban structure shaped by ancient Greece that did not follow a rigid geometry. They emphasized the urban "room," including plazas (the agora and forum of ancient Greece), monuments, and other artistic elements. Outside space was more than residual space for ornamental sculptures. Instead, the three-dimensional aspect of urban form was critical in shaping the city experience. Rather surprisingly, the architectural shape or form of each building was less important than the creative quality of urban space, exemplified by the ancient, more organic shapes of urban form. Sitte attended to the aesthetics of space and the experience it created. His theories countered the sterile formality and dogma of oversized streets and squares as well as the insensitive placement of churches and monuments. Little did Sitte or other shapers of urban design theory know that within ten to twenty years cars would begin to reshape the urban landscape and alter the traditional pedestrian orientation of many cities. The automobile would replace horses. One source of pollution (car exhaust) would replace another source of pollution (horse excrement).

3
TWENTIETH-CENTURY TRANSFORMATIONS

Americans have been living car-centered lives for so long that the collective memory of what used to make a landscape or a townscape or even a suburb humanly rewarding has nearly been erased. The culture of good place-making, like the culture of farming, or agriculture, is a body of knowledge and acquired skills.

—James Howard Kunstler, *The Geography of Nowhere*

With the advent of the automobile in the early twentieth century, the vision of the city changed. Efficiency of car movement demanded wider streets, and the car took priority in city design in both some European and North American cities. These model plans would be precursors of later western "freeway" approaches that would not only create dysfunction and alienation of many downtowns but also spread to other parts of the world, from China to Saudi Arabia, as progressive transportation models that governed urban design. Le Corbusier's romantic Plan Voisin for Paris of the 1920s (fig. 3.1) and Frank Lloyd Wright's conceptual Broadacre City, first presented in 1932, both reflected the linear and the mobilized city. Consisting of freeways and skyscrapers surrounded by parks, Le Corbusier's urban design model lacked a sense of human scale and livability. Broadacre City had the same dominant road systems with large building parcels designed for the efficiency of movement and had little to do with the livability of the human being. Broadacre City previewed suburban isolation of residents, divided by roads and dominated by single uses, so driving is mandatory to obtain services. These visions essentially wrote off the city as it was. Instead, they previewed things to come—in particular the urban renewal movement that wiped out sections of New York City in the 1950s and 1960s in favor of new high-rise apartments, displacing generations of families in the process.

Figure 3.1. Le Corbusier's Plan Voisin (Vision Plan) for Paris (1924). The Voisin Plan created what has become well-known as the "tower in the park" concept, where high-rise residential towers allow for maximum green space and an efficient, car-dominated landscape.

Birth of the neighborhood unit

Countering these dream plans of the car city were practical post–First World War village and neighborhood plans. These provided quality, diverse housing in a complete community environment with support services within walking distance and, in some cases, support industry to provide the necessary local jobs. In many cases, these communities were located along a railway line for convenient public transportation.

In 1929, the American planner Clarence Perry developed a neighborhood model based on a population of 5,000 residents (fig. 3.2). The model was designed to house 1,500 families on 160 acres (64 ha). It featured a comfortable walking distance of 1,320 feet (400 m) for residents to school, dedicated open space, and support facilities, including a church

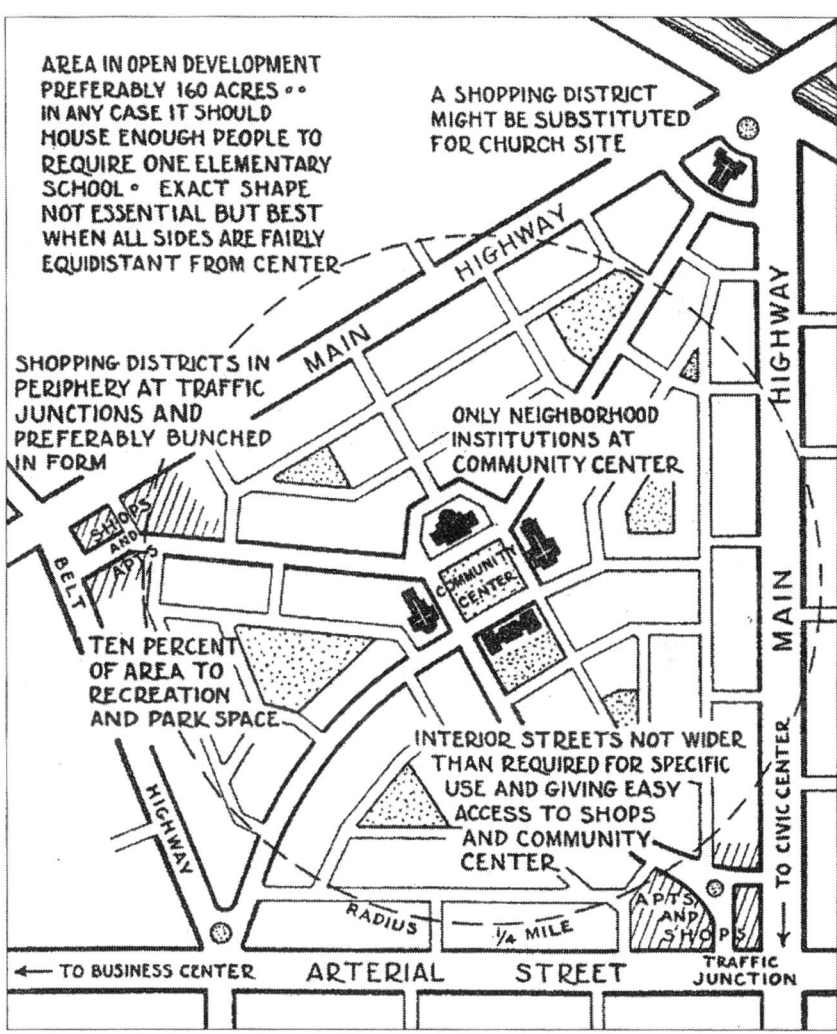

Figure 3.2. Clarence Perry's plan for new neighborhoods (1929). Perry organized the neighborhood around a five-minute walk, a 10 percent open space dedication, central community facilities, and convenient shopping at the edge.

or a library. Shops were located on the edge of the neighborhood, and an internal residential road network protected pedestrian flow, because the main streets did not pass through the neighborhood. Andrés Duany and Peter Calthorpe would rediscover these unique villages and towns in the New Urbanism movement of the late twentieth century.

Clarence Stein, another American urban planner, gave some innovative thought to the neighborhood unit and pedestrian orientation in his work, creating Radburn, New Jersey, in 1929. The development provided an entirely separate pedestrian system through a green space network. Part of this pedestrian model is echoed in more recent projects. For instance, it appears in the Witchwood subdivision in Winnipeg, Canada, where the front yards face open space and access is through back lanes. It is also echoed in the "pedestrian pocket" and transit-oriented development theories of the late 1980s and 1990s.[1]

Stein's efforts are also reflected in the current greenway movement across North America that gained significant momentum in the 1990s. Many areas are adopting local, regional, and national greenway links, using streets, trails, and railways for pedestrian, bicycle, and, in some cases, equestrian pathways. These greenways vary from county-wide greenways to local city greenways. They include the East Coast Greenway in the eastern United States; the Cross Vermont Greenway; the Capital Area Greenway in Raleigh, North Carolina; and the Cherry Creek Greenway in Denver, Colorado. The most recent urban innovation (known as the High Line) is the conversion of a former elevated railway spur line on the lower west side of Manhattan, New York, into a greenway. The Trans Canada Trail, established in 1992, is in the formative stages of development, with eventual greenway links across provinces, regions, and cities that will total almost 14,000 miles (22,500 km).[2]

New town movement
After the Second World War, decentralization became a trend in some of the big cities to reduce congestion. This direction gave birth to the new town movement and towns such as Stevenage and Milton Keynes in England, and Cumbernauld in Scotland. Results were mixed. The modernist approach to urban design introduced by Le Corbusier early in the twentieth century did

not recognize any history or culture in creating a new community. Instead, building form and street grid were functional and self-evident, with little sense of place, history, or culture. A sense of place and cultural richness are difficult to achieve in a short period of time, especially when starting with little existing town or city fabric. The new town movement led to largely functionalist cities with little creative design. One example, is Runcorn, outside Liverpool, England. As reflected in the plan, the overall pattern of the town is repetitive and very mechanical. Each section is the same, and the materials from sector to sector are also the same—all red brick. Nonetheless, as one small boy remarked to me when I visited the site, "this neighborhood is a lot better than where I was living."

Car-oriented North American suburbs

In North America, the car-oriented suburb was born after the war. The planned community of Levittown, New York, was the model suburban community for the family in the late 1940s. Here on Long Island a lack of local services and jobs forced residents to drive to their destinations. Urban sprawl was born with the ever-expanding federal highways funding programs in the United States. This automobile-dependent development continued to spread as central cities deteriorated, the postwar highway program expanded, and an infinite supply of peripheral land created a cheap alternative to city living. The dream of owning a single-family house was now within reach of the middle-income baby boomers. The North American dream was born.

Single-use large-lot zoning pushed the sprawl model farther and farther out of town. In 1949, the first regional shopping center was developed, in Columbus, Ohio. The Town and Country Shopping Center foreshadowed the eventual decline of many downtown shopping districts across the continent. This issue has escalated over the years through the addition of Walmarts and other big-box stores. Communities have struggled to retain locally owned small businesses while still allowing for economic expansion. The attraction of one-stop shopping, an assortment of uses, and convenience all under one roof was too tempting in our ever-increasing fast-paced life dominated by consumption.

"Bedroom communities" were the neighborhoods of choice starting in the late 1940s with creation of Levittown, Long Island, and roads expanded to meet the growing demand. New communities in Columbia, Maryland, and Reston, Virginia, created by the Rouse Company in the 1960s and 1970s, were improvements in creating complete communities because they provided some services and local jobs.

The problems of urban sprawl are many, and they continue today. Urban sprawl ignores both historical precedent and human experience. Instead, it helps pollute our skies through dependency on the automobile, creates gross inefficiencies and higher costs associated with extending infrastructure, and perpetuates hollow human habitats oriented toward only residential use, with little or no local services or jobs. Driving everywhere is the norm in suburbia and not a real choice because of distance, safety, and empty experience, because these areas lack nearby services and recreational opportunities. This dependence on the automobile creates, in turn, health challenges that include increasing obesity throughout the North American population.

Urban sprawl is not healthy growth and is self-destructive. It tends not to pay for itself financially (creating a net loss in terms of costs and revenues) and consumes land at an alarming rate, creating irreparable traffic problems, social separation, inequity, and growing isolation. The suburban ring expands as the core of the city declines in many American cities. Downtown businesses and residents are attracted to newer and supposedly fresher suburban locations that are cheaper and offer attractive amenities.[3]

Urban renewal

Meanwhile, the deterioration of many depopulated downtowns, especially in the United States, forced some cities to undertake "radical surgery," otherwise known as "urban renewal." This trend of the 1950s and 1960s reflected the belief that "when you get rid of the buildings, you get rid of the problems"—of crime, racial unrest, and poverty. However, such problems were not resolved but simply pushed elsewhere. The large new housing projects in New York and Chicago at that time represent this destruction and replacement of entire neighborhoods. The Renaissance Center in downtown Detroit is another monument to that era of thinking. The results were fortress-like structures with little or no "ownership" of the outdoor community spaces. Such modernist and deterministic approaches to urban design showed their flaws almost immediately as some projects "self-destructed" through rapid physical decline and social dysfunction. The so-called urban renewal movement lacked public consultation and featured little or no social or environmental conscience. It was simply seen as an expedient way to eradicate urban problems by starting all over again.

Jane Jacobs in her seminal 1961 work *The Death and Life of Great American Cities*,[4] attacked the thoughtless approaches to urban planning and design of this time. She advocated the development of the public realm, small blocks, mixed uses, and compact design—radical measures in the 1960s that have since become mainstream. Jacobs gave us the concept of "Eyes on the Street," which still lives today in the principles of Crime Prevention Through Environmental Design (CPTED). Another American, the urban planner Kevin Lynch (most famous for *The Image of the City*, 1960),[5] created a vocabulary of paths, nodes, districts, edges, and landmarks and mapped how the observer reads the city. These works reinforced the notion that the design of the public realm is at the core of urban design.

Bringing nature back into urban design

Ian McHarg's *Design with Nature* (1969) and William H. Whyte's books *Cluster Development* (1964) and *The Last Landscape* (1968) helped resurrect the value of nature in urban design.[6] McHarg advocated environmental assessment and analysis to determine "carrying capacity" or the development potential for a site or region. Whyte explored what he termed "cluster development" and innovative methods of conserving valuable ecological features. These works foreshadowed the birth of the environmental movement of the early 1970s that integrated nature as part of the design process—humans were interconnected with nature and therefore any physical change impacted nature. Environmentalists sometimes neglected to approach social and economic needs and growth in realistic or supportable ways. This unrealistic approach marginalized their cause, and instead of receiving support, they were dismissed as radicals. Both Anne Whiston Spirn and Michael Hough would expand on the importance of natural processes in urban design in the 1980s through their research and fact-based conclusions.[7] Both landscape architects and professors, Spirn and Hough effectively illustrated the direct connections between urban growth, natural processes, and potential negative or positive impacts through thoughtful urban designs. They illustrated the value of urban forests, unstable slope sensitivity, and the design of natural areas in urban storm water management as part of environmentally based urban design.

These science-based approaches would have revealed the original location of New Orleans as a delta below sea level or St. Petersburg as marshland. The locations of these cities were not based on scientific fact-finding but politically motivated by either royal single-mindedness, as in St. Petersburg, or through strategic location, as in New Orleans. Disregarding these sensitive relationships can end in disaster, as witnessed in 2005 with Hurricane Katrina in New Orleans. Science and ecological relationships play a key role in urban design. Disregarding nature's powerful forces can have disastrous effects, as we are seeing with constant reminders of climate change in rising sea levels, increased temperatures, increased earthquakes, and erratic weather conditions.

Downtown revitalization and pedestrianization

During the 1970s and 1980s, more sensitive development methods continued to evolve, with some breakthroughs on the importance of heritage in the North American countryside and cities. Smaller towns and villages were now being affected by the extent of urban sprawl. The earlier trend of urban renewal destruction was then transformed into downtown revitalization. Moves to revitalize downtowns extended across North America in the 1980s with various adaptations of "Main Street" programs, as in Danvers, Massachusetts (fig. 3.3).

Bigger Canadian cities such as Montreal and Quebec City discovered the value of their original townsite's history. Ottawa rediscovered

Figure 3.3 Downtown revitalization plan, Danvers, Massachusetts.
(Plan A) This plan improves access, safety, public realm, and storefront
design. (Photos B and C) Photo B shows previous conditions and photo
C shows improvements.

Lowertown and transformed Sparks Street into a pedestrian mall like Nicollet Mall in Minneapolis. The move to make cities more pedestrian-friendly spread across the continent but was short-lived in some cases, as pedestrian malls caused some business areas to decline. By this time, convenience and car access were driving forces for retail sales. Pedestrian malls often eliminate the car and associated convenient parking, which made stores more difficult to access.

In Canada, given the intense winter season, cities such as Montreal and Calgary chose to shift pedestrian movement below and/or above ground. Montreal adopted an underground system with the landmark mixed-use Place Bonaventure project and in Calgary the +15 Skywalk system that connected downtown buildings above the ground. The streets became the victim in both these instances, as pedestrian flow moved indoors, but these alternatives certainly competed with enclosed suburban shopping malls, especially during the colder winter months. In North America, the addition and expansion of outlet malls, power centers, and lifestyle centers (a combination of large-format specialty stores based on common themes) continue to drain business and activities from downtown cores.

Small-town renewal

In smaller towns across North America, downtown revitalization programs sponsored by the state, provincial, and federal governments stimulated facade restoration, streetscape reconstruction, and an improved pedestrian realm. Many towns uncovered their distinctive history, attracted new uses, created unique themes, increased ease of access, and introduced special events with a new organized approach through Business Improvement Areas (BIAs) or similar organizations that represented the business communities. This economic foundation, complemented by cooperation among business owners, spurred innovative approaches to funding improvements and created a collective will to improve entire downtown areas. Work by Harry Garnham, a landscape architect and professor at the University of Colorado, in small towns emphasized analyzing "genius loci" or "spirit of place" in determining urban design directions and priorities. The emergence of national and international advocacy groups such as the

Nature Conservancy, located across North America, and the National Trust for Historic Preservation in Washington, DC, further reinforced this work, as these groups took action to save land and buildings in the public interest.

Public realm returns to the forefront

The downtown revitalization movement brought renewed prominence to Main Street and public space once again. Further work by planners and architects such as William H. Whyte, Jan Gehl, and Allan Jacobs explored the social, physical, and psychological aspects of public space in North America and in Europe from 1960 to 2000.

William Whyte's work, starting in the early 1960s and gaining the most recognition in the late 1970s and early 1980s, suggested the importance of movable seating, sunny orientation, and activities as critical to successful public places. He observed the street and public spaces very closely—specifically how humans interacted in these places. I remember him presenting a video of what he referred to as people "schmoozing" on a street corner. These observations led to design guidelines for plazas and parks in New York City and elsewhere to make them safer, active, and more attractive. Connectedness to adjacent spaces, shade trees, and attractive amenities such as fountains or tables for activities all contributed to the positive transformation of North American public spaces, especially in New York.[8]

Jan Gehl, a Danish architect, emerged as the scientist of pedestrian and bicycle movement, as he observed and helped transform pedestrian and bicycle movement in Copenhagen, Denmark, over almost thirty years. From the mid-1960s to the late 1990s, the summertime use of the streets and squares of the city increased 3.5 times in step with improvements in the quality of public space. Bicycle traffic increased by 65 percent between 1980 and 2001, handling 33 percent of commuter traffic.[9] Gehl embraced the detailing of materials, activities that stimulate pedestrian activity, conditions that extend pedestrians outside during colder months, and public policy strategies that win back our public spaces. Providing heaters and blankets during colder weather to increasing the number of doors to the street are among the strategies Gehl discovered in his countless observations from Barcelona, Spain, to Córdoba, Argentina. Central to these pedestrian strategies are fewer cars, more transit, bicycles, and pedestrians, as part of a sustainable city strategy. A people-centered city is part of Gehl's unified city strategy of interconnected public corridors and squares.

The American planner and former director of planning for San Francisco, Allan Jacobs brought new meaning to streets and boulevards throughout the world with his classic *Great Streets* in the early 1990s as not only places for cars and transport but also as living places where people meet and observe the city. He said if we design streets properly, we have designed 25 to 30 percent of our cities. His analytic drawings and descriptions created a window on the anatomy of different streets' form, function, and intricacies that made them unique places in time and location. Appreciating the delight and grandness of some multiway boulevards to the intimacy of smaller streets, Jacobs revealed that streets can both combine a human scale as well as accommodate the automobile in different ways.[10] He also defined great streets of the world as, first and foremost, helping to make a community, then as comfortable and safe, encouraging of participation, memorable, and lastly, as representative of type and best in class.[11]

For Jacobs and other urban advocates like Whyte and Gehl, the social design and programming of public spaces is of critical importance to their vibrancy and success. This research helped build detailed street, plaza, and park designs, plus it emphasized programming and animating public space to create vibrant and safe environments. Today, Projects for Public Spaces (www.pps.org), headquartered in New York, continues such research and project analysis worldwide. Their Power of Ten concept requires public spaces to have ten activities to be successful. And it reinforces the need to comprehensively program and design the public realm. In other words, and to reemphasize, we should pay the same attention to designing outdoor rooms as we do interior rooms.

Pattern language and good city form
More theoretical urban design work also emerged during the 1960s and 1970s. Christopher Alexander's work on reading the city in *A Pattern*

Language and the benefits of incremental development and an "organic" approach embraced a new and evocative route to finding a better and more sensitive way to design urban spaces. The 253 pattern languages Alexander presented in *A Pattern Language* described a problem and then offered a solution, from the scale of the region to the scale of houses.[12] Taken together, these patterns form a language or a way to understand and synthesize design solutions. They are inherently a means to an end rather than a prescriptive collection of solutions. Their power is in their ability to be adapted and modified to face change over time.

Kevin Lynch's further work in *Good City Form* discussed seven performance criteria for city form—vitality, sense, fit, access, control, efficiency, and justice—to define settlement quality.[13] Although quite abstract, this research by Lynch, an MIT professor, brought forward the importance of evaluating and informing urban planning and design from a physical and social perspective (in both measurable and nonmeasurable elements). For example, the work of Oscar Newman in preventing crime through urban design revealed that good city form through visual access, physical design, and a sense of territory could reduce crime.[14] The value of this research would resurface again in the mid-1990s, as Crime Prevention Through Environmental Design (CPTED) became a mainstream method to reduce crime and increase safety and security across North American cities. This social dimension of urban design, combined with further environmental urgency in the 1980s, foreshadowed the sustainability movement that began to combine environment, society, and economics into a call to action that would be resilient and dramatically change how we view and act in our world.

Sustainability, Smart Growth, and New Urbanism

The rising tide of sustainability, born in 1987 out of the internationally supported Brundtland Commission, spawned a reconsideration of urban patterns and design worldwide. The California-based architect and urban designer Peter Calthorpe explored the importance of ecology, the region, and a move to transit-oriented development (TOD) as major urban design form-makers.[15] Andrés Duany and Elizabeth Plater-Zyberk, Miami-based architects, renewed the importance of traditional neighborhood design, emphasizing a pedestrian orientation, street grid, mixed uses, and a more compact urban form.[16]

About the same time, in the early 1990s, the term "Smart Growth" emerged, especially at the government level, as a policy tool to counter urban sprawl and no-growth advocates. Smart Growth aimed to ensure that neighborhoods, towns, and regions accommodated growth in ways that were economically sound, environmentally responsible, and supportive of community livability. Smart Growth included the following proactive design processes:

- collaborating on solutions
- mixing land uses
- encouraging infill development and redevelopment
- building master-planned communities
- conserving open space
- providing transportation choices
- creating housing opportunities
- encouraging smart development by lowering barriers and providing incentives
- using high-quality design techniques

Austin, Texas, has been a leader in Smart Growth. The city adopted a growth strategy in Smart Growth zones in the 1990s, a land development simplification project, land conservation zones, neighborhood planning, and Smart Growth incentives as parts of a tool kit to advance appropriate growth in their city.[17] Smart Growth has had a significant impact on regional and city planning across North America, as the associated initiatives have created many regional growth management and containment policies. It indirectly affected urban form and location through enlightened land use policies. Maybe most beneficially, Smart Growth affected all levels of government in helping them to manage growth rather than artificially limit growth, with unintended consequences, such as pushing development to an adjoining municipality or county.

This New Urbanism (or neo-traditional town planning), as was discussed in chapter 1, believes in the same principles as Smart Growth but translates those principles into urban design directives that are more specific. New Urbanism is based on the neighborhood planning and design of the early twentieth century. Traditional neighborhood design created easy access with a street grid pattern. It embraced different house designs and types, including lane-oriented housing closer to the street, narrower residential streets, convenient services within a five-minute walk, and overall a more walkable community. New Urbanism built on these principles and included the values of conserving historic buildings, preserving environmentally sensitive areas, and promoting a transit orientation. The goal was to create more self-sufficient, less car-reliant communities that were safer and had more active residents. Through place-sensitive design, New Urbanism aimed to bring more meaning back to individual neighborhoods.

Improvements to the design of new neighborhoods and community elements through the New Urbanism movement have been significant, from the early Seaside neighborhood in Pensacola, Florida, in the early 1980s, to the later Kentlands, Maryland, outside Washington, DC. Unfortunately, the challenge remains to decrease car domination, as the majority of New Urbanism projects are located in the suburbs, with limited transit access.[18] (See also chapter 11, which highlights innovative urban design projects at urban, suburban, and rural locations.)

Calthorpe's and Duany's efforts converged in 1993 with the twenty-three Ahwahnee Principles, which conveyed community, regional, and implementation principles necessary to help reverse uncontrolled urban sprawl and the associated environmental and cultural decay. These principles were further refined in 1996 with the publication of the *Charter for the New Urbanism*,[19] which outlined twenty-seven principles of good urban design, including the region, neighborhood, district, corridor, block, street, and buildings.

The rural cluster and saving our countryside

Meanwhile, rural areas were increasingly coming under attack through the 1970s and 1980s from urban sprawl patterns, with valuable agricultural land and rural character being threatened as buyers were moving farther and farther beyond city limits to find a home or a second residence. The

American landscape planner Randall Arendt brought renewed visibility to the importance of clustering development and recognizing the local traditional built form.[20] He reversed the typical development approach by conserving valuable green space first. His process determined primary and secondary areas of protection, located remaining development areas, and finally created the most efficient access (fig. 3.4). Contrary to traditional development, this approach was nonetheless effective in determining more efficient development patterns and increasing market value, while conserving rural integrity. This cluster approach is being widely adopted as a viable option to rural sprawl by many rural counties across North America.

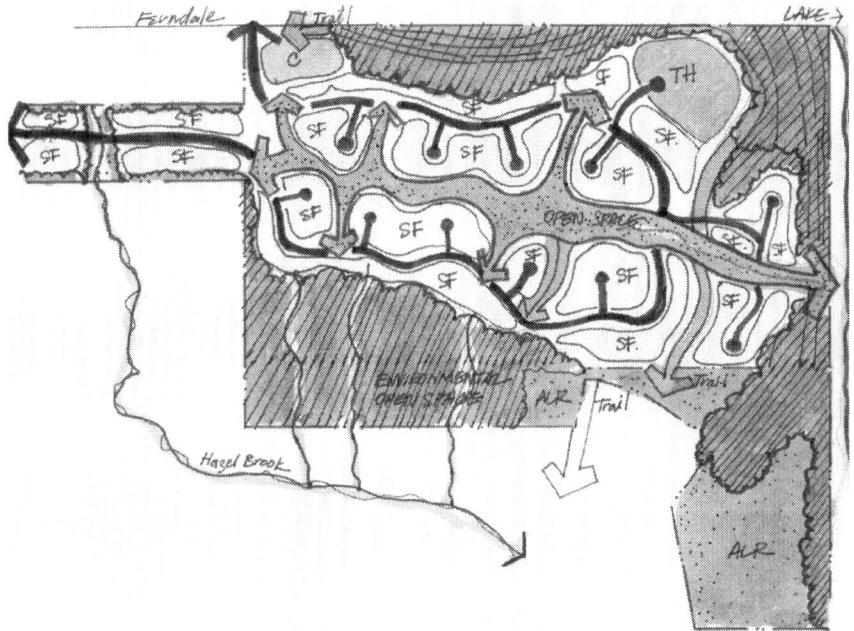

Figure 3.4. Rural cluster concept, Mission, British Columbia. This concept Illustrates the importance of nature conservation, usable open space, diversity of housing types, visual connectivity, and cluster development to create a more efficient and sensitive rural form.

Lessons for the future

The move to conserve the sense of place and nature in our cities, towns, and villages is gaining momentum. At the same time, and ironically, this positive "conservative" trend tends to resist emerging innovative urban design plans that strive to accommodate both growth and sustainability. For instance, increases in density associated with New Urbanism threaten existing residents, who see such density as lowering real estate values and adding more traffic to their neighborhood.

New Urbanism projects received initial praise from designers, planners, and politicians, but these views are now tempered with caution, as developers are not convinced that New Urbanism addresses diverse and changing markets. Other critics see the New Urbanism approach as a "Disney" typology (akin to places such as Celebration and Seaside, Florida), with the aim of creating "Pleasantvilles" that are insensitive to place-making or building on existing site patterns. The process, they argue, is social engineering, with limited flexibility in building codes and overstructured, deterministic patterning. It caters to the affluent and fails to include other social strata. Furthermore, critics argue that New Urbanism is a convenient response to market forces to create value but is generic in type of land use, streets, and building form response. Despite such critiques, New Urbanism has spurred a renewed sensitivity to the pedestrian scale of neighborhoods. Celebration in Florida, for example, protects valuable natural features and integrates mixed uses and densities, while creating significant public amenities and support services (fig. 3.5).

Sustainability is also starting to gain momentum. What was formerly only rhetoric is becoming policy in many cities around the globe. From Curitiba, Brazil, to Chicago, cities are making their downtowns safer and cleaner by reducing waste, increasing maintenance, improving transit, and beautifying the area. The push toward a more sustainable future is grounded in a more comprehensive urban design approach that encourages high-performance buildings, an inclusive public process, and sustainable urban forms.[21] Sustainable community design is now developing realistic frameworks for implementation, as shown in University of British Columbia professor and landscape architect Patrick Condon's recent *Seven Rules for Sustainable Communities.*[22] Condon's seven rules to create sustainable communities are, in short form, the following:

- restoring the streetcar city
- designing interconnected street systems
- making services convenient, within a five-minute walk, and providing frequent transit
- creating good jobs close to affordable housing
- providing diverse housing types
- developing a linked system of natural areas and parks
- investing in lighter, greener, cheaper, and smarter infrastructure

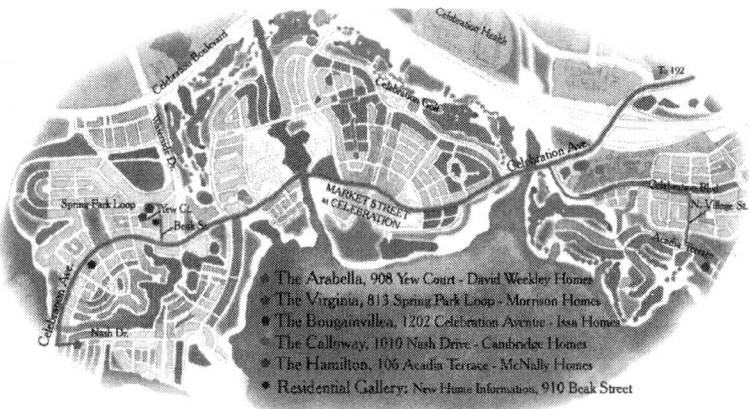

Figure 3.5. Celebration, Florida. An example of the New Urbanism movement, Celebration, in Florida, has made improvements to suburban community design through mixed uses, more compact housing, central amenities, and the creation of a central downtown core with local services, akin to a traditional small town. (Source: Celebration, Florida.)

Alternative development standards are viable ways to save nature, save money, and contribute to the most efficient development pattern that matches the place. Through research and project case studies, the Congress for the New Urbanism (CNU) is furthering efforts to make our communities safer and more fiscally responsible. Resistance to change remains, but the need to move in alternative directions appears to be gaining momentum, especially with climate change moving from myth to daily news. Municipalities and real estate developers, faced with increased state and provincial climate change legislation, are putting their bylaws and building codes under increased scrutiny to improve environmental performance.

UniverCity, the new community at Simon Fraser University (SFU) in Burnaby, British Columbia, has taken the lead in developing the first comprehensive "green" zoning bylaws in North America, which require that all buildings outperform the model national energy code requirements by 30 percent. If developers add a further 15 percent in energy efficiency performance or add other environmental features, such as green roofs, the SFU Community Trust (which manages development) may authorize up to 10 percent density as a reward.

The new UniverCity Childcare Centre is a "net zero footprint" building in that it generates more energy than it consumes. The building also recycles more water than it uses. Described as "the greenest childcare centre on the planet" by the author of the International Living Future Institute's Living Building Challenge, the UniverCity Childcare Centre is aiming to be the first designated "living building" in Canada. The community's recently launched District Energy System will provide heat and hot water to buildings while reducing greenhouse gas emissions for future development by more than 60 percent compared with standard electrically heated buildings. The UniverCity's award-winning storm water system mimics nature by returning nearly 100 percent of the rainfall to the ground, thus cleaning and replenishing local streams.

Since 2005, more than 3,200 residents have moved into UniverCity, which has a projected population of 10,000. Nearly 40 percent of the residents are SFU students, staff, and faculty who now walk to work. Approximately 36 percent of the residents use transit as their primary mode of transportation. In addition to the aforementioned childcare center, the community features a high street of shops, parks, a farmers' market, personal and professional services, an elementary school, and a wide array of recreational and athletic facilities, as well as a library through the university. The housing includes market, nonmarket, and rental units. On the economic side, the SFU Community Trust to date has generated over $26 million as an endowment to SFU for teaching and research (figs. 3.6 and 3.7).

Figure 3.6. Verdant at UniverCity, Simon Fraser University, Burnaby, British Columbia. This housing project for faculty and staff combines green technology and affordability in compact urban design.

These recent trends away from sprawl development patterns and toward smart community design bode well for thoughtful and comprehensive urban design solutions. However, these solutions will require a comprehensive set of tools and techniques to develop compact urban forms that enhance and celebrate the physical, social, and economic place that is already there or needs to be there. This book provides such tools, especially in Parts 2 and 3. But first, the next chapter examines principles and elements of urban design that provide a foundation for the process.

Summary of concepts and theorists

As an addendum to these two history chapters, refer to table 3.1 for a chronology and detailed list of individual theorists and their contributions. A second table describes the major approaches in the late twentieth century and early twenty-first century that include downtown, suburban, and rural design movements (table 3.2).

Figure 3.7. Master plan for UniverCity, Simon Fraser University, Burnaby, British Columbia. This community has 3,200 existing residents in a mix of market, nonmarket, and rental housing units. Supported by an elementary school, local shops, and services, it is expected to have a population of 10,000 residents. (Printed with permission.)

Table 3.1 is a snapshot of some of the key contributors to urban design theory. Theorists are listed in chronological order. Their theoretical contributions, or "isms," are classified under five categories based partially on the work of Jon Lang and defined in the glossary.[23] Good theory provides a way to organize a complex world, enables us to process complex problem solving, and helps us predict (to the extent possible) the outcomes of specific design responses. These classifications of theoretical concepts give us a way to understand the commonalities and contrasting attributes of each contributor. Maybe more importantly, they let us begin to understand the basic principles and concepts shaping the contributors' ideal and/or pragmatic urban design approaches.

The tables are by no means comprehensive and focus mainly on contemporary twentieth-century thought. These lists reflect the depth and breadth of urban design thinking not only in the physical/ecological dimensions but also in the social and cultural dimensions that are frequently neglected in our discourse. The economics of urban design has been explored peripherally at best by a few of these contributors but not as a focus of urban design discussions.[24] The reason is logical. Money and profit or the allocation of resources is a study that has normally been delegated to business schools, not design schools, which have traditionally focused on the "art and science" of design. Economics deals with mathematical abstractions and theory rarely appreciated by urban designers, let alone understood. These attitudes must change.[25]

Table 3.1. Summary of theorists and contributors

Players	Time Period	Approach(es)	Projects/ Location	Contributions
Pope Sixtus V	1500s	Formal city (classicism)	Rome, Italy	Axis, landmark, dominance, civic buildings (formal and restrained)
Georges-Eugène Haussmann	Mid-1800s	Grand revitalization (classicism)	Paris, France	Grand boulevard, terminus
Camillo Sitte	Late 1800s	Outdoor rooms in urban design (phenomenological contextualism and typological empiricism)	Vienna, Austria	Informed major urban design through Austria and Germany (medieval and Baroque designs)
Frederick Law Olmsted	1850–1900	City Beautiful (ecological empiricism) Nature in city design	Central Park, New York City; Mount Royal, Montreal, Quebec; Boston's Emerald Necklace	Design and nature in the city, parks, public realm
Daniel Burnham	1890–1910	City Beautiful (ecological empiricism)	World Exposition, Chicago, Illinois	Importance of public realm and city beauty; regional structure and a comprehensive physical plan
Ebenezer Howard	1900	Garden City (social utopianism)	Letchworth, United Kingdom	New towns with an agricultural greenbelt combining the best of town and country
Clarence Perry	1920s	Neighborhood unit (social utopianism)	New York, New York	Interrelationships between location and functionality of land use and walking distance
Clarence Stein	1920s	Pedestrian orientation (ecological empiricism)	Radburn, New Jersey	Pedestrian pathways, separate systems
Le Corbusier	1920s	Towers in the garden (modernist rationalism)	Plan Voisin, Paris, France	Elitist, high-rise, modernist, mechanical city—a tool
Frank Lloyd Wright	1920–1950s	Transportation city (modernist rationalism)	Broadacre City, USA	Functional "megastructure" (organic modernist)

Table 3.1. (*continued*)

Players	Time Period	Approach(es)	Projects/ Location	Contributions
Lewis Mumford	1950– 1990	Regional city, social, culture (ecological empiricism)	New York, New York	Social, culture city; regional planning in design
Gordon Cullen	1960s	Townscape observation (phenomenological contextualism)	English townscapes	Sense of place, serial vision, and contextualism (postmodern design)
Kevin Lynch	1960– 1970s	People's image of city: paths, edges, districts, nodes, landmarks; design methodologies and performance measures (phenomenological contextualism)	Boston, Massachusetts; San Diego, California	Analytic frame, vocabulary, theory, design methodologies and finally performance measures of urban form: vitality, sense, fit, access, control, efficiency, and justice
William H. Whyte	1960– 1980	People places (phenomenological empiricism)	New York, New York	People place requirements and cluster residential development, responsive to sensitive landscape areas
Jane Jacobs	1960– 2006	Social and economics (ecological empiricism)	New York, New York; Toronto, Ontario	"Eyes on the Street," mixed uses, positive density, functional open space, small block/scale; city as economic engine
Ian McHarg	1969– 2000	Design with nature; eco-regional city; social/culture (ecological empiricism)	Philadelphia, Pennsylvania	Analytic layers for ecology; regional planning in design
Jonathan Barnett	1970–	Political city (ecological empiricism)	New York, New York	Urban design as political process and product
Christopher Alexander	1975–	Pattern language (typological empiricism)	San Francisco, California	Timeless rules and cross-cultural vocabulary of incremental design
Léon Krier	1978–	Architecture communities (typological empiricism)	Poundbury, United Kingdom	Civic design; classical recognition and timeless patterns woven into contemporary interpretation

Table 3.1. (*continued*)

Players	Time Period	Approach(es)	Projects/ Location	Contributions
Jan Gehl	1980–	Pedestrian city (phenomenological empiricism)	Copenhagen, Denmark	Testing pedestrian qualities in quantitative measures in street life
Michael Hough	1984–	Natural processes in city design (ecological empiricism)	Toronto, Ontario	Environment as an important form-maker and basis in urban design
Peter Calthorpe	1986–	Regional city; transit-oriented development (typological empiricism)	San Diego and Sacramento, California	Transit center, sustainability, five-minute town, New Urbanism
Andrés Duany, Elizabeth Plater-Zyberk	1990–	Traditional neighborhood design principles; neo-traditional town planning (typological empiricism)	Seaside, Florida; Kentlands, Maryland	New Urbanism, including the traditional grid street pattern, pedestrian orientation, diversity of architecture, services integrated into neighborhood, local parks, and amenities
Patrick Condon	1995–	Sustainable urbanism (ecological empiricism)	Vancouver, British Columbia	The renaissance of the streetcar city, sustainable urban systems; seven rules—streetcar city; interconnected street system; walking distance to local services; connected jobs and housing; diversity of housing types; linked system of natural areas and parks; and lighter, greener, cheaper, and smarter infrastructure
Douglas Farr	2000–	Sustainable urbanism (ecological empiricism)	Chicago, Illinois	Green systems and urbanism; high-performing buildings; LEED-ND (Leadership in Energy and Environmental Design for Neighborhoods)

Table 3.2. Summary of recent approaches

Location	Approach (Place/Players)	Components/Contributions
Urban	**Neighborhood centers/ EcoDensity** (city of Vancouver)	Infill, densification, mixed use, transit orientation, heritage, housing variety, employment and service proximity, greenways, LEED building standards, and pedestrian/ bicycle priority
Urban/ Suburban	**Regional town centers** Reurbanization and employment centers (city of Toronto and Metro Vancouver)	Intensification, infill, mixed use, transit corridors and multimodal linkages, high-rise concentrations, employment centers and retail concentrations, and other levels of density
Suburban	**New Urbanism** (Duany, Plater-Zyberk, and the Congress for the New Urbanism)	Traditional neighborhood planning with grid streets, pedestrian orientation, compact/higher-density development, distinctive architecture, common greens, variety of housing, local services, and commercial development
	Transit-oriented development (TOD) (Peter Calthorpe, city of San Diego; Freiberg, Germany; Collingwood Village at Joyce Street SkyTrain transit station in Vancouver, British Columbia)	Higher-density mix of housing, offices, and retail development amassed around a transit station; development within a five-minute walk or quarter mile (0.4 km) of the transit stop
Rural	**Hamlets** (Anton Nelessen, New Jersey and New England)	Participatory do-it-yourself town-making; more concentrated clusters of commercial, residential, and institutional uses following earlier patterns; town green in the central area surrounded by civic buildings, 50 to 100 single-family housing units in each hamlet
	Rural cluster and villages (Randall Arendt, New England)	Clustering of housing and commercial uses to conserve rural character and landscape; minimize visual impacts, preserve agriculture, and reflect architectural heritage and landscape qualities; higher densities in two-story structures and retention of larger proportion of open space; parking to the rear; and use of farm cluster patterns

4
SUCCESSFUL PLACES

The simple organization and limited choices provided by traditional urbanism will no longer do. We need both dispersal and concentration in cities—places to get away from each other, and places to gather—and it's time to stop assuming that one necessarily precludes the other.

—Witold Rybczynski, *City Life*

Having reviewed the evolution of urban design in the previous two chapters, it is time to catalog the enduring elements that contribute to successful urban design. This chapter also examines key principles of urban design and place-making.

Nine key elements of urban design

The following nine elements describe some of the key ingredients required to make a successful "place." The elements might vary in emphasis from place to place, or in exceptional circumstances (for instance, where there are no heritage buildings) a particular element may not be readily applicable. However, collectively, these elements work in harmony to create the great places of the world.

1. People (the heartbeat)

The heart and soul of a place dwells in the inhabitants who live there. When we learn about the people, their culture, and their ancestors who settled the area, we can better understand why the urban form is the way it is and how it evolved. The form is a product of social, cultural, economic, and environmental forces. Current residents can also be the long-term "stewards" of the urban design vision if it is developed with them. There are different places in urban design defined by the people combined, whether it be at home, work, or play. For example, the recently coined term "third places" refers to meeting places for people other than home or work (fig. 4.1).

Figure 4.1. Third places. Beyond home and work, these outside or inside areas are where people can meet, mix, and match.

2. Heritage (the past physical and symbolic place)

What to retain, reuse, or replace is important to the core of an urban design plan. Urban designers need to research the history of a site and its context. For instance, buildings and landscapes may be on a local heritage register, or regionally, nationally, or internationally designated. Degrees of heritage protection and conservation incentives vary depending on locale, but it is critical to weave the old and the new (fig. 4.2). These elements also help define the social, cultural, and spiritual/symbolic underpinnings of what makes the place special and/or unique.

Figure 4.2. Contemporary interpretation. To respect heritage, this conceptual study demonstrates how new buildings can be infilled behind old buildings in a small-town context. (Drawing by Calum Srigley.)

3. Mixed land use (including mixed horizontal and vertical uses)

The land use plan (describing the location and use of land) and urban design guidelines (outlining the design directives) set an important basic framework for future land uses and design. General policies and plans, design guidelines, and implementation programs establish a context for the type and extent of present and future activities. Mixing residential, commercial, and institutional uses creates a more vibrant and safer place day and night (fig. 4.3).

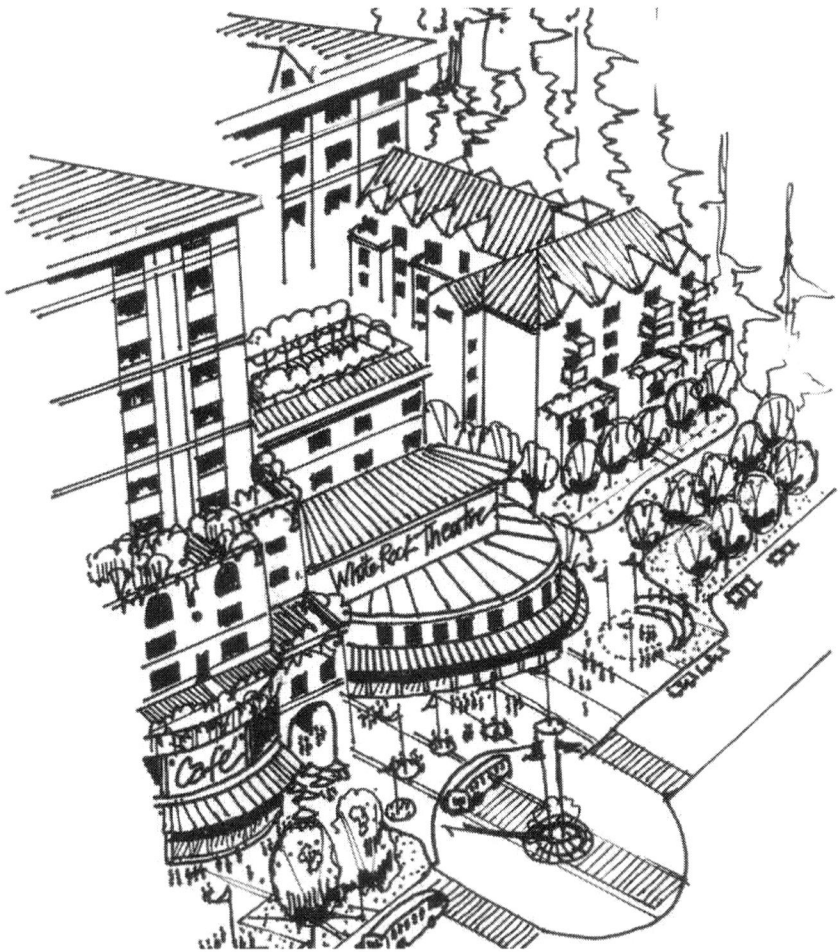

Figure 4.3. Mixed land uses, Vancouver, British Columbia. From residential to public open space, land uses are layered vertically and horizontally.

4. Ecological framework (natural form-makers)

Vegetation, water, soil, wildlife, and microclimate all affect the form and capacity for development. Critical elements in eco-urban design are as follows:

- sun orientation and weather protection
- significant trees and other plants (fig. 4.4)
- water as an excellent public-realm amenity
- storm water features as well as soils for form and relief

These natural form-makers are frequently ignored, especially in downtown projects.

Figure 4.4. Car park, Vancouver, British Columbia. This temporary display brings importance and special interest to the aspect of food and nature in the city.

5. *Building form and massing (from the outside in—integration)*

Buildings constitute the "inside" of urban design and are traditionally thought to be at its core. The following are important building components when weaving together an effective plan:

- appearance (bottom, middle, top) and materials
- height, bulk, setbacks, and layout (fig. 4.5)
- orientation to the street
- degree of integration (amenities, programming, weather protection, lighting)[1]

Figure 4.5. High Street, South Surrey, British Columbia. This highly articulated building face creates an animated street wall and varied setbacks at the second level for terraces, defines storefronts, and defines privacy and interest. At the same time, it creates a coherent and unified block pattern.

6. Circulation, transit, and parking (move people, not cars)

Shifting from a car orientation toward a pedestrian, bicycle, and transit orientation as part of a multimodal approach is mandatory in urban design and transportation planning (fig. 4.6). The following are all important considerations in balancing single-occupant vehicle demands with a safe and desirable pedestrian environment:

- ease of site or community access
- proximity to essential services, such as food stores or basic necessities
- roadways designed with a public streetscape in mind (e.g., incorporating trees or furniture to match function)
- roadways as a critical orientation element (using width, signage, vistas/views, landmarks, and landscape design to inform location in the neighborhood and greater community)

Figure 4.6. Transit interface, Ottawa, Ontario. The Ottawa area has developed a highly successful rapid-bus system that has high ridership and intermodal efficiencies.

7. Public realm (public, semiprivate, and private)

Parks, plazas, roof decks, streets, and parking lots all provide opportunities for interim and permanent uses integrating public, semiprivate, and private open space (fig. 4.7).

Figure 4.7. Cambridge Center, Cambridge, MA. The public realm creates the valuable interfaces between buildings and communities.

8. Pedestrian ways and bikeways (greenways and blueways)

Footpaths, bike lanes, and waterways form essential means to move around the city without a car. Many accessible public lands exist to create these public ways, from conventional streets to other rights-of-way, lanes, pathways, and easements, both linked and continuous. These pedestrian arteries are what will become the "greenway freeways" of the future (fig. 4.8).

User types include the following:

commuter pedestrians	visually impaired or otherwise
in-line skaters	physically challenged pedestrians
commuter bicyclists	wheelchair users
recreational bicyclists	boaters
strollers	kayakers
runners	canoeists
mountain bikers	

These users will be part of the complex and growing diverse groups that utilize "nonvehicular" freeways on water and land throughout world cities.

Figure 4.8. Central Valley Greenway concept, Vancouver, British Columbia. A regional greenway system creates alternative transportation links alongside the SkyTrain rapid transit system.

9. *Activities and activity generation (urban magnets)*

We end these nine key elements of urban design where we started—with the people who live, work, and play in cities, towns, and villages. People generate people, activities generate activities, and safety and excitement result. Uses and activities strengthen urban spaces; they can include street vendors (fig. 4.9), musicians, and other entertainers—which are against the law in some cities. The following provisions are all part of designing an effective and safe urban activity network:

- coordinated activities complementary to surrounding uses
- linkage with activity nodes
- mixed uses along the street to include destinations such as coffee shops, retail shops, restaurants, beauty salons, and fitness studios to draw people at different times of the day
- extension of indoor uses outdoors, such as outdoor cafés, restaurant patios, and displays

Based on the Power of Ten concept of Projects for Public Spaces, headquartered in New York City, think of at least ten activities that will empower your place—and help make the space successful.

Figure 4.9. Street vendors, New York. Introducing vendors in areas of street crime significantly reduced the incidence of crime. Positive activities push out negative activities.

Measurable and nonmeasurable elements

As mentioned in chapter 3, Kevin Lynch describes seven aspects of "good city form" in his eponymous book: vitality, sense, fit, access, control, efficiency, and justice.[2] While none of these elements may have a specific meaning, collectively these terms describe, beyond physical indicators, what makes a "good city." The irony is that nonmeasurable elements are actually measurable but not in physical terms, as in the height of a building or the width of a sidewalk. Instead, the terms of vitality, sense, fit, access, control, efficiency, and justice represent a collection of factors. For instance, vitality is the result of not one activity on the street but normally a number of different activities at varied times to create a place full of life. Through research and observation, urban designers can define measurable and nonmeasurable elements that should be included in site improvements to attain good city form.

The elements set out below form a useful checklist when examining what makes a place successful or unsuccessful from a social, ecological, and economic standpoint. These three components (social, ecological, and economic) are discussed in more detail in chapter 5, on urban design site analysis. The checklist is presented here especially to foreground those elements frequently ignored in urban design projects or examinations.[3]

Measurable elements

- Land use and mix
- Density or intensity of land use
- Size of open space and building
- Building setbacks and height
- Bulk, form, and coverage of buildings (normally measured as floor space ratio)
- Building materials and colors
- Vehicular, pedestrian, and bicycle counts
- Street design
- Number of parking spaces and design of parking lots/garages

Nonmeasurable elements

- Safety and access (some measurement)
- Distinctiveness and character
- Clarity, continuity, and enclosure
- Visual interest and beauty
- Comfort and livability
- Vibrancy and adaptability
- Equity and accessibility to land uses (e.g., private versus public open space)

Frequently missed elements

- Context and connectivity (pedestrian/bike, land uses, buffers, visual connections)
- Pedestrian activity and presence during different parts of the day
- Number of street trees and landscape elements
- Green roofs
- Weather protection
- Lighting coverage
- Street furniture (bike racks, trash receptacles, pedestrian lighting)
- Seating (beyond benches, seating walls, steps)
- Open space programming (specific functions and target groups)
- Transparency and articulation of building form at ground level
- Articulation of public, semiprivate, and private space (inside and out)
- Use of water lots and "blueways" (greenways on the water)

Ten poor form-makers: What not to do

Preceding sections of this chapter have outlined numerous positive elements of urban design, including those sometimes overlooked. Form-makers are those positive or negative elements that help shape urban form, whether they are cars, people, or streets. The following list, in contrast, itemizes indications of *poor* urban design that is unsustainable. Where these "negative elements" are in evidence, there is room to make improvements in any urban place. This catalog of deficiencies in current site conditions can be used as a tool to help analyze what is wrong with a site before we attempt to fix it through design alterations or other means, such as site activities programming or land use changes. After the list, the discussion moves into the overarching principles of urban design.

1.   Unsafe streets that do not fit their specific function in the community

Extra-wide streets focus on the automobile, with little consideration for beauty and pedestrian safety.

2.   Car dominance

Garages and parking are up front, there is parking galore, and people drive everywhere—making the area unsafe for pedestrians.

3.   Single uses

Housing, jobs, and shopping are all separate and distant.

4.   Contemporary building in fantasyland

Place has no sense of history or culture, no reverence for materials and details that fit the location and respect the context.

5.   No natural legacy and bioregional connection

Natural features have been eliminated, resulting in a place that is airless, treeless, valueless, and desolate, with no natural heritage.

6. No "heart"

Place lacks visual orientation, vitality, "center of town," hierarchy of spaces, and interconnections.

7. No civic programming

There is no network of activities and indoor/outdoor programming to prompt social interaction (no walkways, outdoor cafés, theaters, connections to amenities, a central common plaza, or sitting and meeting areas). Place lacks civic spaces or buildings set in important areas with gathering spaces. Programming is limited to summer or daylight hours. Informal street entertainment is not encouraged.

8. Recreation isolation

The space is not central or connected; it is inconvenient, unsafe, and not programmed for multiple user groups. The space is dead (not designed for interaction or contemplation), with little sunlight and exposed to prevailing winds. There are either no facilities or no free and inviting facilities (e.g., splash park or public washrooms).

9. Wildlife separation

Wildlife and nature are fenced off, broken up, or kept out of sight—there is no balanced vision of designing with nature.

10. No real walking, biking, and transit: Disconnected

Alternative modes of transportation are an unsafe afterthought and inconvenient. Distances are too far to walk, with no attractions en route. Transit is unsafe, inconvenient, and costly. No bike racks or lockers are available. No seating areas or weather protection are provided. There is no pedestrian-scale signage or orientation.

Ten key principles of urban design

As badly as we have been shaping our built environment, we still possess the ability to do it right. The principles and techniques of true urban design may have been forgotten, but they are not lost; they can be relearned from the many wonderful older places that still exist.

—Andrés Duany, Elizabeth Plater-Zyberk, and Jeff Speck,
*Suburban Nation: The Rise of Sprawl and the
Decline of the American Dream*

Principles are the guiding rules of the game. They set a framework for urban design, and they set the theoretical foundation for urban design plans. Without principles, we design in a void, with no rules to guide our process or measure its success. Principles, like anything else, may easily be abused. I have seen many urban design principles that can be applied to almost any project around the world. Through community and political process, well-defined principles are diluted so as not to offend or exclude. This approach should be avoided, because the resulting principles will have little meaning or durability.

The principles that follow set a framework to guide sustainable urban design decisions. They are also touchstones to evaluate results.

1. *Context determines site form*

The pattern, age, and value of the surrounding buildings, local ways of moving around or transport systems, natural features, and underlying ecology determine the most appropriate urban design. There are three levels of context: the regional context (or "big picture") of macro patterns, the intermediate level of community context (neighborhoods), and the smaller local patterns that envelop the site. Each level contributes clues as to what the site is and should be.

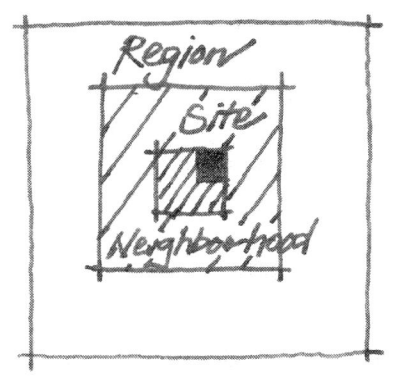

2. Design should save and celebrate the place

The physical and psychological elements that collectively form the "spirit of place" or "genius loci" are the foundations for outstanding urban design. Place is both a center of meaning and a context formed by people's actions. The discovery of meaning comes from detailed inventory and critical analysis of the site and context that identifies the significant cultural, historical, and physical place-makers.

3. Design recognizes natural features as critical form-makers

Innovative urban design requires the conservation of significant landscape features, such as trees, rock outcrops, or water elements. These features, combined with storm water management and recreation, can save money and generate premium values for a unique product.

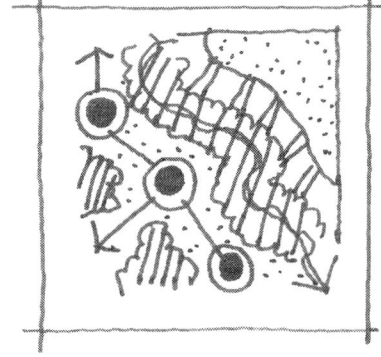

4. *The design needs to fit the scale and location*

Urban design consists of more than downtown design of high-rises. It encompasses cities, towns, and villages within the categories of urban, suburban, and rural. Each of these has unique qualities and can be experienced within the city or the country. They each require a different solution to match the place and the various interacting elements that define their special qualities.

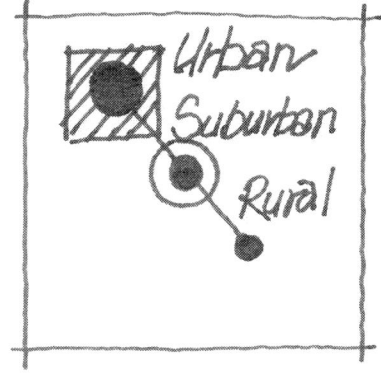

5. *Movement systems should move people, not cars*

The pedestrian should be the first priority, with bicycles, transit, goods movement, and single-occupant vehicles following in that order. Urban design plans should consider each of these movement patterns in detail and have an implementation strategy for each.

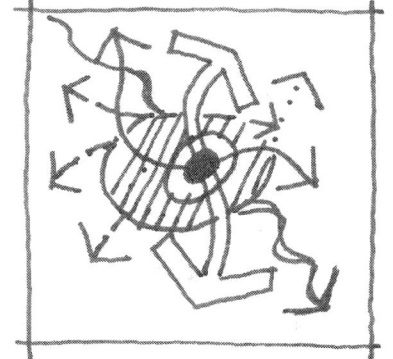

6. *Multiple, flex, and mixed uses are keystones to sustainability*

Sustainability in urban design means balancing jobs and attainable housing, encouraging live/work proximity, and providing recreational facilities and services within walking distance. At the same time, flexible design for buildings and open space provides the opportunity to change urban form or use with the least

waste or expense. This allows the urban design to respond more easily to changing market demands and demographic shifts.

7. Diversity needs to be planned for

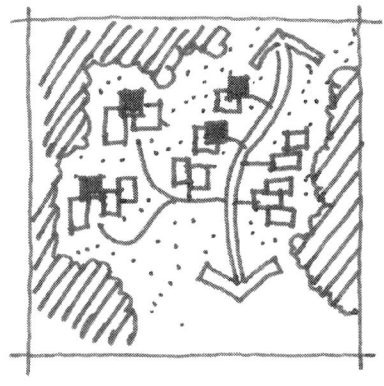

Design for a diverse population that is changing and evolving in the community. Life-cycle housing and aging in place are important components of housing choice. Affordability and various ownership or rental options are also important components of complete communities, as they add to the full breadth of local employment and a rich culture.

Diversity also applies to the ecological, physical, and economic composition of the community. The underlying ecology of a site is diverse by nature. This structure should be nurtured and enhanced through a green infrastructure plan from the beginning of implementation. A variety of building forms, street types, and open space programming should contribute to a central theme of diversity. The economic strategy should estimate realistic demand and provide a broad foundation for businesses to flourish or change.

8. The public realm should be incorporated as a central component

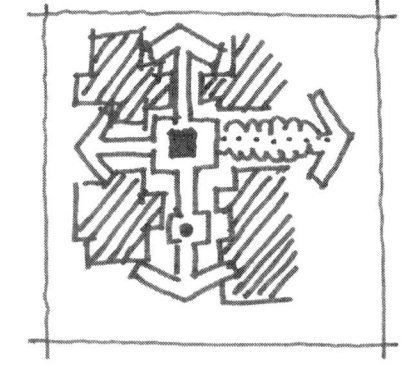

Outdoor spaces such as the street, yard, park, plaza, and alley are the critical glue that ties the elements of neighborhood and community together. Without them, we would just have buildings and no interactive spaces. Outdoor space is the social space of the city, town, and village. The sidewalks, pathways, street trees, seating, and lighting are part of the design tool kit of these areas. At the grander scale, gateways, landmarks, and activity nodes are signatures of a sense of sound visual orientation in the larger city, town, or village urban design—making it more legible, coherent, and attractive.

Design civic spaces and civic buildings at important intersections in the community as a matter of convenience, orientation, and attraction. Create meaningful spaces by programming them for specific activities reinforced by buildings and landscape design.

9. *The urban form should be compact and safe*

To obtain optimum results, sustainable design intervention must be balanced with efficient land use and the retention of valuable ecological elements, such as streams, trees, and significant landscape features. This principle normally leads to cluster development or density transfer, where a variety of multiple and single housing forms are possible. It also determines 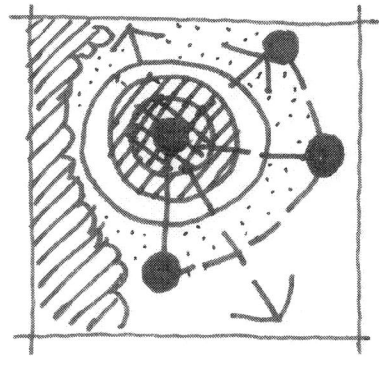 more compact, pedestrian-oriented communities. These forms create a better sense of ownership and visual surveillance, part of Crime Prevention Through Environmental Design (CPTED).

10. *Community building is an integral part of the urban design process*

People are at the core of any community or neighborhood. They come together to create great cities, towns, and villages. Current and future residents and business owners have a significant stake in where they live and work. They are the local experts, as they live and work there. Communities are developed by formal and informal partnerships, stewardship programs, and community gatherings.

The place test: Twenty-five questions

As a tool similar to others in this chapter (e.g., measurable and nonmeasurable elements, poor form-makers), the following questions are intended to test the "placeness" of a space or a combination of buildings and spaces that collectively define an area. These questions, grouped into five categories, aim to define the successful and unsuccessful aspects of the space, as well as identify qualities that are missing.

Character, identity, enclosure, and connections

1. What are the unique identifiers of the place?
2. Does it have a specific boundary that defines the edges?
3. What makes the place memorable (microclimate, ecology, views, buildings, activities, feelings, streetscape, etc.)?
4. Is the place connected to surrounding land uses (visually/physically, socially, and economically)?

Activity and access

5. Are people walking and biking in the neighborhood?
6. Is the area easily accessible (pedestrian, bicycle, transit, car), and if not, why not?
7. Do people say hello in passing while walking or biking?
8. Do people gather or meet (in groups of two to five) in the street frequently?
9. Do street vendors and other entertainers in the street create excitement and animation?
10. Are there outdoor cafés that punctuate the streetscape?
11. Are there a variety of uses and businesses that extend out onto the street and invite you in?
12. Is the place adaptable to other uses?

Streetscape and ecology

13. Are there flowers planted in the public street?
14. Is there a rich streetscape with pedestrian-scale elements, such as benches, pedestrian lighting, trash receptacles, etc.?
15. Are there street trees and a diversity of paving materials?
16. Is there a sense of nature in the street?
17. Is the place noisy? And what causes the noise?
18. How do vehicles fit into the area (dominant, secondary, etc.)?

Buildings and connections

19. Is there specific area defined by unique signatures (landmarks, signs, etc.)?
20. Do the buildings relate to the place in style, form, and massing?
21. Are the buildings connected to the ground-level activity via windows, entranceways, space articulation, materials/textures, and lighting?

Psychological factors

22. Does the space or area feel big or small?
23. Does the area feel safe, or if not, what does it feel like?
24. Do you feel the sense of ownership and territory in the area? If so, why?

And, as a final, overarching question:

25. What is missing? How can the place be improved?

This chapter discussed the elements that go into making a successful place and the principles behind all successful and sustainable urban design. It provided a few initial tools (lists) to guide place- and form-making. The next section delves into the analysis and plan-making process in much more detail, with case studies that illustrate the process at work.

II

ANALYSIS AND INTEGRATION

5
SITE ANALYSIS

According to the summary of wholeness that we have given, it is clear the wholeness will have to come from the process. And, concretely, the process will have to guarantee that each new act of construction becomes related in a deep way, to what has gone before.

—Christopher Alexander, Hajo Neis, Artemis Anninou, and Ingrid King, *A New Theory of Urban Design*

The first part of this book reviewed the history and theory of urban design and explored the elements and principles that should shape the urban design process and products. This chapter lays out a comprehensive process to use this rich historical and theoretical framework in tandem with the principles and elements. The dynamic urban design approach requires that social, ecological, and economic analysis unite in a coherent and practical strategy.

The centerpiece of this chapter is a sample "neighborhood" urban design task list that illustrates the steps required to develop a complete plan. The process includes substantive (qualitative and quantitative) analytic elements. Part of the analytic process examines the SEE (social, ecological, and economic) elements mentioned earlier that go beyond the normal physical analysis of urban design and explore further sustainable development dimensions (table 5.1). An interactive and highly communicative public process parallels the technical process to review results as the process proceeds. This template has been customized and applied to numerous award-winning projects with outstanding results.

Table 5.1. Detailed SEE (Social, Ecological, and Economic) process components (This table provides a framework for the analysis and synthesis of complex information that informs various components of the urban design plan.)

INVENTORY: Data Gathering	ANALYSIS: Strategic Selection	SYNTHESIS: Choices Selection	PLAN RESULTS: Planning for Change
SOCIAL			
People's values Needs History Future vision Sustainability (including governance)	Meaning of data Trend lines Culture/public needs Values Important elements	Public elements What stays What is added Themes	Public systems: amenities, infrastructure, and services Social housing and public facilities Programming activities: festivals, events, and equitable treatment Governance
ECOLOGICAL			
Soils Water Vegetation Wildlife Air Systems/units Sustainability	Classification Landscape units Development potential/ capacity Land uses	Transformation Restoration Enhancement Protection	Site planning and design Building forms and systems Greenways and blueways Eco-stewardship Tree management Wildlife aquifer protection stream stewardship
ECONOMIC			
Market Costs Finance Sustainability	Supply/demand Demographics/costs Sources of funds *(Also see Appendix A: Economics Checklist)*	Program of uses Return analysis Partnerships	Land use feasibility Costing/options Financing Partnerships Funding strategies

INVENTORY: Data Gathering	ANALYSIS: Strategic Selection	SYNTHESIS: Choices Selection	PLAN RESULTS: Planning for Change
URBAN DESIGN PLAN RESULTS			
Buildings Land use Mobility Nodes Character areas Options Sustainability (Also see Appendix B: Sustainability Scorecard)	Building footprints/ land use Building heights/ density Shadow analysis Orientation and slopes Character areas Movement Hard/soft analysis: what will stay or go High-performance buildings	Building form and massing/land use Density and distribution Mobility systems plan Public realm plan Phasing and Implementation Sustainability components	Urban design master plan: principles, goals, land uses, character, features Sustainable design guidelines Historic restoration and management Public realm: street, parks, open space, plazas, gardening Transportation: four tiers (pedestrians, bicycles, transit, goods, and single-occupancy vehicle) Implementation and "Living Sustainably" plan

Table 5.1. (continued)

The goal of the analytic process is to provide a comprehensive foundation for the urban design plan that evolves and grows over time, as illustrated in the sustainable urban design tree diagram (fig. 5.1). Here the tree is intended to be a metaphor for the dynamic process. As in fruit trees, the fruits of urban design will vary depending on the inputs (nutrients) to the plan, such as management, maintenance, monitoring, and stewardship.

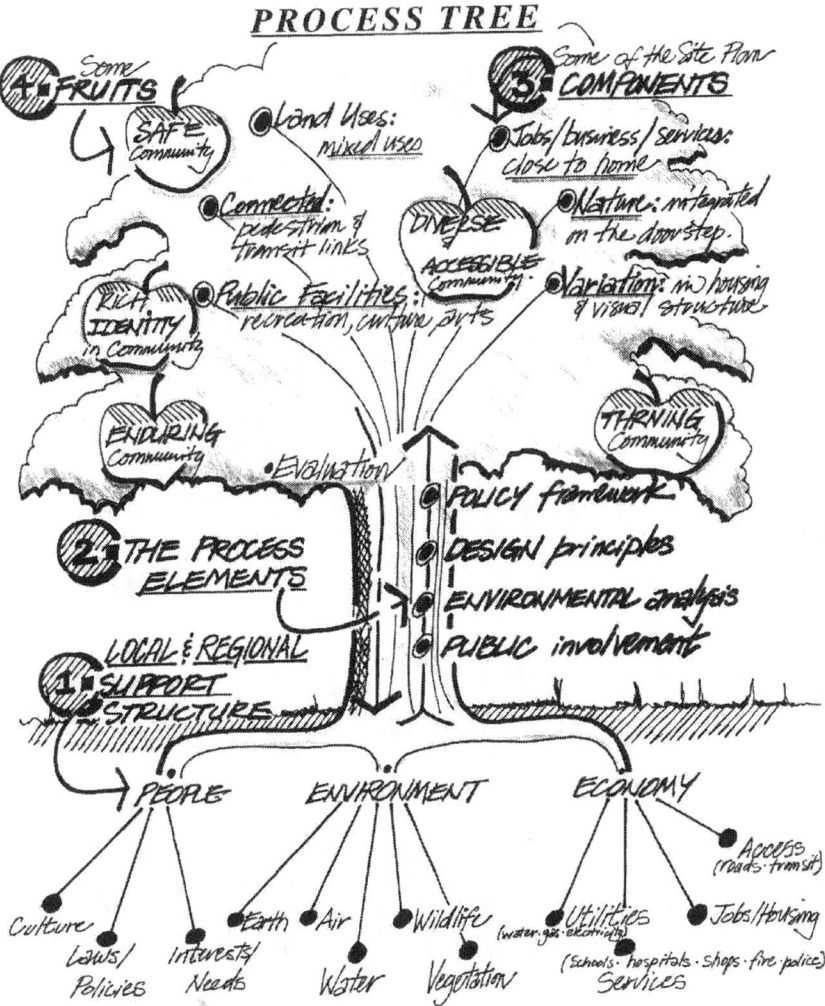

Figure 5.1. Urban design process tree. Metaphorically, the complex and dynamic urban design process starts at the roots (support structure) of people (social), environment (ecological), and economy. These roots feed nutrients into the main trunk of the tree (process elements) and then, through photosynthesis and other processes, convert nutrients (community values and physical elements) into community components and fruits, which change with each season, depending on the nutrients and sunlight (the process).

Sample neighborhood analysis task list

The following is a generic urban design process task list that focuses on a "neighborhood" urban design plan. It follows the urban design process from the initial site inventory and analysis (part A) through to public review (under part E)—forty-four tasks overall. The task list does not reflect the true interactive (feedback) process described in the next chapter, but it does reflect a process that incorporates public review.

Part A. Inventory and analysis

The purpose of part A is to gather and analyze the necessary information to determine the development or redevelopment potential of the land.

1. Project start-up

Task 1: Start-up meetings
Organize two start-up meetings: the first with the consulting team to provide them with project orientation and base information, and the second with the client to address the process, schedule, information requirements, and outcomes.

Task 2: Further information
Generate a list of further information and past studies requirements (including digital photos, surveys topography, and market analysis).

Task 3: Consulting team
Retain an architect, a landscape architect, a planner, an engineer, an economist, and a sociologist (and other specialists as needed) as part of the urban design team, with an urban designer as the lead consultant, coordinating the team.

Task 4: Project scope and purpose
Clearly state and confirm the problem statement, scope, and expectations in terms of goals, objectives, deliverables, and timing, as well as roles and responsibilities of both consultant and client.

2. Social/cultural (policy), ecological/physical, and economic analysis (SEE analysis)

Task 1: Existing improvements and base mapping
Obtain orthographic photos (aerial photos with survey-accurate topographic data overlaid) and geographic information systems, as well as an evaluation of existing housing and building stock. Complete base plans for the site that are adaptable to large- and small-format presentations with selected information (e.g., existing topography, roads, buildings, servicing, special features, and trees).

Task 2: Legal survey
Confirm property boundary, area of parcels, easements, rights-of-way, and property description.

Task 3: Geological and soil conditions
Verify the following through previous studies: subsurface material, drainage characteristics, foundation conditions, engineering properties, erosion qualities, depth to water table during seasonal high, and depth to bedrock.

Task 4: Slope analysis
Obtain topographical map and complete site reconnaissance.

Task 5: Hydrology
Verify previous studies with respect to 100- to 200-year floodplain, status on wells in the vicinity, existing surface drainage and features (if any), and existing wetlands or low-lying areas.

Task 6: Climatic conditions
Confirm microclimate, including wind and sun orientation for site planning and energy-efficient neighborhood design.

Task 7: Wildlife
Review existing studies to ensure compatibility with local wildlife values.

Task 8: Archaeology
Review information on archaeological sites.

Task 9: Vegetation
Undertake a tree survey (to be completed by a certified arborist) to detail condition and value of individual trees on-site, as well as review current municipal tree policy.

Task 10: Existing access and circulation
Review previous report and confirm any changes since the earlier report, including capacities along adjacent roads and pathways/walkways. Confirm capacity for expansion and improvements necessary to accommodate growth.

Task 11: Utilities and infrastructure
Confirm existing and proposed service lines, including sanitary, water, storm drainage, gas/electric, telephone, cable, and other applicable utilities.

Task 12: Cultural review and development regulations
Review development policies, including regional plan; city, town, or village plan; neighborhood plan; zoning bylaws; heritage regulations; commemorative elements on-site; and other regulations, including federal and provincial/state regulations (e.g., streams, waterfront, wildlife).

Task 13: Visual analysis
Identify significant features, visual orientation/gateways, and views in and out of the site.

Task 14: Opportunities and constraints summary
Complete a summary of opportunities and constraints affecting the site's development potential.

Task 15: Character areas

Define areas that have unique attributes that should be conserved and/ or enhanced in any further development considerations. These unique attributes can relate to land use, culture, activities, history/meaning, and/ or natural features.

Task 16: Developable land summary

Identify the following:

- Protection areas, including primary and secondary trees, landscapes, structures, and buildings
- Building development sites with some constraints
- Building development sites with few or no constraints

Task 17: Market and economic verification

Review previous reports and other information from the local area and region regarding demographic patterns; job growth and associated population growth projections; supply, demand, and absorption of housing units; commercial, industrial, and institutional floor space and other uses; emerging economic growth drivers; and specific urban services requirements for projected population growth in the institutional, business, and residential areas.

Part B. Program development

The purpose of part B is to translate the social (including cultural), ecological (including physical), and economic factors into a viable mix of land uses (program development) for the site. The type, amount, and timing of the specific land uses will provide a concrete development program. Two visioning workshops, one for the site and one for the surrounding land uses, explore site opportunities. Products include a vision statement (what the development will be like in future perfect terms); goals and targets (end results in quantifiable terms); principles to guide site planning, design, and development; and a program diagram that reflects the desirable land uses applied to the site.

Task 1: Site vision workshop
Organize a workshop with core design team to generate the preliminary site vision, goals/targets, principles, and design/planning and marketing/communications strategies.

Task 2: Context vision workshop
Organize and execute a workshop with broader participation of community representatives (e.g., city staff and council) to confirm that initial ideas and directions are supported.

Task 3: Neighborhood vision statement
From the two workshops, develop a vision statement that describes the future neighborhood in terms of image and quality of life—for example, "High Meadow is a residential neighborhood that provides a safe, affordable, and active lifestyle for the residents who live there. Neighborhood recreation and support facilities are conveniently located within walking distance of every house and ..."

Task 4: Development goals and targets
Develop goals and targets that set explicit benchmarks for development and be reference points as development proceeds. They will set the standard for development and be flexible to respond to changing market conditions. See goals and targets outlined in appendix B (Sustainability Scorecard), which provides a template for sustainable urban design measurement for other projects.

Task 5: Development principles
Formulate site planning, design, and development principles to provide important guides throughout the process. Principles relating to the development of a sustainable neighborhood plan should be incorporated, including considerations for the following: adaptive reuse, energy efficiency, resource and waste management, nature enhancement, green infrastructure, green buildings, affordability, housing choice, pedestrian orientation, proximity to services and jobs, and heritage conservation. (See Garrison Crossing case study in chapter 11 for a detailed list.)

Task 6: Land use programs
Develop a potential land use program that includes physical, cultural, and market components. Explore land use programs as follows:

- Residential: quantity, reuse potential, type, ownership, market, and nonmarket
- Recreation: indoor and outdoor quantity, reuse potential, and type
- Commercial: quantity, type, and ownership
- Institutional: school and church demand (verify district and local needs)
- Industrial/high technology: heavy, medium, and light industrial uses

Task 7: Program diagram
Diagram the size and interrelationships of the various land uses, as they apply to the site. The diagram should be supported by written information that describes the program in further detail.

Task 8: Preliminary marketing strategies
Develop a more detailed marketing strategy based on the development program that sets out the key messages to the future buyers or renters and portrays the qualities of living or working in this neighborhood, focusing on the sense of place, healthy lifestyle values, and the facilities within walking distance.

Part C. Neighborhood plan/site plan development

Various physical and economic alternatives and strategies explored in part C assume different conceptual and program approaches. Computer image studies and sketches illustrate the existing and proposed building/site interrelationships. Final products include at least two plan options, with an additional recommended neighborhood plan (normally the best combination of elements in the first two options). The recommended neighborhood plan/site plan incorporates the following elements: land use plan, historic conservation/adaptive reuse plan, proposed building zones and massing, parking and circulation, pedestrian and bicycle routes, transit, recreation facilities, and an overall landscape concept, including street trees, parks, and greenways. The plan should also include a servicing/infrastructure plan, phasing plan, and parcel (subdivision) plan.

Task 1: Neighborhood plan options
Develop initial land use and architectural concepts at the beginning of the site planning process. Program assumptions supplied by the previous step generate massing and density alternatives. These options or concepts are measured against the goals, targets, and principles established earlier. They are also measured against the opportunities and constraints generated in the inventory and analysis step.

Task 2: Alternative servicing, road layout, landscape network
In combination with task 1, explore the other pieces to the neighborhood puzzle as part of an integrated design process including the following:

- Servicing plan (civil engineer with hydrological engineer and geotechnical engineer, as well as landscape architect)
- Streets plan (civil engineer and landscape architect)
- Landscape and recreation plan (landscape architect)
- Heritage conservation plan (heritage architect)
- Building prototypes (architect)
- Land economics (economist)
- Schools, places of worship, cultural programming (sociologist)
- Sustainability (sustainability planner)

Task 3: Preliminary parcel plan and phases
Identify land development parcels and phasing based on the developable land summary of part A, program requirements of part B, and neighborhood plan options.

Task 4: Parcel site testing
Test prototypical buildings to determine the true development potential of each site, especially in those areas where building infill, adaptive

reuse, or relocation is being considered. Prototypical unit plans include layout, height, massing, and building sections. Discussions with potential developers explore early the feasibility of concepts in relation to potential or existing market demand.

Task 5: Preliminary neighborhood plan
Formulate the recommended preliminary neighborhood plan from review and discussions with team members, clients, the community, and the approving jurisdiction. This plan provides further details in the following areas:

- Structure for the development pattern, including access, road layout, building footprints, building setback requirements, and amenity areas
- Infrastructure requirements for servicing
- Development potential in terms of number of units, density, coverage, and floor space ratio, as appropriate
- Development parcel layout and phasing

Detailed subplans include the following:

- Building and block plans
- Servicing/infrastructure plan
- Landscape and recreation plan
- Adaptive reuse plan (retention, relocation, or replacement)
- Detailed parcel plan and phasing
- Public amenities plan (recreation, greenways, gateways, and landmark features)

Task 6: Community enhancement
Develop a "public benefits" strategy that goes beyond the bounds of the development. The development should enhance the character of the surrounding community. Design guidelines, community recreation, and nature conservation strategy are three elements of interest to the greater

community. These elements can also be presented to developers and other parties as part of the marketing strategy.

- *Needs assessment:* Assess the needs of the community and how the potential development can contribute in parallel with the development program.
- *Public benefit package:* Outline what the development will contribute to the community; these contributions can be public facilities, such as day care space, community recreation centers, street improvements, park development, performing arts centers, and subsidized rental space for nonprofit organizations.

Task 7: Organize public open house in liaison with jurisdiction
Organize, implement, and evaluate a public open house to review the preliminary neighborhood plan/site plan.

Part D. Neighborhood site plan: Urban design documentation

The purpose of part D is to communicate the detailed information of the neighborhood plan in a way that can be clearly understood and evaluated by the approving authorities, as well as other affected stakeholders, including members of the surrounding community. The neighborhood site plan and associated plans in slide, wall, and booklet presentations address the different presentation requirements of the rezoning approval process. This plan consists of the overall plan and the other subplans, as outlined in part C, to provide the necessary detail for review. Supporting text and illustrations further detail each of the plan's elements.

Task 1: Planning approval document
Complete the rezoning approval document, which includes all the plans and supporting text for submission to the city, town, or village.

Task 2: Wall presentation
Develop a large-format presentation, mounted on foam core board, which includes an introduction and conclusion in addition to the main plan illustrations.

Task 3: PowerPoint presentation
Create a PowerPoint presentation for various audiences as an overall explanation of the approach, plan, and implementation of the plan.

Task 4: Review and refinement of presentations and documents
Review these documents and presentations with the client and the consulting team, and refine documents and presentations in accordance with last-minute adjustments.

Part E. Communications and marketing
Communication is a unifying element that permeates all parts of this process but is especially important as the neighborhood plan is refined and is ready to present to both approving authorities and other affected parties. An action plan is important from the beginning. The marketing consultant develops a marketing strategy. The Stage I action plan focuses on the initial marketing strategy and communications. Important elements to help present the development and generate support for the necessary approvals are image, theme, naming, and the communications associated with marketing, meeting notification, and general information (e.g., newsletter), plus the development of a presentation center that is easily accessible.

Task 1: Marketing and communications strategy initiation
- Develop a database of potential customers and media partners to share the story about the neighborhood plan.
- Create a series of presentations for different audiences, including the surrounding community, municipal staff, municipal council, and potential purchasers of property.
- Refine the image, name, and themes for the neighborhood plan so there is a consistent series of key messages and presentation of materials.
- Develop a customized website that draws the attention of viewers on the home page and is easy to navigate.
- Use social media, such as Facebook and Twitter, to project to different audiences.
- Reach out to the media with key messages.

- Monitor and evaluate marketing progress by reviewing the project inquiries, media coverage, and profile of potential purchasers.

Task 2: Approving authority meetings
- Ensure that the project team meets with the approving authority prior to formal application to review the requirements, process, and any significant challenges.
- Define a project meeting schedule and preapprove the schedule with the approving authority to manage expectations for the time and content of approvals.
- Respond to and deliver on items identified at each meeting as soon as possible to maintain momentum and a sense of commitment from all parties.

Task 3: Other parties
- Ensure that the members of the immediate neighborhood are kept abreast with progress through continuous updates on the project website and associated media, as well as periodic telephone conversations with important members (residential associations, school groups, etc.).
- Extend the communications to local service groups in the greater community (Rotary clubs, nature clubs, etc.).
- Invite other cultural groups and First Nations (or other indigenous cultures) into the process, as appropriate, keeping in mind special outreach needs such as language, customs, and food.
- Include any other special interest groups that could be interested in the development (affordable housing groups, youth, and environmental stewardship, etc.).

Task 4: Public meetings or workshops
- Plan the meeting location, agenda, audience, purpose, and outcomes, keeping in mind the specific needs of the participants.
- Ensure that the location and facilities accommodate the number of people and the activities, and create a comfortable, welcoming atmosphere.

- Plan the sequence, size, and content of displays so that they can accommodate multiple viewers and in different languages if necessary.
- Invite the participants at least two weeks in advance, with an agenda attached to the invitation so that the participants know what to expect.
- Review the agenda with the project team to define roles and responsibilities, including setup team, greeters, registration table monitors, table facilitators, technical specialists, and cleanup team.
- Provide for appropriate light refreshments or a meal for the participants so that their energy level can be maintained and they feel supported in their efforts.
- Invite feedback using a simple survey or comment sheet with specific questions that are directed to the content and purpose of the meeting or workshop.
- Evaluate the feedback, and improve the next meeting or workshop based on the recommendations.

Summary of sustainable process and product elements

The following list highlights a general approach incorporating sustainable community development into urban design. It is a beginning to see what process, physical, and ongoing management elements are required to integrate urban design with sustainable community development.

Process—responsive and dynamic

- *Natural theme.* Identify site character and sense of physical place.
- *Community-based focus.* Work with the community to reflect community values and sense of social place.
- *Site-specific programming.* Develop site programming in the following sequence: nature space/cultural areas, living units, working places, pedestrian system, and streets/access.
- *Soft-touch construction and local help.* Use tree and landscape/soil protection, sensitive construction techniques and local help, and responsible materials. Minimize waste.

Physical product—enduring and evolving

- *Retrofit, adaptive reuse, and intensification.* Focus first on the creative reuse of existing urban infrastructure, such as buildings, parking lots, and unnecessary roads that transform to new housing, commercial buildings, clean industry, greenways, bikeways, and waterways.

- *A connection to local and regional ecology.* Connect the site to the bioregional and local natural patterns of vegetation, waterways, topographical features, and views.

- *Variety of forms and places.* Encourage a diversity of fine-grain building forms, scales, and tenures, plus a mix of open spaces for active and passive recreation.

- *Efficiency of streets and access.* Minimize street surfaces, and create a hierarchy of streets that relate to function and place in the community.

- *A pedestrian and bikeway network.* Create a backbone for local mobility that is safe, convenient, and accessible.

- *Transit priority and service connections.* Locate transit within one-quarter to one-half mile (400 to 800 m) of each residence. Provide modal interconnections that include bike storage, efficient service, and support services.

- *Designed for density.* Implement quality design that has a variety of forms and tenures, balance jobs (one-to-one ratio) and shopping, and support the community by a natural greenbelt system that heightens the quality and convenience of clustering or intensification.

- *Landscape design.* Incorporate low-water-use plants, a ratio of 80 percent planting areas and 20 percent grassed or natural grasses, low-maintenance native plantings, and perennial ground covers. Recycle gray water if possible, and retain natural landscapes where possible.

- *Greenfrastructure.* Encourage green roofs, streams instead of pipes, ponds instead of reservoirs, and multiuse and multifunctional open space and recreational space.

- *Urban streams.* Open up, expose, expand, restore, and revitalize natural watercourses.
- *Energy efficiency.* Use local materials, as well as building orientation, energy cogeneration, fixtures, and incentives.
- *Locally grown food.* Where appropriate, create community gardens, grazing land, *and* market gardens, and integrate agriculture in the open space system.
- *Construction materials.* Consider life-cycle maintenance costs, durability, toxicity, and indigenous qualities.

Management—ongoing responsibility and evolution
- *Organization.* Create an entity to maintain the property and streets and manage the ongoing natural evolution of the neighborhood.
- *Eco-responsibility.* Make it easy to recycle waste, and adopt low-water-use landscapes.
- *Plan implementation.* Ensure that the green standards and guidelines are followed; respond to changes and define revisions.
- *Activities.* Continue the community-building process that nurtures vitality, ownership, responsibility, and mutual education.

Community and neighborhood are used interchangeably in this text. Community can be defined as a collection of neighborhoods with larger common commercial, industrial, and institutional components, while a neighborhood is normally a smaller unit that has a residential emphasis. The next section explores how to build support in a community or neighborhood through a process that listens to the residents and businesses.

Interactive stakeholder process
"Hello, Michael. I just want to let you know that all your hard work paid off and we not only got full approval for the project, but we also got unanimous approval, with every councillor supporting it." This feedback marked the culmination of a successful community-based process involving more than thirteen community groups that ended with full support by the Halifax Regional Municipality in Nova Scotia in early February 2011. This

course was not easy. It took more than a year of public process (a short time compared with other projects of a similar scale)—for one of the largest urban redevelopment projects in Halifax. This project is further profiled in chapter 12.

Not all projects finish this way, with full endorsement from the local politicians and broad support from the community. The public process is becoming even more challenging in urban design. With multiple stakeholders even inside the sponsoring organization, the general public is only a small part of the interested parties. The scale and intensity of public interest normally depends on the location, size, and scale of the project. Simply put, bigger means more complex. Yet this is not always the case. In my experience, relatively small subdivision projects can draw the attraction of all neighbors in some instances. Hence, smaller projects can be just as complicated and can take just as much time or more.

The best way to approach the consultation and interaction aspect of the urban design process is in an organized and constructive manner. My earlier writings explore this subject in depth.[1] One of the current and popular methods is a "design charrette," an intensive, hands-on series of workshops that involve a variety of professionals and stakeholders to define design options and strategies. I have explored effective design charrette techniques and processes since 2002 on projects of various scales—from downtown urban design plans to large-scale projects up to 35,000 acres (14,000 ha). When used properly, design charrettes can be an effective tool in working closely with stakeholders on a number of levels. Charrettes also develop buy-in while generating locally based ideas in a very short period of time. Keep in mind that design charrettes are just one tool in what should be a comprehensive public engagement process tool kit that truly engages the "publics" (many different organizations—informal and formal). These organizations need information to understand the scope of the project and exercises to inform them and help them contribute in a valuable way.

Ten best practices for public engagement

The following is adopted from *Public Process Playbook* (2007), coauthored with Sylvia Holland: a list of the ten best practices for public engagement, and a list of questions necessary to customize your own plan.[2]

1. *Process plan is comprehensive and also customized*
    *   Use different tools for different phases (e.g., open space technique to identify issues in engaging phase, not to make final decisions).
    *   Choose the right process for the problem (e.g., design charrette to generate breakthrough ideas).
    *   Carefully select venues for their welcoming qualities (e.g., development workshop in council chambers, after refusal of first proposal by council, is the wrong place).

2. *Process is inclusive*
    *   Invite more than just insiders. Connections are strengthened by including the old and the young, the established community leaders and the newcomers.
    *   Do multicultural outreach (e.g., Vancouver CityPlan materials translated into five languages).

3. *Process is responsive to changing public landscape*
    *   As the process unfolds, adapt it to respond to additional needs of the public that are within reason.

4. *Decision makers approve the process*
    *   Make the rationale for, and benefits of, public involvement part of initial client consultations. Resources for the process are thereby secured.
    *   Have decision makers agree to use the recommendations in their review and approval processes.

5. *Process focuses on informed awareness*

- While unanimous agreement is an ideal, it is rarely a realistic goal. Keep the focus on *how* to decide, not a specific outcome. If some participants still disagree, they know why the option preferred by most is approved.
- Build learning steps, not just feedback mechanisms, into the plan.

6. *Process uses principle-based decision making*

- Set guiding principles together, as a precursor to design.
- Base agreements on objective criteria and factual information.
- Define specific community benefits that correspond to specific community needs (e.g., Weyerhaeuser Lands development in Ucluelet, British Columbia—see case study on page 164).

7. *People are heard and acknowledged*

- Document and archive all ideas, even if they are not part of the final design.
- Report survey results to the stakeholders and interested parties as soon as possible after completion to validate process and plan directions.

8. *Capacity building takes place through the process*

- Help participants deepen their understanding of their community, thus improving their planning ability.
- Design events and working groups to foster new connections and new partnership possibilities.
- Teach participants how to facilitate, and help them improve their teamwork skills.

9. *Rules of engagement are agreed on at the outset*

- Establish "how to plan" agreements with stakeholders (nature of process to use, ground rules for collaborative work) before seeking input on actual designs.

- Develop a set of specific goals for the process, including target timing.
- Clearly state what the process will and will not accomplish.

10. *Social aspects are integrated into the process*

- Incorporate fun, food, and prizes to make a "normal" planning process outstanding.
- Integrate planning with local traditions, and consider babysitting services to widen participation (figs. 5.2 and 5.3).
- Encourage community members to name the plan.

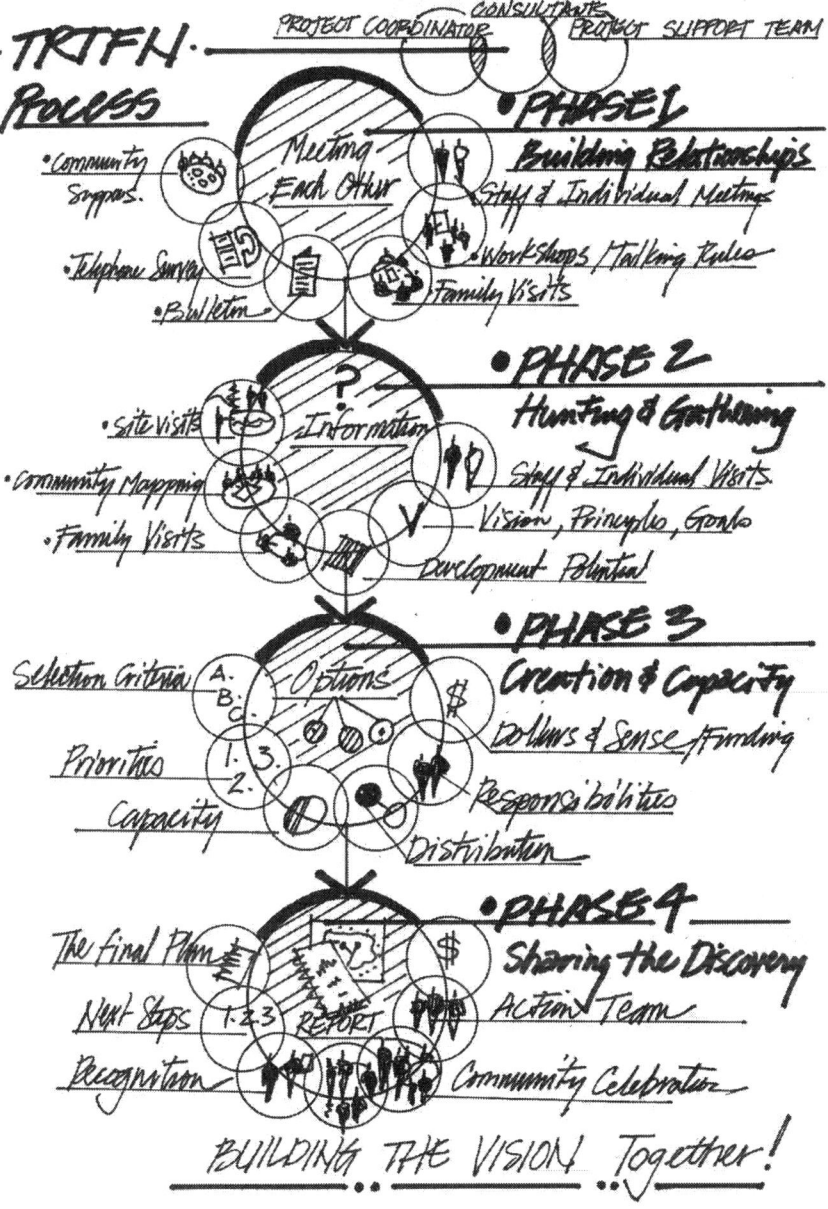

Figure 5.2. Comprehensive engagement process diagram. The First Nations engagement process in the rural community of Atlin, British Columbia, used familiar language and various ways to reach out to the community, including a telephone survey, community suppers, group workshops, family visits, community mapping, "dotmocracy" exercises (everyone placing dots on a list of issues, challenges, and action items to determine priorities), campfire discussions, the teaching of talking rules, and elder storytelling.

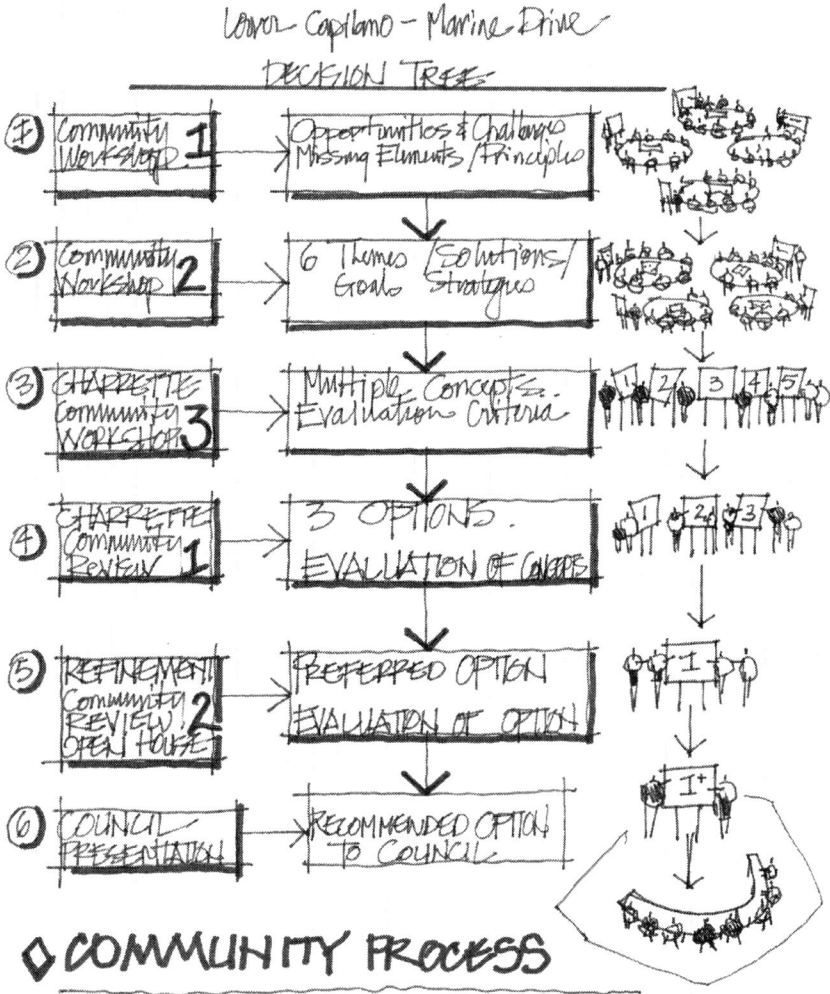

Figure 5.3. Decision tree process diagram. This urban public engagement process included a series of interactive community workshops, a design charrette, and an open house to reduce multiple options to one option supported by the community.

Ten key questions to help design your customized public engagement plan

1. What is the problem, challenge, or opportunity?
2. Who are the stakeholders?
3. How can stakeholders become involved, and what are their potential roles and responsibilities within the project?
4. What information will be needed to make an informed decision (versus provide an opinion)?
5. What is "on the table" as part of the process, and what is "off the table" (e.g., sidewalk improvements versus the building of a new civic center)? Consider the different intentions and assumptions held by various parties, and ensure the project's scope is defined clearly.
6. Who are the final decision makers, and what do they have to know during the process and to approve the recommendations that emerge (e.g., council requirements)?
7. What resources are required to get the job done properly (financial, people, in-kind)?
8. What is the process *before* and *after* the various stakeholders are consulted?
9. What objective criteria could be used to ensure the final decision is equitable under the specific circumstances?
10. How will the process carry on after your involvement? (Who will the team members be? What will implementation and stewardship involve?)

Any genuine public engagement makes best efforts to invite the public into the process. This world of public engagement in urban design can be complex and politically driven. It is important to have a public engagement specialist on your urban design team who develops and manages the program. Otherwise, the public engagement process often becomes a sideshow, ineffective in generating informed public decisions and a broadly supported plan.

This chapter examined the various tasks that go into site analysis and discussed ways in which the process can lead to more sustainable and accountable urban design. It visited the complex and critical area of public engagement, offering best practices and guiding questions. The next chapter tackles the fundamentals of plan-making. Where does the creative spark behind great urban design plans come from? What steps can we follow to ensure that the final plan is functional, sensitive, and, above all, sustainable?

6
PLAN-MAKING IN THEORY

To influence the growth of cities, the designer must have a clear concept of the underlying design structure that must be produced to set in motion the involved processes of city-building.

—Edmund N. Bacon, *Design of Cities*

I remember walking into the National Gallery of Canada in Ottawa in the late 1980s, when the gallery was still under construction. Members of my group were all mesmerized by the structure and the details. I was consumed by the sense of space and place—the context and how the gallery fit into the fabric of Ottawa and the adjoining Canadian War Museum and Major's Hill Park. As I walked up the entrance ramp into the gallery's natural light–filled atrium, I noticed a man seated on a chair in the center of the high-ceilinged space, intently focused on the dazzling play of light all around him. On further study, to my amazement, I recognized the man as Moshe Safdie, the architect for the National Gallery.

Safdie was the director of the Urban Design Program at Harvard, where I had gone to school, so it was easier for me to recognize him than the rest of my group. No one else seemed to notice; they seemed interested in other things as they walked off down one of the gallery's branch corridors. I decided to respectfully and quietly go over and introduce myself. My hope was to get a firsthand response from the architect on the quality of the space. After some pleasant introductions, Safdie looked up in wonder and commented on the atrium space. "You know," he said, "I wasn't sure if it would work until now."

His statement summarized for me the wonder of design and the associated experimentation and evolution involved to get it right. At the same time, the discussion gave me an intimate awareness of the magic of design and showed me that even the greatest designers do not have all the answers prior to construction. As a designer, we become part of a task that is greater than ourselves, and this leads to new possibilities.

Processing complex information: The "making" process

The mark of a good designer, unlike a scientist, is the very ability to make final decisions without all the requisite information, because it is rarely all available at the proper time.

—Douglas Kelbaugh, *Common Place: Toward Neighborhood and Regional Design*

The "design" in urban design is something that always appears elusive—just beyond the grasp of many planners and designers. More than a few see it as some sort of "magic moment"—the revelation of a great architect in the early hours of the morning. The "vision" is scribbled on a hotel napkin, and the image is imprinted as the turning point in the project. The big idea can also come from a small piece of sculpture or a landmark on the site. Certainly the urban design of a project can come together in these ways, but they have inherent risks, including missing important cultural, physical, and economic form-makers—critical to the enduring success of the plan.

Malcolm Gladwell in his books *The Tipping Point* and *Blink*[1] points out the importance of how little things can make a big difference and the power of "thinking without thinking." In other words, there is merit in knowing when we have enough information to make a decision and also in trusting our trained intuition to respond to a challenge in the most effective manner. The important distinction here is *trained* response. This can be the inspirational design idea that comes from extensive experience and training (call it wisdom). And sure enough, I have been in many intensive team situations where what I call the "big idea" inspires a whole design story line for the urban design project. The big idea is inspired as one member of the design team makes an observation based on analyzing the site. Listening to community members in a workshop can also reinforce or elevate these site ideas to inspire a whole array of other ideas that *collectively* define a story, with the help of other team members. This is part of the synthesis process, where data intersects with observations and community input to create a set of urban design components that set a foundation to the plan, illustrated by A3 in figure 6.1.

This urban design plan-making process can be compared to preparing a meal together. First, the ingredients are agreed upon (the inventory and analysis portion). Without the right ingredients, the meal does not have the basic elements for success. It does not match the mood and tastes of the guests. Care has to be taken to balance short-term aspirations (political motivations) with longer-term aspirations (needs of the community) in the ingredient selection. This could mean retaining significant heritage buildings while replacing other buildings that do not have the same importance in the community.

The second step is to mix the ingredients and cook them (the synthesis process). As we know, too many cooks can spoil the broth. Have the design team (qualified professionals) assemble the plan alternatives, for they have the skills, knowledge, and abilities to shape the plans. During the making, the food deserves some sampling as it is cooked (input from the broader community). This taste test (or interim design review) gives the community the opportunity to modify the ingredients emphasis (mobility, building form and use, extent of development, etc.). With this input, the cooks (design team) adjust the ingredients, amount, and spices. The meal preparations are completed, and the dinner is served (public presentation). With this interactive and collaborative process, the result is generally pleased dinner guests. The community (dinner guests) then respond constructively with further refinements to the menu, ingredients, and preparation methods, while fully supporting the general directions. Details are the focus, not the conceptual framework or analysis behind the plan.

The diagrams in figure 6.1 illustrate some of the traditional ways to develop the "design" in urban design.

A. *Four Different Points of View*

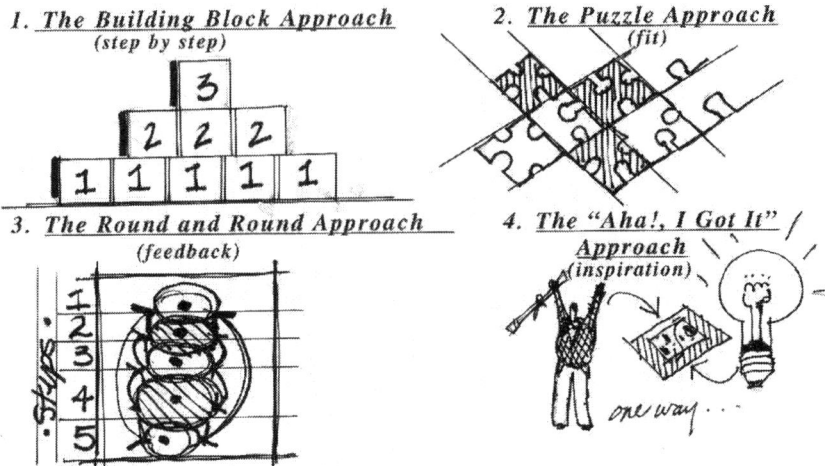

1. **The Building Block Approach**
   (step by step)

2. **The Puzzle Approach**
   (fit)

3. **The Round and Round Approach**
   (feedback)

4. **The "Aha!, I Got It" Approach**
   (inspiration)

B. *Side by Side Activities in the Process*

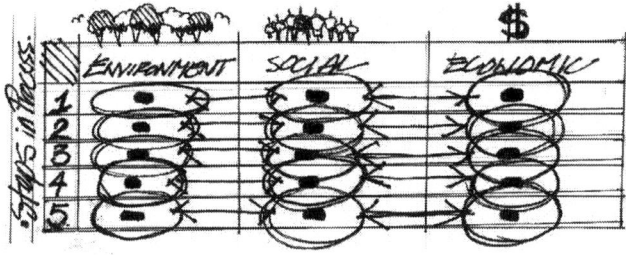

Figure 6.1. Process thinking and problem-solving approaches. Diagram A1 illustrates the logical and linear sequence of thinking, where each component of the process is separate and builds on each other. A2 exhibits the puzzle piece approach, which does not necessarily follow a logical order of decision making or a linear sequence. A3 illustrates the synthesis/process approach, with a constant feedback loop that checks decisions against earlier work. A4 portrays the inspirational idea approach that discovers the idea without the comprehensive process (based on wisdom). Finally, B describes a combination of rational linear thinking (A1) and the iterative feedback loops of A3 for each of the social, ecological (environmental), and economic (SEE) processes, as well as horizontal cross-connections.

Form-makers and a "family of plans"

Now let us look at the outputs from (i.e., products of) the synthesis process. We will leave behind the meal analogy and focus on the specific components of the "family of plans" that constitute the comprehensive urban design plan. Through the site analysis (see chapter 5), the design team assembles extensive sets of data (and interpretations of this data). This information forms the foundation of a comprehensive urban design plan—constituting major elements or "form-makers" that distinguish this urban design plan from others and can help create signature elements. These form-makers can include natural and cultural features, heritage buildings and landmarks, land uses, mobility patterns, solar orientation, and many others. When analyzed together, the form-makers start to shape the plan in physical, social, and economic terms.

The design process translates these important elements into a number of different plans, each with a focus, that together form the "family of plans" that constitute the urban design plan. These constituent plans may include, but are not limited to, the following (each project requires different plans depending on its location, size, and complexity):

- *Development capacity plan.* This plan itemizes what existing elements should be saved and what can be replaced, and the extent or intensity of development proposed within the *carrying capacity* of the site (balancing social, economic, and ecological factors).
- *Development areas plan.* Where development should be placed, the associated land use, and how much development should be permitted are all articulated in this plan.
- *Built form plan.* This plan explores form, massing, and character on the site.
- *Movement (or mobility) plan.* Five layers of mobility are analyzed here—transit, pedestrian, bicycle, goods movement, and single-occupant vehicle.
- *Implementation plan.* This plan lays out the order of development, timing, organization, funding, and allocated responsibilities.
- *Sustainability plan.* Social, ecological, and economic components as well as governance components are summarized in this plan, which should be translated into a manual for living sustainably as part of implementation.

In this plan-making process, across North America, a very important policy phase can include amendments to policy documents and additional design guidelines:

- *Community plan amendments:* official designation of new land uses, policies, objectives, or densities
- *Zoning bylaw amendments:* comprehensive development zone
- *Design guidelines:* general guidelines with specific design conditions tied to the development agreements or covenants on title that direct the prospective builders

This chapter illustrates the urban design process from inventory to the final product. The SEE technique, outlined in chapter 5, is used, incorporating social, ecological, and economic information throughout the process and in an iterative way so that the urban design strategies are rich in physical and cultural form and have sound and enduring economic grounding. The whole dynamic urban design process in essence is iterative in that it checks back and forth between analysis and synthesis to obtain the best solutions. Information uncovered in the analysis—including goals, principles, and targets, as well as technical data—supports and synthesizes the ultimate, most robust urban design options.

Five-step comprehensive urban design process
The five-step urban design process starts with defining the place, progresses through a process of analysis and synthesis, and arrives at an urban design plan that addresses the needs of building, living, and legacy. A logical linear process is one way to examine complex information from built form analysis to market information (see A1 in fig. 6.1). The synthesis process (fig. 6.2) is an alternative where each step refers back to the former step to ensure nothing is lost in the evolution of the design in substance and original intentions. Of course, the resulting products vary from process to process, depending on the particular needs and scope of the project.

Step 1. Clear vision and goals as foundation blocks
A study of twelve communities across the country in 1995 by the Canada Mortgage and Housing Corporation revealed one central common success factor—the most successful communities had a clear vision and goals to guide them. Here is one example of a vision of the future: *This project will be*

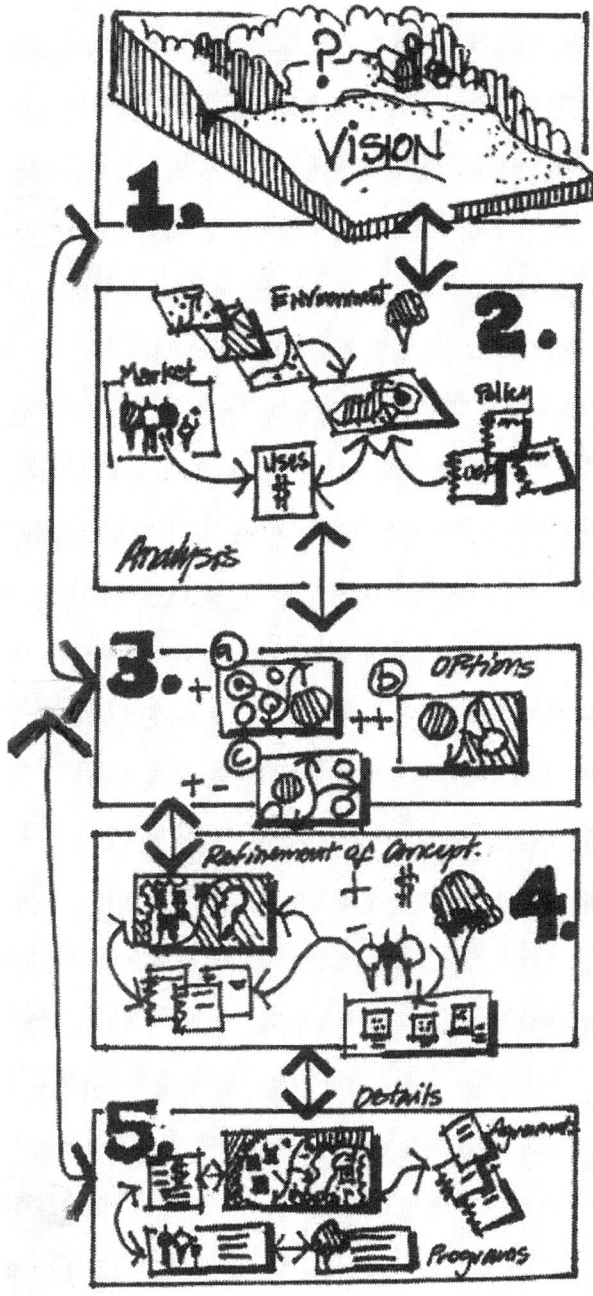

Figure 6.2. Five steps to site design. These steps provide a summary of the progression from inventory and analysis to the specific site concepts and design.

a unique, diverse, and thriving neighborhood that complements its surroundings, contributes to the healthy growth of the area, and builds on its rich heritage of the site. It will be a model of responsible development that seeks to respect the natural environment, connect to its neighbors, provide for housing choice, as well as some local employment, and reuse the existing built and natural assets where possible.

Urban designers must be careful to customize the vision to the specific. Too often visions are generic and too general; they could apply to many communities rather than the one under study.

Here are a dozen sample design goals for various aspects of the site (e.g., housing, roadways). As with the vision, such goals, envisioned as the end results of the urban design process, should be specific to the site yet incorporate adaptability and sustainability.

- *A sense of unique identity.* The form responds to the sense of place defined by the landscape, architecture, culture, associated local signatures, distinctive boundaries, visual continuity, and well-defined public spaces.
- *Connectiveness.* The design encourages people to walk with a variety of convenient options and interconnections, with a five-minute walk tolerance.
- *Safety.* The design provides a variety of housing closer to the street without major walls, garages set back, public buildings, and mixed use to provide people with "eyes on the street," as in traditional towns.
- *Local services and employment.* Residents have access to what they need on a daily basis within a five-minute walking distance, and the site provides a variety of land use types, ranging from service providers to larger corporate employers with specific resident/ employment targets.
- *Diversity of housing.* The site includes different types and tenures of housing in a variety of settings and densities for changing needs relating to residents' life cycle.
- *Road size to fit needs.* Pedestrians have priority in residential neighborhoods. Road types vary, with street specifications for specific needs.

- *Integrated parking.* Longer-term parking is in the rear of the buildings, out of sight, and reduced where possible, broken up into small clusters (parking courts), and richly landscaped to provide pedestrian and natural visual connections.
- *Mixed uses.* Site provides a collection of uses adjacent and above for intensity, proximity, diversity, activity, and integration.
- *Public and cultural facilities.* Design features civic buildings—including cultural and recreational spaces, fire and police facilities, and schools—as focal points associated with civic plazas, green spaces, and other meeting places.
- *Comprehensive open space system.* Site has multiuse systems incorporating walking paths, bikeways, playgrounds, and natural areas.
- *Ecological infrastructure.* The following are incorporated into the site: recycling, waterways, drainage, forest and tree retention/planting, restoration, wildlife, food generation, energy conservation, and agriculture.
- *Sustainable lifestyle.* Site features transit orientation, progressive building materials, and energy conservation. It also incorporates food purchasing and growing, solid and liquid waste management, nature stewardship, water use and recycling, and equity/justice in resource/shelter allocation.

Step 2. Site analysis

This step analyzes the ideas and data for the site gathered during the site analysis. The analysis brings together conflicting and harmonious elements that determine the capacity for development or redevelopment. It is important at this stage not to miss a critical aspect that could undermine future development concepts. Constraints to development could include soil contamination, wildlife habitat, recent or pending rezoning, public sentiment, or market saturation of specific land use segments.

An important step is to quickly "scan" the critical site factors, attending to ecological (environmental), economic, and social factors that limit the site's potential. This process could include, as time and budget permit:

- observing the site at different times of the day and night, if possible
- examining the historic evolution of the site and its context
- reviewing local policy and current/past development applications
- sketching the site from different perspectives
- cataloging the site with photographs

Summary of analysis process

A. Enviro-scan: Natural capacity
    i. All the natural air, earth, water, plants, and wildlife elements critical to development
    ii. Overlay of potential land uses with the site constraints and opportunities

B. Eco-scan: Market forces and local programming needs
    i. General regional and local analysis of population trends and preferences, history, and business prospects—competitors, land use patterns, land trading prices, and rental/vacancy trends (supply/demand analysis)

C. Social scan: Policy status and social deficiencies
    i. Regional plan, municipal plan, local plan, and zoning status
    ii. Other federal and provincial policies
    iii. Community services and amenities needed (fire, police, schools, libraries, open space/recreation, day care, arts and culture facilities)

D. Red flag summary: Key factors limiting development
    i. Summary of challenges and opportunities
    ii. Opportunities for cooperation and innovative solutions
    iii. High, medium, and low development potential, with qualifiers

Step 3. Site concept development

The site concept interprets information assembled in step 2 and translates it into a number of broad development/urban design strategies. These illustrations, or "bubble diagrams" (fig. 6.3), capture the preliminary exploration of design ideas and land use relationships. They give stakeholders with an interest in the project the opportunity to review and comment on basic assumptions and possibilities before further details are explored. As a colleague reminds me, "people like choices. Give them options." Fundamental to the urban design process is the concept of measuring choices and trade-offs. Examining each concept's trade-offs and testing them against the established goals and principles (step 1) should yield the preferred concept for further refinement in step 4.

Site concept development process

A. Land use location: Land use programming in "bubbles"
   i. Location of land uses, access, and circulation
   ii. Development densities and interrelationships
   iii. Land use summary and percentage uses/densities

B. Economics basics: Land use and minimum return on investment
   i. Highest and most appropriate uses
   ii. Return-on-investment goals and infrastructure planning/phasing
   iii. Structure of financing and rental/ownership

C. Imaging: Different design responses
   i. Ideas and design principles that reinforce place
   ii. Photo imaging to reflect the principles
   iii. Combination of natural and man-made elements

D. Flow: Mobility, energy, water, and waste
   i. Movement of people, goods, and waste
   ii. Concepts of site treatment and minimum-impact analysis

E. Public services: Common facilities
   i. Planned central public and other semiprivate facilities
   ii. Services that address local and regional demand

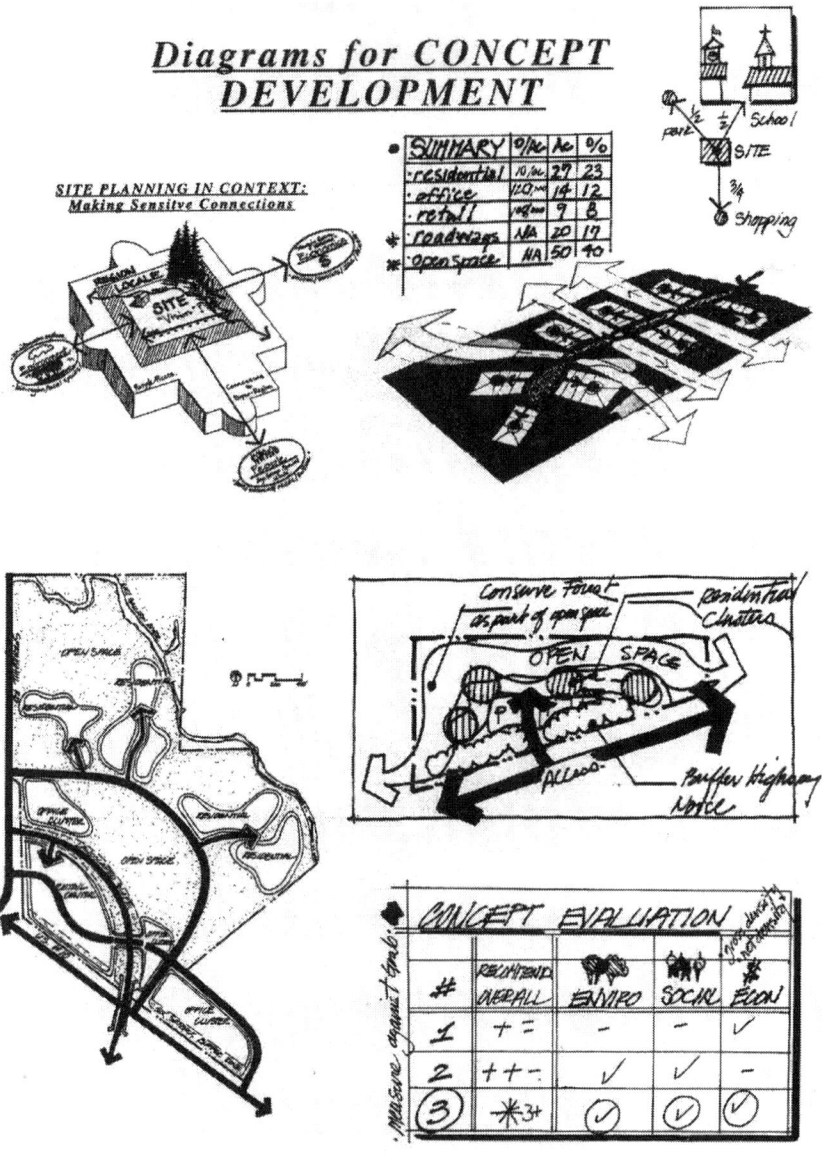

Figure 6.3. Diagrams for concept development. Site "bubble diagrams" simply illustrate land use locations and transportation (mobility) so that different options can be easily compared, especially by the public, who normally have more difficulty reading drawings.

F. Minimum standards: Design prototypes and activities
 i. Character ideas (photo imaging)
 ii. Prototypes for infrastructure (roadway, lot sizes, and other regulations)
 iii. Review and approvals strategies (community, buyers, municipality, and other agencies)

Step 4. Master urban design plan development

The master plan takes the "bubble diagrams" from the concept stage and brings them to life by adding building and landscape details. It makes concrete the "vision" of the full landscape in the following ways:

- *Buildings* are dimensioned and illustrated in their basic forms.
- *Public realm* is articulated with greenways, streets, walkways, and trees.
- *Transportation systems* are scribed, showing bus stops, transit ways, and other movement patterns/design elements.
- *Ecological greenfrastructure* is detailed. Natural systems' conservation, enhancement, and restoration should be at the core of the plan, even in downtown locations, if possible.
- *Community benefits and phasing* are described. The actual building timing and areas can be refined in the master plan, along with financial (public and private) benefits and social programming.

As provided for steps 2 and 3, here is a summary list, showing the various components that go into the master plan, followed by a sustainable master plan checklist.

Master plan process

A. Testing: Form, density, land use, and interrelationships
 i. Land uses and circulation
 ii. Building footprints
 iii. Landscape and architectural character/styles

B. Refinement of urban design
   i.   Buildings dimensioned and illustrated in their basic forms
   ii. Public realm articulated, with greenways, streets, walkways, and landscaping
   iii. Transportation systems with bus stops, transit ways, pedestrian and bicycle ways, and a hierarchy of streets
   iv. Ecological infrastructure showing natural systems conservation and enhancement
   v.   Community benefits and phasing, including social and cultural programming and other associated public facilities and improvements

C. Real impact: Phasing, financing, and organization
   i.   Return-on-investment analysis on phasing and overall
   ii. Financing structures (servicing, public facilities, and private)
   iii. Ownership and rental, as well as other potential tenures
   iv. Partnerships (recreation, community facilities, and servicing)
   v.   Net gains analysis for public and environment (triple bottom line)

D. Policy changes: Alternative directions
   i.   Consideration for amendments to existing policy documents
   ii. Discussion of impacts and benefits to others

E. Measurement against goals, principles, and vision
   i.   Test the design against goals (end results) established at the beginning of the process
   ii. Review the design against project principles established to guide the process outcomes
   iii. Evaluate the design against the project vision that outlined the qualities of the project in the future

Sustainable master plan checklist

This master plan checklist inspires alternative ways of looking at urban design and sustainable development in an integrated way that builds a sense of belonging and identity. Think of it as another tool to creating sustainable urban design.

1. Craft a natural theme that reflects the sense of place, conserves energy, manages resources best, and creates a responsible home and workplace that fits with the surrounding community.
2. Connect to the surrounding community by a comprehensive transit and pathways network.
3. Develop detailed architectural guidelines that reflect and enhance the surroundings.
4. Create detailed landscape guidelines for everything from streets to plant materials, including signs that provide genuine responses to the landscape, specifying enduring materials.
5. Define public and private spaces with design features such as low fences, street furniture, and plantings, rather than walls.
6. Bridge specific land uses such as town houses and single-occupancy dwellings by creating positive and mutually complementary transitions between building form and landscaping.
7. Enhance the natural amenity structure of the land with a comprehensively programmed passive and active recreation system.
8. Preserve the best natural aspects of the site, including view areas, significant stands of trees, natural drainage ways, and environmentally sensitive areas, to provide visual order and a sense of regional connection.
9. Create a sense of entry to the site that captures the distinctive spirit of the place through the special design of entrances that reflect their primary or secondary functions.
10. Develop in small sections and phase development so that each unit is as self-sufficient as possible and has its own identifiers.
11. Leave areas for future development open to new programming as the need arises.

12. Shape the land to minimize site disturbance and reduce costs associated with excavation and moving excess soil material off-site.

13. Develop streetscapes and furniture, including lighting, mailboxes, utility boxes, benches, signs, walls, and fences, along with guidelines for their sensitive design and placement.

14. Capitalize on existing facilities on or adjacent to the site, such as heritage sites, school grounds, and/or parkland systems, that complement site improvements.

15. Cluster development and increase density to conserve natural features, but not without high-quality site planning.

16. Create individual cluster identities by modifying road, lot pattern, and housing type, or by emphasizing landscape features.

17. Design street widths and associated features to indicate, visually and perceptually, location in the community in terms of local residential street versus a main street.

18. Ensure that the overall master plan has a series of features that bring a certain "wow" factor to the design and add to the special design "signatures" on-site.

19. Include social and cultural aspects in the design and planning that outlines housing diversity, equity, and a variety of tenures as well as inclusivity of all age groups in the project and associated master plan process.

20. Develop an economic prosperity plan that creates jobs close to home, includes live/work opportunities and also creates an affordability component in the master plan strategy.

21. Incorporate energy, waste management, solar orientation, water conservation, local building materials, and other resource conservation strategies as integrated parts of the master plan.

The master plan is illustrated in figures 6.4 to 6.6 in a number of different ways, as they apply to various sites, providing alternative tools to present ideas.

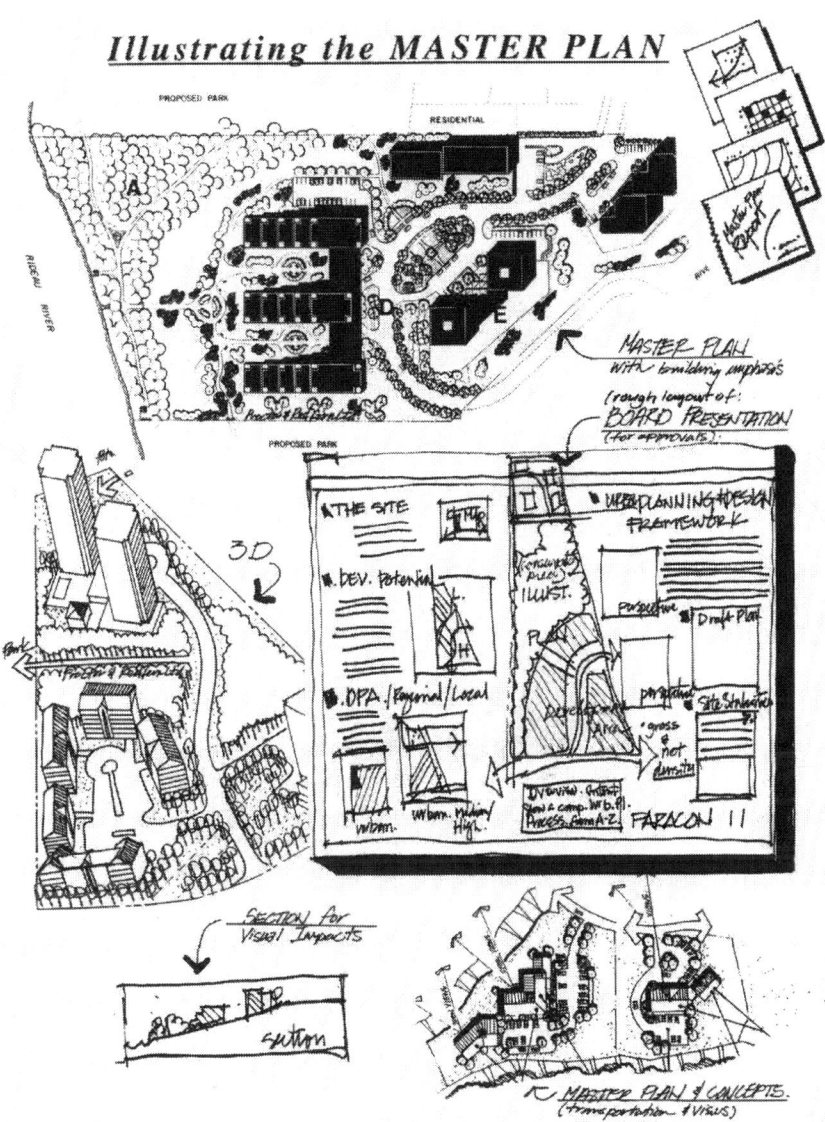

Figure 6.4. Master plan sample illustrations. This figure shows different aspects of the plan drawn in sections, and perspective to further clarify intentions.

1. DETAILED DESIGN

• *Overlays: relationships*

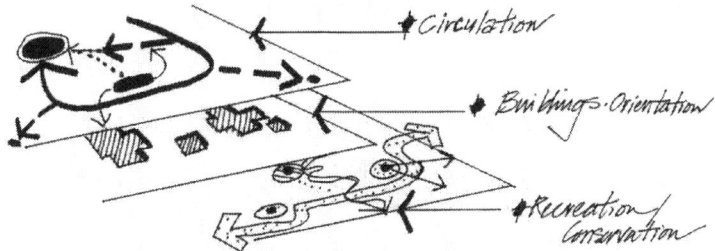

• *Templates: repetitive elements*

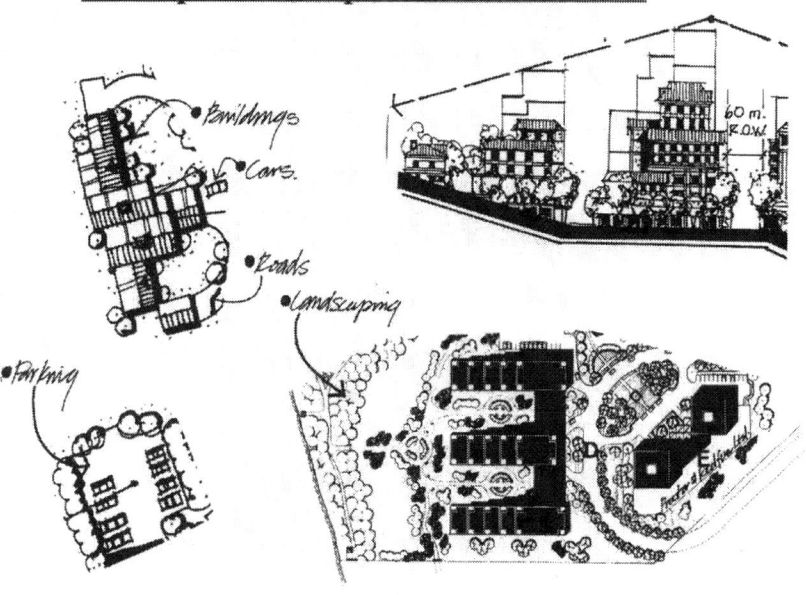

Figure 6.5. Master plan elements and templates. These elements provide further details on various aspects of the master plan. The templates can be applied to various aspects of the master plan (i.e., parking).

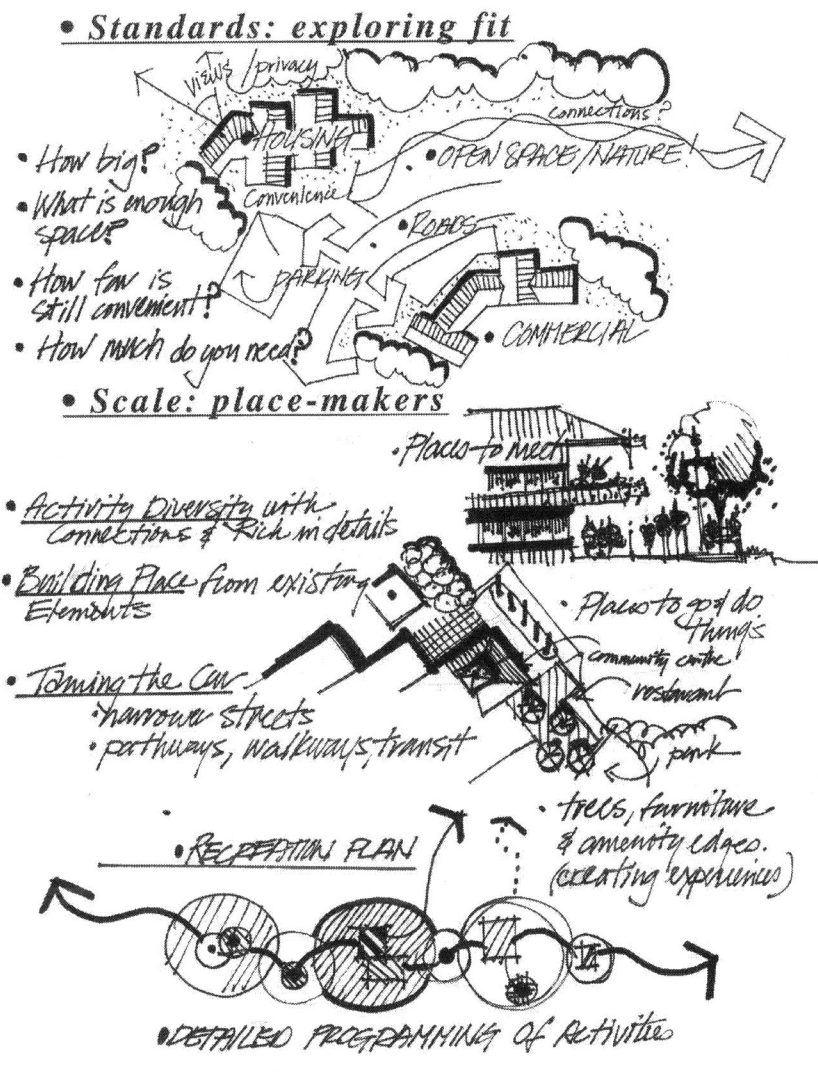

Figure 6.6. Master plan programming detail. This figure illustrates the various activities (e.g., recreation) that can relate to land uses within the plan.

Step 5. Final site plan

Frequently, the site plan is not included in urban design plans, as it is used at the development and building stages of the project. However, many rezoning applications require this level of detail to ensure follow-through and commitment to the concept and master plan. The site plan is very important in testing the detailed design of the master plan.

The final site plan provides all the explicit site design details to implement the project. These include building envelopes and schematic design of buildings, schematic street design and pedestrian/bicycle pathways, parking facilities, recreational and public facilities, and schematic landscape design, including lighting, planting, pathways, plazas, and courtyards. The site plan is the technical basis for detailed construction drawings to build the project and reflect the zoning and subdivision regulations.

Further detailed refinement in this phase of the project includes the public facilities plan and the financial pro forma (cash flow) and phasing of development. At a glance, here are the multiple components of the final site plan.

Site plan process

A. Best option: Detailed site plan with land use summary
    i.   Land uses, building envelopes, and 3-D character of buildings
    ii. Restoration and conservation strategies for buildings and landscape
    iii. Landscape development, including planting, lighting, and surface materials
    iv. Street design and parking
    v.   Transit, bicycle, and pedestrian systems design
    vi. Wayfaring plan
    vii. Servicing drawings for water, storm water, sanitary sewer, and other utilities
    viii. Recreation, open space, and public facilities plan
    ix. Energy and waste plan

      x. Sustainability implementation manual for residents and business owners, including operation, maintenance, and stewardship of energy, waste, and natural systems

B. Corporate returns: Pro forma return on investment and financing
      i. Detailed financial pro forma, including return analysis and cash flow projections
      ii. Financing strategy linked to phasing of development and partnerships/purchase agreements
      iii. Marketing strategies, including presales, pricing, absorption, and positioning

C. Public gains: Summary of benefits and net gains
      i. Public benefits plan and development agreement
      ii. Environmental restoration and recreation linkage
      iii. Transportation and other infrastructure linkage and contributions

Detailed dimensioning and scale

Figures 6.7 to 6.9 show the level of detail in the site planning stage and pose key planning questions. As the final stage of the detailed design of the site, the site plan incorporates the technical expertise of a variety of professionals for detailed construction documentation. As noted earlier, in many instances it is not part of the normal urban design process but is illustrated here to represent the importance of keeping the end result in mind.

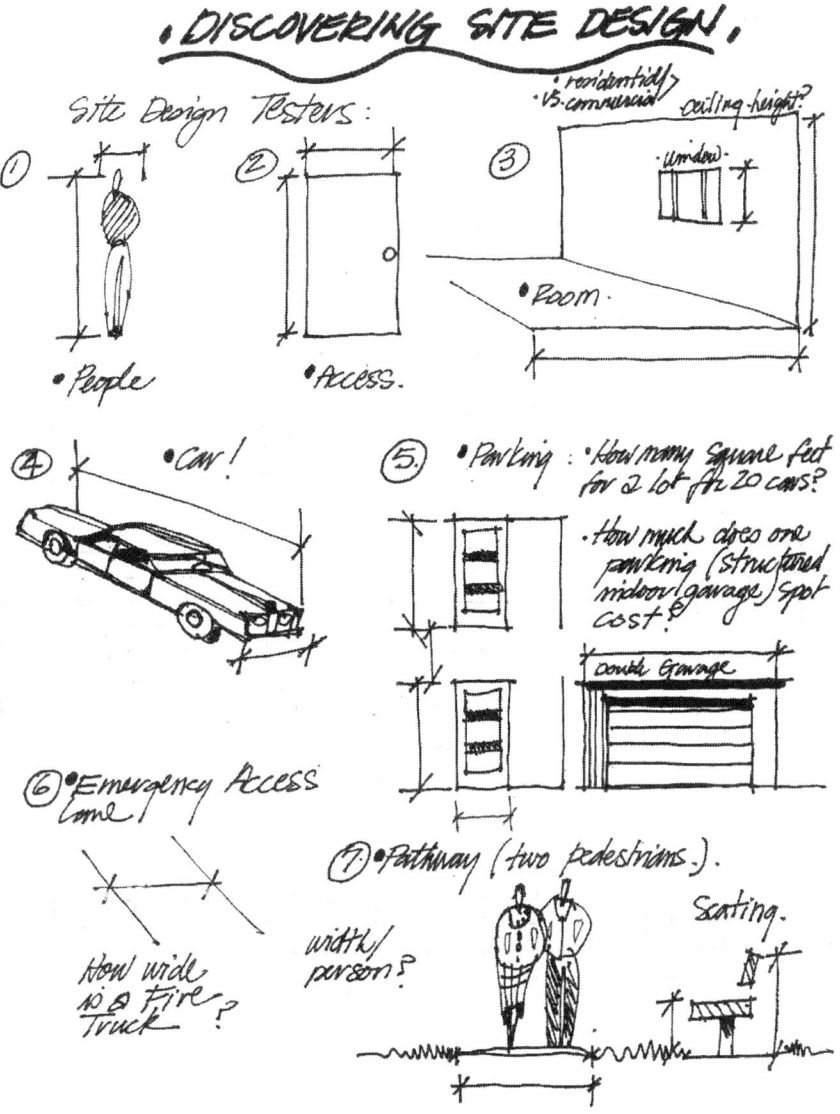

Figure 6.7. Exploration of site plan core dimensions. Design starts with human dimension and should work with "nature" to find optimal form. Much of our urban design today is driven by emergency access, and car and truck dimensions. How do we change that?

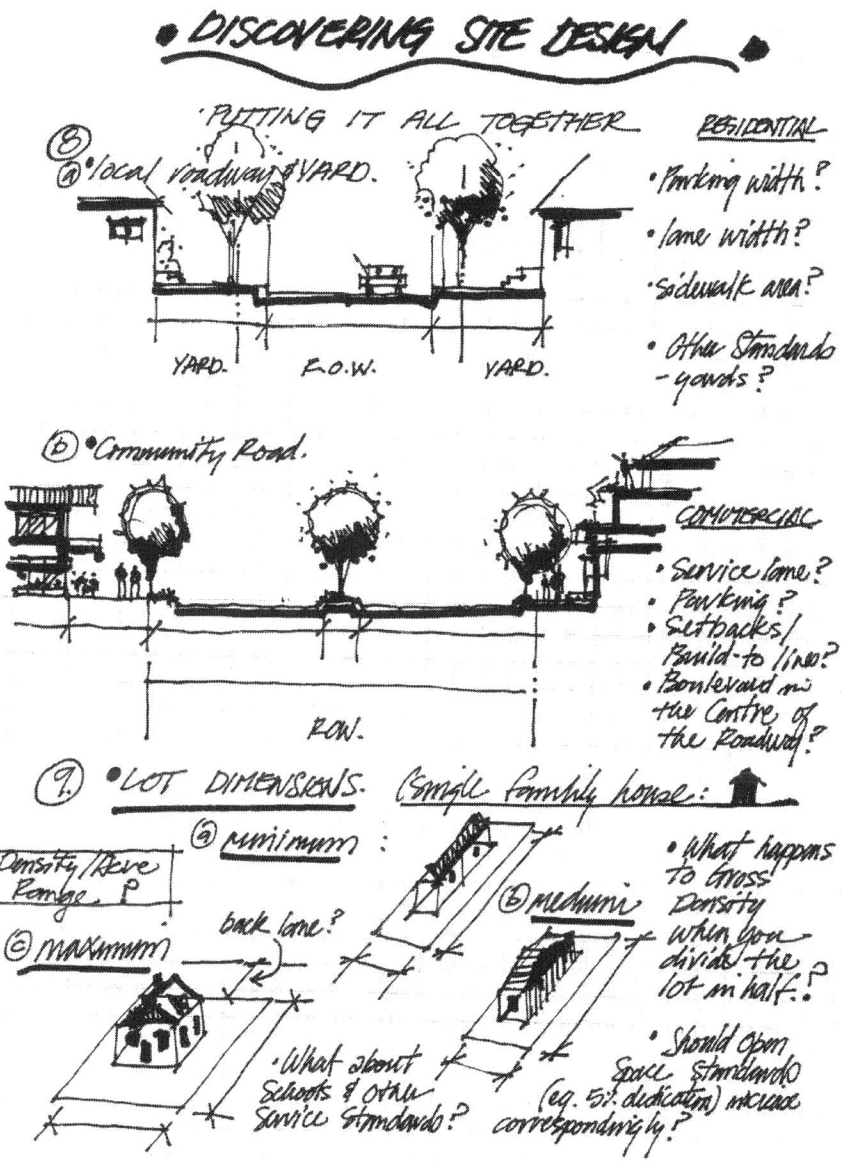

Figure 6.8. Exploration of site plan lot and street design dimensions.
Discover how a car or truck dimension determines much of our urban design by answering questions in this diagram.

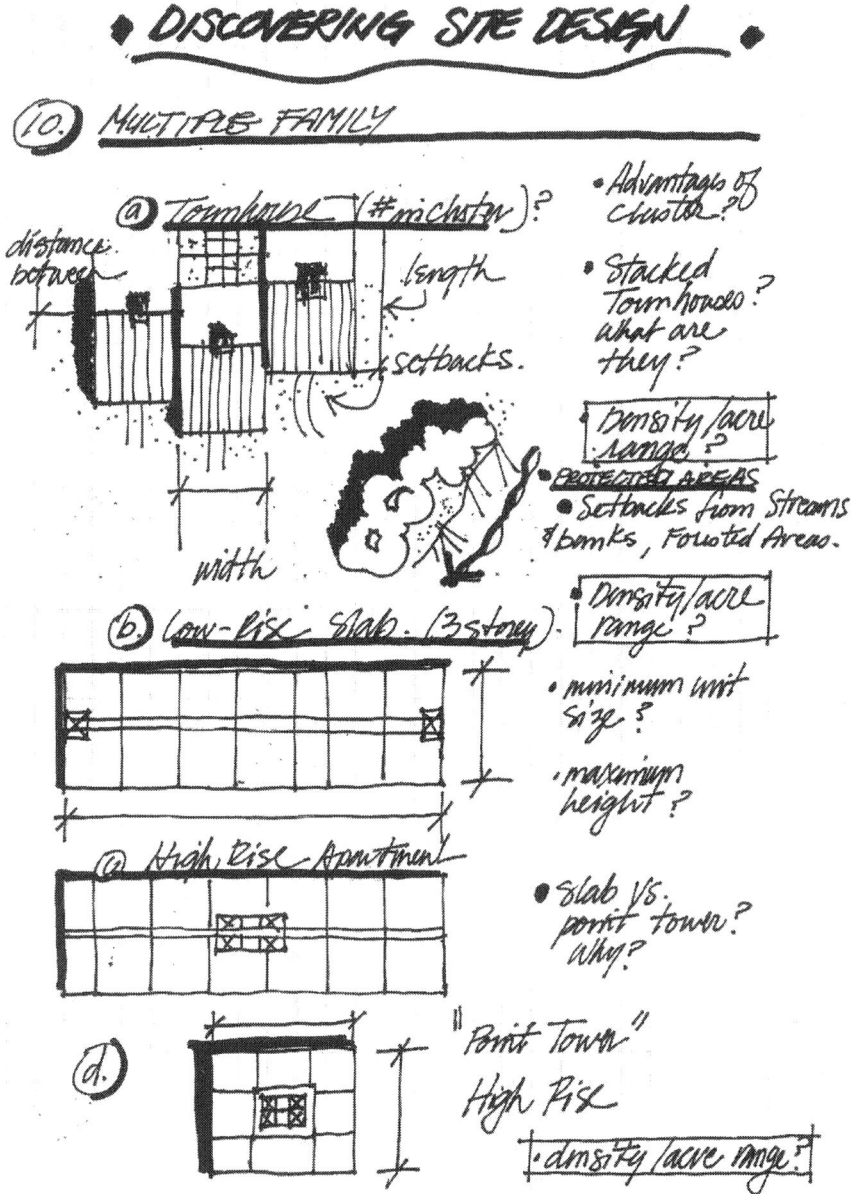

Figure 6.9. Exploration of family of building design dimensions.
Some fundamental dimensions are derived from building codes and standard living dimensions. Again, this diagram lists the questions for consideration.

Case study: Concept to master plan, New Elita, Krasnoyarsk, Russia
I have the honor to continue to work in Russia. It is a land with a rich
cultural history and vast natural resources. Russia is also a country of
extreme climates and distinctive local culture. Krasnoyarsk is a natural
resource–based industrial city of over 1 million residents located in south
central Siberia. Temperatures can range more than 130°F (50°C) between
summer and winter months. New Elita is a proposed new community
located on 1,366 acres (553 ha) of land about 7.5 miles (12 km) northwest
of Krasnoyarsk. Figures 6.10 to 6.21 illustrate the concept development
for New Elita—a measured and sequential process that ends in a "family"
of supportive detailed plans.[2]

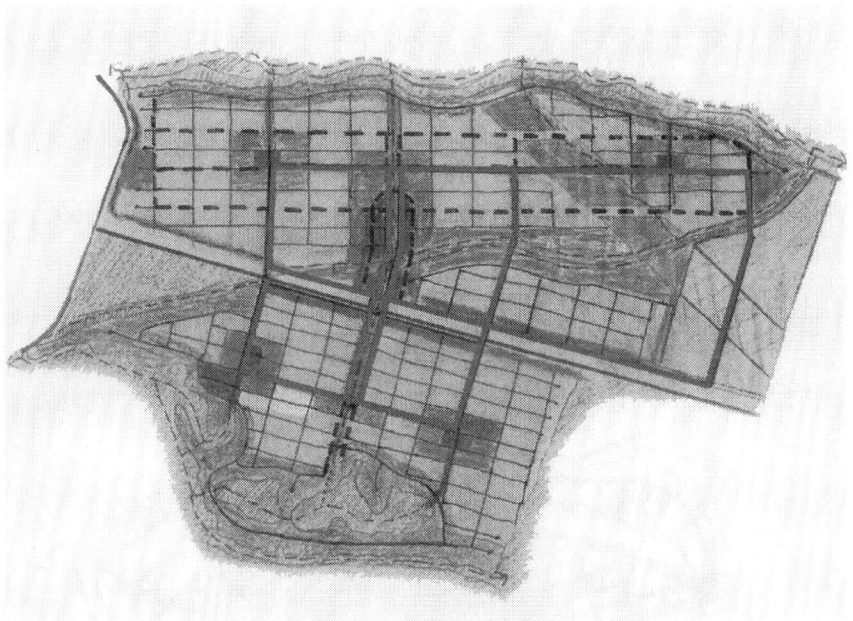

**Figure 6.10. Neighborhood centers and central town center concept
1, New Elita.** Concept 1 shows one town center and four neighborhood
centers connected by a standard street grid. (Drawing by Paul Turje.)

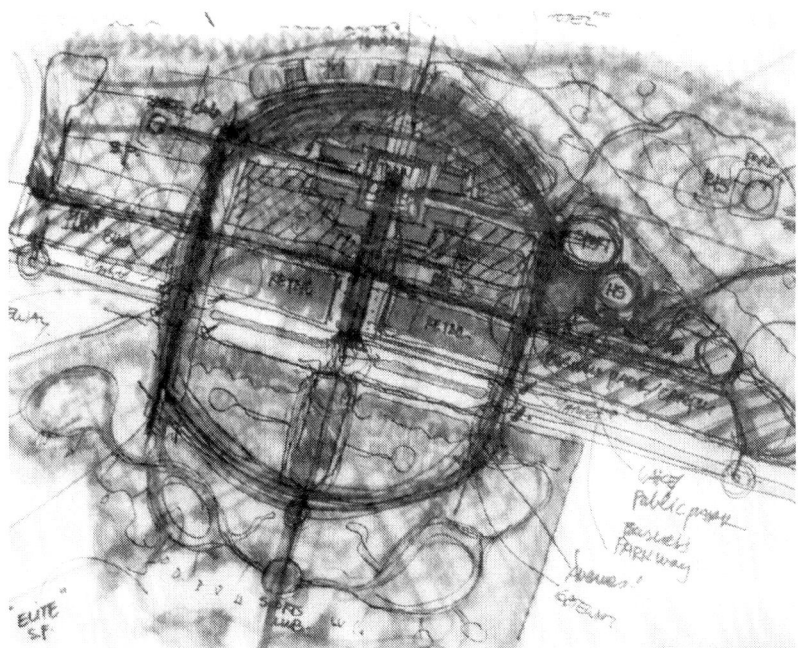

Figure 6.11. Town square concept 2, New Elita. Concept 2 illustrates one large town center within surrounding neighborhoods connected by a circular boulevard. (Drawing by Calum Srigley.)

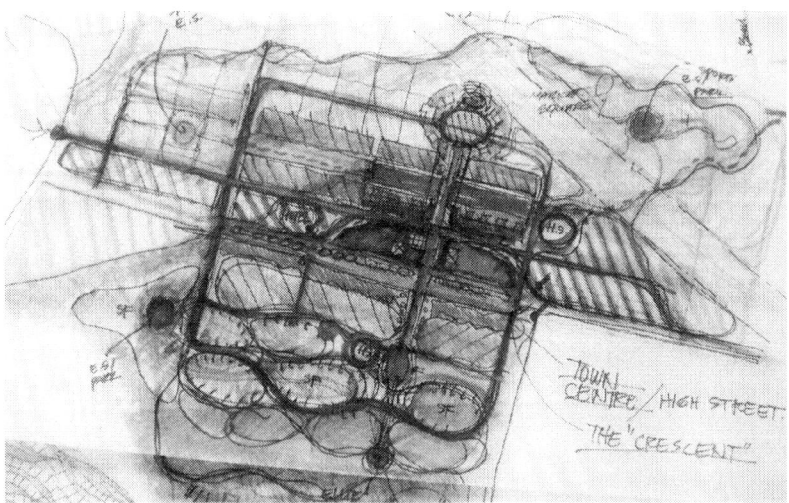

Figure 6.12. High street concept 3, New Elita. Concept 3 creates a central high street that cuts east-west across one town center, with a surrounding road network and multiple land use districts. (Drawing by Calum Srigley.)

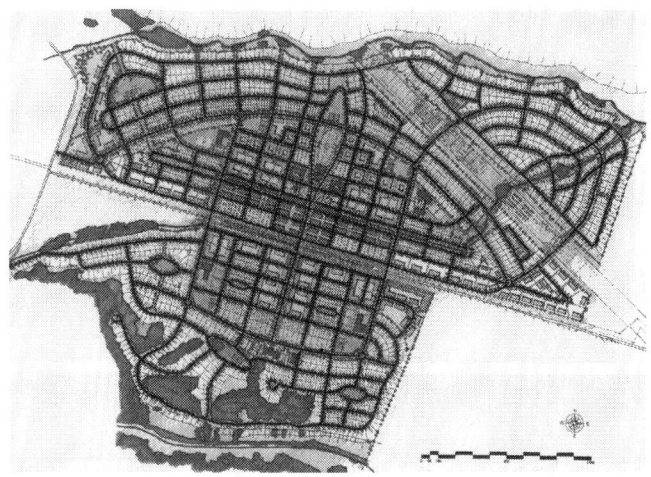

Figure 6.13. Urban design master plan (the bow-and-arrow concept), New Elita. The final approved master plan combines two town centers (one north and one south of the central existing highway) with an elegant connecting street system. The central street grid creates easy access and adaptability to different land uses, while the peripheral, more organic street layout protects the natural features and slows cars in the residential areas. An integrated network of parks, trails, open spaces, and recreation spaces interconnects schools, town centers, and surrounding neighborhoods. (Drawing by Don Wuori.)

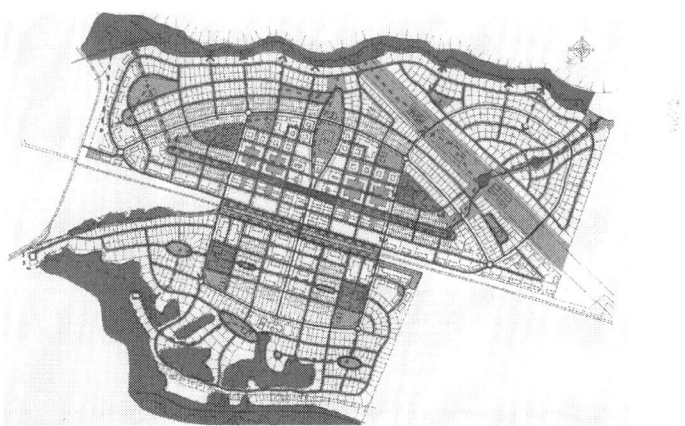

Figure 6.14. Green network plan, New Elita. The green network starts with tree-planted streets with sidewalks and expands to neighborhood playgrounds, parks, community gardens, a tree nursery, sports fields, and a central indoor/outdoor sportsplex with swimming pools, ice rinks, and a football field. Elementary schools are located within a five-minute walk for every New Elita resident. (Graphics by Dolores Altin.)

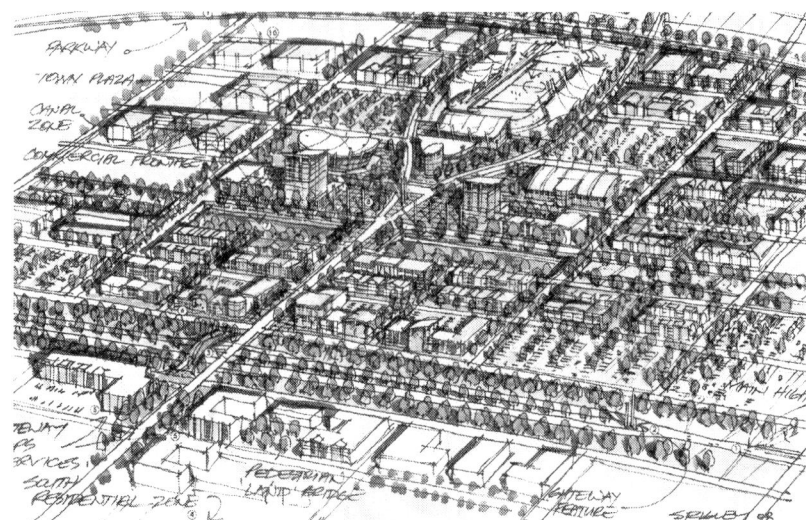

Figure 6.15. Town center concept sketch with central canal, New Elita. The town center will be the business and cultural gathering area for New Elita. Mixed business and residential uses will provide for an active, safe, and engaging area seven days a week throughout all four seasons. (Drawing by Calum Srigley.)

Figure 6.16. Canal promenade concept sketch, New Elita. A central canal amenity will cool the crowds in summer, provide recreation skating in winter, and provide storm water management for the new community. (Drawing by Calum Srigley.)

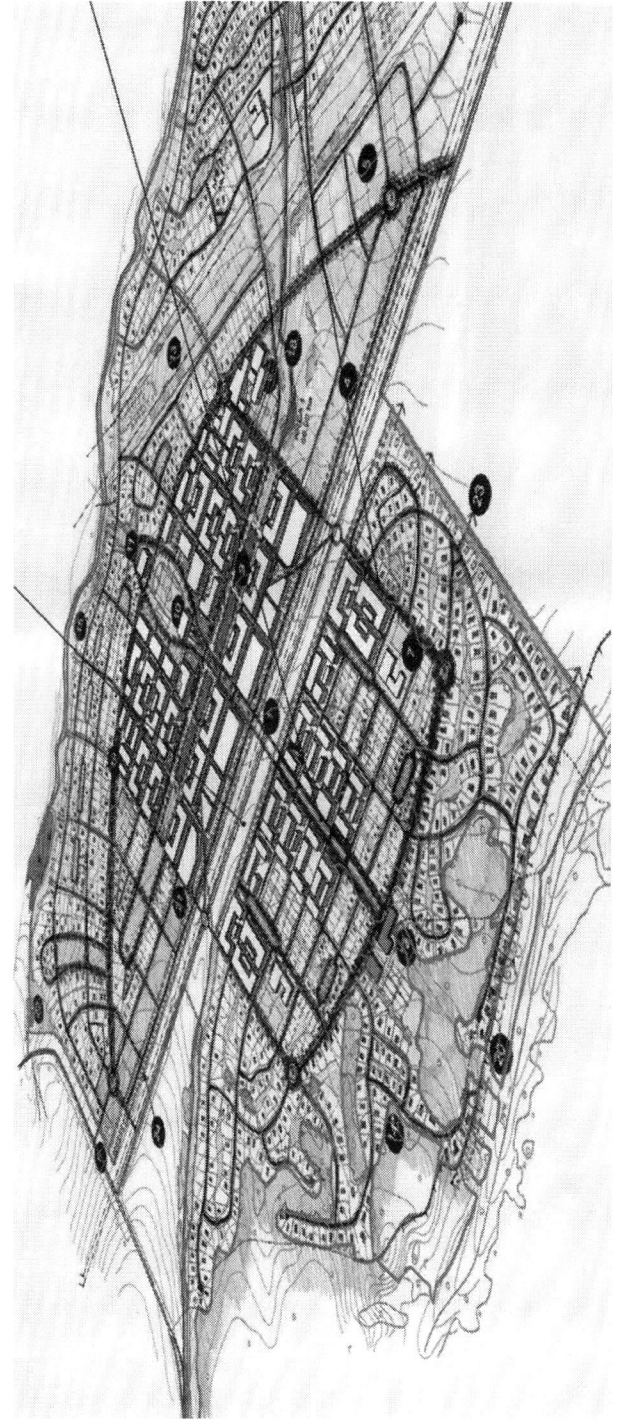

Figure 6.17. Working sketch for aerial perspective, New Elita. A working aerial perspective provides a basis for design refinement. (Drawing by Don Wuori.)

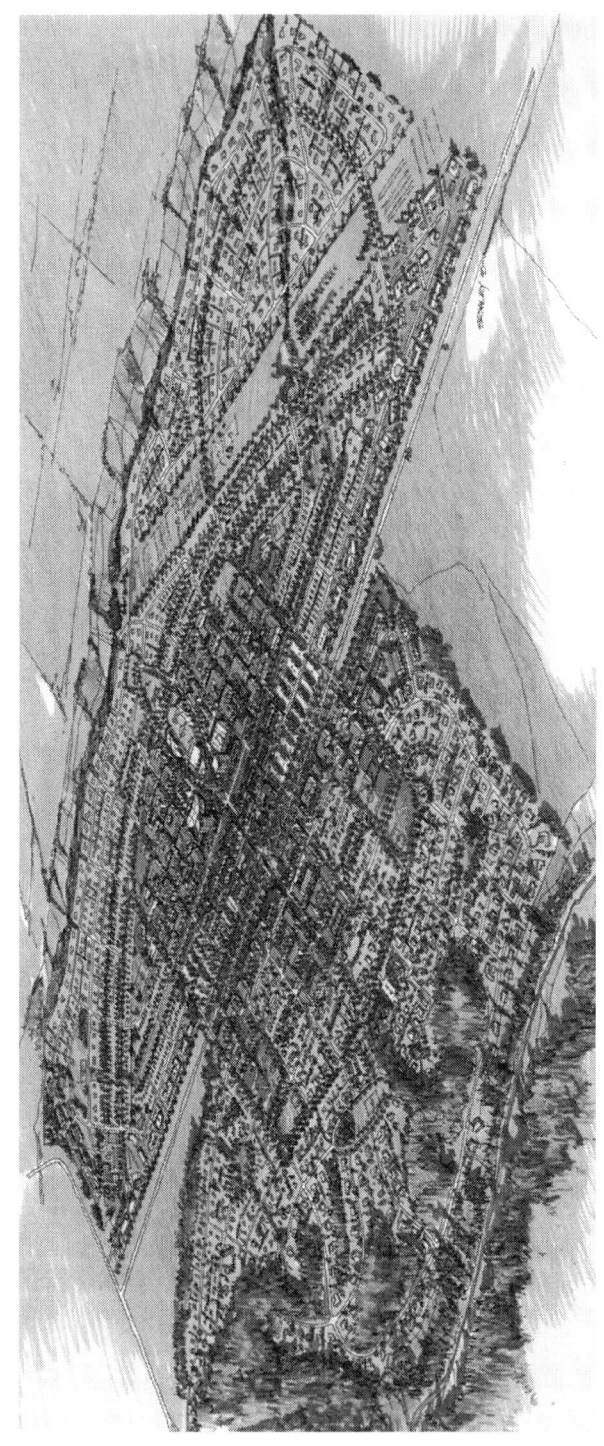

Figure 6.18. Aerial perspective sketch of New Elita. The final aerial perspective sketch illustrates how New Elita fits into its surrounding context and conserves as well as enhances natural features. (Drawing by Calum Srigley.)

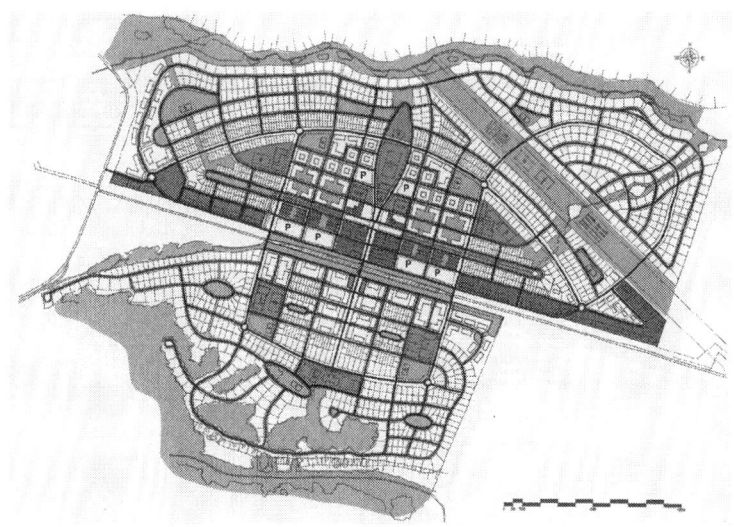

Figure 6.19. Commercial, industrial, and recreational network zoning, New Elita. This plan provides a diversity of land uses, including industrial and commercial uses to provide local jobs to encourage a degree of self-sufficiency. The concept is for many residents to live, work, and play in close proximity. (Graphics by Dolores Altin.)

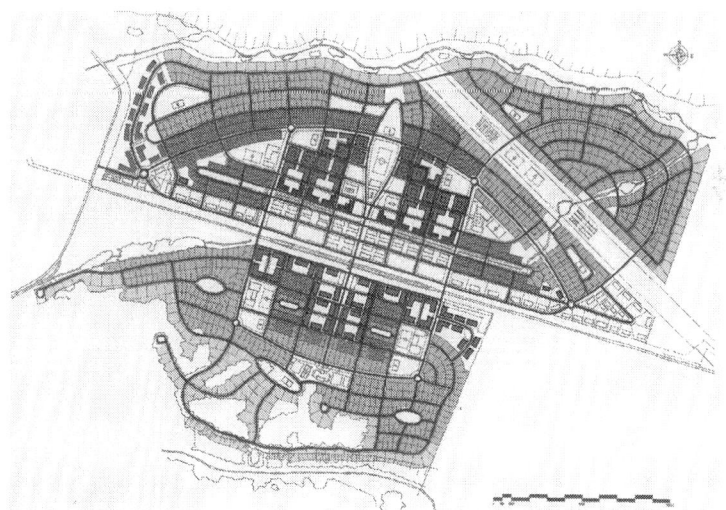

Figure 6.20. Residential zoning layer with flex blocks for swing uses, New Elita. Residential blocks are built for flexibility. Although there is a diversity of residential zones, the central blocks can be adapted for single-family, town house, or apartment uses to respond to demographic changes and market demand. (Graphics by Dolores Altin.)

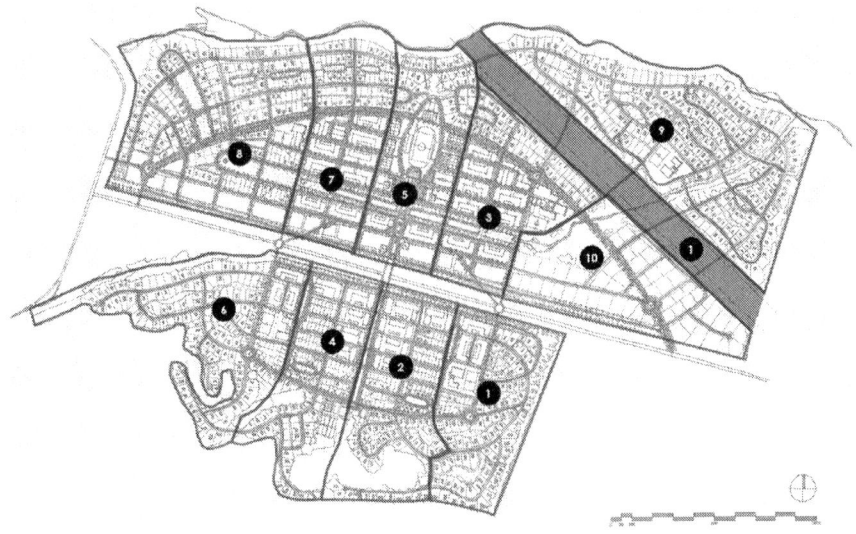

Figure 6.21. Phasing layer, New Elita. Phasing for New Elita is reduced to small, sequential steps so the community can be built in stages, with appropriate services. (Graphics by Dolores Altin.)

This chapter walked you through the plan-making process in five comprehensive steps:

1. Establishing a clear vision and goals at the outset to guide the project
2. Analyzing the environment, including critical factors
3. Developing a site concept in "bubble diagrams"
4. Developing a master plan with building and landscape details
5. Creating a final site plan with all site design details required to implement the project

The New Elita case study illustrated the concept development for a brand-new, planned community in south central Siberia. Of course, urban designers do not always have such a blank slate on which to try out their ideas. But no matter the site in question and the challenges associated, success can still be achieved when this comprehensive planning process is followed, as two case studies in the next chapter reveal.

7
PLAN-MAKING IN REALITY

Since Sustainability Change Agents are often working in organizational settings, where social power dynamics may be the decisive factor in determining success or failure, a capacity to see and recognize power dynamics for what they are is crucial.

—Alan AtKisson, *The ISIS Agreement*

You read one case study in chapter 6, for a planned community in Russia. This chapter provides two more case studies that demonstrate a successful planning process, both in my home province of British Columbia, Canada. These case studies examine the process of working with social power dynamics in the community and at the municipal government level. The first, an urban design plan in the city of New Westminster, is a true "urban" plan to upgrade, intensify, and better utilize land in a redevelopment area. The second, a plan for private lands in the coastal community of Ucluelet, was a more controversial attempt to integrate resort, recreational, and residential uses. But first, let's look at some preferred methods for plan generation.

Jump-starting design

So how do you begin your plan-making process? Do you sit down at your computer and open a computer program and just start your design process based on a template from another similar site and series of land uses? Alternatively, do you start with a sketch pad and design from memory or inspiration? Do you analyze data and background information? Do you visit the site and talk to the people who live in the area? Each one of these methods has a role in jump-starting a project. I like to use a combination of tools, depending on the scale and size of a project. I call this approach using "the right tool at the right time."

The right tool at the right time means that I might use my sketchbook initially to capture ideas that build on-site observations and information. I visit the site very early in the process. I visit the site not once but at different times of the day and during different seasons if possible. My camera and sketchbook capture various aspects of the site through different media and "lenses." This series of site visits may be followed by detailed computer analysis through aerial photos, census data, and geographic information systems review. The sketching tools then come out again on the drawing board as I overlay tracing paper on maps and aerial photographs to sketch over natural features and buildings to understand the various elements and their interrelationships, as well as their context. This step is followed by analysis of land use, zoning, transportation and mobility, site orientation and topography, natural features and ecological systems, and other applicable elements.

The products at this stage can be a series of hand drawings that are translated into computer drawings. Drawings are in two dimensions and three dimensions. The two-dimensional drawings are flat plans. They show no vertical form, only horizontal dimensions and relationships. Section drawings cut through the site, like cutting through a layer cake, revealing vertical and horizontal relationships. These drawings can be invaluable to show important vertical and horizontal differences between site features, buildings, and across a street. For instance, a section drawing can easily reveal that an important building can be set above a street on a ridge to retain important views. A plan drawing cannot show that vertical relationship, except that the building is adjacent to the street. The perspective drawings and models illustrate three dimensions. The three-dimensional drawings and models are easiest for the public to read. Although they are interpretations, through them the viewer can better experience the place.

The final project documentation may integrate a variety of different media, combining technology with hand drawing. These media can include video, PowerPoint slide presentations that can be posted on a website, web-based interactive social media such as Twitter and Facebook to invite comments, and print documentation. I use multiple tools focused and dependent on the specific project needs and associated audience demands.

Two essential requirements stand out in all urban design processes. First, you need a story about the future experience, and second, the story needs to be told in images, plans, maps, and hand sketches. The story is a collection of experiences. Images bring life to the story. Hand-drawn images illustrate the possibilities of the future. The sketches also represent conceptual ideas, especially at the early stages of the project, and can be refined as the project progresses. In contrast, computer drawings can be seen as more final or defined and, therefore, can be perceived as being less flexible or open to change. The computer-generated image may be most appropriate toward the end of the urban design process, when detail is better defined. Again, "the right tool at the right time" is always my test to define what tool to use and when, depending on resources, goals, and time limits.

The format, scale, and orientation of the maps and plans associated with the story must be consistent so that they can be readily understood. Consistent format means a standard size and layout for all drawings. Consistent scale means that the size of the elements remains the same in all drawings or plans. However, three scales can be used to differentiate regional context, local context, and site design. Consistent orientation means that north is always in the same direction, normally at the top of the plan. Collectively, format, scale, and orientation are the first challenges in any project. Organize these three elements, and the project foundation is set. Otherwise, the plans can be confusing, which can lead to misunderstanding, frustration, and wasted time.

Combining two approaches

A systematic method is required to help successfully develop the urban design ideas, since they are complex by nature and involve many factors. Add sustainable community development to the mix, and you have yet more complexity. The previous chapter reviewed various methods of generating and organizing ideas, from the logical building block or puzzle approach to the more inspirational approach (see fig. 6.1). These methods work differently for different people. The logical and sequential thinker uses more the left side of the brain—normally seen as the engineering approach to problem solving. This approach is based on scientific data and carefully measured observation. The more creative person uses the right side of the brain—normally seen as the architectural, creative, or artistic approach to problem solving. This method tends to be more intuitive, based on other precedents and/or an evolving sequence of inspirational ideas.

Either method—call them logical and creative—can be seen as correct, but combining elements of both creates a more substantial result in terms of sustainable urban design, with more possibilities. The substance is in the data and the facts, which is the engineering approach. The possibilities are in the expansion of current ideas and projects to a new dimension, which is the architectural/artistic approach, although it must be stated that some architects are very practical and take an engineering approach to projects. Because they come at problems from different perspectives, these two methods, when combined, result in a powerful chemistry that leads to well-informed and innovative solutions.

Case study: Collaborative community process, Lower Twelfth Street, New Westminster, British Columbia

Here I share my plan-making experience with the Lower Twelfth Street project in the city of New Westminster, just outside Vancouver. Starting in August 2003 and ending in April 2004, the consulting team completed a successful urban design process that included the formation of a support group, the scheduling/instigation of a community historic walk, and the utilization of community newsletters and the city's website to keep the community informed. The team also completed a four-day design charrette process to actively engage the residents and businesses in shaping their future. The plan took shape through this active engagement of the community and local government in an interactive and open process. Any social power dynamics of fear and loss of neighborhood control were dissipated by a number of possibilities of participation that were flexible and respectful. From the historic walk led by a local historian to the community solutions workshop, public presentation, community questionnaires, or final public open houses, there was a concerted effort supported by the community to ensure different ways of participation.[1]

In many urban design projects, synthesis of all the elements into an urban design plan is often left until late in the process, and members of the design team have forgotten much of the detail. To avoid this typical scenario, I decided to sketch the whole urban design plan framework midway through, after the major public participation took place. The whole sketching exercise took place on the plane on the way back from Playa del Carmen, Mexico, where I was working on a sustainable development project. These sketches took me three to four hours of focused time, and the whole story came together in a series of drawings. The results formed the basis of the award-winning plan for Lower Twelfth Street.

This case study site is located in a transition area of New Westminster, dominated by car dealerships, and one of the busiest streets borders its southwest edge. The site has a desirable southwest exposure, dominated by steep to moderate slopes. It is well situated for growth and redevelopment, but current land uses and perceptions of the area had limited its potential. The vision for the area is to transform it into a higher-density residential community with a rich streetscape and community amenities linked to services and nearby transit.

Although the substance is always important in any plan, the focus of this case study is the synthesis part of the process. Here I want to get at the essence of the plan-making process rather than the substance, which I cover extensively in other parts of this book. I share the following Lower Twelfth Street drawings for three reasons. The first is to inspire you to trust your intuition about a site and get to the plan-making process earlier rather than later. In my experience, if you do not sketch and explore in a loose manner early in your process, you tend to limit the exploration and generation of innovative ideas. The second reason is to prove that the combination of the logical and creative methods can make for a powerful and compelling sustainable urban design story. The final reason is to show that the process of synthesis does not have to take long if you have done your homework in site inventory and analysis. The series of plans come together in a sequence of related drawings that collectively form the "family" of plans and tell a colorful story for the project (figs. 7.1 to 7.5).

You will notice that the early analysis (the logical approach) is combined with some "creative" work, especially in the final urban design framework plan. Each plan sketch delineates specific information and sets a basis for thinking of what could happen in the future.

For example, the building coverage plan (fig. 7.1) illustrates how underutilized the site is in terms of potential additional development. The dark areas represent the buildings, and the rest of the plan is white, representing vacant land and streets. The development potential plan (fig. 7.2) reveals how relatively few owners control major blocks of land, making it easier to redevelop the area (noted as "H" on the plan—indicating high relative development potential). In contrast, if there were many landowners, it would normally be more difficult to consider redevelopment, since smaller parcels limit redevelopment options (noted as "L" on the plan—indicating low relative development potential). The slopes and orientation map (fig. 7.3) reveals the potential views of the Fraser River, slopes, floodplain, and the positive, sunny orientation of the site. The character areas and existing land use plan illustrate the variety of land uses and differing characteristics that should be recognized in redevelopment (fig. 7.4). These plans are the key ingredients for the final urban design and land use concept. This concept synthesizes the analysis into a composite plan that optimizes the potential of the area while respecting its existing character and capacity for redevelopment (fig. 7.5).

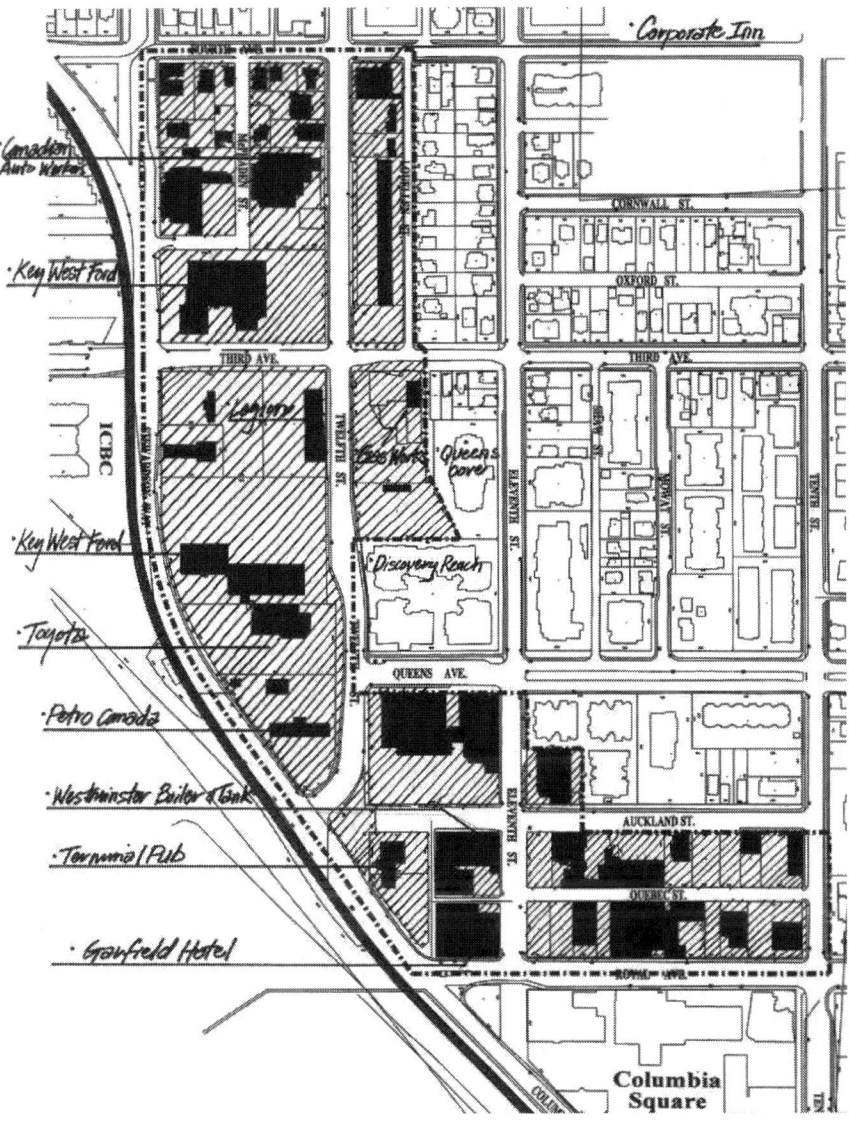

Figure 7.1. Building coverage, Lower Twelfth Street, New Westminster, British Columbia. Low building coverage indicates underutilized land and opportunities for redevelopment with a more compact and efficient building form.

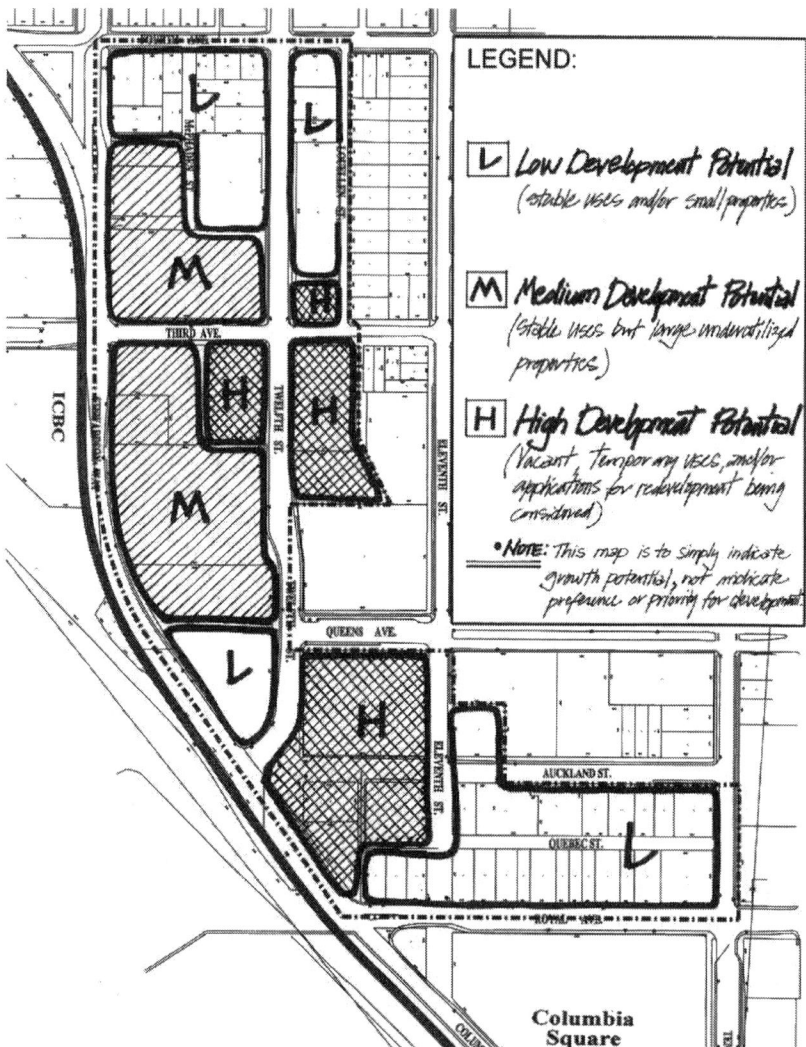

Figure 7.2. Development potential, Lower Twelfth Street, New Westminster, British Columbia. Examining the social, ecological, and economic capacities for redevelopment should inform the priorities for redevelopment, such as location, demographics, history, and market potential.

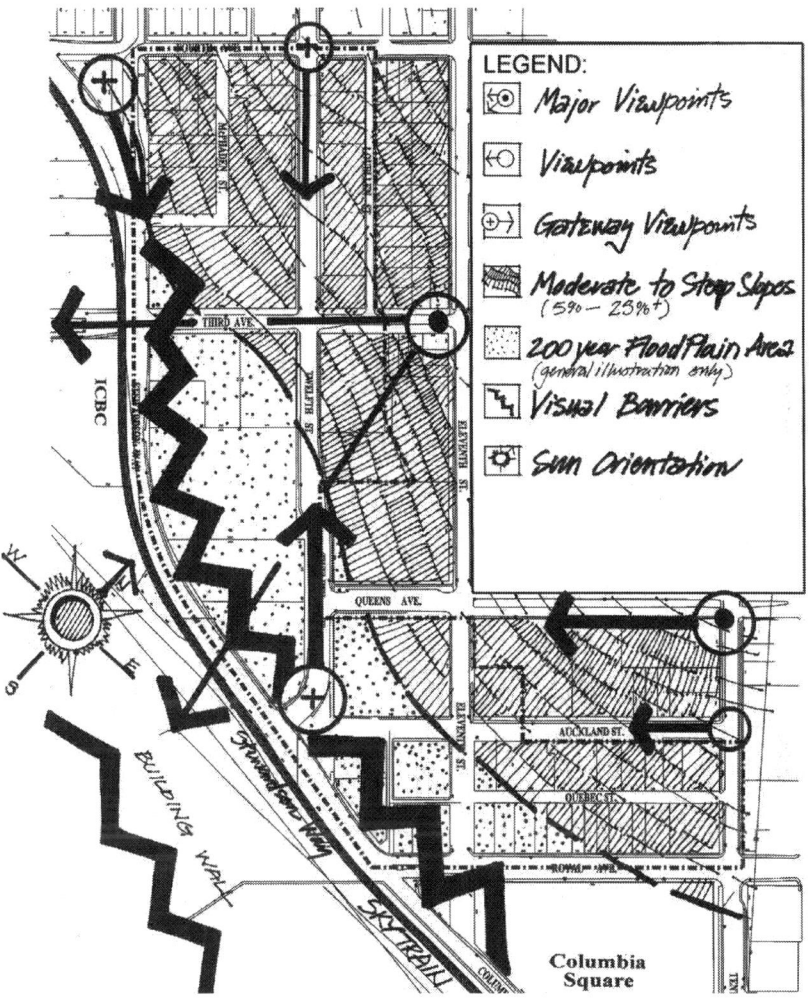

Figure 7.3. Topography, views, and orientation, Lower Twelfth Street, New Westminster, British Columbia. Physical aspects of the site, such as views, slopes, microclimate, and floodplain location, inform development challenges and opportunities.

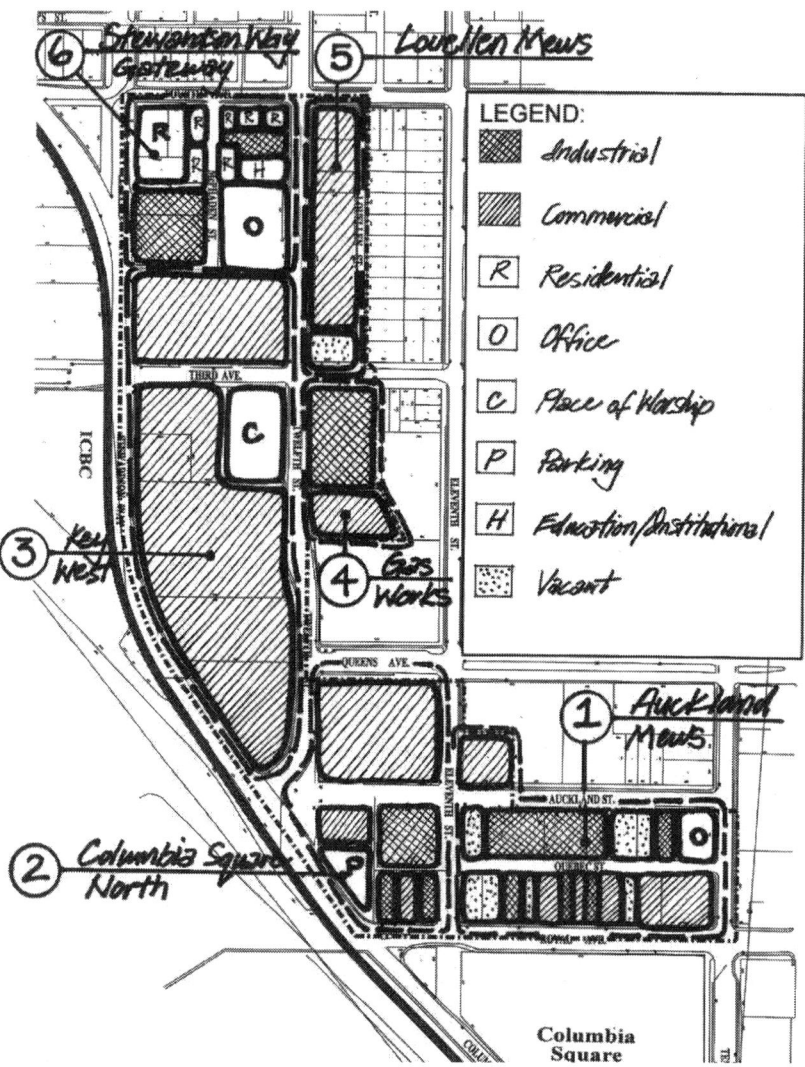

Figure 7.4. Character areas and existing land use, Lower Twelfth Street, New Westminster, British Columbia. This community has unique elements, such as block size, south orientation, history, current land use, and street type, that shape its character subareas.

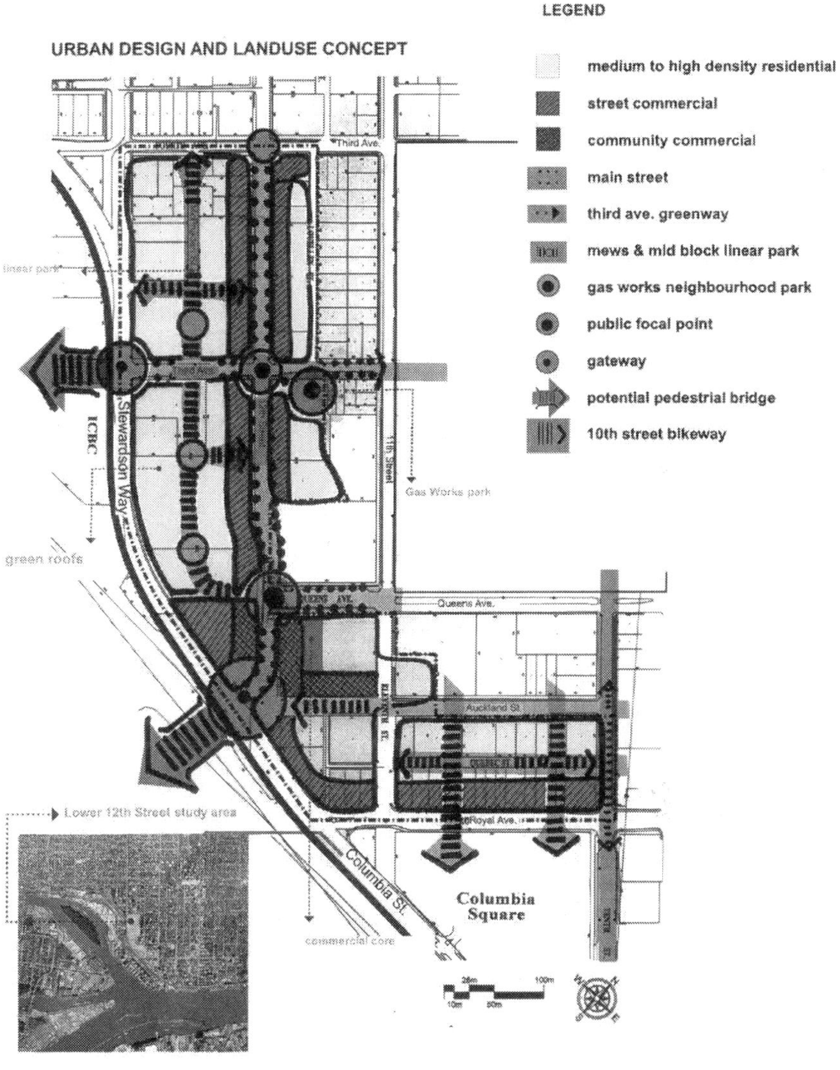

Figure 7.5. Urban design and land use concept, Lower Twelfth Street, New Westminster, British Columbia. The final concept has many different elements that collectively shape the plan, such as block size, existing and potential land use, location, orientation, and capacity for redevelopment. (Graphics by Dolores Altin.)

Case study: Resort and housing development, Weyerhaeuser Lands, Ucluelet, British Columbia

The next case study counters what is happening in many resort areas around the world, where developers often disregard the local character, culture, and geography. Driven by preset hotel standards and formula design, the result is often a prepackaged resort that can be experienced around the world. I have experienced many such resorts and wonder why I am enticed to return. Reasons include food safety and personal safety, as well as predictable accommodations and amenities measured on an international standard. After all, the last thing you want to worry about is your well-being when you visit these resorts to relax and enjoy yourself. Most often, I am drawn to the more "natural" resorts that fit into the community landscape and culture.

This case study combines resort planning with local community needs and aspirations. The results build on the community character and contribute to healthy growth. This healthy growth is spurred in part by a community amenity package and associated strategies that extend beyond the bounds of the property. Specifically, eight strategies in sustainable urban form (see page 172) served as a framework for a new community plan on the west coast of Vancouver Island in the town of Ucluelet, British Columbia.[2] The case study takes us from a project that was at first turned down by the local council to an award-winning project with unanimous council approval within the remarkably short time frame of six months. Normally, these processes take up to three to five years!

I have an expression: "If my clients don't have a fire, I don't have a job." In this case, I ran into a firestorm. It was not good news. I had to assess first whether I would take on the assignment. The director of planning, Felice Mazzoni, was a former student of mine at both the University of British Columbia and Simon Fraser University. I remember distinctly when he first approached me at a planning conference. He said, "I think we might need your help." My mind immediately went to the scene of either a hospital or a grave site. My initial thought was *Could this foundering ship be rescued, or should we simply let it sink?* As Felice described the status of the project, the situation did not look promising. All the facts seemed against the project's future feasibility. The project had been turned down by unanimous vote of the local council. The prior developer had ignored the advice of the landowner—Weyerhaeuser Lands—as well as council, staff, and the community. The trust in the community for the previous developer appeared to be gone.

When I looked at the aerial photo of the 376-acre (152-ha) property, my feelings changed instantly. The property looked spectacular—set out on the Ucluelet peninsula on the edge of the Pacific Ocean, with nothing between it and Japan. Enormous, brooding surf and a pristine coastline drew me to imagining its potential. As I started to dig for information, my first step was to meet with Charles Smith of Weyerhaeuser, the director of the project and landowner. Weyerhaeuser is an international forest resource company that had owned the land for many years, originally for forest resource purposes. I had to see whether the company was willing to develop a project that followed sustainable development principles and a process that I would custom-design for success.

The first meeting with the company was a real test. Charles Smith was an accountant and director of Canadian lands for Weyerhaeuser. Charles told me about the previous project developer, under contract to Weyerhaeuser, who had created a plan with little consideration for the community. He also told me that Weyerhaeuser, under his direction, would be the master developer of the project. In other words, instead of contracting out the project, Weyerhaeuser would take on the approvals and development land sales coordination themselves. As I soon found out, Weyerhaeuser had always had a good relationship with the town council and staff. Felice Mazzoni, director of planning, and Geoff Lyons, the town manager, were very supportive of Weyerhaeuser proceeding with the rezoning of the property again. They intended to leave a legacy. This all showed promise, until Charles told me that they needed approval within six months, before the next council election. Not only was I going to need a miracle to get this project approved, but the miracle was supposed to have happened the previous week! Despite the political history and timeline challenge, somehow I held out hope for the project.

I told Charles that a measured, tactical response was the only way to right the ship quickly and put it back on course. I knew rebuilding trust at all levels in the community was critical to success. With trust reestablished, I figured the project team could then use our site-sensitive design skills to work with the community to create a supportable land use plan and design for everyone. I told Charles that we needed to create a local consulting team with local contacts. Charles was an active contributor throughout our process—a key ingredient to our eventual success. I also found out that no biophysical investigation had been completed for the property. In other words, there was no summary of environmental opportunities or challenges based on factual information. At the same time, the Wild Pacific Trail, the important trail network along the west coast, had not been adequately recognized in the past planning process. The community and council were not pleased.

Streamline Environmental Consultants soon completed a biophysical analysis overview of the property. I knew we could use this data and site understanding to develop a well-founded plan. We built a local team that included Shine On Consulting to help with public consultation, a local architect (Wayne Wenstob), and Streamline Environmental Consultants. One of our biggest victories was in retaining the local Wild Pacific Trail expert "Oyster Jim" (Jim Martin). Jim owns an oyster farm, and he helped us gain credibility and trust with the local community. Oyster Jim was the initiator of and remains the driving force behind the Wild Pacific Trail.

We took the results of our biophysical information to a community ideas workshop on June 22, 2005, to identify the key opportunities and challenges, as well as to develop concepts for the property based on community values, economic viability, and environmental capacity. We had a number of challenges identified, among them land uses, affordable housing, types of accommodation and hotels, as well as open space and trails. We tried to find solutions for each one. One of the major challenges was the Wild Pacific Trail organization's goal to retain 100 percent of the trail along the Pacific Ocean. I told my team we had to exceed their expectations. "How can that be done?" they asked. We eventually met my goal. We at least doubled the trail length by creating a series of trail loops within the property and retaining 80 percent of the trail along the waterfront. We also developed a policy that the first, more affordable lots would be offered to local residents. These were among some of the concessions and community benefits that emerged from the discussions. We were moving in the right direction.

The consulting team developed five different concepts over a series of meetings and open houses that eventually became a basis for the final plan. A major part of the plan was anchored on eight development strategies that responded to local needs and development capacity. These strategies were supplemented by a community amenity package that extended to improvements to the town and its recreation and social infrastructure. Now we were looking for approval at the community and council level. We felt the ship was back on course. We had a series of three land use concepts that refined to a fourth concept and finally a fifth concept over the summer of public engagement. At a public open house on July 7, many participants added further ideas and information. We also set up a booth at "Ukee Days" on July 23 and 24 for broader public input. Finally, two additional public open houses were held on August 4 and 16 in parallel with staff and council's review of the application, to ensure the public was informed and commented on the refined development concepts (figs. 7.6 and 7.7).

Was there a storm brewing that could sink the ship again? We did not know for sure until the public hearing. It was held in the local recreation center on October 5, 2005, and attended by nearly 300 people, or approximately 25 percent of the town's population. Everyone was seated in neat rows, with council members at the front of the room behind a long table. I felt like I was attending a trial and did not know the evidence that would be presented for or against the project. I was seated adjacent to Charles Smith, just a few rows from the front, next to the podium where the community members would speak. The mayor, Diane St. Jacques, called the meeting to order, and the "trial" of the Weyerhaeuser project proceeded. You could feel the tension in the air. The future of the Weyerhaeuser property rested on the next few hours.

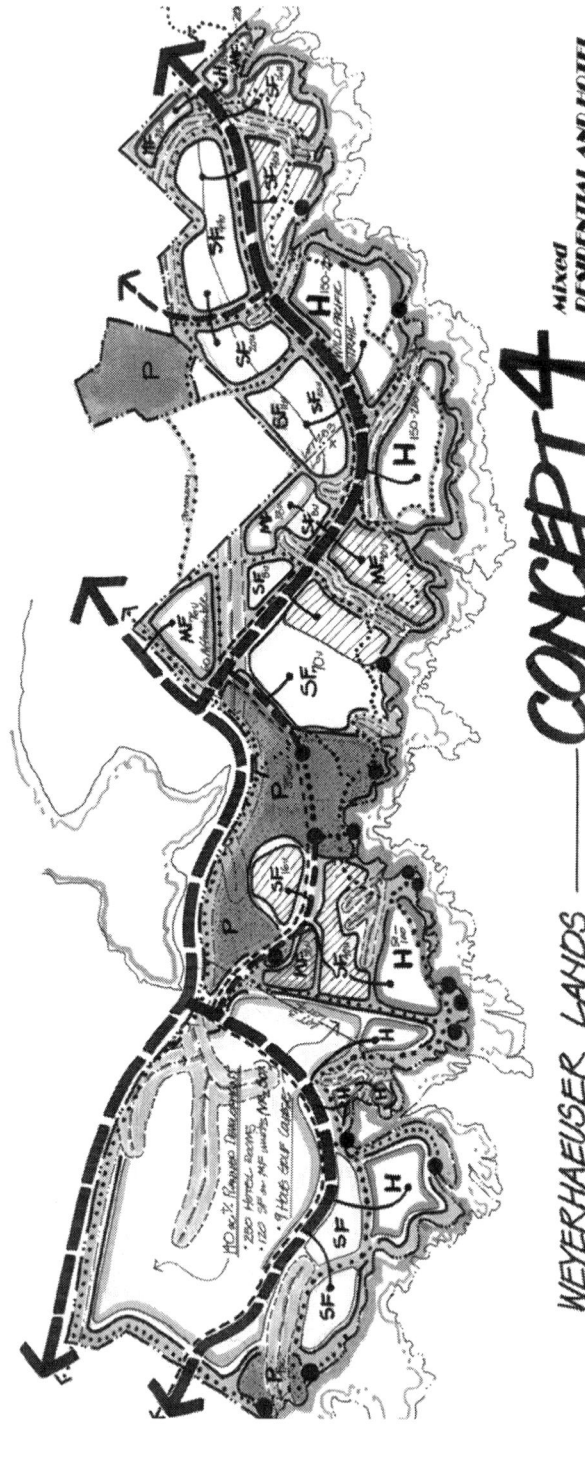

Figure 7.6. Land use concept, Weyerhaeuser Lands, Ucluelet, British Columbia. This plan illustrates the overall land uses, streets, and trails network.

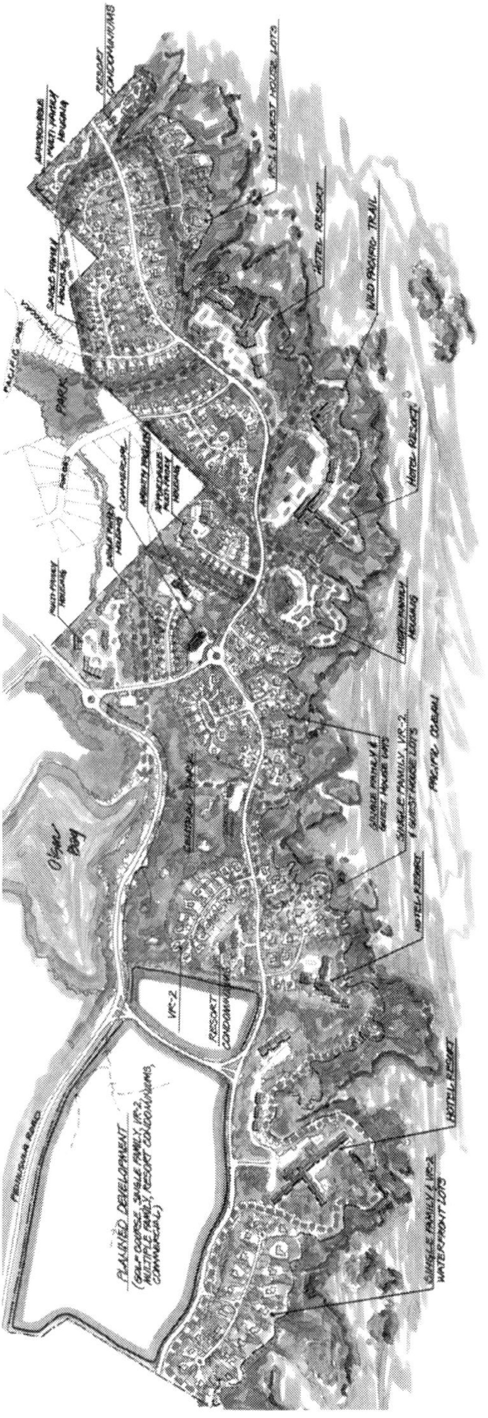

Figure 7.7. Illustrative concept plan, Weyerhaeuser Lands, Ucluelet, British Columbia. This plan takes the bubble diagram in Figure 7.6 one step further and shows a more detailed site plan with building design, from hotels to houses, streets, parking, and open space design.

Public hearings should be about hearing from the public, and that evening the public spoke their mind. Even if Charles and I did speak a few words, I don't remember, as my memory is fixed on what the public said that night, not what we said. The meeting was one of my greatest experiences in democracy. Each person stood up and gave their views on the development in a civil way, listening carefully to and building on the previous points. Comments addressed too much growth, the character of development, and impacts on the town in terms of traffic and competition with other developments and the existing town. I really did not know what the verdict would be. The conversation resembled a teeter-totter—going from negative to positive and back again, with no clear resolve one way or the other.

Finally, after what felt like two hours of speakers, someone rose and said, "We elected you guys [referring to council] to make these difficult decisions." After patiently waiting for hours, it seemed, the council asked whether there were any more speakers. One community member came to the podium and repeated his concerns about the development. Not a good sign to finish on a critical note. Oyster Jim stood up toward the end and made a supportive speech that appeared to sway things toward approval, but still the outcome was uncertain. The mood in the room was quiet, as everyone was anticipating what would come next. The finish was a surprise to me and maybe to all those in attendance.

Everyone was focused now on the front of the room. Council had listened intently for the entire time. To my surprise, they all appeared calm and composed. What came next was a measured and careful response by council—something I was not expecting. One by one, council members gave their closing comments. I knew after the third councillor had spoken that there was promise in the air. Each one had prepared specific comments about the risks and rewards of the project. They recognized the process and the final development plan but, maybe most importantly, what the project would do for the community. The plan had value and substance. It was very different from the previous proposal, and the community amenity package that accompanied it would make a big difference for Ucluelet. The boat was back on course, and the sun came out at that point. The final council vote was five to zero in favor of the project. The miracle had happened within the specified time!

The Weyerhaeuser Lands development plan was completed in September 2005 (a portion now is called Ocean West). The plan provides housing choice and affordability, protects environmental assets, and creates complementary tourism/recreation development. The intent of the rezoning application was to create a comprehensive development (CD) zone that permits a variety of land uses that are sensitively clustered into the landscape. Specifically, the plan

- protects valuable ecological and visually sensitive areas, as approximately 56 acres (22.5 ha) of the land will be protected as open space, trails, and parks—including a 22-acre (8.9-ha) central nature park that will help naturally connect Olsen Bay to the Pacific Ocean;
- provides an alternative to rural sprawl housing and protects the natural resources of the site while providing a variety of necessary cluster housing, including affordable housing—small-lot and multiple-family housing, employee housing linked to the hotels, market town houses, and market single-family housing;
- expands hotel resort opportunities as part of economic diversification for the local economy, enhancing tourism, recreation, and the associated employment in the area;
- creates a necessary and logical extension to the community of Ucluelet that extends its form and character, as well as connects the Wild Pacific Trail, other recreation facilities, and transportation links with the site;
- provides a unique cluster design that fits into the landscape and complements the rural character of the adjoining Ucluelet community; and
- introduces a customized development framework to minimize any impacts on the landscape and reinforce the local rural character (e.g., tree retention and natural storm water management where possible).

The Weyerhaeuser Lands proposal includes the following land use mix:

- 236 single-family residential lots
- 225 multifamily residential lots
- 700 hotel rooms
- 120 resort condominiums
- 10 guesthouse lots
- 108 employee residential units at full development
- 90 affordable residential units at full development
- 30,000 square feet (2,788 m^2) of commercial uses
- 56 acres (22.5 ha) of parks or open space
- Golf course on the northwestern portion of the site and more than 6.5 miles (9 km) of Wild Pacific Trail
- 68 vacation rentals

Eight strategies for sustainable urban form

To advance sustainable urban form, explicit urban design and planning strategies need to be embedded into zoning and development agreements that are legal documents. These legal documents become the requirements for development permit and construction drawings. As we know, legal documents are not the only instrument to implement sustainable design, but they represent binding agreements between parties to ensure they follow through with agreed-upon intentions and satisfy community expectations. These documents continue as property development requirements even though the property owners may change.

In the case of the Weyerhaeuser Lands plan, eight strategies were established to ensure that the plan's policies and guidelines are implemented in the specific site planning of the rezoning proposal. These land uses and other aspects of the proposal follow the Official Community Plan policies and guidelines.

Strategy 1: Create a natural extension of Ucluelet

- Extend the road network of Marine Drive and Cynamocka Road to provide secondary local and emergency access.
- Extend the Wild Pacific Trail through the property, and provide an extensive series of loops and access points for parking, viewing, and nature interpretation (fig. 7.8).
- Connect to the bike trail along Peninsula Road (Pacific Rim Highway), and provide a secondary bike trail along the proposed internal roadway system.
- Connect to the sports field along Forbes Road and the related recreation facilities.

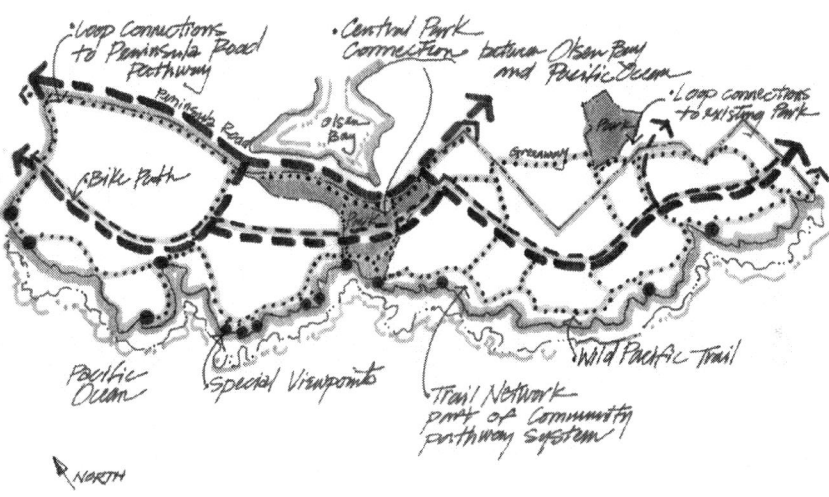

TRAIL NETWORK OF LOOPS CONCEPT

Figure 7.8. Trail network concept, Weyerhaeuser Lands, Ucluelet, British Columbia. The trail network completes the Wild Pacific Trail along the waterfront, and a series of trail loops connect to the interior of the property.

Strategy 2: Maximize environmental sensitivity

- Enhance and extend the Wild Pacific Trail alignment in a 50-foot (15-m) right-of-way, with viewpoints, trailheads, and interpretative areas (e.g., special specimen cedar area and north beach area; fig. 7.9).
- Retain trees where feasible in site development by creating nature parks, buffer strips, conservation areas, and covenanted areas.
- Reduce road widths and length where appropriate to reduce environmental impacts and maximize the soil permeability.
- Cluster developments into compact forms to maintain significant green space.
- Protect the stream corridors with appropriate building setbacks.

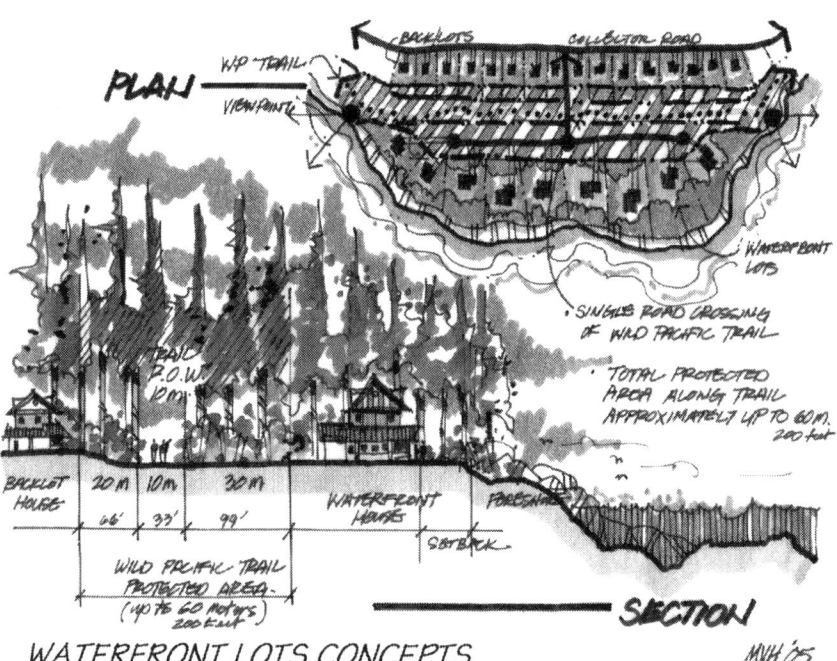

Figure 7.9. Waterfront lot concepts, Weyerhaeuser Lands, Ucluelet, British Columbia. The Wild Pacific Trail–protected area of 200 feet (60 m), consisting of 33 feet (10 m) of trail area and 164 feet (50 m) of natural area, was dedicated from the two adjoining lots on either side of the trail.

Strategy 3: Provide housing diversity

- Provide affordable multifamily housing closer to town in two parcels of approximately 7 acres (2.8 ha).
- Provide employee housing associated with the hotel resorts close to the hotels (fig. 7.10).
- Create a variety of smaller lot (more affordable) single-family housing adjoining existing development (fig. 7.11).
- Provide a mixture of market multifamily options (town houses, stacked town houses, and other strata-type development).

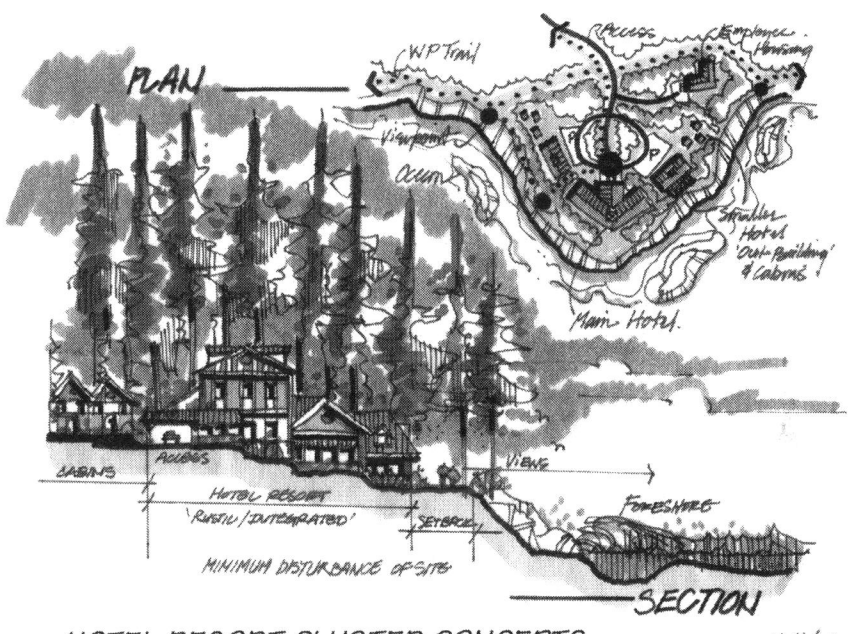

Figure 7.10. Hotel resort cluster concepts, Weyerhaeuser Lands, Ucluelet, British Columbia. Hotel sites integrate employee housing in key waterfront locations to maximize the west coast experience.

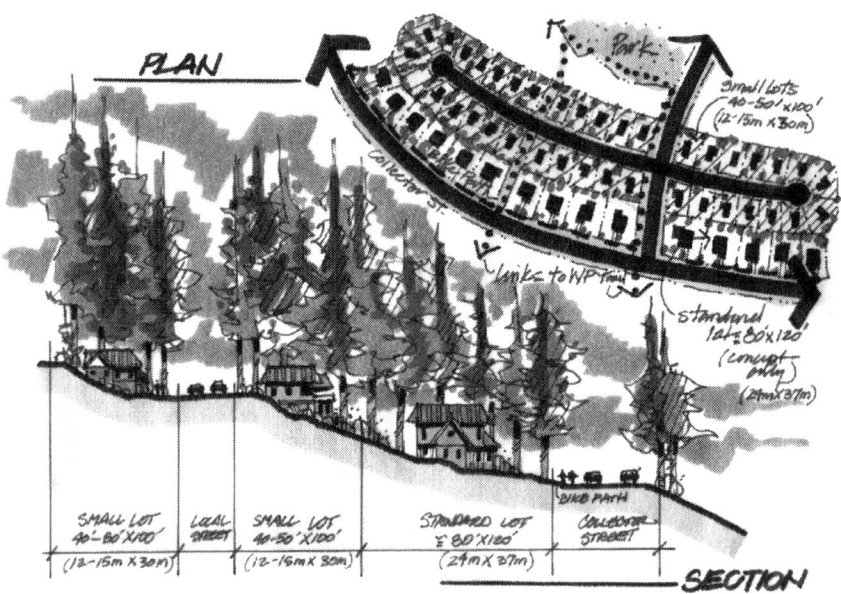

POSSIBLE SMALL LOT UPLAND CONCEPTS   MVH '05

Figure 7.11. Small lot concepts, Weyerhaeuser Lands, Ucluelet, British Columbia. The plan provides some smaller, more affordable lots that local residents have the first right to purchase.

Strategy 4: Contribute to economic diversification

- Create a series of large and small hotel resort opportunities along the shoreline that fit with the unique Ucluelet west coast character (fig. 7.12).

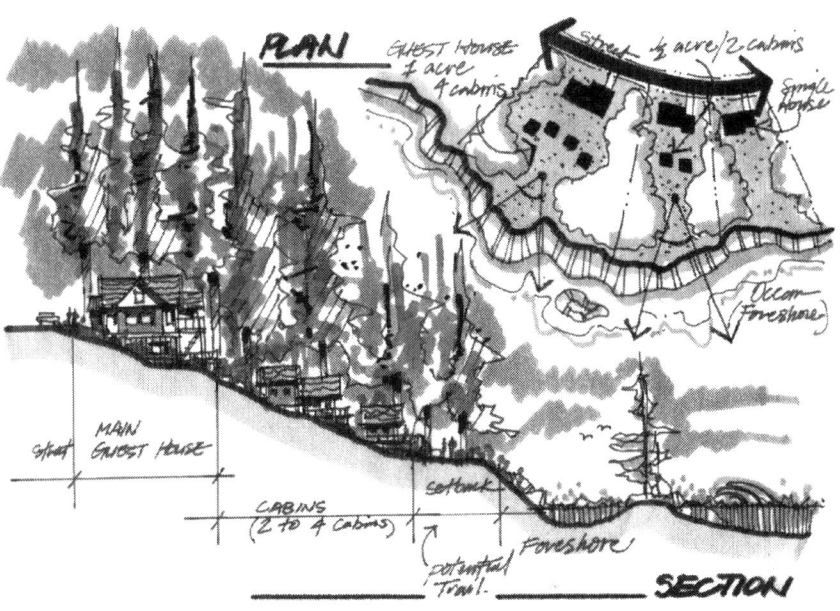

GUEST HOUSE CONCEPTS

Figure 7.12. Guesthouse concepts, Weyerhaeuser Lands, Ucluelet, British Columbia. The guesthouse lots provide an innovative alternative resort accommodation integrated with the local housing. The main guesthouse is located near the road, and guest cabins are tucked in behind.

Strategy 5: Improve mobility

- Create an extensive on-street and off-street walkway and bike pathway system to make walking and biking convenient and safe (fig. 7.13).
- Use the Wild Pacific Trail and the Pacific Rim Highway bike trail as the building blocks for an extensive pedestrian and bikeway system.

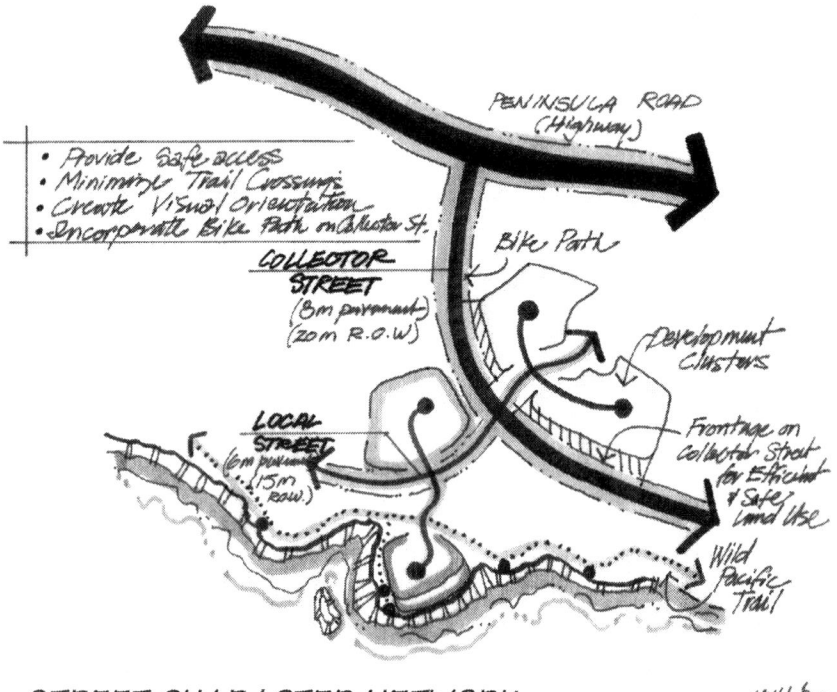

STREET CHARACTER NETWORK   MVH 05

Figure 7.13. Street character network, Weyerhaeuser Lands, Ucluelet, British Columbia. The main collector street performs as a central spine, with a bike path, and intersects with smaller local streets to access more housing and hotel sites.

Strategy 6: Integrate flexibility and innovation

- Provide diversity in the comprehensive development zone to allow for single-family housing, multifamily housing, and hotel lots or units, as well as smaller guesthouses.
- Ensure the vacation rental zoning is limited to specific areas and adequately buffered from adjoining uses.
- Provide for commercial space in a central location that allows for appropriately scaled neighborhood commercial uses that are integrated into the community.

Strategy 7: Conserve energy and reduce waste

- Maximize solar orientation, as the site is facing south/southwest.
- Encourage energy-efficient design and retention of trees to maximize where appropriate for solar gain.
- Encourage alternative energy sources (heat pump and geothermal) if feasible to reduce conventional energy load, especially in larger hotel and strata developments that can gain economies of scale.

Strategy 8: Create enduring value

- Phase development so that water and sewer are provided in a logical and timely manner over the next ten to twenty years.
- Ensure that buildings are efficiently designed and sited to minimize storm damage and maximize the protection of trees and the natural environment.
- Coordinate community facilities planning to maximize efficiencies and minimize duplication by providing a significant contribution of $2.3 million to the construction of the Ucluelet community center.

Additional community amenity benefits

In addition to these strategies, Weyerhaeuser will make the following contributions to the Ucluelet community:

- Construct the Wild Pacific Trail at the time of development of the lands, as part of 56 acres (22.5 ha) of open space, park, and trail contributions.
- Provide 7 acres (2.8 ha) of affordable housing (90 units at full development).
- Provide $25,000 each to the Westcoast Community Resource Society, the District of Ucluelet for facilities associated with the new multipurpose field, bursaries for postsecondary forestry studies for Ucluelet students, and the Ucluelet and Area Childcare Society.
- Contribute $20,000 for the highway rescue truck (provides emergency rescue services for highway accidents) and $100,000 for the District of Ucluelet's Social Reserve Fund.
- Donate 10 acres (4 ha) to the district for community uses.
- Restrict the marketing of any small lots less than 7,000 square feet (650 m²) to Ucluelet residents for 60 days.

In summary, the land use plan for the Weyerhaeuser Lands provides for an innovative series of land use clusters that are sensitive to the surrounding landscape and create a dynamic mix of residential and hotel uses. The Wild Pacific Trail will be integrated with the development and extended into a comprehensive loop network, better serving the local and visiting community. More detailed biophysical studies are being completed as the land is developed, and an archeological study has since been completed to determine any First Nations issues (indigenous people).

The plan integrates supporting commercial services and employee housing with the hotel uses so that the uses are appropriately scaled and maximize compatibility within the neighborhood. Other support education services, like a suggested trade school, would be most compatible with the existing Ucluelet High School, more centrally located in the town. Without the Weyerhaeuser contribution of $2.3 million to the community center, this facility would not have been built, and it is clearly the center of activity for the town.

In addition, the plan provides affordable housing close to town, along with more affordable, smaller lots adjoining existing development. Larger waterfront single-family lots will conserve and provide adequate room for the Wild Pacific Trail, while multifamily housing will provide for different buyers and further conserve sensitive landscape features by clustering the units in less sensitive areas. Many steps are required to realize the Weyerhaeuser Lands plan on the ground over the next one to two decades, but a comprehensive framework is now in place, along with a 100-page development agreement to help ensure the plan is implemented properly.

As these two case studies illustrate, plan-making is a complex and situational task, but there are ways of ensuring, from the ground up, that principles of sustainability are incorporated throughout the plan. For a reminder of ten principles that can guide sustainable urban design decisions, see chapter 4. Even when the master plan is finalized, it remains only that—a plan. The next chapter discusses the policies, design guidelines, and regulations necessary to realize any urban design plan.

8
POLICIES AND GUIDELINES

Unintentionally, ... the lawyer, the surveyor, and the engineer have determined the basic design of the American city, through a combination of local zoning regulations and the street pattern, neither of which has been enacted with its design principles in mind.

—Jonathan Barnett, *Urban Design as Public Policy*

As mentioned in chapter 7, urban designers or consultants are often hired to do only the urban design plan plus accompanying sketches and specific site plans that further convey its purpose and functions—not the detailed documentation of design policies, guidelines, regulations, and action plan that should accompany the plan. This is the point where the urban design process can often fall short of a truly comprehensive and sustainable urban design. Without these essential implementation elements, the plan becomes what is referred to as "shelf art"—a beautiful plan that gains dust on a shelf.

Catalysts for action
At the end of the previous analysis and synthesis process, two distinct steps remain as part of implementation. The first step is to develop the policies, design guidelines, and regulations required to realize the plan. They create a framework of words for the plan that range from goals and objectives to design requirements and legally enforceable regulations. However, they do not create physical actions. The second step is to create the action plan required to move the plan ahead to a physical

improvement on the ground. The action plan requires organization, resources, and an evaluation method that reflects back on the vision, goals, and targets established earlier in the analysis process. The action plan is described in further detail in chapter 14. This chapter and the next focus on the policy framework, design guidelines, and development of standards, progressing from more general design intentions to specific design requirements.

The first section of this chapter describes policies required for urban design. These are statements that set out the goals and objectives necessary to attain all the dimensions of the urban design plan, from overall urban design and heritage conservation to development of housing and parks. The design guidelines that follow in the second part of the chapter are the more specific directives to attain these goals and objectives.

Guidelines should cover innovative sustainability components, such as

- overall site planning and building orientation, including compact design to encourage walking, biking, and transit use, as well as an improved jobs/housing balance within the community;
- a mix of uses as part of a more compact land use form to increase social interaction, support local services, and improve transit viability;
- housing diversity for different ages and family sizes;
- rainwater management to improve water quality and reduce flooding;
- energy conservation to reduce nonrenewable energy use and increase renewable use;
- materials selection and purchase to buy more environmentally sensitive materials locally;
- social and cultural programming, as well as increased community facilities, to build community strength and increase safety and a sense of belonging; and
- construction processes that recycle and respect the site's environmental and social dimensions.

Other, more basic design components covered by guidelines are built form and massing, heritage conservation, parks and open space, streets, parking, loading, storage, transit, traffic circulation/mobility, schools/social amenities, and landscaping.

Design "guidelines" are regarded by definition as being somewhat flexible in interpretation and equivalencies. Design guidelines are not normally *approved* by council bylaw but normally *adopted* by council. This means that the design guidelines are not enforceable by law. The language in guidelines varies from "should" to "shall"—with "should" being a desired alternative that is desirable and "shall" a requirement.

The results and the use of guidelines depend on local government staff's knowledge, skill, and abilities to ensure development applicants follow the guidelines. In contrast, *regulations* (see chapter 9) are approved by council bylaw and can also be referred to as "standards." They set out specific requirements that are mandatory and may be flexible to a limited degree (e.g., up to 10 to 15 percent) only in cases where the project will be rendered unfeasible. In these cases, the specific degree of flexibility is normally reviewed by a formal board of "variance" that reviews each situation with regard to specific criteria of hardship—physical or economic. Progressive design guidelines cross-reference requirements to help the applicant and council connect the policy, guidelines, and regulations. For instance, design guidelines may refer to the zoning bylaw or land use district regulations (depending on where you are in North America) or similar statutory documents (approved by council and enforceable). In this way, those aspects that are requirements are referred to within the governing legal documents. Where there is conflict, the regulations take precedent.

Design guidelines continue to run into challenges since they are viewed as subjective or overextend the public domain into private property interests and rights. Many municipalities are choosing to view design guidelines as "requirements" rather than optional and measure most development applications against the guidelines for approvals. To further reinforce this trend toward high-quality design, urban design review panels are emerging throughout North America to advise councils on the merits of development applications.

Case study: Downtown master plan, Langley, British Columbia

The following policies, guidelines, and regulations are drawn from a successful downtown master plan that included all three elements. This urban design plan for the city of Langley, British Columbia, married physical, social, and economic elements to support redevelopment in this community of about 20,000 in the central Fraser Valley, 27 miles (43.5 km) east of Vancouver. My consulting team not only completed the master plan in 2009 but also a subsequent economic feasibility analysis and a public realm plan in association with other firms. These urban design tools proved a successful combination to attract development. Credit the city of Langley for leading the process and supporting all three urban design components as well as associated initiatives. Business retention strategies protected existing businesses while inviting new ones to join the successful momentum.

Our team completed an economic analysis of seven key redevelopment sites quickly after the master plan was approved unanimously by council. We wanted to examine how economic factors, such as construction cost, location, density, and use, would affect each of the seven sites, especially considering the limited height of fifteen stories and underground garage limitations of one story based on soil conditions. The study examined architectural options for building form and parking, as well as land use, as they related to return on investment. The outcome of the site analysis proved the economic attractiveness of the majority of these sites for redevelopment. The study also indicated the need to consider further height relaxations on specific sites.

As a result of the master plan and economic analysis, changes to density, height, and parking requirements made redevelopment even more attractive, with the support of the community. The development of the public realm plan followed. The resulting "gray to green" strategy recommended transforming the hard surfaces into treed streets, greenways, and squares to enhance walking and biking in the downtown. The sidewalk details laid out in the public realm plan became mandatory requirements for any new development and established a template to be followed throughout the downtown. Other important features of the public realm plan were bicycle and pedestrian connections to the surrounding neighborhoods, gateway features, seating, lighting, decorative paving, and wayfaring signage.

Mayor Peter Fassbender championed the plan's implementation along with Gerald Minchuk, the city's director of planning and development services. A breakfast sponsored by the city to introduce and promote the plan had the largest attendance ever of any breakfast event supported by the Vancouver-based Urban Development Institute. The city was not only open for business; it was actively seeking business with a supportive approval process. The results of this process have been outstanding. Since 2010, following the approval of these initiatives, $160 million of development permits have been issued and/or are under construction. The master plan, economic analysis, and public realm plan helped visualize and measure the potential of the city of Langley.

Numerous awards recognized the planning and design, as well as associated economic strategies. The city of Langley council and staff truly embraced the city's vision of "The Place to Be." The policies, guidelines, and regulations subsequently became the frame for implementation.

Regard the policies, design guidelines, and regulations that follow not only as an urban design plan but also as critical instruments in successful projects, as demonstrated in the city of Langley. They can be applied in different form to other downtown projects but need to be specifically and carefully crafted to the specific place to obtain the right results.

Figure 8.1 illustrates the eight design districts developed for the city of Langley's downtown. Interestingly, although our design team had completed a detailed master plan illustration, in this case the design districts plan became the preferred plan illustration for the project. The reasoning becomes clearer when you compare the level of detail in each plan. The detailed master plan illustration (not shown) was very detailed and site specific. In contrast, the design districts plan was a concept that left room for many alternatives to be considered within the framework of the master plan's policies, design guidelines, and regulations. Its flexibility made it more attractive to the community, council, staff, and developers.

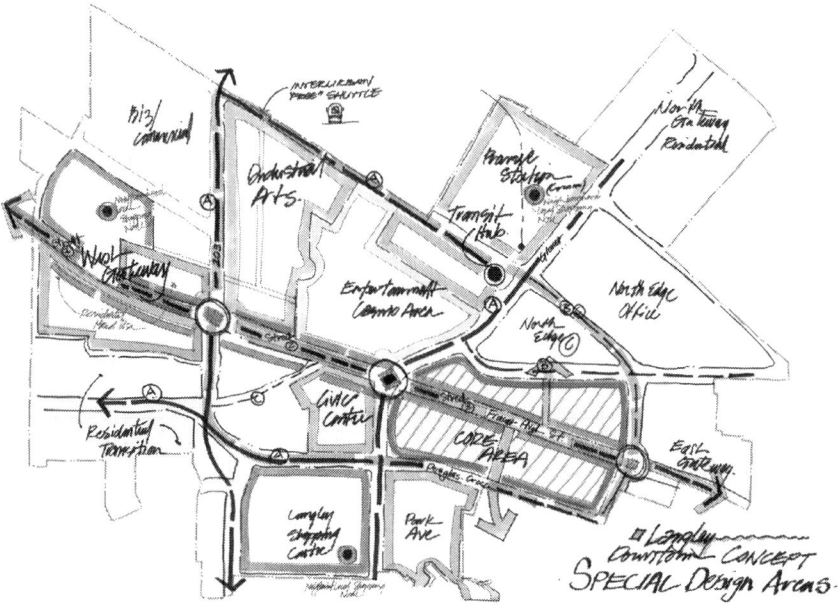

Figure 8.1. Special design areas in the city of Langley, British Columbia. This conceptual "design districts" plan was favored by council and other stakeholders because it allowed them to consider alternatives.

Examples of design policies

Design policies are explicit statements of goals and objectives. In the case of Langley, these policies were categorized into nine topic areas, each with a specific urban design application:

- Urban design
- Heritage conservation
- Housing and redevelopment strategies
- Parks, green links, bikeways, and connections
- Servicing, streets, parking, and traffic circulation
- Environment and greening downtown
- Commercial and downtown core focus
- Schools, social amenities, and community facilities
- Business/light industrial activity and "Good Neighbor" program

In every urban design plan, the details of each policy area should be different and/or refined. Other topic areas may be added specific to the location requirements. Each policy has a definition at the beginning followed by an "objective" statement that outlines the expected results and summary of means to get there. The policies that follow detail the requirements for each development application in the city of Langley.

Urban design

Public and private open spaces, as well as the buildings that shape them, define the character and identity of the downtown. The design framework for the downtown is important in establishing reference points that build on the strengths and "sense of place" of that neighborhood.

Objective: Improve the overall safety, identity, and attractiveness of the area by revitalizing the streetscape, increasing pedestrian orientation, and introducing compatible building forms that reinforce the special sense of place in the downtown (figs. 8.2 to 8.4).

Policies
1. Create a nonvehicular and safer pedestrian environment by extending the landscaping along the major streets and bordering streets and avenues, with the specialty retail concentrated in the current core retail area.
2. Create diversity through a mix of uses and housing types along the streets, with a specific street orientation, emphasizing entrances along the street by incorporating porches and overlooks.
3. Use Crime Prevention Through Environmental Design (CPTED) techniques to improve public safety, including the following:
   - enforcing standards of maintenance on properties that aren't keeping their sites clean and free from graffiti
   - increasing "eyes on the street" by requiring street entrances and orientation of residential and commercial units
   - upgrading sidewalks in the area and considering a "street gardening" program that improves the sense of ownership in the area

- hardening up the existing buildings and new buildings against crime by reducing places of concealment, enhancing landscaping and security, and fencing off specific areas
- improving the lighting in the area, including pedestrian lighting and security lighting, especially in highly traveled areas

4. Design with human scale in mind by
   - using a variety of materials;
   - incorporating higher-quality materials where pedestrians can see them (e.g., first story of buildings);
   - providing transparency along the street by a variety of windows or openings;
   - limiting building size;
   - creating minimum distances between buildings;
   - limiting building heights to three to four stories along the street; and
   - stepping back any buildings from the building setback line.

5. Use building forms to define public space (courtyards, pocket parks, plazas), and create a variety of building forms, roof pitches, and materials that reflect the city's history in contemporary interpretations.

6. Reinforce the gateways, lanes, major intersections, and lookout points with landscaping, street furniture, activated pedestrian signals, and traffic calming to emphasize the pedestrian orientation of these important nodes in the community.

7. Promote building forms and heights that enhance public views and minimize intrusion on adjacent views.

8. Retain and enhance public views (e.g., street-end views and views to the surrounding mountains).

9. Create a rich streetscape theme, and emphasize the use of a coordinated public art program (e.g., building on the previous revitalization efforts in the core retail area) with banners, coordinated lighting, special sidewalk treatments, and bench and trash receptacles, unified by a strong street tree and landscaping program.

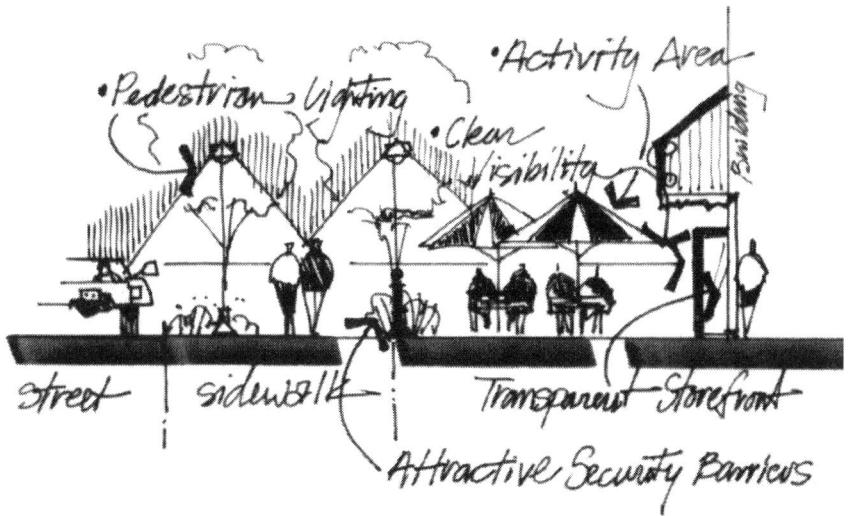

Figure 8.2. Crime Prevention Through Environmental Design, Langley, British Columbia. Clear visibility and improved pedestrian lighting are two means to improve public safety and security.

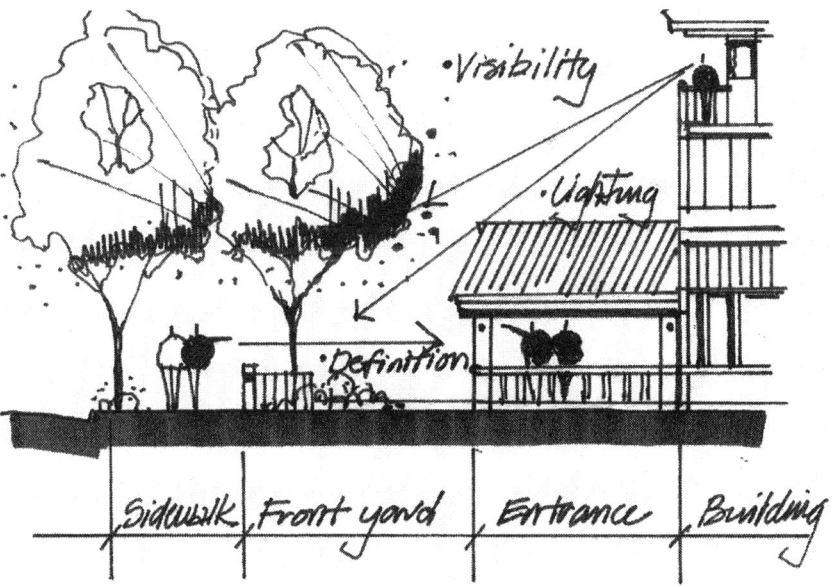

Figure 8.3. Apartment street orientation, Langley, British Columbia. Residential buildings oriented toward the street provide ease of access and help to establish a "sense of place."

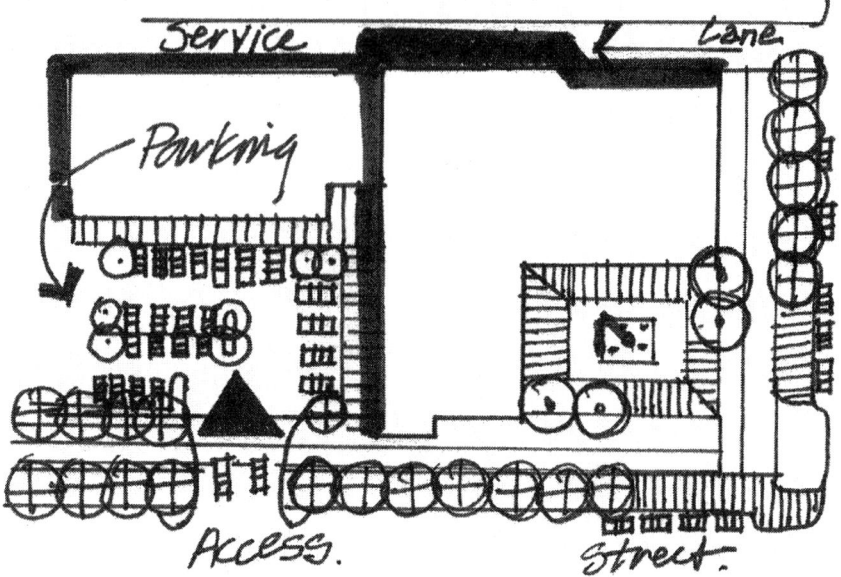

Figure 8.4. Building forms to frame corner public space, Langley, British Columbia. Corner buildings can frame street corners and extend public space along the street into active south-facing courtyards.

Heritage conservation

The soul of a neighborhood is found in the historical references that hark back to its beginnings. Downtown does not appear to have many heritage buildings, but the heritage theme in its downtown core retail area creates a basis for continuity in that area, while areas outside the core could take on a more contemporary character.

Objective: Encourage the conservation of important heritage buildings and landscapes of interest as community resources to be revitalized and adaptively reused (fig. 8.5).

Policies
1. Identify and complete a heritage inventory of important heritage buildings or buildings and landscapes of interest in the downtown if necessary.

2. Encourage new developments to redevelop sites in keeping with the history of the area, reflecting traditional materials, colors, and forms.
3. Continue to encourage the use of historical names (individuals and buildings) in the naming of public open spaces and new developments.
4. Incorporate historical references in a special wayfaring and public art program that builds on the city's historical roots.

Figure 8.5. Recognizing heritage in public art installations, Langley, British Columbia. Installations and signage on a human rather than epic scale contribute to an appreciation of local history.

Housing and redevelopment strategies

The downtown, especially some of the areas around the core retail area, is targeted for significant residential growth over the next ten to twenty years. Variety, diversity, flexibility, and affordability of new housing will be encouraged as part of the Downtown Plan.

Objective: Encourage a wide variety of housing forms and tenures that maximizes quality, flexibility, and affordability.

Policies

1. Direct residential densities in accordance with the Downtown Land Use and Growth Plan and the associated Special Design Districts, as illustrated in figure 8.1. Promote a diversity of residential development that respects and supports adjacent residential and commercial uses and forms, especially during the transformation of the downtown core area from commercial uses to residential mixed-use neighborhoods.

2. Encourage a variety of housing units that cater to the life cycle, from singles and young families to empty nesters and seniors.

3. Encourage home businesses in residential areas adjoining the downtown core.

4. Promote the inclusion of affordable housing, including smaller units and units that are flexible for use and design, defined by the Canada Mortgage and Housing Corporation (CMHC) as costing occupants not more than 30 percent of their income. (Note: Each municipality can define its own measure of affordability or simply create a diversity and choice of housing to improve affordability. Housing affordability is a complex issue that requires careful measure of issues as well as government and private development support to ensure implementation.)

5. Encourage a provision of a percentage of housing for people with special needs (e.g., five percent of units should meet design standards that are higher to that required by code for accessibility).

6. Create medium- to high-density housing in the downtown area that is street-oriented, with entrances directly facing the street, and with porches, overlooks, windows, and other design features that highly articulate the facades and bring a friendly neighborhood scale and comfort to the street face.

7. Ensure that housing is scaled to the street, with a maximum height of three to four stories at the street edge, and adjacent properties stepped back to higher levels as necessary.

8. Discourage long blocks of housing without courtyards or some break in the block pattern that creates sterility and long block faces.

9. Use classic and timeless colors that are earth tone–based with simple highlights.

10. Encourage the provision of private, semiprivate, and public open space as components of residential developments that provide recreation and amenity on-site.

11. Promote and expand local lanes and mews as part of public access and open space systems through some of the character areas to break up the block and provide necessary pedestrian access through the blocks.

12. Promote usable "green roofs" in the neighborhood to increase public and private open space and improve the green overlook from adjacent developments.

13. Require developers to provide plans that show shadow impacts on adjoining properties, view analysis, and impacts on the adjacent owner's views; a public realm plan that includes improvements to the streets coordinated with the city's street tree planting program; and a green roofscape plan. In addition, require the submission of a complete set of landscape drawings for proposed developments.

Parks, green links, bikeways, and connections

The redevelopment of the downtown offers the opportunity to extend existing parks and open space system into the downtown area over the longer term through a comprehensive green links (pedestrian way) and bikeways program. The amount, type, location, financing or dedication, and ongoing maintenance of park and open space will be a challenge for the area as it transforms, with a diverse set of community needs.

Objective: Create a park, bikeway, pedestrian way, and open space system over time that reinforces a more pedestrian orientation in the downtown, with a rich green aspect to the program for all ages (fig. 8.6).

Policies

1. Develop and refine the proposed park, bikeway, and pedestrian way program in association with the current trail, bikeway, and Trans Canada Trail initiatives.

2. Develop a major park in the current area north of the downtown.

3. Develop a street tree master plan that identifies the tree species, spacing, and requirements on the major pedestrian-oriented streets.

4. Encourage the provision of additional publicly accessible open space and parks along the street (e.g., courtyards and plazas).

5. Encourage the development of green roofs, both public and private, to maximize amenity space for adjoining residences.

6. Orient the park and open spaces to a sunny south orientation to create inviting spots for sitting, strolling, and other recreation activity, while providing optional shade and weather protection.

7. Ensure that the public and private open spaces are programmed and designed for activity that is appropriate for the location, size, and maintenance program.

8. Expand the tree-planting program in association with pilot programs, including areas west of the existing core retail area.

Figure 8.6. Pocket parks add meeting and rest areas, Langley, British Columbia. Southern orientation, shade, comfortable seating, visual access, and adequate amenities—such as colorful planting, public art, and views—are considerations when developing green spaces and parks in the downtown area.

Servicing, streets, parking, and traffic circulation

Servicing requirements to accommodate the projected growth include sewer, roads, water, and drainage. From preliminary review, it appears that servicing capacity for sewer, water, and drainage requires further study to accommodate the projected growth.

Objective: Improve the infrastructure services, pedestrian safety, and traffic function within the downtown area by upgrading infrastructure where necessary and improving street design, parking, vehicular access, and pedestrian crossings (fig. 8.7).

Policies

1. Examine the traffic circulation and street design improvements required for the projected new development as part of a comprehensive specific downtown traffic analysis.

2. Complete new street designs and other potential pilot street beautification projects that could include the following:
   - Traffic calming (bulges and central boulevard)
   - Pedestrian-activated signals
   - Gateway entrance designs (e.g., special bulges with appropriate landscaping, civic art, and signage)

3. Develop a downtown parking structures plan as part of the downtown redevelopment strategy that is not exposed to local streets and limit access points. Where parking entrances exist, they should be properly landscaped and designed to mimic a normal building facade.

4. Create parking pockets[1] where possible to extend the pedestrian boulevards and narrow the perception of street width.

5. Upgrade the sewer, water, and drainage systems in association with new development.

6. Examine the feasibility of introducing a local bus system (or streetcar) that completes a downtown area loop (fig. 8.7).

7. Encourage power-smart (energy-smart) development and associated conservation measures for new development in the area.

8. Provide the necessary fiber-optic utility servicing to the area to support home-based businesses that require state-of-the-art Internet support services.

9. Separate local residential and truck traffic as much as possible.

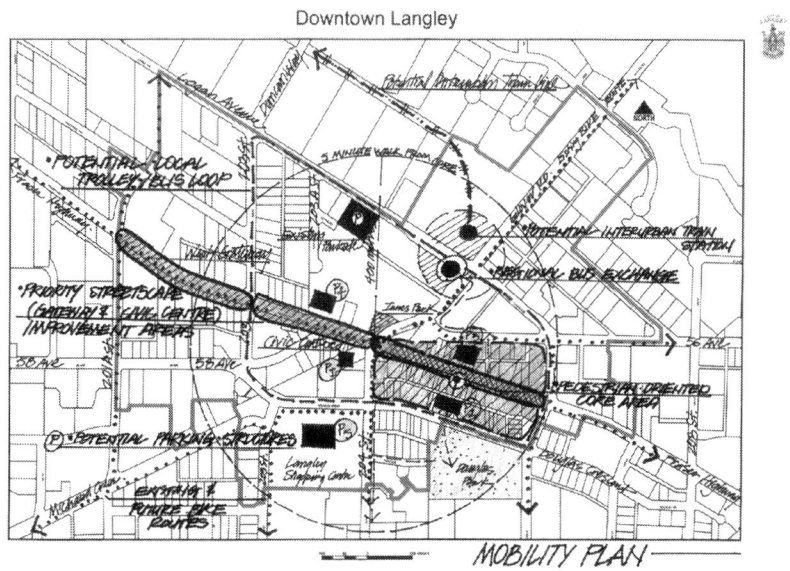

Figure 8.7. Mobility plan concept, Langley, British Columbia. The mobility plan includes a transit hub for high-speed buses and a local shuttle, existing and potential bike and pedestrian routes, pedestrian nodes (meeting places), and traffic nodes (major intersections).

Environment and greening downtown

The downtown area redevelopment provides an opportunity to bring nature downtown and "green" the streets as well as clean up incidences of soil contamination because of past commercial and industrial activity (fig. 8.8).

Objective: Create soil contamination cleanup requirements that are as practical as possible for redevelopment yet protect the public interests in the long term.

Policies

1. Ensure that a proper site profile and associated studies are completed in conformance with provincial legislation for soil contamination.

2. Encourage the creation of low-maintenance naturalized landscapes, using native plants that require less watering and provide habitat for birds.

3. Encourage the retention of existing trees and other vegetation during redevelopment if possible and as appropriate.

4. Maximize green planting areas in the public and private realm that increase natural drainage and groundwater recharge.

Figure 8.8. Maximizing landscape opportunities and pedestrian connections in parking lots, Surrey, British Columbia. Through simple means, even parking lots—traditionally "gray" areas—can become "green."

Commercial and downtown core focus

Specialty retail, entertainment, pedestrian-oriented restaurants, and civic uses should be focused in the downtown core area.

Objective: Concentrate specialty retail and complementary entertainment, restaurant, and civic uses in a pedestrian-friendly downtown core area through measures such as special street treatments (fig. 8.9).

Policies
1. Reinforce the existing pedestrian-oriented shopping district (core retail area) by limiting specialty retail uses to that area.
2. Limit other major commercial development (office and retail) to the three nodes outlined in the Urban Design Concept Plan.
3. Review and consider upgrading special streetscape treatments, including special street paving, signalized crosswalks, and traffic calming measures where necessary.
4. Encourage commercial and residential mixed-use redevelopment in the core area (maximum four stories).
5. Require commercial redevelopment to incorporate decorative sidewalks, appropriate street furniture, and street trees, and supply planting plans for trees and other landscaping.
6. Support the inclusion of home businesses (in some of the Special Design Districts, fig. 8.1) in combination with street-oriented residential development, not to exceed 20 percent of the floor area and be reserved for the ground floor.
7. Require a traffic impact study for each major development application to determine appropriate measures for turning, pedestrian crosswalks, signalization, access, servicing, and parking.
8. Restrict off-street parking between the street and the building, with any off-street parking required in underground parking, structured parking (or cash-in-lieu contribution), or surface parking behind the building that is unobtrusive and screened from public view.
9. Entertain the provision for shared parking if the applicant demonstrates justification by conducting a traffic study by a qualified engineer.

10. Limit servicing areas for commercial uses to lanes or areas out of public view or buffered by screens or landscaping.

11. Respect the existing commercial and industrial activity in the area while integrating new commercial development.

12. Encourage commercial development that has multiple storefronts and that is transparent and inviting to pedestrian traffic.

13. Encourage outdoor cafés and other similar uses that create pedestrian activity on the sidewalk and adjoining courtyard areas.

14. Support a safety and security awareness program to improve security for commercial properties.

Figure 8.9. Special streetscapes with wide sidewalks, trees, and lighting, Langley, British Columbia. Such elements complement specialty retail, entertainment, and restaurants in a pedestrian-friendly downtown core. (Drawing by Calum Srigley.)

Schools, social amenities, and community facilities

The downtown area will add significant new residents over the next ten to twenty years and beyond.

Objective: To provide adequate community facilities and associated social amenities in association with the residential development needs of the area (fig. 8.10).

Policies

1. Investigate the capacity and potential for increased enrollment from this area in the local schools in the longer term as residential redevelopment occurs.
2. Encourage the development of other cultural facilities in the downtown core area (e.g., performing arts and culture center, children's museum, and park).
3. Improve pedestrian and transit linkages to the surrounding areas to take advantage of other local facilities.

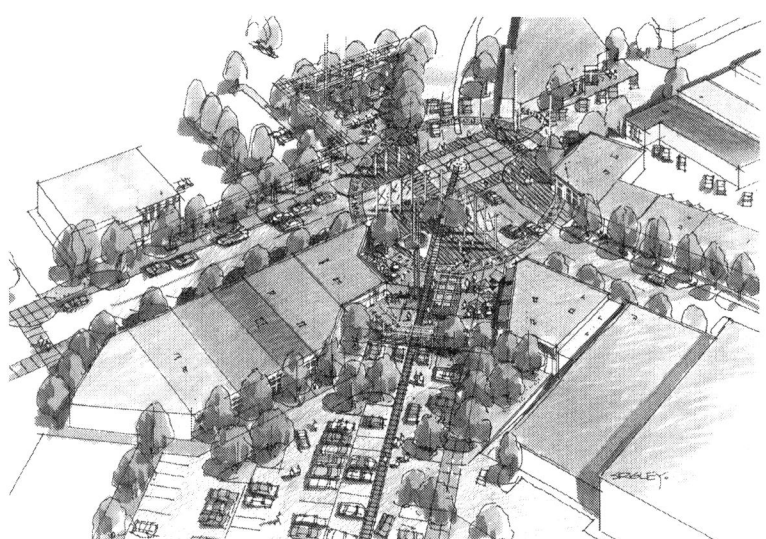

Figure 8.10. Adding significant public amenities as part of redevelopment, Langley, British Columbia. As a regional hub, Langley is preparing for a larger population in the next two decades. (Drawing by Calum Srigley.)

Business/light industrial activity and "Good Neighbor" program

Industry has been a tradition on the northwest side of the downtown area. It will continue to be there in different forms (from heavy to light industry) or transform to residential and commercial uses. During the transformation of the area, existing industrial uses should be supported. Special attention should be given to the existing and potential nuisances and associated residence complaints that could increase with residential redevelopment.

Objective: To minimize potential conflicts between existing industrial and new residential redevelopment in the area, while supporting existing industrial uses (Figure 8.11).

Policies
1. Create a "Good Neighbor" program that promotes clear communication between the residential groups in the area and existing industrial and commercial businesses to reduce or eliminate nuisances associated with their businesses (e.g., delivery hours and industrial truck traffic).
2. Support the existing industrial uses in the area during the transition period.
3. Encourage cleanup and enhancement of existing industrial properties in association with new development and the general beautification of the area, including the screening of parking and loading areas and general landscaping.
4. Promote the ideas of existing industries sponsoring the "Green and Safe Streets" theme by building naturalized landscapes and features on their properties.
5. Support a safety and security awareness program to improve security for industrial properties.

Figure 8.11. Business uses integrated sensitively into community fabric, Langley, British Columbia. Landscaping can help to beautify and "naturalize" industrial and commercial premises.

Examples of design guidelines

While design policies set out the goals and objectives necessary to realize the urban design plan, design guidelines set out the specific design requirements for the development area. The design consultants, including the architects, landscape architects, and engineers, must pay close attention to the details associated with the guidelines, from building massing to streets and landscape treatments. New to many design guidelines are sustainable design features. The following guidelines from the city of Langley's downtown master plan highlight the need for sustainability considerations by beginning with them rather than ending with them. This positioning creates a direct priority and backdrop for the other design considerations that follow.

When applying these guidelines elsewhere, it is important to handpick ones that apply; otherwise, the guidelines will be dismissed as being unrealistic, insensitive to local customs, or unattainable. It is better to recommend less and have success than recommend a lot and have little or no success. This lesson specifically applies to geographic locations throughout the world where weather conditions or very limited resources require different design responses.

The indigenous ways of building are great sustainability instructors, for these timeless ways of building have hundreds, if not thousands, of years of tested experience. These historical forms, landscape, and associated water, sewer, and other infrastructure precedents should inform the specific sustainable urban design guidelines. These guidelines can be advanced by current technological innovations where applicable and available. For example, the slums of New Delhi have a unique form and governance structure. To attempt to radically alter its form would probably prove disastrous. A more gentle evolutionary approach in line with local residents' customs would be more effective. It would empower residents to improve their own homes and community within their context. The wholesale eradication of slums and sections of cities, as in New York in the 1950s, revealed the shortsighted nature of these strategies (see also discussion of urban renewal in chapter 3).

The design guidelines that follow should be read in the context of the specific city of Langley case study. They are intended to present a structure, format, and content that may be instructive to other city downtowns worldwide but, as stated, will also need to be adapted to local circumstances. Specific sustainable community strategies here, as with the preceding policies, are grouped into several topic areas, namely sustainability; downtown built form; parks, open space, and amenity areas; and streets, gateways, parking, and transit. As with the policies, each area of design guidelines opens with several clear objectives.

Sustainability

Objectives

1. Consider sustainable development principles in the planning and design of the downtown area.
2. Contribute to the socially sustainable community by providing housing for a range of household types, ages, and physical abilities.
3. Design the downtown to facilitate walking, bicycling, and transit use.

Overall sustainability elements

- The downtown should be a walkable, mixed-use development area with opportunities to live, work, play, and learn in close proximity to home or business.
- A mix of housing types should be provided, including street-oriented row housing, stacked row housing, as well as low-, medium-, and high-rise apartments.
- Universally accessible design should be considered in the architecture of buildings and the design of open spaces, parks, and amenities.
- Where possible, buildings should be designed to include on-site alternative energy sources, such as solar heat, solar electricity, and geothermal energy.
- The incorporation of features such as daylighting, recycling, reuse of water, low-water landscaping, low-water fixtures, and energy-efficient lighting and materials should be considered in building and site planning in the downtown area to reduce the consumption of energy and materials.
- On-site infiltration of storm water should be considered in the site planning.
- To encourage alternatives to the automobile, each development should be walkable, bicycle-friendly, and well connected to transit and local services and should consider a car-sharing program to reduce further automobile use.

Specific sustainable community strategies include the following:

Site environmental strategies
- Minimize construction disturbance by protecting areas (tree retention areas) with fencing.
- Specify light-colored, high-reflective roof materials to minimize "heat island" effect.

Storm water
- Use permeable pavers in parking areas where appropriate and feasible.
- Use grassed swales where appropriate.
- Require storm management detention on-site, as appropriate.

Water
- Choose drought-resistant native plantings for landscaping to reduce water use.
- Mulch planting beds to a depth of 2 inches (50 mm) to reduce water loss.
- Use recycled water or rainwater for irrigation (e.g., rain barrel program).
- Limit the area of grass within a landscaped area to a maximum of 50 percent.
- Incorporate water use reduction features in buildings and on-site (e.g., include gray water recycling system and install low-flow fixtures).

Energy
- Improve energy efficiency through design and building orientation (e.g., energy-efficient LEED standard and south building orientation).
- Include energy-efficient fixtures in buildings.
- Use shade trees to shield buildings during summer months and reduce solar heat gain.
- Utilize programmable thermostats in individual living or commercial units.
- Install energy-efficient refrigerators and laundry machines.
- Use energy-efficient lighting for internal and external lighting.
- Use renewable energy features, such as solar and geothermal energy.

Construction material and waste reduction
- Reuse existing building materials where possible.
- Use construction materials with recycled content where possible.
- Ensure construction waste is recycled where feasible.

Healthy buildings, landscapes, and practices
- Improve air quality by using materials that reduce off-gassing for such elements as flooring and paint.
- Design windows so they can be opened for fresh air circulation.
- Require one secure bicycle parking space for each apartment unit.
- Install clarifiers or water/oil separators on each drain.
- Provide landscaping that includes wildlife habitat.
- Provide flexibility in design and universal accessibility of units so that occupancy can change over time (e.g., live/work units, physically challenged).
- Provide a "resident's handbook" to each new resident to outline environmentally sensitive practices.
- Include a provision for a community garden in the residential site planning.

Downtown built form

Objectives

1. Ensure that buildings and streetscapes are of a high-quality design.
2. Ensure that medium- and high-rise buildings have relatively small floor plates to permit for increased ground-level open space, maintain view corridors, and mitigate against adverse microclimatic conditions.
3. Maximize solar penetration and avoid adverse microclimatic effects related to wind and shadowing on- and off-site.
4. Enliven the street by providing attractive streetscape treatment, active storefronts, and multiple doorways and windows.
5. Ensure that the tallest high-rise buildings are treated as signature landmarks with distinctive architecture.

Guidelines

Building height and massing

*   The development should provide a transition in building height and massing in relation to the surrounding neighborhoods and uses, with a transition to the general four-story norm or lower for adjoining commercial or light industrial areas (fig. 8.12).
*   The taller buildings should be located outside the core retail area on designated sites.
*   Floor plates of high-rise buildings should be relatively small to allow for increased ground floor open space, maintain view corridors, and reduce adverse microclimatic impacts.
*   Buildings should be sited in such a way as to maximize solar penetration and to avoid adverse microclimatic effects on- and off-site related to wind and shadowing.
*   Perceived height and massing should be minimized through such things as building setback variations at the upper levels, building orientation, roof treatment, and choice of exterior materials and colors.

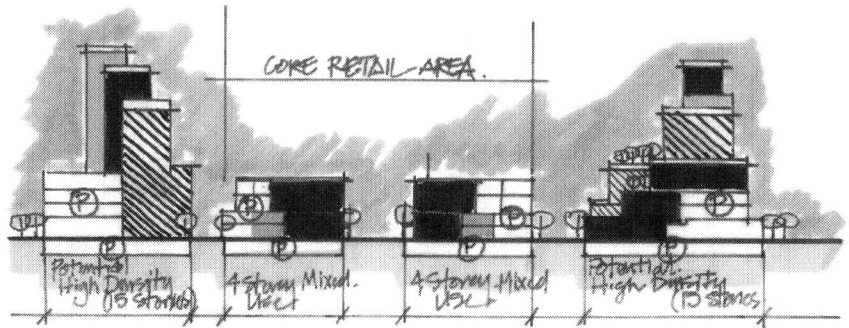

Figure 8.12. Transition of densities, Langley, British Columbia. This concept drawing shows the saddle form of built densities—medium in the center and higher on the outside edges.

Architectural treatment of buildings

- All building facades should use compatible and harmonious exterior finishing materials.
- Building colors should provide visual interest.
- Mechanical equipment on the roof of any building should be concealed by incorporating it within the building roof, or by screening it in a way that is consistent with the character and finishing of the building.
- High-rise signature buildings should have distinctive architecture that includes sculpted tops.
- The design at rooftops visible from higher buildings should be carefully considered. Where feasible, rooftop gardens, "green roof" technology, and patios should be designed to improve rooftop use, look, and sustainable function (fig. 8.13).
- Dwellings and other elements of the development should be sited and oriented to minimize their impact on other dwellings, considering such things as daylight, sunlight, ventilation, quiet, visual privacy, and view.

Figure 8.13. High-density building forms and rooftop gardens, Vancouver, British Columbia. The city of Vancouver requires that all roofs require active programming and landscaping where possible.

Building relationship to the street

- To provide active and inviting streetscapes at the ground level, buildings should feature doorways, porches, and windows at ground level, as well as weather protection features, such as awnings, canopies, and arcades (figs. 8.14 and 8.15).
- Larger buildings with long street fronts should be designed with detail and articulation to create an attractive streetscape.
- Blank walls should be avoided by wrapping active retail or residential areas around above-grade parking structures to maintain an active and attractive streetscape.
- Residential high-rise buildings should be generally integrated with row housing, stacked row housing, or low- to mid-rise apartments to provide a pedestrian street scale and transition.
- Any low-, medium-, or high-rise should be designed to provide an inviting and interesting street presence/entrance, as well as attractive building facades facing the street.

Figure 8.14. Street-oriented development with multiple entrances, Vancouver, British Columbia. Multiple residential entrances facing the street create a safer and more active streetscape.

Figure 8.15. Defined street entrance, Vancouver, British Columbia. Special treatment of street entrances help to add pedestrian scale and detail to the street front.

Parks, open space, and amenity areas

Objectives

1. Provide a safe and pleasing pedestrian environment that encourages walking and biking.
2. Create strong linkages connecting the site to the downtown transit exchange and other community amenities.
3. Provide a variety of open spaces and amenity areas.
4. Ensure that many of the open spaces are accessible to people who do not live or work on the site.
5. Ensure high-quality activity programming and design is incorporated into the areas.
6. Minimize the ground surface area necessary for vehicular circulation, access, and parking to increase the area devoted to open space and recreation amenities.

Guidelines

Pedestrian circulation

1. Safe and attractive pedestrian linkages should be provided between various land uses within the downtown area and surroundings neighborhoods (fig. 8.16).
2. The internal street system should foster connectivity from various parts of the downtown area to the transit exchange and future transit hub area.
3. Pedestrian linkages should include both pedestrian mews access limited to emergency and service vehicles only and sidewalks included as part of the road rights-of-way.
4. Crime Prevention Through Environmental Design should be considered in the design of open spaces, parks, and amenity areas. (See previous discussion on page 189 for further details.)
5. The primary pedestrian spaces should be well lit, visible, and linked in a comprehensive network where possible.

Figure 8.16. Pedestrian connections within a development, Surrey, British Columbia. Pedestrian connections within a development should have clear visual access as well as proper lighting to ensure safety and security.

Open space, parks, and amenity areas
- Development should include a variety of open spaces, amenity areas, and parks, such as plazas, courtyards, pedestrian mews, greens/commons, and community gardens designed for the four seasons.
- Secure interior courtyards should serve as focal points for residents of a series of buildings.
- Open spaces should feature a high level of activity programming where appropriate, as well as high-quality landscape architecture to make them functional, safe, and enjoyable. These spaces should include a rich palette of planting for different seasons, abundant street furniture, and local public art.
- Site entrances and edges should receive special design attention to help ensure that the developments present a safe, attractive, and distinctive face to the street.

Figure 8.17. Centralized park and amenity areas, Vancouver, British Columbia. A central park within a housing complex can provide a secure space for safe and supervised play.

- Internal streets in specific developments should have tree-lined boulevards and should be lit at night with pedestrian-level lighting.
- Open spaces, amenity areas, and parks should be designed to discourage negative and criminal activities (fig. 8.17).

Streets, gateways, parking, and transit
Objectives

1. Provide a high degree of connectivity among the site, transit facilities, and the core retail areas.
2. Provide a safe and pleasing pedestrian environment that encourages walking and biking.
3. Design developments for effective access and egress of automobiles, including service and emergency vehicles.
4. Provide adequate parking for new residential and commercial uses that also encourages transit use and walking.

Guidelines

Streets and parking

1. Traffic calming measures and pedestrian mews (access limited to service and emergency vehicles only) should be provided in the design of the downtown area to create a safe and attractive pedestrian environment.
2. Streets should be designed to accommodate bicycles, and bicycle parking should be abundant and obvious.
3. A variety of parking options—surface behind buildings, structured, underground (one floor maximum feasible), and street parking—should be provided to maximize choice and convenience in the downtown area.
4. Short-term street parking should continue to be provided.
5. Where possible, parking should be shared by users with staggered peak hours of demand.
6. Service and emergency response vehicles should have clear and effective access to the downtown area.
7. Parking, loading, and passenger drop-off areas should be easily accessible and designed to minimize pedestrian-vehicle conflicts (preferably situated at the side or rear of the buildings).
8. Potential traffic impacts on adjacent roadways resulting from development should be designed for in advance and minimized where possible.

Integration with transit and future transit hub

• Clearly defined and attractive pedestrian connections should be provided among the various parts of the downtown area and adjacent neighborhoods to provide safe and attractive access to transit, trolley, and the major transit station.
• Consideration should be given to exploring opportunities to introduce an "interurban train" to connect other municipalities in the medium to long term.

Gateways

- To define these gateways, the preferred design would be to plant evergreen trees on either side with a ground-mounted sign on the side boulevard with background foundation planting, such as shrubs or accent perennial flowers.

- These areas will have special paving and sidewalk treatments to announce arrival at the downtown area. A special "rumble strip" across the pavement in the roadway could also announce a decrease in speed to 30 mph (50 km/hr) through this town center.

The downtown policies and guidelines set the framework for the specific regulations in the next chapter. The city of Langley Official Community Plan (overall goals, objectives, and policies) and the zoning bylaw (land uses, setbacks, density, and other special provisions, if any) set the overall legal directions for the specific downtown policies and guidelines. The downtown master plan is a subset or more detailed implementation plan for the overarching Official Community Plan and Zoning Bylaw. Each of these plans has different names across North America and around the world.

9
DEVELOPMENT REGULATIONS

No set of rules can anticipate all the situations and conflicts that will eventually surface and there is a tendency that rules designed to prevent something bad will also prevent something good from happening.

—Richard Hedman, with Andrew Jaszewski,
Fundamentals of Urban Design

As compared with policies and design guidelines, development regulations are requirements that are not flexible unless there is a substantive reason that makes development infeasible. In those cases, urban design can deviate from the regulations. As outlined in the previous chapter, in North America, committees such as a board of adjustment or board of variance review the application in question. Sometimes they will have a tolerance of up to 10 to 15 percent variance from the regulation. This applies to exceptional hardship cases. These cases may include a building setback or height variance due to specific site conditions, such as significant retention of trees, conservation of an existing historical structure, or an awkward lot configuration. The word "shall" in most of these regulations that follow emphasizes their general inflexibility.

The previous chapter provided the overall policies and design guidelines to direct design implementation. This chapter provides a sampling of two sets of regulations as the next step of achieving design intentions. These regulations are requirements unless worded otherwise. The first regulations refer to downtown Langley, British Columbia—an extension of the previous policies and guidelines. The second regulations refer to housing infill regulations for the Flats neighborhood in Medicine Hat, Alberta.

The regulations for Medicine Hat are more stringent than those for the city of Langley. The Medicine Hat regulations require conformity to specific land use district standards (zoning requirements), while the city of Langley is more responsive to creative solutions that meet the intent of the regulations. The city of Medicine Hat's stringent regulations are understandable, as the city has seen redevelopment in the Flats neighborhood that has not met the expectations of the residents. Any intensification or increase in density is required to fit into the character of the neighborhood. With varying lot dimensions, specific setbacks and building height requirements are necessary to fit new development into the existing character. Any deviation from these regulations could result in a larger home or multifamily building being too close to an existing house or too high compared with adjoining houses. The issue is sensitive, so the regulations have to be exact.

In somewhat of a contrast, the city of Langley is inviting higher density on the outside of the downtown core area but still within limits. The historic character of the downtown core area will be maintained, but outside the core retail area, density and intensification are not significant issues. High-quality design is still mandatory, and a proposal that fits with the adjoining context is required. Therefore, the regulations are specific in most instances, but there are some instances where wording such as "encourage" or "may be permitted" is included to leave some flexibility where the regulation cannot be met or another equivalent design option is chosen that matches the intent of the regulation.

Comprehensive downtown development district

The following regulations apply to the same city of Langley downtown master plan introduced in chapter 8 and represent one more step in requirements to shape the downtown. Keep in mind that the format, content, and range of regulations must change when we consider applying these regulations elsewhere in the world. We begin with a table that illustrates land use and proposed density in the nine major areas of the downtown (table 9.1). This is followed by the development regulations for these downtown areas, which proceed from general to specific.[1]

Table 9.1. Land use and growth plan, Langley, British Columbia (This chart outlines the specific character, land use, and permitted residential density for each one of the nine areas in downtown Langley.)

Area	Character	Land Use	Residential Density*
Core area (Main street area)	Specialty retail with residential uses, following an arts and culture theme	Commercial and residential	Medium—four-story development
Civic center	Civic, office, and hotel	Institutional (public use) and commercial office/hotel	Only hotel uses on western edge
Entertainment casino district	Commercial, entertainment, and hotel	Commercial, entertainment, and hotel	Medium long-term potential
Festival park and industrial arts district	Recreation, education, commercial, and light industrial	Public uses, commercial, and light industrial	None (provision for some work/live units)
West gateway	Residential	Residential	Medium
Prairie Transit station	Residential	Residential/commercial mixed use	Medium to high
Park Avenue	Higher-quality residential	Residential/commercial only on Douglas Crescent	Medium
Langley shopping center	Commercial short-term; mid-rise to high-rise residential in medium to long term	Short-term commercial pods on Douglas Crescent; long-term residential/commercial mixed use	Medium- to long-term potential for medium to high
Transition to residential areas (outside downtown area)	Residential	Residential and commercial	Medium (transition to adjoining neighbors)

* Downtown residential density for medium and high density; medium: up to 60 units per acre (148 units/ha) with a four-story maximum height (current RM3 Zone); high: up to 150 units per acre (370 units/ha) with a 150-foot (46-m) maximum height determined by airport limits (current C1 Zone), with a maximum of fifteen floors (on some sites the maximum height has been increased).

Examples of development regulations
Core retail area, Langley, British Columbia

General
- The form and character of building design and site planning shall coincide with the character of the downtown.
- The permitted uses include all those included in the downtown commercial zone.
- A variety of institutional uses may be permitted, provided they are compatible with neighboring uses.
- Institutional uses shall be multipurpose, if possible, to maximize community benefits.
- Heights in the core retail area will be limited to four stories.
- Conflicts with adjacent residential land uses (where applicable) shall be avoided through effective architectural design and landscaping.
- Access for the disabled shall be provided for in building and site design.
- Parking lots are required to have significant landscape plans to provide a safe and attractive pedestrian/automobile environment.
- A traffic impact study may be required to evaluate the developments and the associated traffic circulation improvements.
- Crime Prevention Through Environmental Design (CPTED) principles shall be applied.
- Mixed-use buildings up to four stories are encouraged, with retail maintained on the ground floor.

Building form and exterior finishes
- Developments shall feature an attractive and unified architectural presentation, with continuous weather protection where possible.
- Overly abrupt facade changes between Commercial Retail Units shall be avoided.
- Blank building facades shall be articulated with materials or graphic definition.
- Signs shall complement the architectural design and be approved by the project architect.

- High-quality exterior finishes shall be used to ensure the integrity of the building envelope and to present an attractive appearance.

Landscaping
- Landscape plans shall be prepared by a registered BC landscape architect.
- Landscaping shall be in accordance with standards of the British Columbia Nursery Trades Association (BCNTA) and the British Columbia Society of Landscape Architects (BCSLA) and should be equipped with an inground irrigation system.
- All trees shall be a minimum 2.5-inch (6.0-cm) caliper, and one tree is required for every six parking spaces.
- Landscaping shall screen parking areas from adjacent streets and "soften" the overall appearance of the development.
- Landscape plans shall emphasize shade tree species in order to moderate the summer climate.
- Entrances shall be distinctive but not overstated, using ground-mounted signs, apron walls, and rail fences, complemented by generous landscaping to create emphasis.
- Lighting shall be safety focused for visibility and use nonglare and direct lighting to minimize impacts to adjoining residential properties in accordance with the existing exterior lighting impact policies.
- Pedestrian areas shall feature distinct surface treatments (concrete, brick, or stone) from vehicular parking and maneuvering areas.

Crime Prevention Through Environmental Design (CPTED)
- The city may require development projects to be reviewed by a qualified CPTED consultant.
- Target hardening measures to prevent break-ins should be considered in plans.
- Unsightly bollards (posts) and window bars shall be avoided.

Specific building design
- New buildings shall complement existing buildings.

- Buildings shall have distinct bases, middles, and tops, with gabled roofs.
- Buildings shall have large windows along the building facade to create large airy and inviting volumes with slightly recessed building entries.
- The windows shall be larger on the ground floor for commercial uses but should not extend to the upper level.
- The construction shall use high-quality materials and craftsmanship, including molding and cornice detailing in wood or other appropriate materials.
- The primary materials shall be wood, with some stone detailing, secondary cladding, ornamental glass, concrete, and metal siding.
- Continuous overhead weather protection shall be incorporated into the heritage area, preferably a wood porch arcade extension of the building, but awnings and canopies are acceptable in discontinuous buildings. The awnings or canopies shall be designed as simple flat planes of durable fabric or wood. Glass or plastics are not permitted.

Signage

1. Signs shall identify businesses or activities and shall be in keeping with the character of the area.
2. New development shall ensure that signage is
   - an integral part of building and site design and that its form, material, and character complement the types of activities being advertised;
   - wood (painted, stained, sandblasted, or carved), metal (cast, painted, embossed, or enameled), fabric, or painted/etched on windows or glazed door panels;
   - not plastic, internally illuminated, back-lit awnings/canopies, electronic or moving signs or messages, or neon;
   - primarily oriented to pedestrians on the sidewalk, except gateway boulevard signs;
   - illuminated externally by concealed fixtures with a heritage theme; and

- in compliance with the sign bylaw and otherwise in accordance with the following: marquee/under-canopy signs (8 feet, or 2.4 m, clearance above grade; 8 square feet, or .74 m², maximum per business; .5 foot, or 0.15 m, maximum height of letters); fascia/awning and canopy signs (1.5 square feet, or 0.14 m², maximum sign area per linear meter of building frontage); projecting signs (10.5 feet, or 3.2 m, minimum clearance distance above grade; 3 square feet, or .28 m², maximum sign area per linear 3.5 feet, or 1 m, of building frontage); and entry signs (ground-mounted as part of entry feature, with landscaping and fence details).

Medium- and high-density residential regulations

Multifamily four-story development will be recommended as a basic standard in the downtown, with mixed use being focused in the core area, where the first floor is retail with three stories of residential uses above. There are opportunities for mid-rise and high-rise development in the longer term. As described in this section, mid-rise and high-rise developments (maximum of fifteen stories, or higher in specific locations) will only be permitted with adherence to the specific regulations outlined here.

Density, form, and character

1. The maximum density for medium density is 60 units per acre (150 units/ha) in accordance with the applicable zone and not exceeding four stories, with a setback from the street of 10 feet (3 m) on the fourth floor (fig. 9.1).
2. The maximum density is 150 units per acre (370 units/ha) and fifteen stories (150-foot, or 46-m, height limit), in accordance with airport regulations.
3. Front setbacks should reflect pedestrian-oriented street presence; therefore, front setbacks for town houses may be approved at 6.5 feet (2.0 m) to verandahs and 11.5 feet (3.5 m) to units, and for buildings higher than two stories, front-yard setbacks of 13 feet (4.0 m) for the first two levels, and even 20 feet (6.0 m) may be approved.

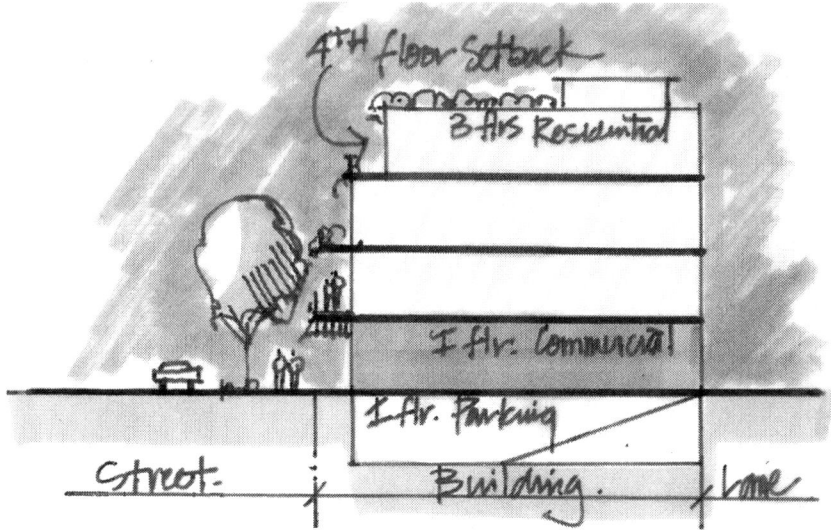

Figure 9.1. Stepped-back top floor, Vancouver, British Columbia.
This feature reduces massing of a multistory building.

4. Buildings should have clearly identified front entries and yards related to the street and specific private open space for townhomes.
5. New developments should be integrated with surrounding land uses but buffering to lower-density uses.
6. Conflicts should be minimized with existing single-family land uses in transitional areas.
7. Building design and site planning shall complement adjacent multifamily residential developments.
8. Access for the disabled shall be provided for in building and site design.
9. Crime Prevention Through Environmental Design (CPTED) principles shall be applied.
10. Child play areas shall be provided for projects over 100 units, with a minimum size of 2,691 square feet (250 m^2).
11. Green commons (local parks) shall be a minimum of 65 by 65 feet (20 by 20 m).
12. Building separation shall be a minimum of 20 feet (6 m) unless otherwise approved.
13. The residential developments shall have a strong street presence through extended porches, recessed entries, and ground-oriented units (fig. 9.2).

Figure 9.2. Separate street entrances in multifamily residential developments, Vancouver, British Columbia. Street entrances improve "eyes on the street" and activate the street.

14. Mechanical equipment on the roof of any building shall be concealed by incorporating it within the building roof, or by screening it in a way that is consistent with the character and finishing of the building.

15. Parking shall be to the sides or rear (or underground/structured), with the parking requirements following in accordance with the parking bylaw—no direct access to arterial roads will be permitted. Consolidated vehicular access in the form of frontage roads or lanes is required.

16. Parking pockets on one or both sides of the street shall provide additional parking, with visitor parking evenly distributed throughout the development.

Specific mid-rise and high-rise requirements

1. Residential towers should consist of three distinct vertical zones—the base zone, mid zone, and top zone (see fig. 9.3)—with regulations as follows:
   - The base zone shall be a maximum of three stories with a minimum setback of 10 feet (3 m) at the top of the base on the sides of the building facing streets, to create a strong horizontal street wall expression.

2. The mid zone (ten to eleven stories) shall be differentiated from the base zone through the use of a different architectural style and articulation of the facade and building massing. At the same time, it should reinforce some of the architectural expression, details, and materials below for continuity and unity. Floor plates will be generally limited to 90 percent of the base zone.

3. The top zone shall be one to two stories in height. Generally, the top zone should noticeably step back from the mid zone to create a distinctly different top to the tower. The area should be generally 90 percent of the mid zone and step back on the street fronts. A change in materials or architectural detailing can be used to emphasize and distinguish the top zone but should not dominate the building.

Exterior finishes and building envelope

1. High-quality exterior finishes should be used to ensure the integrity of the building envelope and to present an attractive appearance (fig. 9.4).

2. The finishing material shall consist of glass and glazed window wall systems, brick, stone, architectural concrete, precast colored concrete, stucco panels (to a maximum of 15 percent of the building exterior surface areas), or prefinished metal.

3. Although stucco is not encouraged, where it is used, the applications shall be inspected and certified by a qualified independent consultant.

4. Roof materials shall be "architectural grade," including ridge caps and shadow lines.

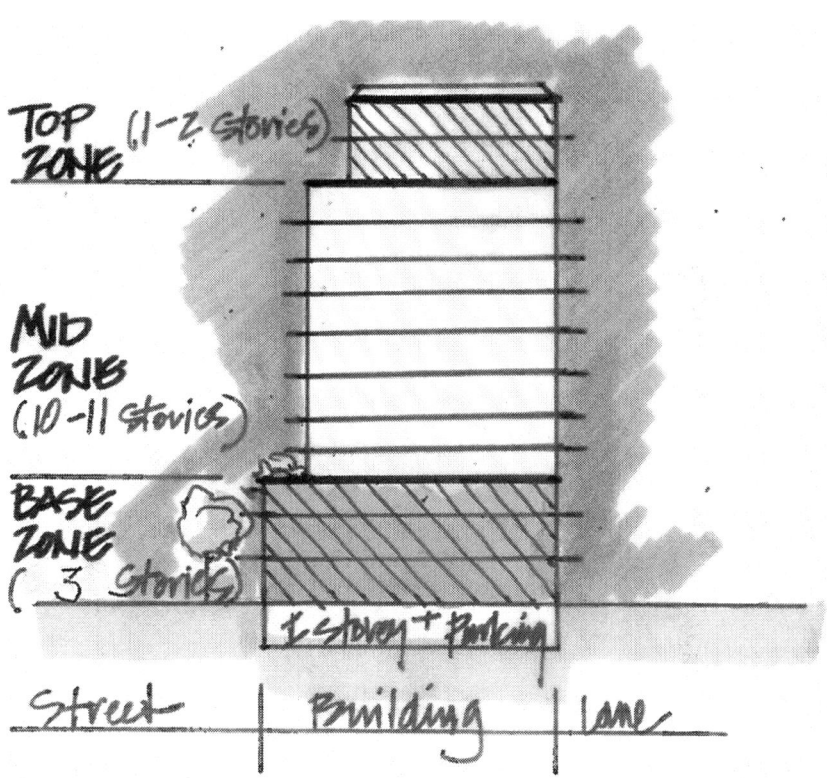

Figure 9.3. High-density illustration of building form, Langley, British Columbia. This drawing clearly shows the three distinct vertical zones of mid- and high-rise buildings.

Figure 9.4. High-quality exterior finishes and materials, Langley, British Columbia. One cost-effective approach is to concentrate high-quality materials at the ground-floor level, but still maintain continuity and different materials on the facade to the roof level.

Landscaping

1. Landscape plans shall be prepared by a registered landscape architect.
2. Landscaping shall be in accordance with the local standards of the professional landscape/nursery association and equipped with an inground irrigation system.
3. All trees shall be a minimum 2.5-inch (6.0-cm) caliper, and a landscape strip of 5 feet (1.5 m) is required adjoining a public road.
4. Entrances shall be articulated with appropriate low see-through fencing and high-quality features to provide distinction between private and public space.
5. Walls are not permitted adjoining streets; low fencing, not exceeding 4 feet (1.3 m), is encouraged in combination with hedging and foundation planting adjoining the street to reinforce the rural theme.
6. If security fencing is required in storage areas, etc., then chain-link may be approved (black vinyl covered), combined with hedging materials.

7. Landscaping shall be rich and context sensitive to enable viewing to the street and have a pedestrian-oriented edge, with a variety of materials and dimension to define public and private space.

8. Clearly defined pedestrian connections are required in all residential areas.

9. Developers shall provide special miniparks and green space within the developments as common public areas to socialize and gather.

10. Parking areas visible from a street, lane, or adjacent residential area uses shall be screened.

11. Mature trees and vegetation shall be retained wherever possible.

12. Parking and garbage areas should be appropriately screened, preferably by evergreen vegetation.

13. Developers shall incorporate a variety of hard and soft elements.

14. Private outdoor living space shall be encouraged.

15. Courtyard and trellis work shall be encouraged.

16. All wood applications shall be pressure treated.

17. Where applicable, fencing shall be wrought iron, aluminum, or an approved alternative, and retaining walls shall be kept to a minimum height.

Mixed-use development regulations

1. Individual commercial units shall not exceed 4,844 square feet (450 m²) on street level, with private residential space required for each unit.

2. Horizontal stretches of uninterrupted facade should be limited to 39.5 feet (12 m) in length.

3. At least 50 percent of the ground-floor building facade shall be glazed to the exterior on street frontage sides to provide visibility into the building and create a more inviting pedestrian environment.

4. The commercial uses may be in the form of live/work spaces, with the residential component visually integrated with the commercial uses.

5. Parking shall be provided on the street and via access lanes to the rear of the building so that the building can be set close to the street and emphasize pedestrian orientation.

6. Parking structures may have differentiated access for the residential and commercial units (e.g., third- or fourth-floor residential connection to residential lobby at the rear of the building; fig. 9.5).

7. Lot coverage may be up to 70 percent, with underground or structured parking to ensure street frontage continuity.

8. Residences will be accessed via a separate entrance from the commercial uses, excepting the live/work situations, which may combine the entries.

9. Awnings and/or canopies will provide continuous weather protection along the street front.

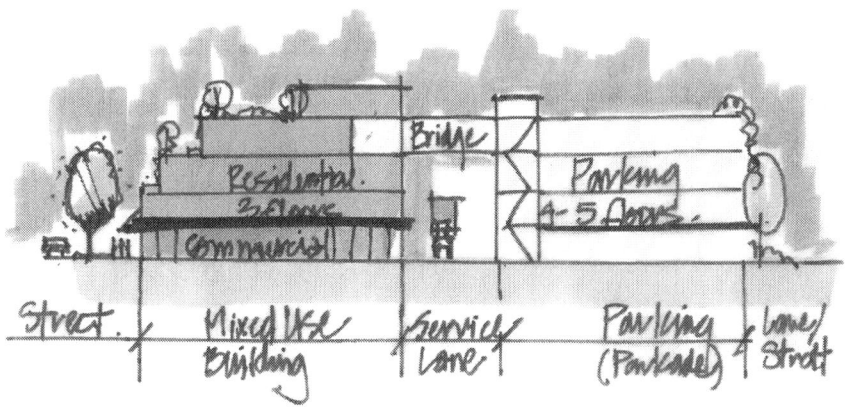

Figure 9.5. Parkade concept connected to residential, Langley, British Columbia. The concept of a parkade separate from the building but connected provides convenient parking for both residents and businesses. The top floor is a community garden/green roof.

Case study: Low-profile housing infill regulations, Medicine Hat, Alberta
The purpose of the following regulations is to present alternative forms of housing in existing neighborhoods. Every effort should be made to create appropriate housing alternatives that fit with the existing neighborhood character and the local market demands. The goal is to provide a diversity of housing choice to broaden affordability and type, yet increase density and enhance quality of place in the existing neighborhoods where services and utilities are already in place to support redevelopment. These guidelines highlight eight types of housing that are limited to residential infill development up to four stories (table 9.2).

Redevelopment does not happen in isolation. Built form establishes important relationships with many components of a place, including neighboring streets, houses, open space, and the overall character of the area. The success of these relationships will directly affect the neighborhood quality of life and sense of being in the specific place.

These guidelines were developed by MVH Urban Planning & Design in association with the city of Medicine Hat, Alberta, to inspire creativity and encourage adaptability to a number of specific situations in the Flats area of the city.[2] Medicine Hat is a city of approximately 60,000 people located in southeast Alberta on the Trans-Canada Highway. It is an area rich in natural gas and is known as the "Gas City." The South Saskatchewan River runs through its downtown, set in a picturesque river valley setting.

The development regulations for the Flats area west of downtown are intended to enhance current character while providing for a diversity of housing forms that further enhance community richness (fig. 9.6). Each begins with a definition.

Table 9.2. Development standards summary for proposed dwelling types, Medicine Hat, Alberta (This table summarizes the specific standards for different land use districts (zones) within the city of Medicine Hat. Minimum lot size in the second column relates to specific land use district requirements.)

Proposed Housing Types	Min. Lot Size in Square Feet	Max. Height	Max. Floor Area Ratio*	Front Yard Setback	Side Yard Setback	Rear Yard Setback	Coverage (%)
Large house Small house	330-L 420-LCS 441-NL 535.5-NLCS	2.5 stories	.60			18–24.5 feet (5.5–7.5 m)	
Coach house (with large house) Legal suite (with large house)	225 450-L 540-LCS 567-NL 630-NLCS	35 feet (10.5 m) on slab	.60 .75	11.5 feet (3.5 m) w/ garage setback of 18 feet (5.5 m)	5 feet (1.5 m) 3.0-CS	Coach house 8 feet (2.5 m) setback from lane; 13 feet (4 m) between house and coach house	45 percent
Semidetached (2 units) Quad-plex (4 units)	450-L 540-LCS 567-NL 630-NLCS	2.5 stories 35 feet (10.5 m) on slab	.75 .85	11.5 feet (3.5 m) 11.5 feet (3.5 m)	1.5 3.0-CS	18–24.5 feet (5.5–7.5 m)	45 percent 50 percent
Row houses Courtyard townhomes	225-Internal 315-External	2.5 stories 35 feet (10.5 m) on slab	1.0 1.0	11.5 feet (3.5 m) 11.5 feet (3.5 m)	3.0 5.5-CS	11.5 feet (3.5 m) 33 feet (10 m) between town houses	50 percent
Courtyard row houses Three- to four-story apartment	930 930	3 stories 39 feet (12 m) on slab 49 feet (15 m) on slab	1.0 1.5	11.5 feet (3.5 m) 3.0 6.0	3.0–7.5 or half of building height	7.5-L 9-NL	55 percent

* Floor area ratio (FAR) is the ratio of the building to the lot area. For example, if the building areas cover 100 percent of the site with one floor, that equals 1.0 FAR. Alternatively, if the building area covers half the site with two floors it is still 1.0 FAR. The calculation is total square feet (m^2) of building (area of building) divided by the area of the site. In some jurisdictions FAR is referred to as FSR, or floor space ratio.

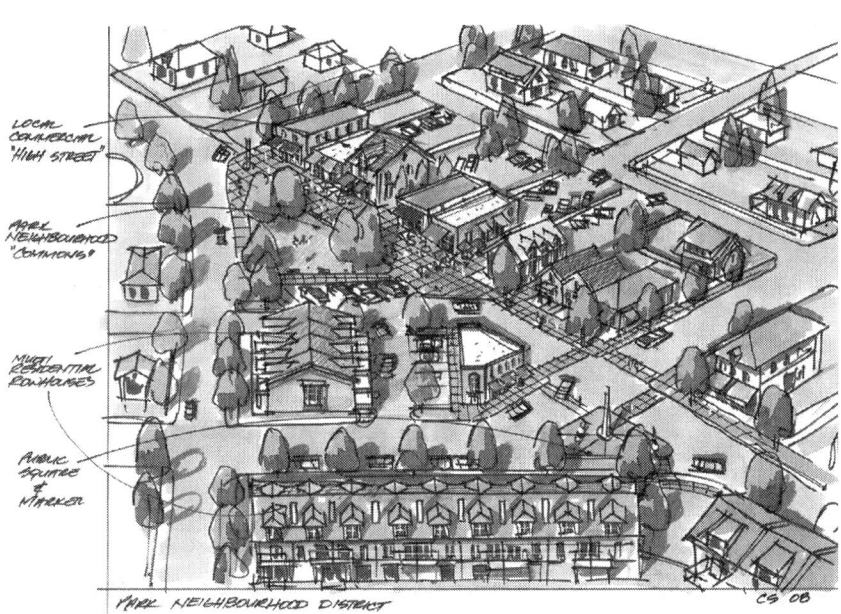

Figure 9.6. Neighborhood center area illustrating potential infill redevelopment, Medicine Hat, Alberta. This neighborhood center shows the potential residential row house infill coordinated with a revitalized commercial area. (Drawing by Calum Srigley.)

Types 1 and 2: Large single dwelling and small single dwelling

Large single dwelling. A single-family dwelling located on a large lot (i.e., 60 feet, or 18.3 m). Categories include legal suites or coach houses with lane access and parking only. Typically a minimum of 2,150 square feet (200 m²) in area (fig. 9.7). A large dwelling can have a legal suite in the dwelling or a coach house along the back lane but not both. A legal suite is a self-contained unit in a single dwelling that has a separate entrance and parking in the back lane only. A coach house is a self-contained dwelling unit located by the back lane, normally above a garage or carport and not to exceed 645 square feet (60 m²). The single dwelling units are limited to a two-and-a-half-story height of 34.5 feet (10.5 m) on slab. These dwellings require a minimum 5-foot (1.5-m) side yard. Coach houses shall be set back from the lane a minimum of 8 feet (2.5 m). Coach houses shall provide two inside parking spaces for the principal residence and one parking space for the lane home or suite. Legal suites (one per residence) are permitted provided they have a separate entry to the side or rear of the home. Street trees shall be retained or planted along the street every 25 feet (7.62 m).

Small single dwelling. A single-family dwelling located on a minimum 30-foot (9.1-m) lot (as illustrated on the right side of fig. 9.7) with single-car garage and tandem parking for a second car in the back lane only. It is typically 860 to 1,300 square feet (80 to 120 m²) in area.

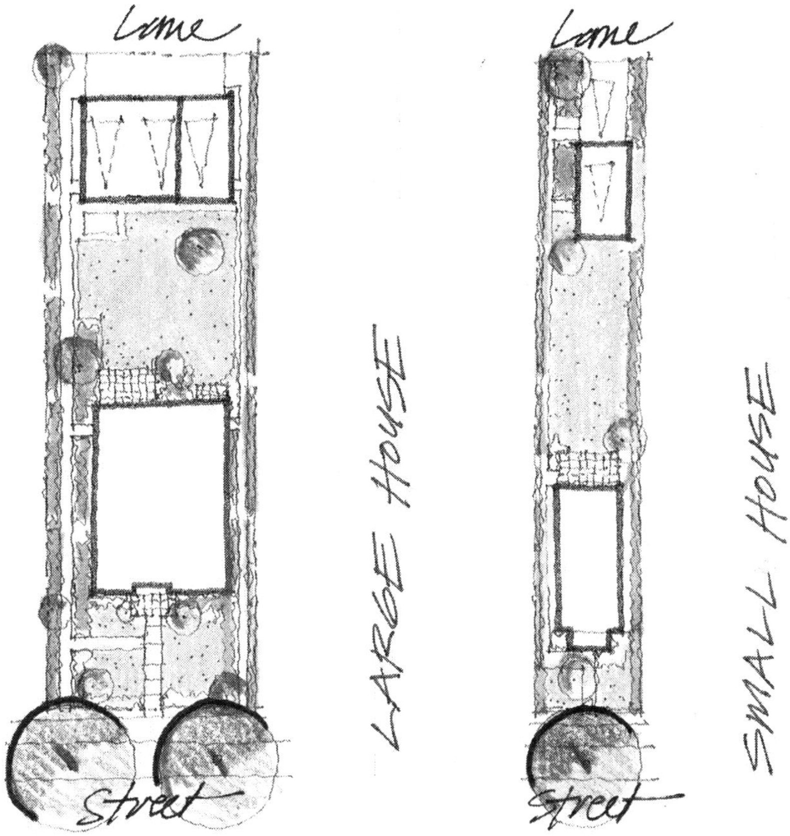

Lane

Lane

LARGE HOUSE

SMALL HOUSE

Street

Street

Figure 9.7. Large single dwelling, small single dwelling, legal suites, or coach houses, Medicine Hat, Alberta. The figure on the left illustrates a large single dwelling with a coach house at the back of the lot. Parking is provided on the ground level. (Drawings by Calum Srigley and Don Wuori.)

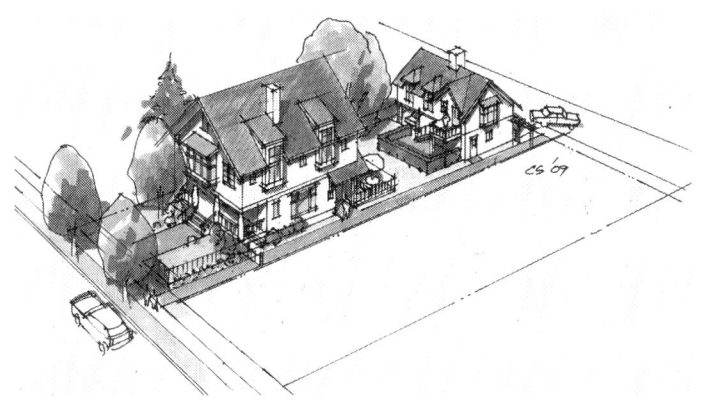

Type 3: Semidetached dwelling units
Two dwelling units side by side with front or lane parking (fig. 9.8).

- Two-and-a-half-story limit in height of 34.5 feet (10.5 m)
- Minimum 5-foot (1.5-m) side yard
- Four-car garage off back lane
- Character of semidetached looks like single dwelling home
- Street trees retained or planted along street every 25 feet (7.6 m)

Figure 9.8. Semidetached dwelling, Medicine Hat, Alberta. Two dwelling units on a lot with lane parking provide double the density with an estate home look.(Drawings by Calum Srigley and Don Wuori.)

239

Type 4: Quad-plex

Four dwelling units back-to-back with lane parking or front and back enclosed parking (fig. 9.9).

- Two-and-a-half-story limit in height of 34.5 feet (10.5 m)
- Parking for cars from rear lane only
- Minimum 5-foot (1.5-m) side yard
- Character of house looks like one large estate home
- Street trees retained or planted along street every 25 feet (7.6 m)

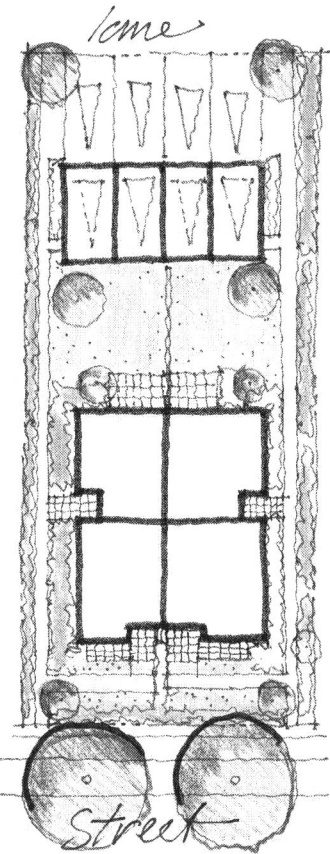

Figure 9.9. Quad-plex, Medicine Hat, Alberta. The quad-plex creates two units in front and two in the back with common walls and parking provided off the rear lane. (Drawings by Calum Srigley and Don Wuori.)

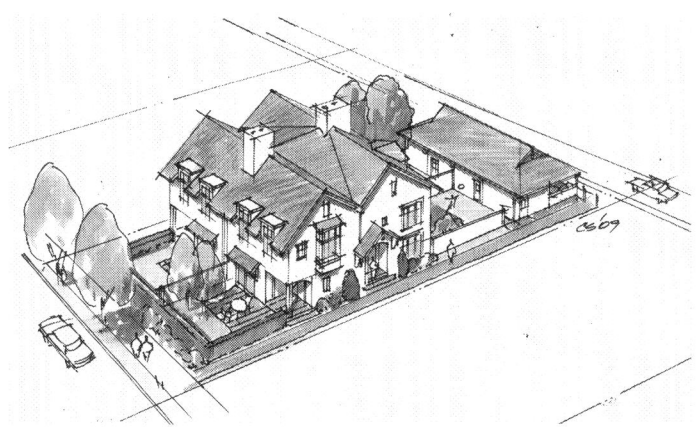

Type 5: Row houses

Street-oriented attached dwelling units with separate entrances with lane or front parking (fig. 9.10).

- Outdoor amenity spaces for each ground-floor unit
- Maximum six to eight units in a row (up to 164 feet, or 50 m)
- Three-story limit in height of 39.5 feet (12 m)
- Minimum 5-foot (1.5-m) side yard
- Parking provided in single garages and behind garages along back lane
- Large rear yard provided for each unit
- Street trees retained or planted along street every 25 feet (7.6 m)

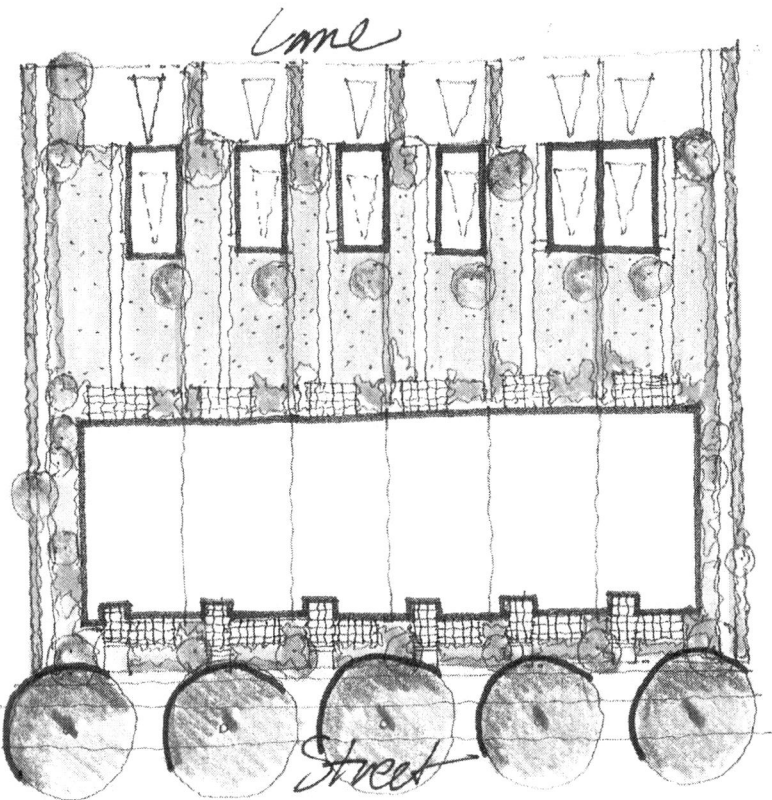

Figure 9.10. Row houses, Medicine Hat, Alberta. These dwellings can range up to three stories with tandem parking provided in the back lane, allowing a more sizable front and back yard. (Drawings by Calum Srigley and Don Wuori.)

Type 6: Courtyard townhomes

Street-oriented and courtyard-oriented attached dwelling units with separate entrances and lane parking with a two-and-a-half-story height limit (fig. 9.11).

- Create outdoor amenity spaces for each unit
- Side yards 5 feet (1.5 m)
- Wrap units around corner of building to create use of side yards and minimize blank walls
- Two-and-a-half-story limit with a maximum of 34.5 feet (10.5 m)
- Parking provided off lane in carport underneath units (see plan)
- Street trees retained or planted along street every 25 feet (7.6 m)

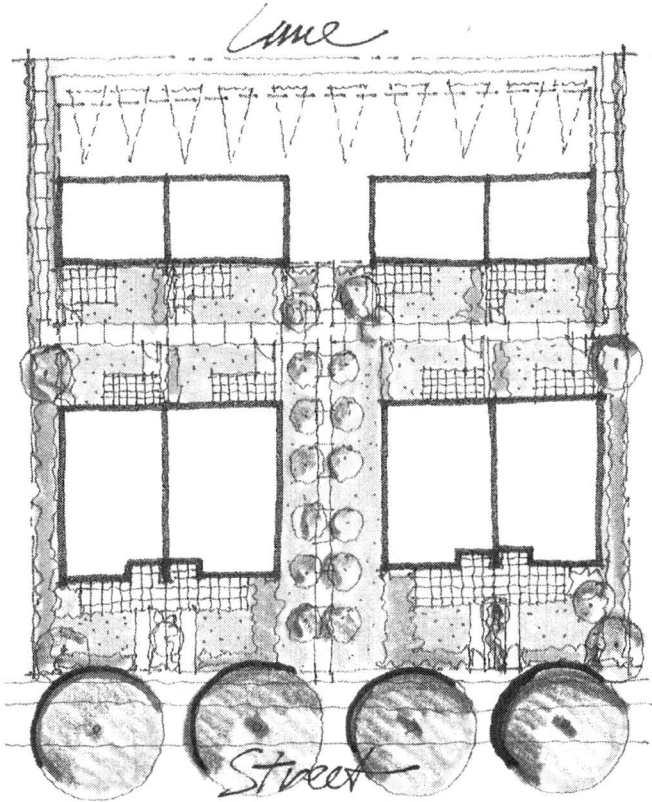

Figure 9.11. Courtyard townhome, Medicine Hat, Alberta. These homes feature carport parking for all residential units along the lane to maximize yard space. This site planning provides housing units in the back and front of the property with the front semidetached (two side-by-side units) appearing to be large estate homes. (Drawings by Calum Srigley and Don Wuori.)

Type 7: Courtyard row houses

Street-oriented attached dwelling units with separate entrances and interior courtyard units with underground parking and three-story height limit (fig. 9.12).

- Create outdoor amenity spaces for each ground-floor unit
- Screen underground parking from rear lane access entry with planting or screen
- Plant narrow pyramidal trees in side yards to buffer adjoining uses
- Maximum six to eight units in a row (up to 164 feet, or 50 m)
- Three-story limit in height of 39.5 feet (12 m)
- Minimum 10-foot (3.0-m) side yard
- Wrap units around corner of building to create use of side yards and minimize blank walls
- Plant street trees along the street every 25 feet (7.6 m)

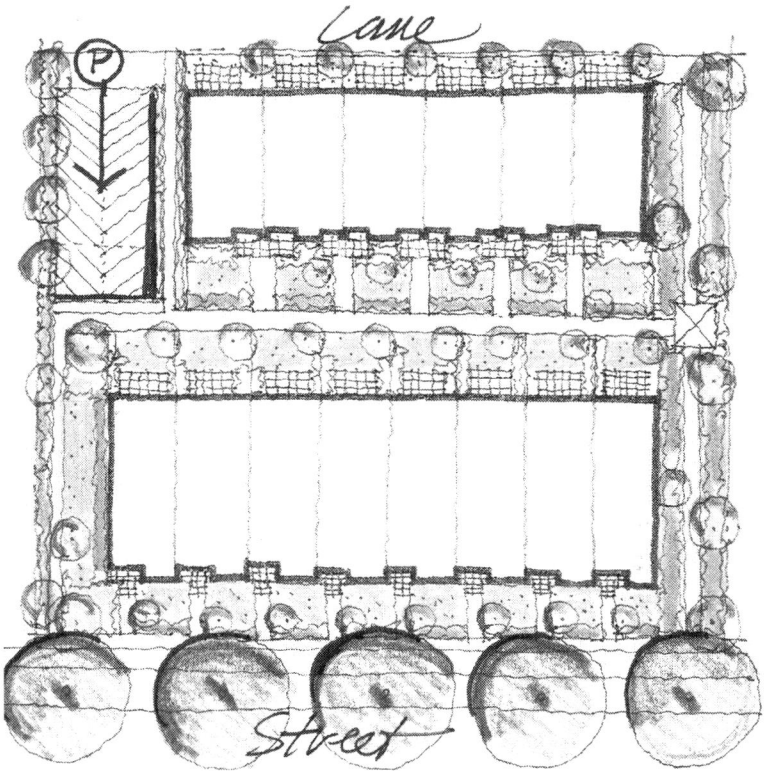

Figure 9.12. Courtyard row houses, Medicine Hat, Alberta. The courtyard row houses provide front yards similar to single-family housing areas, with backyards and common underground parking, assuming redevelopment of back-to-back lots. (Drawings by Calum Srigley and Don Wuori.)

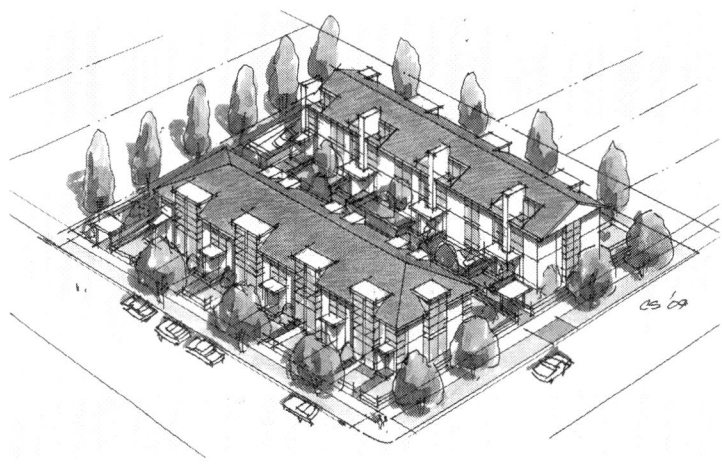

Type 8: Three- to four-story apartments

Three- to four-story apartments with underground parking access from rear lane (fig. 9.13).

- Maximum building length of 164 feet (50 m)
- Street-oriented units with separate entrances where appropriate
- Create outdoor amenity spaces for each ground-floor unit
- Develop common outside amenity area for upper apartment units
- Screen underground parking entry with planting or wood screen
- Plant street trees along the street every 25 feet (7.6 m)
- Plant narrow pyramidal trees in side yards to buffer adjoining uses
- Wrap units around corner of building to create use of side yards and minimize blank walls
- Four-story limit with a maximum of 49.25 feet (15 m)
- Side yard to be 25 feet (7.6 m) or half of the building height
- Underground parking with access along the lane where rear lanes exist

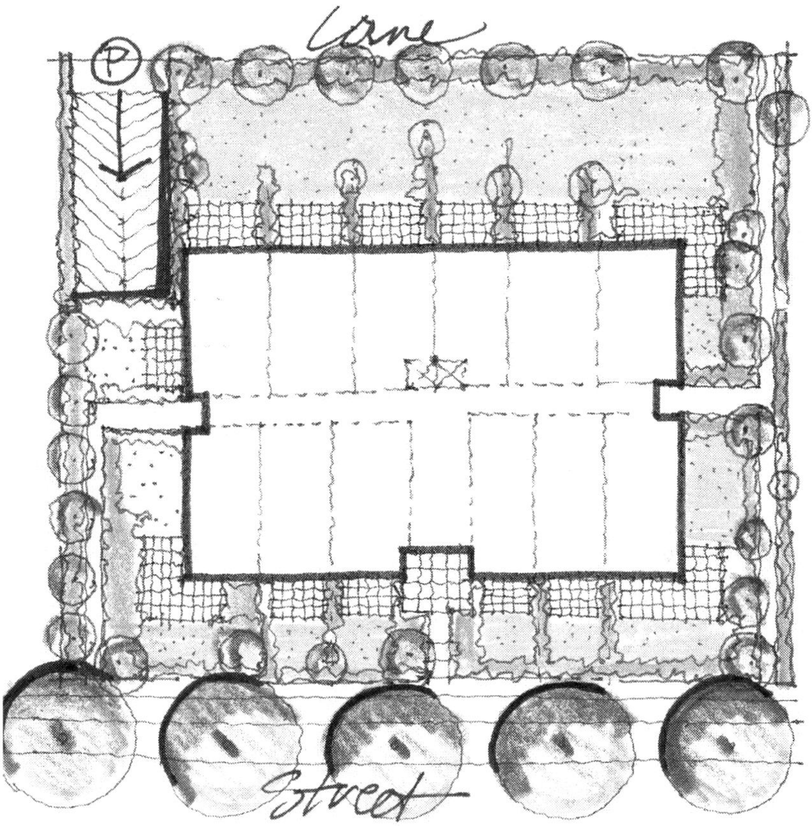

Figure 9.13. Three- to four-story apartments, Medicine Hat, Alberta.
These three- and four-story apartments provide the highest density of
the infill options. These apartments feature underground parking with a
ground orientation for first-floor units to address the street and increase
the building's connection with the street. (Drawings by Calum Srigley
and Don Wuori.)

III

EVALUATION AND INNOVATIONS

.

10
DESIGN REVIEW

Sustainable urbanism represents a generational shift in how human settlements are designed and developed. Its adoption as a societal norm requires all of the many parties to the process of planning and developing urbanism to perform highly specific tasks in tight coordination.

—Douglas Farr, *Sustainable Urbanism*

We have now journeyed through the entire sustainable urban design process of analysis, synthesis, policies, design guidelines, and regulations. We have developed a sustainable urban design sensitive to the locality and context. The community has been actively involved in shaping the plan. The local council has formally approved the urban design plan. Celebrations go on long into the night.

The realization strikes us early the next day: we have promised to develop a sustainable urban development. Lofty goals, principles, and targets have to be satisfied. Those who are to sell the property are more often than not worried about the price of executing development in a different way than is normal. Hence, at this stage it is important to have in place a review structure and requirements that go with the property, not only an agreement with the owner. This is necessary because details can get conveniently lost in transfer to other developers or builders, especially when these details are associated with a perceived or real cost premium and/ or additional approval time. In these cases, good intentions can willingly or otherwise evaporate, and community members, as well as council and staff, will be disappointed. As a result, more and more local governments are learning to hire and/or develop knowledgeable staff and use a defined design review process to ensure better results, especially where sustainable development is involved, as it adds an additional layer of complexity and requires additional attention.

Overview of the process

The following description of the design review process is somewhat simplified but covers its general aspects. A list of classic oversights in design review follows, to highlight important elements often missed or ignored. The final section of this chapter presents a design review matrix that sets out a checklist for the review of urban design plans with an additional specific sustainability component.

The details and players as we move from the planning stage to the development and building permit stages change. Urban design plans eventually transform from colorful animated plans to black-and-white construction drawings. Different professionals are involved, and potential different property owners or new development partners emerge. With all of these changes, a rigorous design review is required to keep the original vision in play; otherwise, it can easily drift.

Such a systematic review is emerging in larger cities and smaller towns. The sophistication varies. More and more cities are forming professional design panels tasked with reviewing significant development applications. Yet even with stringent requirements and documentation, the process is only as good as the quality of review by staff and the commitments of staff and council not to compromise.

The first aspect of design review is to develop a consistent series of steps to ensure that the application is not only complete but is also reviewed with the original goals in mind. A preapplication meeting helps to ensure that there are no major obstacles in the way of approvals. These obstacles can include soil contamination, traffic, and servicing capacity. If the green light is given following the preapplication meeting, the applicant can proceed to submitting a complete development application.

Each application requires a number of technical studies and plans, depending on the scale, location, and complexity of the project. Urban design applications can involve blocks of land or multiple parcels, so the requirements are usually complex. Once these requirements are met, the application goes through initial review to identify any substantial deficiencies that need attention. Once these deficiencies are corrected, the application is circulated to all necessary departments in the municipality, including planning, engineering, fire, police, parks, social planning, and others, as necessary. Feedback from these departments is summarized by the lead development planner and submitted to the development applicant for review and comment.

If there is a design panel or review committee, the application can move forward for formal review, with comments and recommendations from municipal staff. The design panel or review committee is advisory in nature. In other words, these committees have no power to formally approve or refuse an application. Nonetheless, their recommendations are taken seriously and affect the next steps in the application process. Refinements or entire redesigns often happen after design review.

After the internal review, the application can be circulated to external agencies (state/provincial and federal) that have jurisdiction or interest over specific parts of the application (e.g., highways, environmentally sensitive areas, water bodies, agricultural lands, unique wildlife, and significant parks). Finally, with all the comments submitted, the lead development planner assembles the list of preconditions for approvals, sends the lists to the applicant, and the proposal goes forward for approval. The municipality then coordinates with the applicant subdivision of lands to separate public roads, recreation and utility easements, municipal dedicated lands like parks, and environmentally sensitive lands such as wetlands and streams. The municipality then can proceed with the building permit process following the permitted phasing of construction. The total time of this design and development review process from initial design submission to final building permits can take up to five years, depending on the municipal approval requirements and complexities. Straightforward applications in some jurisdictions can be expedited in less than a year, but this is the exception rather than the rule.

Three steps to successful design review
Step 1. Preapplication meeting
The first meeting between the development applicant and jurisdiction is important to discuss any critical constraints, approvals time period, and application content expectations. Other associated approval factors that should be part of this discussion include anticipated community, staff, and council support, reasonableness of the proposal, and amenity contributions associated with the application. This meeting is critical to set up and manage expectations in terms of level of potential support, application requirements, and timing for approvals.

Step 2. Completion of development application
The development application contains the following components:
1. Normal legal information
2. Current survey
3. Photos of the existing site and adjoining sites
4. Aerial photograph
5. Plan illustrating existing services on and adjacent to the site
6. Site plan
7. Building form and massing plans
8. Landscape plan
9. Tree management plan
10. Sun/shade analysis
11. Site analysis including visual, noise, built form, and natural assets (biophysical analysis)
12. Analysis of the proposal as compared with the zoning requirements— existing and proposed (with variances noted)
13. Physical model and materials board if such is required
14. Any other supporting required studies, including the following:
    - Geotechnical analysis
    - Site contamination analysis
    - Traffic impact assessment
    - Infrastructure drawings including water, sewer, storm water, and other utilities

- Biophysical analysis of the environment elements of the site
- Associated management/mitigation strategy
- Crime Prevention Through Environmental Design (CPTED) study
- Lighting study

If any of these required components of the application are not submitted, the application should not be accepted for processing. Without all parts of the application, staff or the advisory design panel members are at a disadvantage and might miss a critical aspect or overlook a flaw in the design.

Step 3. Application review

Initial review. The application review should be first filtered through the staff team (some municipalities, such as the city of Vancouver, British Columbia, have a staff project facilitator). The development application is evaluated initially to ensure that it is complete, containing all the required information. If not, a specific list of deficiencies is sent to the applicant.

Application submission and internal circulation. Once the application is complete and suitable for circulation, it is circulated to assigned individuals in planning, engineering, parks, fire, police, and other departments, as appropriate, to obtain preliminary feedback in written form. If major elements require resolution before proceeding, the applicant is required to resolve these issues at this stage. If not, the development planner or facilitator will assemble the comments in preparation for review by the approving office for the municipality and then forwarded to the design review panel.

Design panel review. A design review panel normally consists of design professionals—architects and landscape architects, as well as planners, police, a disabilities representative, developers, and other members of the public supported by staff, determined by the municipality. This design panel is normally "advisory" only and has no enabling legislation to make decisions. The panel can only make recommendations to the municipal council. Any recommendation by the advisory design panel is forwarded to the municipal council as part of the final application recommendation by staff.

Normally, the advisory design panel's function is invaluable in openly discussing the merits of an application from a number of varied perspectives. This process brings an extra level of design rigor that complements the staff's review. The greater public interests are covered in these advisory design panel discussions, which give the application greater context and richness.

Circulation to external agencies. Depending on the municipality, the level of circulation (e.g., to regional government and state or provincial agencies) varies depending on the scale and sensitivities of the application (state or provincial highways, adjoining federal lands, watercourses, and significant habitats). The circulation requirements take time, and that time should be considered in the overall application approval process. Early investigations of significant potential issues are also encouraged to determine whether the application will be approved or what measures will probably be required for approval (e.g., building setbacks from streams).

Preconditions for approvals. The comprehensive set of preconditions for development approval are important in the rezoning process, for these conditions set the detailed expectations for on-site and off-site infrastructure improvements and/or contributions, community amenities, and detailed tree retention requirements. These conditions have to be carefully crafted and agreed upon by all parties before proceeding to a public hearing or other formal approval process before council. Appeasing any public concerns before the public hearing is also wise through the developer providing appropriate community considerations.

Oversights in design review

As mentioned, a number of important elements can be missed or ignored during design review. This list highlights some typical problem areas that should be considered by development applicants and design review professionals.

Application contents

1. Principles and tenets are not considered at the beginning.
2. Tree retention strategies are considered last, not first.
3. Pedestrian and bicycle analysis/needs are ignored or considered last.
4. Photo boards are incomplete or not submitted.
5. Sun/shade analysis is not comprehensive.
6. Transportation impact analysis is not complete.
7. Transit is largely ignored as a viable mobility support element.
8. Public realm improvements (including seating, street trees, sidewalk treatment, pedestrian-scale lighting, bike racks, and public art) are not included.
9. Site contamination is not scrutinized early enough.
10. Water and sanitary sewer capacity and connections are not fully reviewed.
11. Parks and environmentally sensitive area dedication requirements are not calculated correctly, or assumptions are not clear.
12. Watercourse setback requirements are not represented.
13. Off-site contributions are left until the end.
14. Community amenity contributions are not clear.
15. Fire requirements are not understood.
16. Building materials board is not submitted or not scrutinized.
17. Sustainability expectations are not clearly stated, and the review process is unclear.

Processing of application

1. Public review and comments are received too late for proper response from applicant.
2. Time expectations are not explained in detail.
3. Council or senior management become involved too early or too late.
4. Other agencies are not contacted early to define expectations.

Design review matrix

The following matrix is meant as a general guide to review development applications. The goal in design review is to be as objective as possible in your critique so that it motivates an improvement to the design. Frequently, design discussions can develop into a war of "tastes" rather than an objective discussion of function and more fact-based aesthetics. For example, access and egress have specific spatial requirements for safety and function; the colors of the building should blend with the adjoining palette, especially in a heritage district; and the street tree species and location should be consistent with the pattern on the street.

The matrix that follows (table 10.1) provides a checklist for reviewing specific design elements, including context, function, order, identity, and appeal. The matrix also includes social, ecological, and economic sustainability elements. These elements are all measured in terms of how they are addressed by the proposed site building(s), public realm treatment, and external connections, as well as access. The blank boxes are meant for written comments or simply check marks if elements have been addressed adequately.

Table 10.1. Urban design review (This chart includes urban design and sustainable urban design elements.)

Components	Site Building(s)	Public Realm	Connection/ Access
Context: Surrounding Fit			
Visual			
Ecological			
Context Buildings			
Activity/Pathways/ Streets			
Function: Use			
Security (safety, visibility, privacy, activity)			
Weather (sun, wind, rain, snow, other)			
Comfort (physical ease, visual enclosure, materials, furnishings, friendliness)			

Table 10.1. (*continued*)			
Components	Site Building(s)	Public Realm	Connection/ Access
Diversity (choice, variation, activities)			
Order: Understanding			
Coherence (entrance, edge, landmark, vista, skyline, ground plane)			
Clarity (structure, articulation, closure)			
Continuity (system, sequence, rhythm)			
Balance (patterns/ emphasis)			
Identity: Distinctiveness			
Focus (visual and activity node)			
Unity (continuous elements and repetition)			
Character (integrity, simplicity, restraint, style)			
Uniqueness (historical quality, symbolism, signatures)			
Appeal: Attractiveness			
Scale (human and humanizing)			
Appropriateness (proportion, authenticity, familiarity)			
Vitality (stimulus, contrast, tension, movement, sense of humor)			
Harmony (light, color, texture, line, sound, smell)			
Social Contributions			
Cultural activities			
Heritage conservation			

Table 10.1. (*continued*)			
Components	**Site Building(s)**	**Public Realm**	**Connection/ Access**
Place interpretation and public art			
Social housing			
Park space and connections			
Other (social equity)			
Ecological Contributions			
Water conservation (storm and potable water)			
Energy conservation (materials and recycling)			
Wildlife habitat enhancement			
Air improvement			
Vegetation enhancement			
Community gardens			
Retaining ecologically sensitive land			
Cleaning up contamination			
Other			
Economic Contributions			
Real estate value contribution			
Off-site contributions (services and infrastructure)			
Jobs and safety			
Other			
Overall Green Designation (LEED or local standard)			

Design review has an important role in realizing sustainable urban design. The review process better ensures that design intentions are realized in the details of the approvals documents. Supplemented by development agreements, customized zoning bylaws, and construction supervision, good project intentions can materialize into outstanding communities. The next chapter profiles two successful examples of sustainable urban designs that incorporated these ingredients into their success formulas.

11
NEW URBANISM AND LEED-ND

In the redevelopment of a military base in Calgary, the Canada Lands Company discovered New Urbanism as the road to community building and financial success.

—*New Urban News*, July/August 2002

Now it is time to measure sustainable urban design results on the ground. We hear about so many award-winning projects that fall short of expectations. Well, here are two projects that exceeded expectations. The following two case studies of Garrison Woods in Calgary, Alberta, and Garrison Crossing in Chilliwack, British Columbia, provide a basis to compare and contrast two community designs with interesting common histories but different locations, characters, and market forces. These sites are both former Canadian military bases and are being developed by the same company, the Canada Lands Company. My company was fortunate to be part of a consulting team for Garrison Crossing in Chilliwack, British Columbia.

What is LEED for Neighborhood Development?

LEED-ND, which stands for Leadership in Energy and Environmental Design for neighborhood development establishes one set of standards for sustainable neighborhood design. It originated in the United States as part of the US Green Building Council (USGBC) and is a collaboration among the USGBC, the Council for the New Urbanism, and the National Defense Fund. The standards are set out in a list of measurements that have specific criteria and points associated with each one. The measurements (credits and requirements) are organized in five categories: smart location and linkage, neighborhood pattern and design, green infrastructure and buildings, innovation and design process, and regional priority credit. There are forty-four credits that are given points and twelve requirements. Without the twelve requirements being satisfied, no LEED-ND certification is possible. The points are totaled, with the highest certification level being Platinum (ranging above eighty points), the second highest Gold (sixty to seventy-nine points), and the third certification level Silver (fifty to fifty-nine points). The basic minimum is Certified, with a range of forty to forty-nine points.[1]

The LEED-ND designation is not easy to achieve, especially in suburban locations with lower relative density thresholds than more urban sites. If the proposed project is a "green field" development (on vacant land), on agricultural land or on land including wetlands and other environmental features, these elements create additional challenges for certification. High-density "brown field" redevelopment sites (previously developed sites) in urban settings, where infrastructure and servicing already exist, normally can score the highest.

Other site development measurements in Europe and North America include the Built Green, Living Building Challenge, and Minergie rating systems. However, these systems tend to focus on the green building standards, not so much the overall neighborhood development. Net Zero buildings, or buildings that have zero net energy consumption and zero carbon emissions, are advancing the standard of high-performance buildings. The zero-energy housing in BedZED, United Kingdom, is an example of this applied standard.

The Congress for the New Urbanism (CNU) has made great strides in developing information and awareness about irresponsible development patterns and the New Urbanism alternative.[2] New Urbanism follows the principles of traditional neighborhoods of the early twentieth century, aiming to counteract the negative effects of suburban urban sprawl. Principles of New Urbanism include a more compact neighborhood with a diversity and mix of land uses; a more pedestrian-oriented community that is walkable, convenient, and safe; a respect for environmentally sensitive areas and community parks; the conservation of significant buildings and landscapes; and active citizen-based participation in planning and design. These principles were discussed in chapter 3.

Comparing two New Urbanism projects

The objectives for reviewing the two projects of Garrison Woods and Garrison Crossing are as follows:

- to examine the complexity of process and components in new community design, including LEED-ND and New Urbanism innovations in sustainable urban design
- to discuss the interdisciplinary nature of urban design and the many different actors involved in forming the master plan
- to illustrate the results of building the communities
- to study the "anatomy" of sustainable urban design solutions in two different situations

These two case studies are examples of new community design in Canada. They exemplify the popular movement back to traditional neighborhood design and are two of the first neighborhood designs (the Currie Barracks portion of Garrison Woods) in North America recognized with the LEED-ND certification.

These two new communities represent the next generation of urban design in that they

- recognize their heritage as a point of strength and unique identity in their design signature;
- provide a more pedestrian and transit orientation;
- develop an active and connected local park system, building on the existing assets on-site;
- create convenient services within walking distance, including shopping, schools, and recreation;
- encourage a mix of higher densities and a broader choice of housing;

- require multi- and single-family housing in the same block; and
- define narrower and safer local residential streets.

These developments also illustrate a regional move toward smarter, more sustainable growth that intensifies current land uses in urban and suburban areas with infill and redevelopment, where services are already available.

In this chapter, the two projects are summarized in table 11.1 and then described individually in detail. The first project discussed, Garrison Woods in Calgary, is summarized in an overall project profile. Then its unique features and financial success are described. For the second project, Garrison Crossing in Chilliwack, the case study goes into more detail in terms of vision, goals, principles, existing site conditions, and the resulting plan components. Although the details of the case study profiles are unique, common lessons provide valuable information about the success factors of these two projects and how they have evolved from concept to implementation.

About the Canada Lands Company

Canada Lands is a self-financed federal, nonagent Crown Corporation that optimizes financial and community value through the development and sale of surplus federal properties. The corporation's mandate is to revitalize properties and then manage and/or sell them in order to produce the best possible benefit for both local communities and Canadian taxpayers. As a nonagent Crown Corporation, Canada Lands operates like any other private company, paying taxes to all levels of government.[3]

Table 11.1. Two projects summary comparison

Element	Garrison Woods	Garrison Crossing
History	Currie Barracks (Canadian Forces Base)	CFB Chilliwack (Canadian Forces Base)
Size	175 acres (70.8 ha)*	153.5 acres (62.12 ha)
Location	7 minutes to downtown Calgary (1 million people)	10 minutes to downtown Chilliwack (80,000 people)
Previous Housing Units and Density	500 housing units (3 units/ acre, or 7.4 units/ha)	388 housing units (2.5 units/acre, or 6.2 units units/ha)
Proposed Housing Units and Density	1,700 units (10 units/acre, or 24.7 units/ha)	1,700 units (11 units/acre, or 27.2 units/ha)
Housing Adaptive Reuse	409 units	241 units
Housing Variety	409 refurbished single-family/semidetached; 288 new; 314 street-oriented town houses; 646 apartment units	241 refurbished single family/semidetached; single-family: minimum 400 to maximum 800 units; multifamily: minimum 200 to maximum 1,100 units
Development Status	Started 1998; complete	Started 2003; house construction spring 2004 (ten-year build-out)
Mixed Uses	67,000 square feet (6,225 m²) commercial retail	85,000 square feet (7,897 m²) commercial retail
Parks	11.7 acres (4.74 ha) parks plus 16.0 acres (6.48 ha) of existing hockey arena and military museum	9.0 acres (3.64 ha) of parks and open space
Amenity Package	Tree retention, parks, adaptive reuse (e.g., two private schools), and military legacy program	Tree retention, parks, Cheam Centre precinct, and military legacy program
Design Guidelines	Yes	Yes
Public Process	16 months	12 months

* Numbers may not be absolutely accurate and are only used herein for relative comparison purposes.

Case study: Urban renaissance, Garrison Woods, Calgary, Alberta

The closure of the Calgary "Currie Barracks" Canadian Forces Base in 1995 represented a significant loss to the community but also provided a significant opportunity. The 175-acre (70.8-ha) first stage of the former CFB has since been transformed into a renewed and integrated inner-city neighborhood (fig. 11.1). After a transparent sixteen-month public process, the first stage of this redevelopment process began in 1998 and is now complete. All the land has been sold in advance of the original schedule. Mark McCullough, Calgary general manager for Canada Lands, was a driving force behind the development, along with his dedicated staff.

The base provided housing for married army personnel for more than seventy years. The development was arranged in a park-oriented design at three units per acre. The site was redeveloped into a compact, pedestrian-scaled neighborhood of ten units per acre (24.7 units/ha) that will eventually be home to 3,500 residents (fig. 11.2).

At the northern end of the site, 67,000 square feet (6,225 m²) of retail/commercial space extends an existing Marda Loop retail district into the site. A 45,000-square-foot (4,181 m²) Safeway food store anchors the development, which also features a mixed-use complex of 160 apartments and 16,000 square feet (1,486 m²) of ground-floor retail. The southern edge of the community is not served by retail, but the distance from north to south is one-third of a mile (1,800 feet, or 550 m). The mix of uses is rounded out by two private schools (reusing existing buildings), a hockey arena, a senior complex, and a military museum. Every resident is located within a four-minute walk of a bus stop.

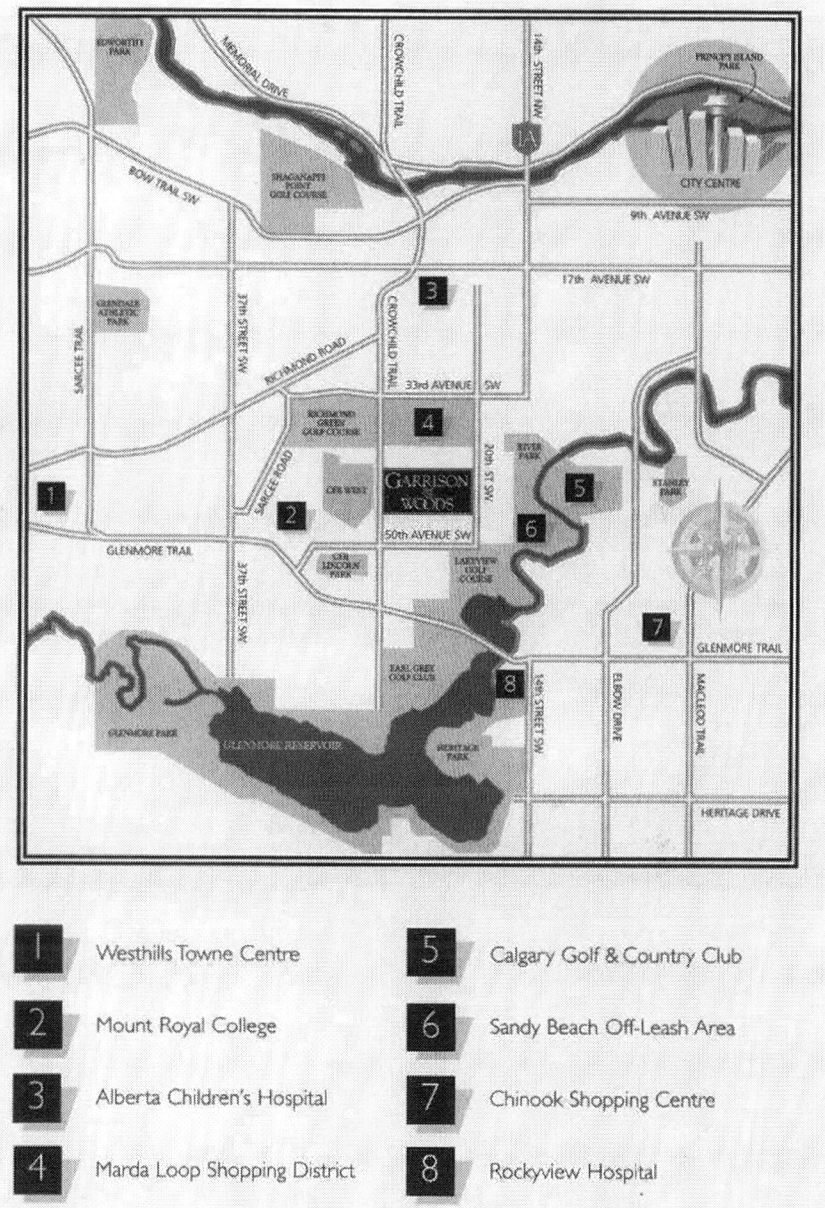

1	Westhills Towne Centre	**5**	Calgary Golf & Country Club
2	Mount Royal College	**6**	Sandy Beach Off-Leash Area
3	Alberta Children's Hospital	**7**	Chinook Shopping Centre
4	Marda Loop Shopping District	**8**	Rockyview Hospital

Figure 11.1. Location: Garrison Woods, Calgary, Alberta. Garrison Woods is located just south of the city of Calgary's downtown. (Used with permission: Canada Lands Company.)

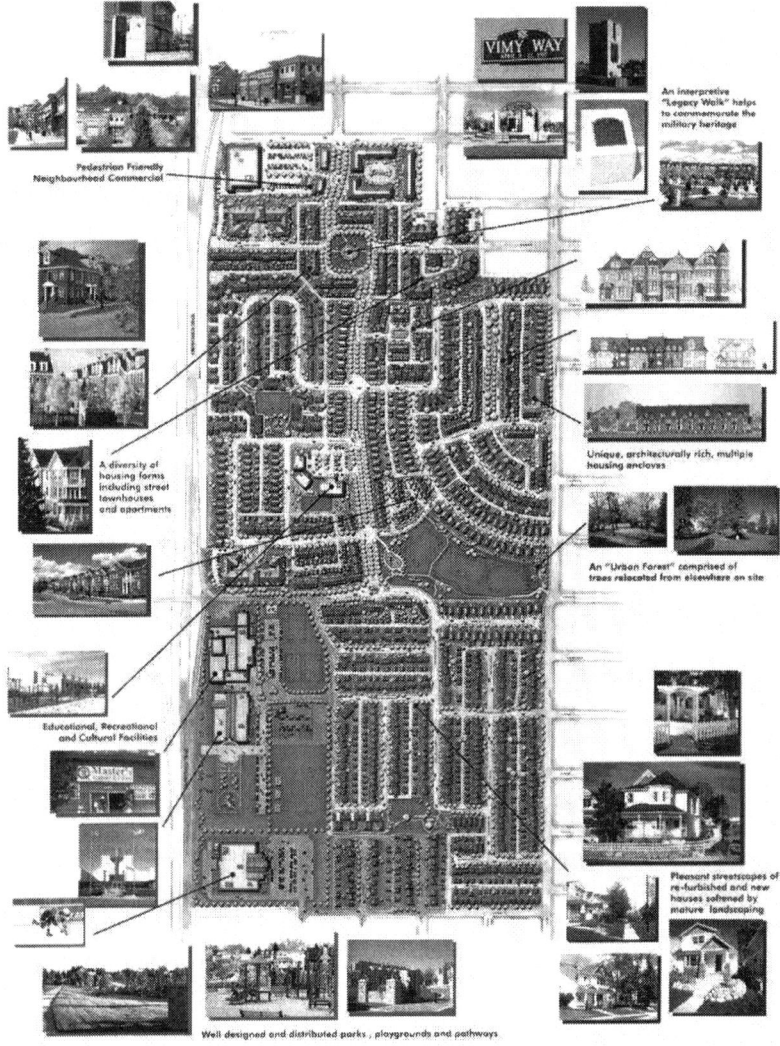

Figure 11.2. Master plan: Garrison Woods, Calgary, Alberta.
Illustrated is the first stage of the Garrison Woods redevelopment plan.
(Used with permission: Canada Lands Company.)

The Garrison Woods neighborhood incorporates many elements of New Urbanism and additional unique features:

- *Efficient land use.* Garrison Woods supports more efficient land use, infrastructure, and services by increasing density in an inner-city location.
- *Protection and enhancement of unique assets.* The development retains unique elements of the site, including the existing homes (all have been retained or relocated on-site or off-site), portions of the historic street pattern (95 percent replaced because of age), hundreds of very valuable trees (forty to eighty years old, some very close to homes), and several community facilities (schools, arena, and museum).
- *Mixed uses.* Garrison Woods incorporates a mix of land uses and a variety of housing types along with affordability levels. The popularity of the development has driven up prices. In 2002 prices ranged from $73,000 for condominium apartments to $435,000 for new single-family homes. The completed community has 1,700 housing units, consisting of 409 refurbished single and semidetached homes, 288 new single-family and semidetached homes, 314 street-oriented town houses, 646 apartment units, 67,000 square feet (6,225 m^2) of retail space, and two schools totaling 68,000 square feet (1,925 m^2). Approximately 80 percent of the existing homes were relocated and upgraded. The refurbished homes were interspersed with new single-family homes and town houses and helped broaden the range of home prices.
- *Transit.* The community is supported by a bus transportation system and a pedestrian-oriented environment that incorporates a linked network of streets and parks. (Transit ridership and private car use appear to be similar to conventional patterns of ridership and car use based on a recent survey.)
- *Parks expansion.* The development has 11.7 acres (4.7 ha) of existing parks, in addition to the existing hockey arena and military museum (16 acres, or 6.5 ha). A variety of parks ensures that every resident is within 650 feet (about 200 m) of a park.

- *Military legacy.* Garrison Woods commemorates the military legacy of the site through park and landscape design features that include monuments and plaques.
- *Public realm emphasis.* The development recognizes the importance of public realm and pays attention to it in the detailed site planning (fig. 11.3).
- *Customized development standards.* The community has customized engineering standards for streets and lanes to conserve unique site features such as trees. For example, streets are 29.5 feet (9 m) wide, with a design speed of 20 mph (30 km/hr), which compares to a wider standard of 36 feet (11m) wide, with a higher design speed of 30 mph (50km/hr). All intersections have bulges for safety. Rear lanes are reduced to 19.5 feet (6 m) from the customary 29.5 feet (9 m).
- *Design guidance and quality.* Garrison Woods has become a special urban place through specific design guidelines and themes (colonial, craftsman, Tudor, and Victorian house architectural codes; fig. 11.4).

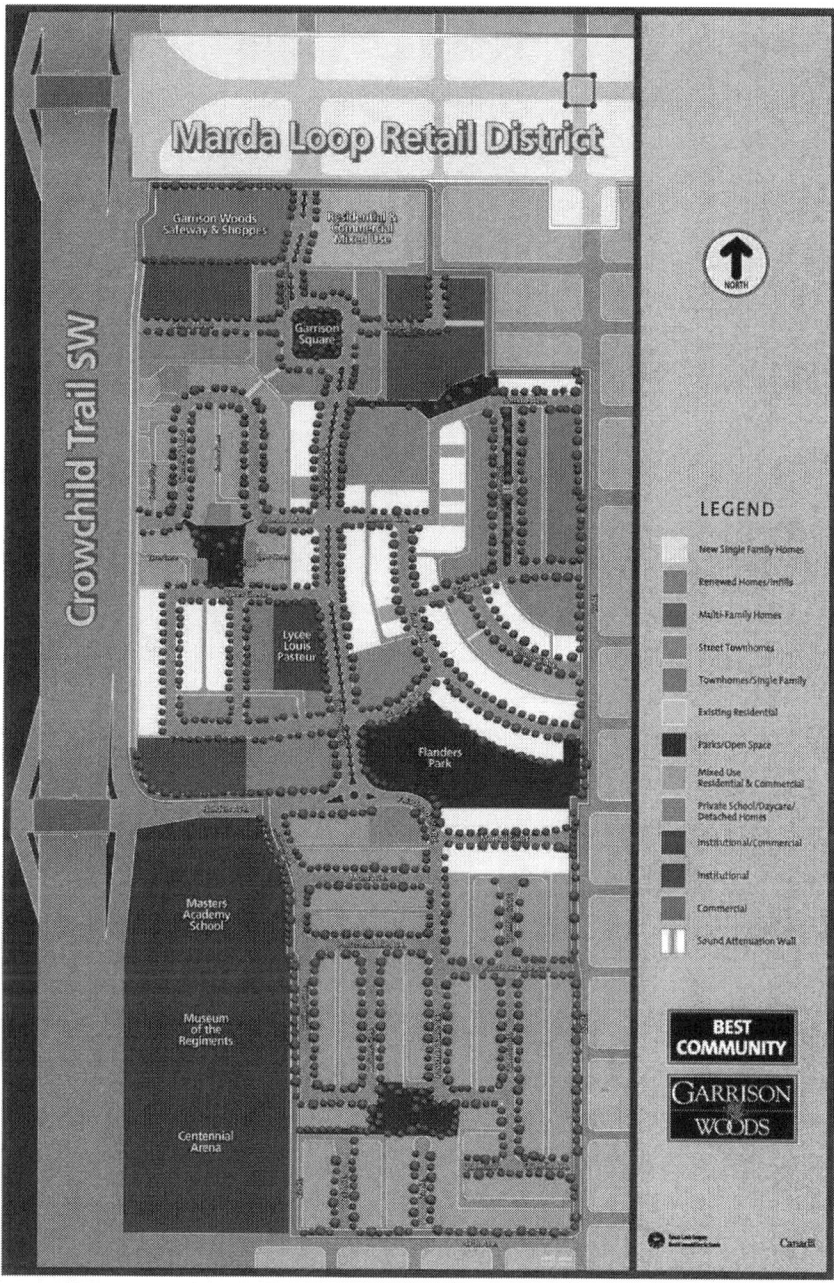

Figure 11.3. Land use plan, Garrison Woods, Calgary, Alberta. The land use plan illustrates the diversity of land uses and proximity to parks and services within walking distance of residents. (Used with permission: Canada Lands Company.)

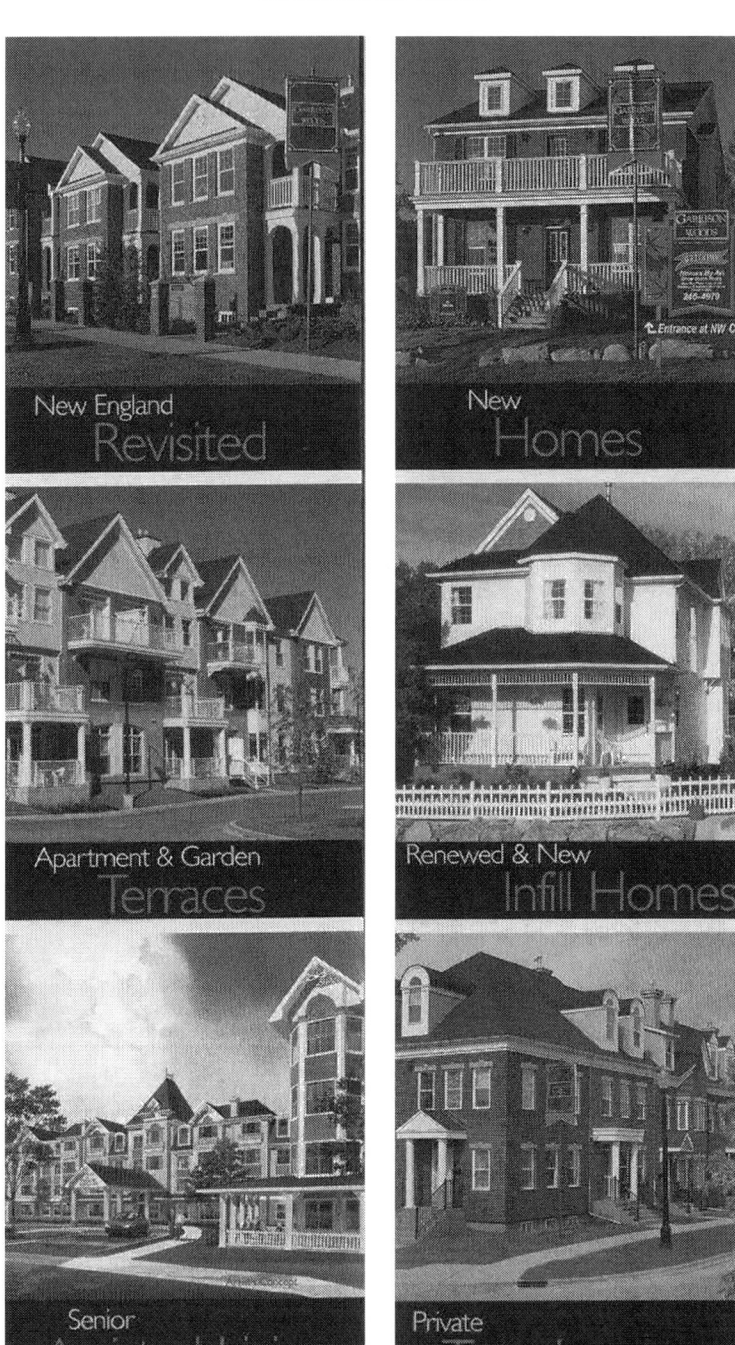

Figure 11.4. Housing choice, Garrison Woods, Calgary, Alberta.
Garrison Woods offers a distinct variety of housing, as illustrated in the housing types. (Used with permission: Canada Lands Company.)

Financial success by design

> Garrison Woods has become our flagship community ... There's a variety of architectural styles, within the active and commemorative parks, land uses, and in demographics. We have empty nesters, young families, professionals ... it's a great urban community.
>
> —Mark McCullough, General Manager,
> Canada Lands Company, Calgary, Alberta

Garrison Woods has also been a significant financial success, exceeding projections even with the substantial investment in public realm improvements and customized development standards. Canada Lands sold all the land in four construction seasons. This represents more than doubling the sales absorption of new conventional suburban projects (300 units versus 120 to 150 units). Since development began, housing prices have increased 25 to 30 percent in subsequent phases and in the resale market. Garrison Woods also proves that front-end investment in public infrastructure (30 percent more and 12 percent premium for back lanes) pays off in presales in advance of construction and value premiums. For instance, the investment of more than $500,000 in the Garrison Square Park feature yielded a premium of $15,000 per unit in the sale of the surrounding fifty-six town houses (fig. 11.5).

Figure 11.5. Town houses as backdrop to Garrison Square, Garrison Woods, Calgary, Alberta. Garrison Square Park added an estimated $15,000 to each of the fifty-six town house units surrounding the park.

Performance evaluation: What the residents say

A post-occupancy survey of the community sponsored by Canada Lands produced the following results:

1. Front porches and rear lanes were well received and considered assets.
2. The traffic circles are the most effective traffic-calming device.
3. Transit, walking, and cycling are only slightly more than the citywide average.
4. Residents feel that they can walk and cycle safely.
5. Parks are safe, well linked, and accessible (even though the linkages are not yet complete).
6. Most residents visit the Marda Loop business area at least once a week, and many visit it at least three times a week.

The development survey reinforced the plans for Garrison Woods and provided a benchmark for other developments in Calgary.

Case study: Suburban renaissance, Garrison Crossing, Chilliwack, British Columbia

Randy Fasan, director of planning and land development for Canada Lands, has been the man who kept the vision alive for the redevelopment of another former Canadian Forces Base, this one in Chilliwack, British Columbia. With the help of his able consulting team—including Mark Ankenman, architect—the vision came to life and presents an exceptional case study from concept to implementation. My firm, MVH Urban Planning & Design Inc., was involved in the initial planning and approvals and helped shape the Neighborhood Plan for the property.[4] Garrison Crossing builds on the sixty years of history at the former base in Chilliwack, located approximately 60 miles (100 km) east of the city of Vancouver. The foundation blocks of an outstanding neighborhood and a complete community were already in place—walkable streets, a variety of housing, active and passive parks, indoor recreation facilities, a grand boulevard, mature trees, conveniently located schools, and adjacent shopping.

A neighborhood and a team with a vision

Here is the vision that guided development of the former military base:

> Garrison Crossing is a unique, diverse, and thriving neighborhood that complements its surroundings, contributes to the healthy growth of Chilliwack, and builds on its rich military past. Garrison Crossing is a model of responsible development that seeks to respect the natural environment, connect to its neighbors, provide for housing choice, and reuse the existing built and natural assets where possible.

The project had the following goals, which included sustainable and New Urbanism goals:

- *Adaptive reuse.* Use the significant natural and built resources of the site in redevelopment, including buildings, roadways, and trees where possible, to create an exceptional and unique neighborhood.

- *Environmental sensitivity.* Respect, conserve, and enhance the significant and valued natural assets of the site.
- *Legacy.* Incorporate the rich military history of the site as an important central theme in redevelopment.
- *Diversity.* Provide for a range of types and styles of homes, local services, and associated amenities that include all age groups and complement adjoining land uses.
- *Connection.* Ensure that future redevelopment continues to provide activities and facilities for the surrounding neighborhoods and the greater Chilliwack community.
- *Innovation.* Explore new and proven urban forms that create a more pedestrian, compact, green, and complete neighborhood that is more efficient, healthy, safe, and livable.
- *Value.* Build an outstanding neighborhood that adds value to the greater community.

Historical development

The history of the existing neighborhood started with the establishment of Camp Chilliwack (later called Canadian Forces Base Chilliwack) in 1942. The threat of war in North America, a need for improved military engineer training, plus the need to provide personnel resulted in the establishment of the base. For the next fifty-six years, until its closure in 1998, CFB Chilliwack was the primary base for training military engineers.

During its time as an active military community, the north section of the property, also known as Parcel A and now Garrison Crossing, was the residential component of the base. Nearly four hundred permanent married quarters units were developed over the years to house military personnel and their families. At its peak, CFB Chilliwack was a thriving military community, with over 2,500 personnel and their families, living or working at the base. The northern residential section had two chapels, a commercial store, a gas station, a hospital, a dental office, a fire station, other industrial and commercial buildings, and the Cheam Recreation Centre. It was a complete community where one could live, work, shop, and play, all within walking distance.

The military base also developed strong relationships with the surrounding Chilliwack community and became a significant contributor to the social and economic well-being of the region. Since the closure of CFB Chilliwack in 1998, the two chapels and the three-story apartment complex have been removed, along with the commercial store, hospital, dental office, and fire station. The Cheam Recreation Centre came under YMCA management, and the remaining 388 residential units were leased to military and nonmilitary personnel. The city of Chilliwack demolished the original swimming pool and replaced it with a new $9 million aquatic center that opened in May 2010.

Predevelopment site conditions

The original site conditions created the important ingredients for the redevelopment of the property (fig. 11.6). The vision and goals (outlined earlier) provided a strong directive to use the natural and built resources on-site. The site receives good sunlight year-round and is relatively flat, with good access and proximity to services on-site or close by. Wooded areas and a host of mature trees provide natural amenity. Existing housing, recreational, commercial, and light industrial uses provided reuse potential. Aging buildings and infrastructure set the stage for redevelopment intensification and renewal.

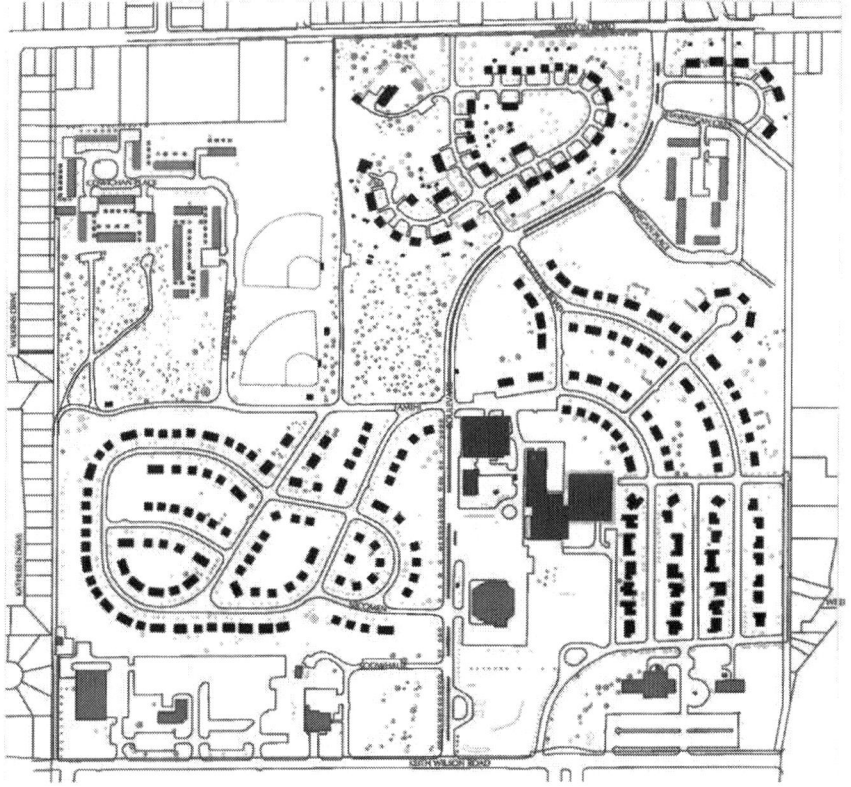

Figure 11.6. Former site conditions, Garrison Crossing, Chilliwack, British Columbia (2003). The former military base had a specific road pattern and open space network that became the basis of the redevelopment plan. (Used with permission: Canada Lands Company.)

Plan preparation process

Preparation of the Garrison Crossing Neighborhood Plan was a team effort. A host of consultants reviewed the site in detail and formed ideas for the future redevelopment of the site in 2002. The city of Chilliwack council and senior staff had an opportunity to review and comment on the early ideas in December 2002. Two public open houses followed at the Cheam Centre on January 14 and 15, 2003, which included separate meetings for the existing tenants and surrounding community. Nearly five hundred people attended these two meetings. Further open houses were held in April. The public feedback was generally supportive, reinforcing the central theme of retaining and enhancing the existing neighborhood character. The following highlights summarize some of the public comments:

1. Retain the trees, the boulevard, and the Cheam Recreation Centre.
2. Provide a variety of housing choices, and retain existing houses where possible.
3. Retain the existing open space and associated recreation facilities.
4. Enhance the walking paths in the community.
5. Retain the existing street structure, and add traffic-calming measures to discourage through-traffic and improve safety.
6. Ensure that housing intensification is sensitively implemented to enhance the existing neighborhood character.
7. Provide adequate capacity for additional students at the adjacent schools.
8. Retain the views to the adjacent mountains.
9. Protect the aquifer.
10. Provide opportunities for existing tenants to purchase or continue to rent in Garrison Crossing.

Planning principles

The following social, ecological, and economic principles continue to guide development and design. The goal of these planning principles is to promote sustainable development that embraces the long-term interests of Garrison Crossing's residents, workers, and visitors.

Social principles

1. Create a diverse and complete community. Provide a range of activities and land uses that enable residents to live, work, and play within a convenient walking, cycling, or transit-riding distance.
2. Celebrate the military legacy. Incorporate the rich military history as a major theme element throughout the neighborhood.
3. Reinforce the neighborhood heart. Enhance the Cheam Centre precinct as a recreational, cultural, ceremonial, and educational heart of the neighborhood.
4. Expand the walkable neighborhood. Provide a safe and extensive network of pathways that encourage walking and biking in the neighborhood with public transit support.

5. Protect the distinctive character. Conserve and enhance the existing unique neighborhood elements, including the significant trees, road patterns, and open space network.

6. Create housing choice. Provide a variety of housing forms and sizes, while also providing different ownership and rental opportunities, that together encourage a range of age groups and incomes.

7. Design for safety and security. Ensure that CPTED (Crime Prevention Through Environmental Design) principles are included in the planning framework, including lighting, traffic calming, signage, and housing orientation.

Ecological principles

1. Promote responsible development. Retain, relocate, and replace significant trees and other natural heritage elements where possible.

2. Protect the aquifer. Provide the necessary development standards to ensure the protection of the Vedder Aquifer.

3. Improve storm water drainage. Reinforce the natural storm water drainage system, where necessary and reasonable, to ensure aquifer protection.

4. Encourage environmental stewardship. Promote continued environmental responsibility and lifestyles, including tree stewardship and transit use.

Economic principles

1. Integrate new uses. Incorporate existing residential and commercial uses into the new neighborhood plan where possible.

2. Use land efficiently. Make efficient use of the land and infrastructure by increasing housing units and other uses, while ensuring that the redevelopment is sensitive to adjoining developments.

3. Integrate public infrastructure. Optimize the use of existing public infrastructure, including roadways, storm drainage, sanitary sewer, water, and other services.

4. Create value by design. Encourage innovative high-quality urban design that fits the existing and future built form, enhances the streetscapes, and refines the open space network.

5. Provide for adaptability. Ensure that Garrison Crossing, as it grows and changes, can renew and adapt itself effectively to new social and economic conditions, programs, policies, and technologies.

Major form-makers and big ideas

Specific elements of the former neighborhood character emerged, both from the site inventory and the public open houses, which formed the major form-makers for future development. These elements shaped the development opportunities on the site (fig. 11.7).

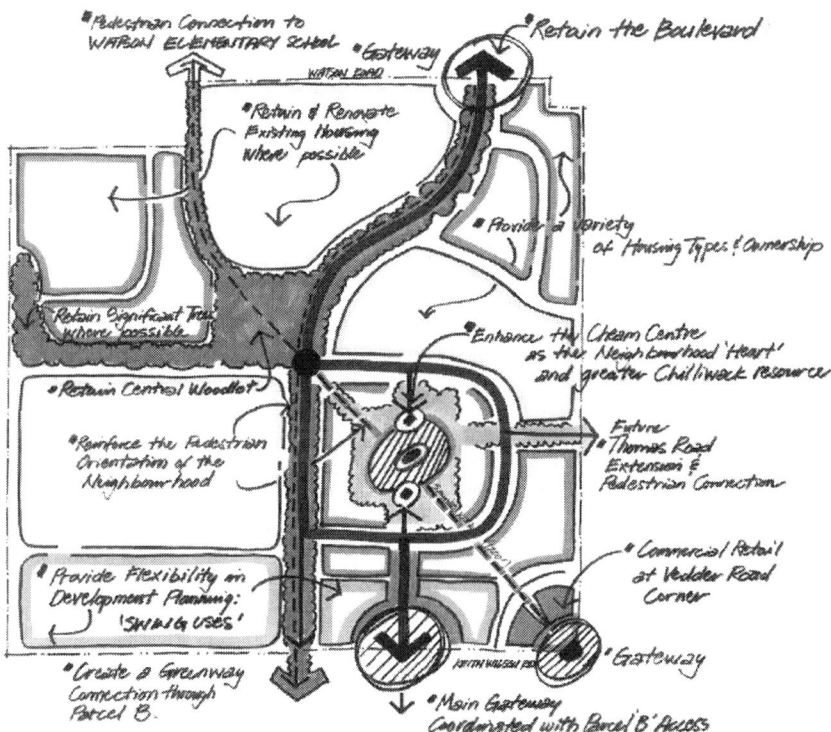

Figure 11.7. Big ideas plan illustrating opportunities, Garrison Crossing, Chilliwack, British Columbia. The early big ideas plan reflected some of the primary elements that the public identified in the open houses.

285

- *The boulevard.* The central boulevard is one of the most memorable elements of the former CFB Chilliwack site. Its broad, sweeping curves, enhanced by mature trees, form the pedestrian and vehicular backbone of the site. The tree-lined central median divides car lanes, adding to the attractive driving and pedestrian experience.
- *The Cheam Centre.* The heart of this neighborhood is the Cheam Centre. Bustling with recreation activity throughout the day, the Cheam Centre serves as a valuable resource for both the immediate area and the city of Chilliwack.
- *Existing housing.* The existing housing units on the site were in relatively good condition structurally but needed upgrades and improvements. These 388 units provided an opportunity to build on the architectural character of the site.
- *Central woods.* Another memory for most residents and visitors was the central woodlot located adjacent to the Cheam Centre. A stand of mature coniferous trees dominated the site, with a variety of trails weaving their way among the tree trunks and the high tree canopy overhead.
- *Significant trees.* The site had a wide variety of mature trees, both healthy and in decline. This "green" aspect of the site created an attractive base on which to build, where trees were retained where possible and replaced in suitable locations so that they could grow and thrive.
- *Existing roads.* The existing local roads had no curbs and gutters. Their relatively narrow road widths contributed to a safer and more pedestrian-oriented neighborhood. Limited through roads also discouraged any cut-through traffic. The neighborhood plan tried to retain and enhance these safer neighborhood-oriented streets.
- *Access points.* There were two major vehicular access points to the site. The boulevard at Watson Road on the north and the boulevard at Keith Wilson Road on the south form the major gateways. These points provided an opportunity for improved traffic and pedestrian movement.

- *Access to Parcel B.* The south section of the former CFB Chilliwack, Parcel B, was not connected with Parcel A at Keith Wilson Road. Access points for future development should be coordinated because of the strong physical connection between the two parcels.

- *Adjacent land uses.* Connectivity to adjacent uses will be important in the neighborhood plan. Pedestrian and bicycle connections to the Vedder Road commercial area, Vedder River Rotary Trail, Watson Elementary School, and Mount Slesse Middle School will help connect the site to the surrounding community. At the same time, any development should be sensitive to adjoining uses and the existing character in the area.

- *Flexibility.* The Chilliwack market for residential, commercial, and light industrial uses will change over time. This residential-focused neighborhood plan for Garrison Crossing should be flexible to respond to these changes in an appropriate manner that fits with the integrity of the planning principles and the character envisioned for the area.

Land use concept

The original Garrison Crossing land use concept (fig. 11.8) reflects the earlier vision, goals, and planning principles. At its core is the commitment to conserve the existing neighborhood character. The Cheam Centre precinct, central woodlot, central boulevard, and road patterns are retained in a residential-focused neighborhood.

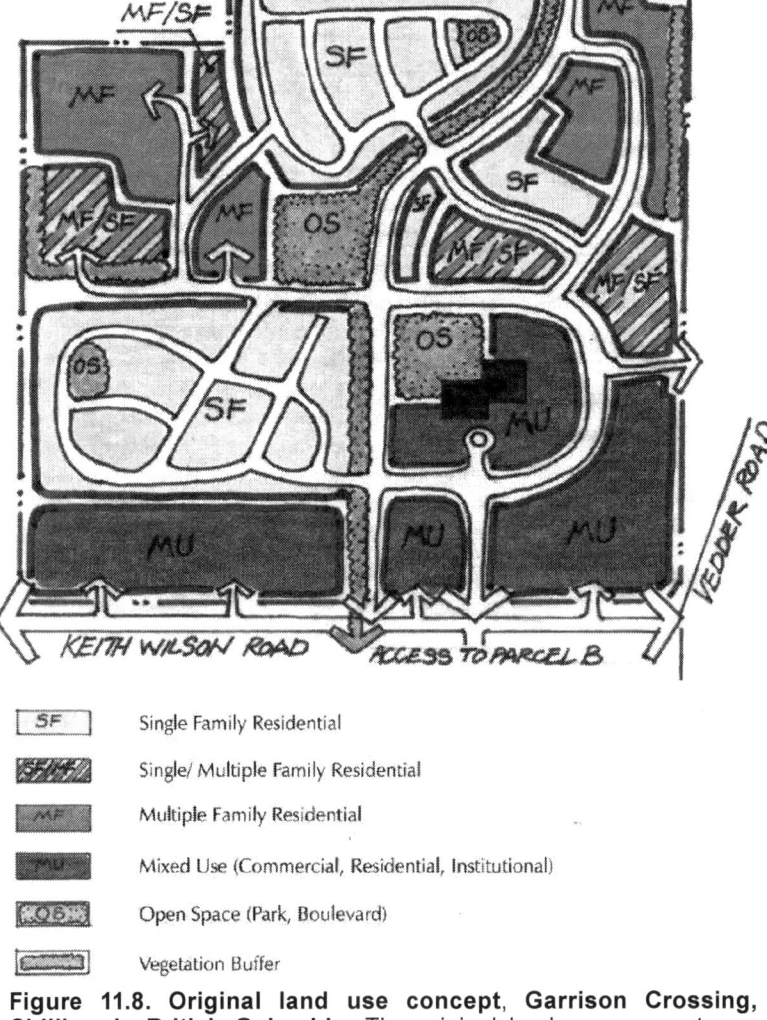

SF	Single Family Residential
	Single/ Multiple Family Residential
	Multiple Family Residential
	Mixed Use (Commercial, Residential, Institutional)
	Open Space (Park, Boulevard)
	Vegetation Buffer

Figure 11.8. Original land use concept, Garrison Crossing, Chilliwack, British Columbia. The original land use concept was modified as the development progressed based on market demand and the local knowledge gained through the development process.

Neighborhood design vision

The accompanying urban design plan (fig. 11.9) provides an illustration of the diversity and richness that builds on the existing neighborhood character. From standard single-family residential units to duplexes, town houses, and four-story apartments, the proposed redevelopment plan provides a wide variety of site planning.

Figure 11.9. Urban design plan, Garrison Crossing, Chilliwack, British Columbia. This plan illustrates rich diversity of land uses and unique features, including the central tree park, the Cheam Centre for recreation, and the Garrison Village mixed-use area in the southeast corner. (Used with permission: Canada Lands Company.)

Highlights of the urban design plan include the following:

- *Residential mix.* The variety of housing units and densities are illustrated in the accompanying plan. The revitalization plan builds around the existing homes where possible and introduces a variety of new units that either infill between existing housing units or replace them when it is not practical to retain or relocate the houses.

The lot sizes vary, as does their orientation to the street or the lane. The diverse types of homes (fig. 11.10) include single-family and duplex renovated units, new single-family and duplex units, renovated row houses (townhomes), new townhomes, and walk-up multifamily units in the three- to four-story range.

Former row houses have been renovated and sold. Some single-family units have coach houses in the rear yard over the garage. Zoning, design guidelines, and covenants strictly regulate residential site planning and uses to ensure compliance with standards over the long term.

Figure 11.10. Housing diversity, Garrison Crossing, Chilliwack, British Columbia. Illustrated here are single-family housing with retained trees (top left); a coach house behind some single-family units and townhomes (bottom left); three-story town houses (top right); and four-story apartments (bottom right). (Used with permission: Canada Lands Company.)

- *Parks and greenways.* The Cheam Centre is the center of neighborhood recreation and cultural activities. The center has undergone major renovations. Surrounding "flex-field" open space and convenient parking will complement the recreation center. The flex-field will provide recreation for a variety of sports and age groups.

  Walking paths encourage residents or visitors to walk or bike to the Cheam Centre. These walking paths are part of a commemorative walk theme that celebrates the military legacy at CFB Chilliwack. Pedestrian lighting, street furniture, and other features create a comfortable and safe walking environment. These paths connect other parts of the recreation network, including the proposed central greenway along the main street that provides a bikeway and walkway north to south through the site; the central tree park, which is enhanced and protected; the pathway connection to Watson Elementary School across Watson Road; and neighborhood parks, like Cheamview Park, that emphasize passive visual space, local activities, and recreation for small children (fig. 11.11).

Figure 11.11. Cheamview Park restoration, Garrison Crossing, Chilliwack, British Columbia. This park is a centerpiece for a restored neighborhood and includes a mailbox and interpretive signage, as well as a children's playground. (Used with permission: Canada Lands Company.)

- *Roadways, access, and transit.* Primary access is retained from Keith Wilson Road and Watson Road with access at Watson Road and the boulevard as well as a new street access along Keith Wilson Road aligned with the access to Parcel B.

  The roadways emphasize a neighborhood orientation that reflects the existing character and standards in the community. The central boulevard acts as a collector road, while the existing road network and improvements function as local streets. Trees are carefully retained where possible in any road reconstruction to retain the richness of the existing landscape (figs. 11.12 to 11.15).

Figure 11.12. Cheamview Crescent before construction (left) and after reconstruction (right). Tree retention and alternative street standards are important features of Garrison Crossing. (Used with permission: Canada Lands Company.)

Figure 11.13. Concept sketch of proposed streetscape before construction, Garrison Crossing, Chilliwack, British Columbia. Compare this conceptual sketch of the street with figure 11.14 (below) and see comparative results in the final construction.

Figure 11.14. Streetscape after reconstruction, Garrison Crossing, Chilliwack, British Columbia. Reconstructed residential streetscape with retained boulevard and trees, as well as houses set close to the sidewalk. (Used with permission: Canada Lands Company.)

Figure 11.15. Residential heart of Garrison Crossing, Chilliwack, British Columbia. High-quality public realm investments include customized pedestrian lighting, underground utilities, traffic-calmed streets with parking pockets, and a comprehensive heritage recognition program. (Used with permission: Canada Lands Company.)

- *Garrison Village and future uses.* Garrison Village, a neighborhood commercial component, has been built in the southeast corner of the site to service Garrison Crossing and complement the Vedder Road commercial corridor adjacent to the site (figs. 11.16 A,B, and C). The future multifamily belt along the balance of Keith Wilson Road responds to a further demand for residential uses on the parcels. The balance of the west side of the site is single-family and multifamily residential, following the existing patterns.

A

Figure 11.16, A, B, and C. Garrison Village near Garrison Crossing, Chilliwack, British Columbia. This mixed-use commercial village at the corner of Keith Wilson Road and Vedder Road is pedestrian-oriented, with a grocery store, professional offices, local retail services, and residential uses above commercial uses on the ground floor. (Used with permission: Canada Lands Company.)

B

C

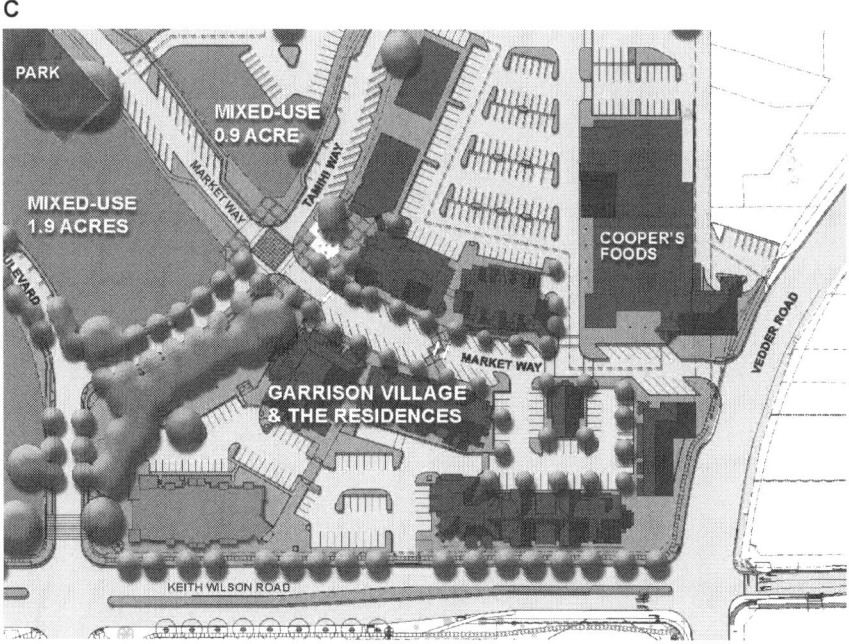

Implementation

> While the wrong kind of suburban development can induce a sense of panic and entrapment, Garrison Crossing feels like the kind of place you'd like to stay and rest awhile.
>
> —*Globe and Mail*, March 12, 2011

Great neighborhoods are a result of good plans, great intentions, and a commitment to carry out the plan with the original intentions. The implementation plans go beyond the neighborhood plan document. The formal Neighborhood Plan for Garrison Crossing provided the basis for the Official Community Plan and rezoning amendments. In addition to the neighborhood plan document, the following continue to support the additional necessary detail for the design and building approvals process:

- *Site development design guidelines.* These guidelines specify the site use regulations, public realm, and private realm site planning and landscape standards, as well as the architectural standards that apply to the subareas. These guidelines are registered on title to ensure that future landowners are aware of their permitted uses and design regulations. The developer, Canada Lands Company, or an appointed agent, reviews building and site planning submissions to ensure that they comply with the design guidelines.
- *CD-10 zone.* This comprehensive development zone specifies the regulations and standards for each of the subareas within Garrison Crossing, including setbacks, density ranges, and other use or site development restrictions. This zone permits the flexibility to retain existing houses, trees, and other elements associated with neighborhood character, and respond to changing market demands and customized development standards in the longer term.
- *Customized engineering standards.* Specific technical drawings will address the specific road and utilities standards for Garrison Crossing.

As in Garrison Woods in Calgary, the Garrison Crossing project in Chilliwack provides an example of the value in sustainable urban design. A committed design and development team, follow-through, and innovation continue to make Garrison Crossing a leading example of successful new sustainable communities in North America. The project illustrates that place-sensitive urban design can provide an excellent return on investment not only to the developer but also for the community and municipality. These two case studies of Garrison Woods and Garrison Crossing will be expanded by others across Canada in the next chapter to provide a basis for potential application elsewhere in the world.

12
URBAN INNOVATIONS

This is no little plan. This is a plan of urban greatness.

—The Central Area Plan, City of Chicago

Case studies in the previous chapter showed how it is possible to rejuvenate existing neighborhoods and increase density while incorporating principles of sustainable design. This chapter continues that discussion with additional, diverse urban examples. We begin with a visit to legendary Chicago, which in recent years has built on the strong foundations established by a city plan envisioned more than a hundred years ago. Likewise, in Calgary, Alberta, city planners have seen the benefits of a visionary nineteenth-century plan and are imagining the city another hundred years hence. Meanwhile, in the far eastern city of Vladivostok, Russia, developers are creating a brand-new community within the city's limits—from the ground up—in a project that demonstrates extraordinary cooperation from federal, regional, and local governments. The chapter concludes with the more common scenario of urban infill and redevelopment, this time in the eastern Canadian coastal city of Halifax, Nova Scotia. All of these case studies aim to demonstrate the possibilities for realizing sustainable urban design principles in very different sites.

Lessons from Chicago

I visited Chicago for the first time in 2004. My daughter, Athena, was attending Ballet Chicago that summer, so I thought we would tour the city before going on to New York. My wife, Laura, had gone ahead in advance of my trip. What happened then surprised me. Laura phoned me not once but several times to rave about the sites, architecture, and life in the city. Her positive and enthusiastic response was somewhat unusual for Laura, which made me curious. I soon discovered for myself that the city was not the past Chicago of race riots and unrest, but a city going through a revival to become one of the great cities not only in North America but in the world.

Central Chicago has a plan to guide growth and invite the right growth over the next twenty years. Since 1980, Chicago has added 43 million square feet (almost 4 million m²) of office space, equivalent to the entire metropolitan-area inventory of Phoenix or St. Louis. Downtown residences are back and growing, contrasting the decline in many American city cores. More than 23,000 new homes added since 1980 make Chicago the leader in American downtown residential development.[1]

The center of the city is going through a transformation, but it has a sound foundation of urban design on which to build. As home to America's original skyscrapers, it has a rich architectural legacy. It is also a showcase of grand public space, parks, and monuments shaped in part by the famous Plan of Chicago completed in 1909.[2] This progressive plan was oriented toward the Lake Michigan waterfront, incorporating parks and recreational uses that integrate with the street system and other city parks. It embraced many aspects of the City Beautiful movement of the late nineteenth century, emphasizing the importance of city appearance, sanitation, and street paving (see also discussion of City Beautiful movement in chapter 2). The small details around beauty matter in embracing the City Beautiful movement. This plan provides a platform for sustainable urban design in its regional scope and depiction of the city as an organism. It reaches beyond normal city boundaries, championing the idea of an accessible public city, and extends parks, streets, transit, and rail into a regional network (fig. 12.1).

Over one hundred years later, the principles of the Chicago plan stand strong and guide much of the development, especially along Lake Michigan. The three themes of the current twenty-year plan—directing growth, strengthening connections, and creating great public places—

Figure 12.1. Chicago's downtown connections. Streets, parks, transit, greenways, and railways connect downtown Chicago to its region.

are evident in the new emerging city.[3] An extensive park system and a series of grand boulevards balance development with amenities. Grand civic buildings, statues, and fountains anchor corners of the public areas, provide orientation points, and bring an inviting civic comfort to the downtown. Millennium Park, along Lake Michigan, with Frank Gehry's landmark open theater architecture and a host of rich interactive public art and park pieces, buzzes with activity and people having fun (fig. 12.2). The Navy Pier redevelopment, stretching into Lake Michigan, brings more visitors and residents to the lakefront and downtown core, where they can experience, along interconnected waterways, Venice-like boat tours of the classic Chicago heritage and modern architecture.

Figure 12.2. Millennium Park, downtown Chicago. This park has set a contemporary standard for downtown park functions and programming in North America.

Off of Lake Michigan in the center of the downtown, a weekend farmers' market animates a formerly inactive plaza, and the "Magnificent Mile" shopping street (Michigan Avenue) throngs with shoppers along its inviting wide sidewalks and boulevards. Hanging flower baskets and wrought iron low-railing features decorate the streets, a legacy of Mayor Richard M. Daley. Maintenance workers are constantly cleaning and caring for the streets. A free trolley connects downtown destinations, and the trolley driver provides such an animated tour that there is a lineup at every stop (fig. 12.3). The activity does not subside at night either in the heart of the city. Restaurants spill out on Michigan Avenue, where warm lighting makes the walking experience feel safe and comfortable.

Figures 12.3. Chicago's downtown farmers' market and free trolley.
The downtown market and free trolley amenities invite local residents
and visitors to participate in the city's many attractions in an open and
welcoming way.

Downtown Chicago well illustrates all the concepts of place-making that collectively define great places (for a list of these elements, see chapter 4). The city provides a current example of a "complete community" design that combines live, work, and play close by. There is no need to travel elsewhere. The Chicago sustainable urban design and planning layers of housing, commerce, public access, public spaces, and public transit are all layers for other world cities to consider and emulate in their own way. That said, these innovations must be carefully examined before being adopted elsewhere. Otherwise, new initiatives can easily become a wasted use of time and resources. Each city, town, or new community is unique and requires special treatment, as the following three case studies show.

Case study: Hundred-year vision, Calgary, Alberta

Like the Plan for Chicago of 1909, the hundred-year Calgary Midtown Plan, completed by MVH Urban Planning & Design as the lead consultant in 2004,[4] provides a good basis for examining the merits of long-term thinking in urban design . Planning documents in North America normally look ahead twenty to thirty years. You would think that great things might take more time to plan and design. To that end, the Calgary Midtown Plan looks forward for three generations of Calgarians.

The rationale for the hundred-year time horizon is that it transcends typical urban planning by providing the opportunity to think big and to proactively address the issues and opportunities that will shape its future. This concept is not new to Calgary, as it is not new to Chicago. In 1914, the British town planner and landscape architect Thomas Mawson presented a farsighted plan for the future development of Calgary. The Mawson Plan was a classic City Beautiful plan that presented a grand vision, richly detailed and illustrated (fig. 12.4; see also chapter 2, figs. 2.10 and 2.11). To get to this vision, Mawson needed to stretch out beyond what built form existed at the time. His elaborate vision was for a future Paris of the Prairies. However, with the start of the First World War, some of the grander ideas were put to rest. Mawson's vision did live on, however, through the early and ongoing appreciation and protection of the natural form of the city, its views, its rivers, and its escarpments. Future inner-city subdivision patterns and land use plans would borrow from his thinking, as well.

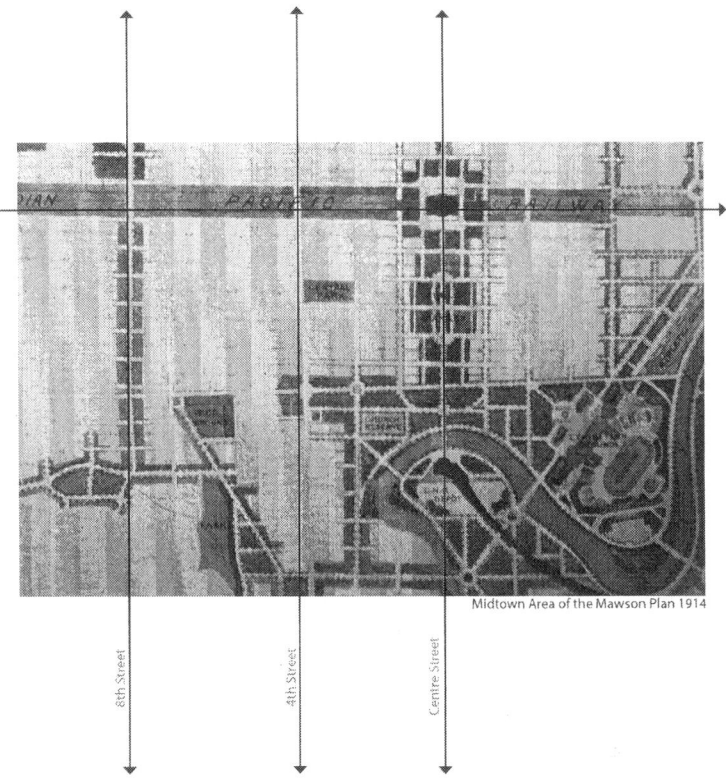

Midtown Area of the Mawson Plan 1914

Figure 12.4. Partial plan illustration of the Mawson Plan, Calgary, Alberta (1914). This portion of the Mawson Plan illustrates the many qualities of the City Beautiful movement, including grand streets, extensive park networks, and formal visual connections with important sites. (Source: City of Calgary)

In January 2004, the city of Calgary joined the +30 Network, a growing group of global cities and regions committed to long-term quality of life. This network is sponsored by the International Centre for Sustainable Cities, headquartered in Vancouver, British Columbia. The goal is to bring together at least thirty global cities, working in partnership through a multistakeholder approach, developing hundred-year visions of sustainability for their communities (fig. 12.5).[5]

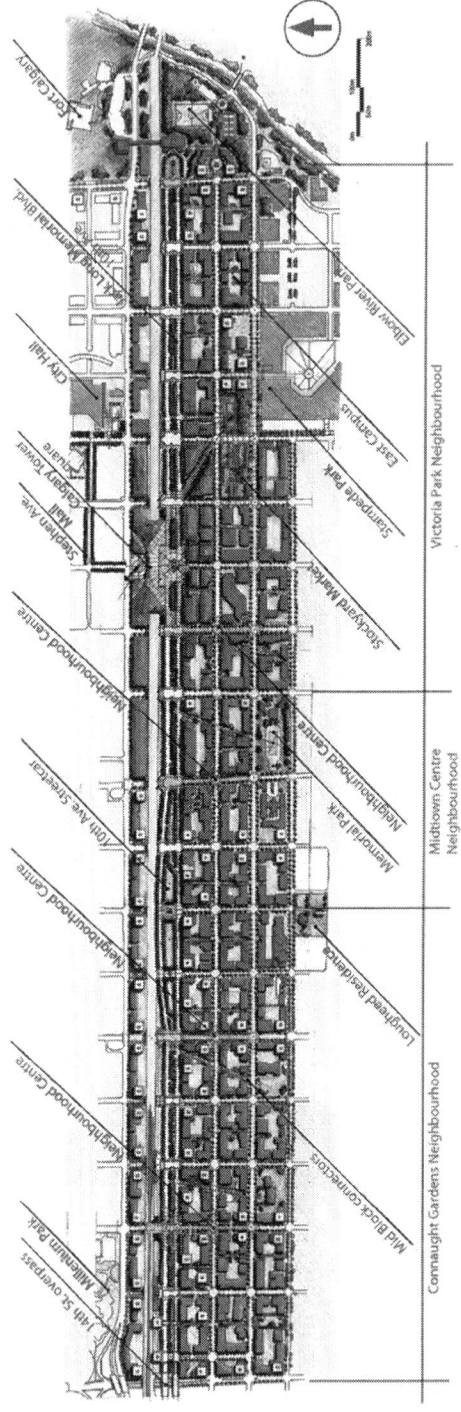

Figure 12.5. The Calgary Midtown Plan. This hundred-year plan defines detailed form and spatial qualities of the area immediately south of the downtown core area, also known as part of the Beltline area. (Drawing by Don Wuori.)

Using the Mawson Plan as inspiration, the city of Calgary's Downtown and Inner City Planning Section wanted to undertake a hundred-year urban design strategy for a large area of Calgary's inner city, known as Midtown. Just south of the main downtown commercial core, Midtown is one of Calgary's oldest areas. It encompasses an eclectic mix of uses and buildings, from heritage warehouses to modern offices and funky retail stores and restaurants. Midtown has immense potential over the long term to become one of Calgary's most authentic urban districts, and the city needed to develop a vision to inspire the development of a truly great urban area (fig. 12.6).

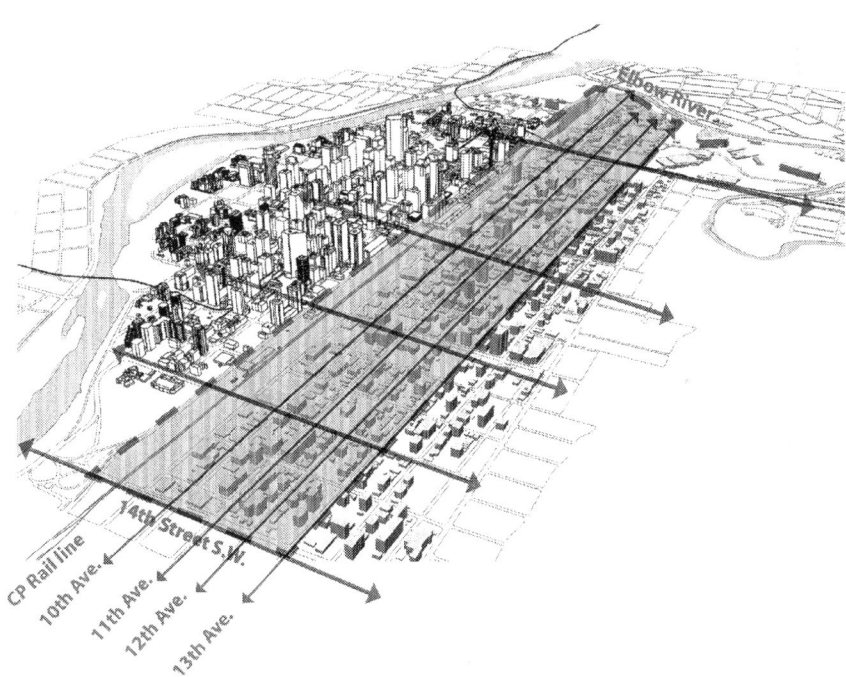

Figure 12.6. Calgary Midtown location. The Midtown Plan consists of 400 acres (160 ha) bordering the south side of downtown Calgary. (Model by Xia Zhang and graphics by Dolores Altin.)

Midtown: An Urban Design Strategy for Midtown Calgary is a landmark urban design document in Canada.[6] Like the Mawson Plan, it is farsighted and reaches out one hundred years. It provides a comprehensive hundred-year vision for a 400-acre (160-ha) section of land bordering the southern edge of downtown that incorporates some of Calgary's most important heritage landmarks (fig. 12.7). The plan includes not only physical urban design but also neighborhood planning, land economics, demographics, and transportation planning/engineering. This comprehensive plan was developed by an interdisciplinary team that brought the necessary expertise to the project. The planning process incorporated a design and planning charrette that involved the major stakeholders, including among them business, community, heritage, and revitalization interests.

The Midtown Plan is concise and well illustrated to inspire the various stakeholders to embrace parts, if not all, of the possibilities it presents. The fifty-five-page document is meant to inspire the potential urban fabric when the full spectrum of opportunities is harnessed in a large inner-city area. The plan is also practical. It proposes an implementation framework that outlines the next steps for each of the ten main urban design features. These ten features can be implemented separately or together, depending on timing, support, and resources.

Figure 12.7. Typical local commercial street, Calgary Midtown, Alberta. This perspective features retail uses on the first floor and residential uses above with a wide sidewalk, including street trees, benches, planting, displays, and convenient curbside parking—reflecting a highly animated and attractive pedestrian environment that is also friendly to bicycles. (Drawing by Calum Srigley.)

Ten features of the Midtown vision

The Midtown Plan consists of ten features that provide separate visions in themselves (fig. 12.8). These ten vision elements collectively define Midtown's future. Each of these features also provides flexibility, as they can be implemented as separate projects or together. Further work is required to establish their detailed feasibility.

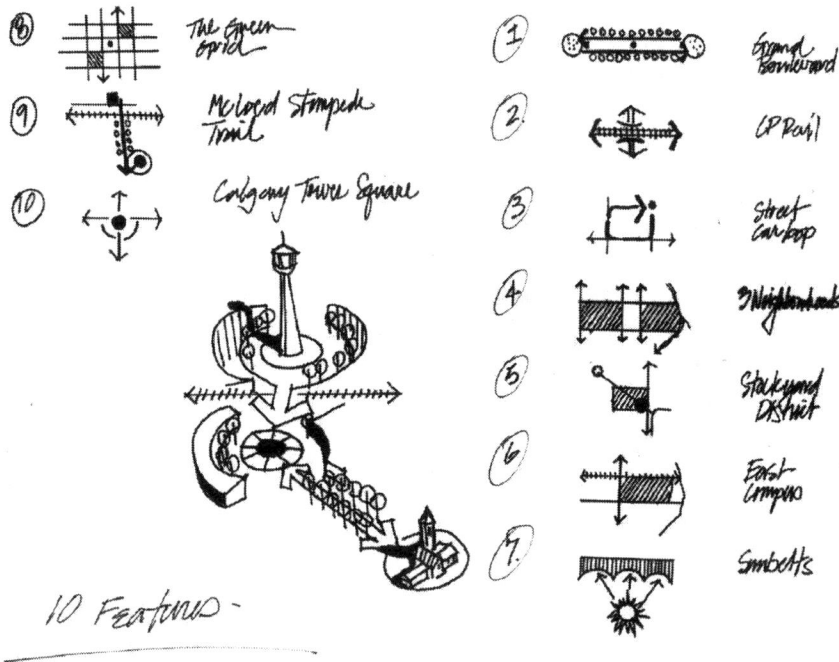

Figure 12.8. The ten features of the Midtown vision, Calgary, Alberta.
This early sketch of icons represents principal features of the Midtown Plan.

- *Grand boulevard.* Tenth Avenue will be transformed into a grand street with a central boulevard (fig. 12.9) at a scale similar to Commonwealth Avenue in Boston, linking adjacent neighborhoods and creating an urban greenway connector from Millennium Park on the Bow River to Stampede Park on the Elbow River.

A

B

Figure 12.9. Grand boulevard proposed for Tenth Avenue, Calgary Midtown, Alberta. Before (A) and after (B) images reveal the potential for creating an "emerald necklace" trail loop around Calgary's downtown that connects the Elbow River and Bow River trail systems via Tenth Avenue while still accommodating vehicular traffic. (Drawing by Alfonso Testada and photo by Calum Srigley.)

- *CP Railway viaduct.* Calgary was built on the railway, and the central concept of this plan assumes that the Canadian Pacific Railway corridor will continue as a transportation corridor in the long term (fig. 12.10). As part of this long-term commitment, consideration for improving the bridges and passageways over and under are described in this plan.

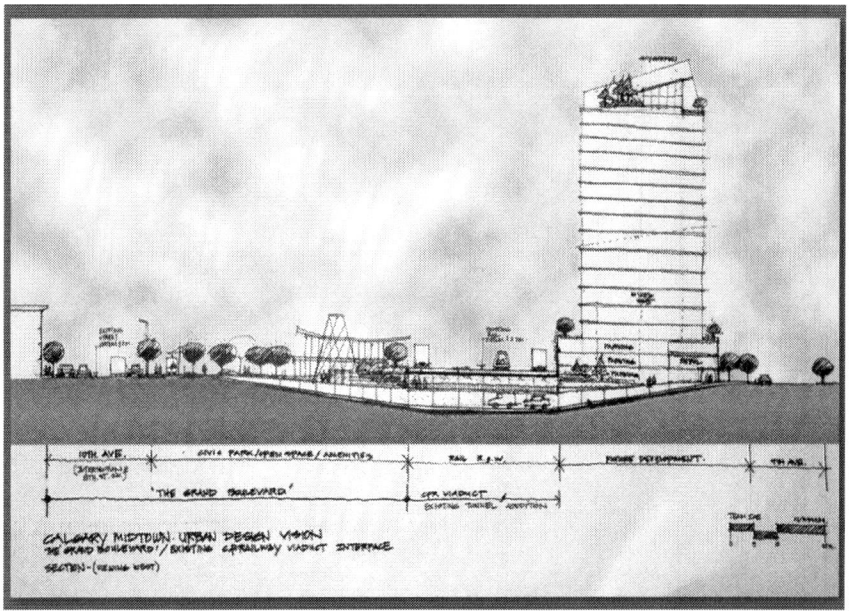

Figure 12.10. Proposed elevated CP Railway viaduct interface, Calgary Midtown, Alberta. Improvements to the CP Railway underpasses will better connect the downtown core area and Midtown. (Drawing by Don Wuori.)

- *Streetcar loop.* The grand boulevard proposed for Tenth Avenue will also accommodate a streetcar on its right-of-way that could be part of an "Inner Loop" for the downtown.
- *Three Midtown neighborhoods.* Three distinct neighborhoods emerge from the existing patterns of uses and character of Midtown (fig. 12.11). Each is grounded in its historical roots and builds on emerging land use patterns. The western neighborhood of Connaught Gardens will continue to have a residential

emphasis; the central neighborhood of Midtown Centre will focus on contemporary commercial development at its core with surrounding residential uses (fig. 12.12); and the eastern Victoria Park neighborhood will mix commercial and entertainment with residential support uses.

| Connaught Gardens Neighbourhood | Midtown Centre Neighbourhood | Victoria Park Neighbourhood |

These three Neighbourhoods will have distinct characteristics with emphasis on different activities:

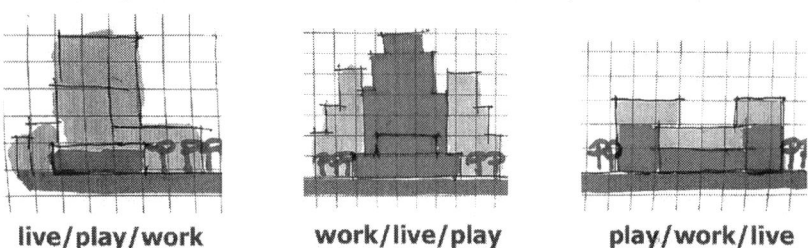

| live/play/work | work/live/play | play/work/live |

Figure 12.11. The proposed three neighborhoods, Calgary Midtown, Alberta. Each of these neighborhoods will have a different combination of residential and commercial land uses.

Figure 12.12. Midtown Centre neighborhood (left) and potential of infill office and residential (right). These sketches of the central neighborhood reflect a work, live, and play emphasis. (Drawing and photography by Calum Srigley.)

- *Stockyard District.* A commercial retail and entertainment zone will be encouraged, adjoining the northwest corner of Stampede Park (Fig. 12.13). The Stockyard District will complement the growing needs of Stampede Park and provide necessary shopping and entertainment for Victoria Park residents.

Figure 12.13. The proposed Stockyard District (left) before and (right) after improvements, Calgary Midtown, Alberta. The Stockyard District provides an entertainment and shopping zone adjoining Stampede Park. (Drawing by Calum Srigley.)

- *East Campus.* Education and business campuses will be encouraged in the Victoria Park area above Stampede Park, as an extension of planned facilities in Stampede Park. The education facilities will infill into the historic building fabric of the area and enhance pedestrian activity, while the business campus will be on the former Canadian Pacific Railway yards.
- *Sunbelts.* Building form and orientation will be an important element in maximizing sun during the winter months (fig. 12.14). A mix of low-, medium-, and high-rise buildings has been carefully placed to maximize sunlight during winter months in the parks, open spaces, and streets.

THE WINTER SUNBELTS

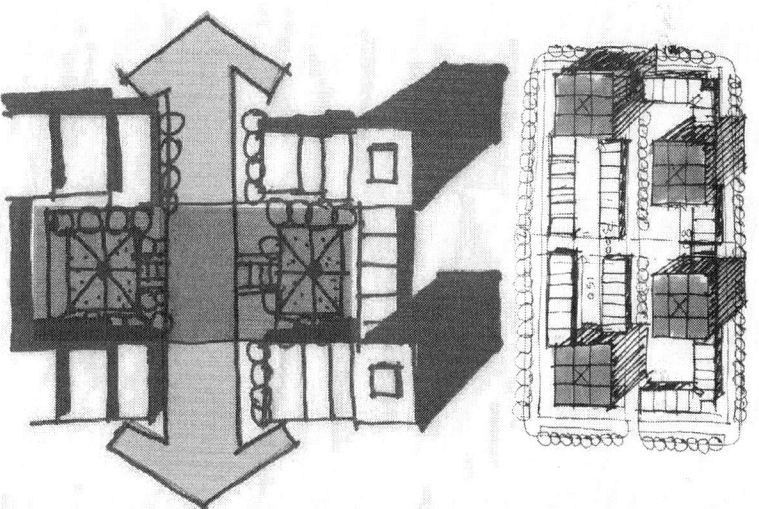

Figure 12.14. Interrelationships between "sun catchers," "green" courts, and connected public realm, Calgary Midtown, Alberta. The sun catchers are south facing courtyards and plazas that are connected along the street. (Drawing by Frank Ducote.)

- *Green grid.* Historic parks and open spaces, such as Lougheed House, Central Memorial Park, and Carl Safran Centre, form a strong foundation to extend a grid of urban street greenways north–south and east–west that will be attractive and complemented by new park additions.

- *Macleod Stampede Trail.* A ceremonial route connecting Olympic Park Plaza in the downtown and Stampede Park in Midtown will be an important pedestrian and celebration route of the future. A generous double-treed boulevard on the east side is envisioned to connect the downtown with Stampede Park.
- *Calgary Tower Square.* The hub of Calgary's downtown may be transformed over time by a pedestrian bridge and square that spills out south to the Midtown area and the Stockyard entertainment district. The Calgary Tower will truly be a central point, connecting the downtown to Midtown.

The Midtown Plan incorporates all three legs of sustainability—social, ecological, and economic—to frame the future of the proposed three residential neighborhoods in the area, bringing nearly 30,000 residents to the border of downtown. Together these new neighborhoods complement and enhance the bordering communities and downtown.

The sustainable features of the plan include enhancing public transit, conserving heritage assets in the area, and creating a grand boulevard along Tenth Avenue that would have multiple uses as a recreation connector, as well as a cultural spine. The proposed building forms and street designs would maximize light to the streets and reduce energy use. The proposed "green grid" would expand the number of parks and pedestrian walkways in the neighborhoods. Finally, the element of lifelong learning as part of sustainability would be introduced in the East Victoria neighborhood in the form of an "East Campus" to complement plans for the Stampede Park grounds.

These sustainable features and the three neighborhood integrated land use strategies (mixed uses and multiple uses) collectively form a complete sustainable community where residents can live, play, learn, and work close by. In working on the Midtown Plan, the value of planning out one hundred years was made evident. It allowed breathing space to think of possibilities that would seem impractical in the typical twenty-year planning horizon. Some of the "big ideas" inspire further thinking and planning policy.

Case study: Cooperation for a new community, Vladivostok, Russia

Innovative and sustainable urban design relies on cooperation among federal, regional, and local authorities. In this area, the transfer of knowledge helps conventional urban design and planning transform into new and varied urban forms, social programs, and land uses. Both cooperation and the transfer of knowledge came into play in the case of a new-community plan for Sunnyville, in the far east of Russia.

Canada Mortgage and Housing Corporation (CMHC) committed to transferring knowledge and technologies to Russia through an agreement between the Russian Federation and the Canadian federal government. This story of cooperation and knowledge transfer started at the federal government level in September 2010. The CMHC sponsored the MVH Urban Planning & Design team trip to Russia to help in a cooperative planning process between the Russian Housing Development Foundation (RHDF) and the regional and local governments in Vladivostok, Russia. The focus of this Russian housing program is to develop new affordable social housing in Russia.

The RHDF owns approximately 988 acres (400 ha) of land 5 miles (8 km) from the international airport and 16 miles (26 km) from downtown Vladivostok but still within the city limits, the proposed site of Sunnyville. Vladivostok is located in the far east of Russia. It has a population of nearly 600,000 people and is home to the Russian Pacific Fleet. The city's strategic location near the border of China, just two hours by air to Seoul, Korea, and Tokyo, Japan, makes it the eastern gateway to Russia.

Our team used a series of workshops and discussions in Vladivostok to demonstrate the value of cooperative planning and design methods.[7] On-site discussions with senior RHDF officials, the vice governor of the Primorsky region and the vice mayor of Vladivostok created the basis for the development concept. A further three days of presentations at the local and regional level refined the concept plan for the Sunnyville site supported by site analysis and a complete community development approach.

The Sunnyville site is surrounded by scenic rolling hills similar to those of Vermont in the United States. These forested hills frame dramatic views of the Amurskiy Gulf. The site itself, of open fields and forested landscapes, is punctuated and bisected by streams. The development concept conserves the forested areas and streams and develops the open areas, preserving the natural areas as much as possible and creating a foundation for a healthy and ecologically sensitive community.

The idea of the "complete community" also emerged from the discussions, a community allowing the majority of residents to live, work, and play close by. Basic services are located within a five-minute walk of every residence. This complete community concept also includes compact urban form, a variety of housing types and tenures, transit orientation, local schools, recreational spaces, nature corridors, and local commercial and medical facilities. The major employment would be off-site in the Vladivostok region.

Four days after landing in Vladivostok, the MVH Urban Planning & Design team presented a preliminary development concept to the vice governor of the region and other senior government officials. The concept and illustrations were well received, and the vice governor envisioned that the final development plan would follow this concept.

Six months later MVH Urban Planning & Design received an invitation from Oleg Drozdov, president of the Dalta-Vostok-1 Corporation, to complete the master plan for the site. Dalta-Vostok-1 had won the bid to develop the lands from the RHDF. We worked closely with Mr. Drozdov and Dalta staff to develop the first new community of this scale in the far east of Russia. This master plan is unique in a region where sprawling suburban development is the norm and traffic jams are the common result, a situation not dissimilar to many regions throughout the world.

Sunnyville, as it became known, is a departure from other developments, as it is planned as a complete community with nine schools and sports fields, two commercial centers, a civic center, medical facilities, recreational trails, and a variety of housing types from single-family housing to high-rise apartments (fig. 12.15). We worked with Dalta staff to ensure our master plan standards met the Russian regulations in setbacks, road configurations, and building orientation, height, and massing. The design team created a variety of streets (fig. 12.16), three types of architecture for low-rise and high-rise apartment buildings, flex-lots that could be converted to different housing, and a "European superblock" model that could be adapted to a number of configurations, with buildings set close to the street and interior secure courtyards (fig. 12.17). A complementary green network of parks and open spaces creates a structure for healthy lifestyle options and places where children could safely walk to school and play close to home. The stream corridors are natural areas with trails that connect throughout Sunnyville. Pedestrian-friendly streets offer places to meet, walk, and sit. A grand central park offers seating, outdoor performance areas, playgrounds, and water features. Commercial uses and day care on the first floor of apartment buildings create convenient shopping and services close to residents (fig. 12.18).

NOTE:

(1) The Master Plan features are conceptual and locations of roads and limits of development should be refined during detailed design in order to conform to Russian norms and engineering requirements.

(2) Avoid development on steep slopes next to streams, within flood plain and within environmental corridors.

(3) Ensure that the structural members of the lowest building floor are at least 0.5 m above the 1:200 year flood level. A flood analysis is required to define this level.

200m

1 EXISTING SEWAGE DISPOSAL PLANT, TO BE ABANDONED	9 COMMERCIAL / RETAIL	17 TOURIST ZONE OR FUTURE LOW RISE APARTMENT
2 SURFACE PARKING	10 GRAND BOULEVARD & PARK	18 TOWN HOUSE OR ROW HOUSE (RM1)
3 HIGH RISE APARTMENT (RM3)	11 DALTA VOSTOK HEADQUARTERS	19 SINGLE FAMILY HOUSES (COTTAGE) (SF1, SF2, SF3)
4 UTILITY AREA ON HILLSIDE	12 SCHOOL AND SPORTS FIELDS	20 WATER RESERVOIR SITE (IF REQUIRED)
5 ACCESS HIGHWAY TO M60	13 POLYCLINIC	21 ELECTRICAL CORRIDOR USED FOR GARDEN PLOTS, PLANT NURSERY AND PUBLIC SPACE
6 HIGHWAY TO RESORT AREA	14 TRANSIT CENTRE	22 BURIAL GROUND CONSERVATION AREA
7 ENVIRONMENTAL PRESERVATION CORRIDOR AROUND STREAMS	15 CIVIC CENTRE	
8 HAZARD CORRIDOR AROUND STEEP SLOPES BESIDE STREAMS	16 LOW RISE APARTMENT (RM2)	

Figure 12.15. Sunnyville land use concept plan. This plan has a diversity of housing types, as well as different local shops, support services, a child day care, and schools within a convenient five-minute walk for residents. (Drawing by Don Wuori and graphics by Paul Turje.)

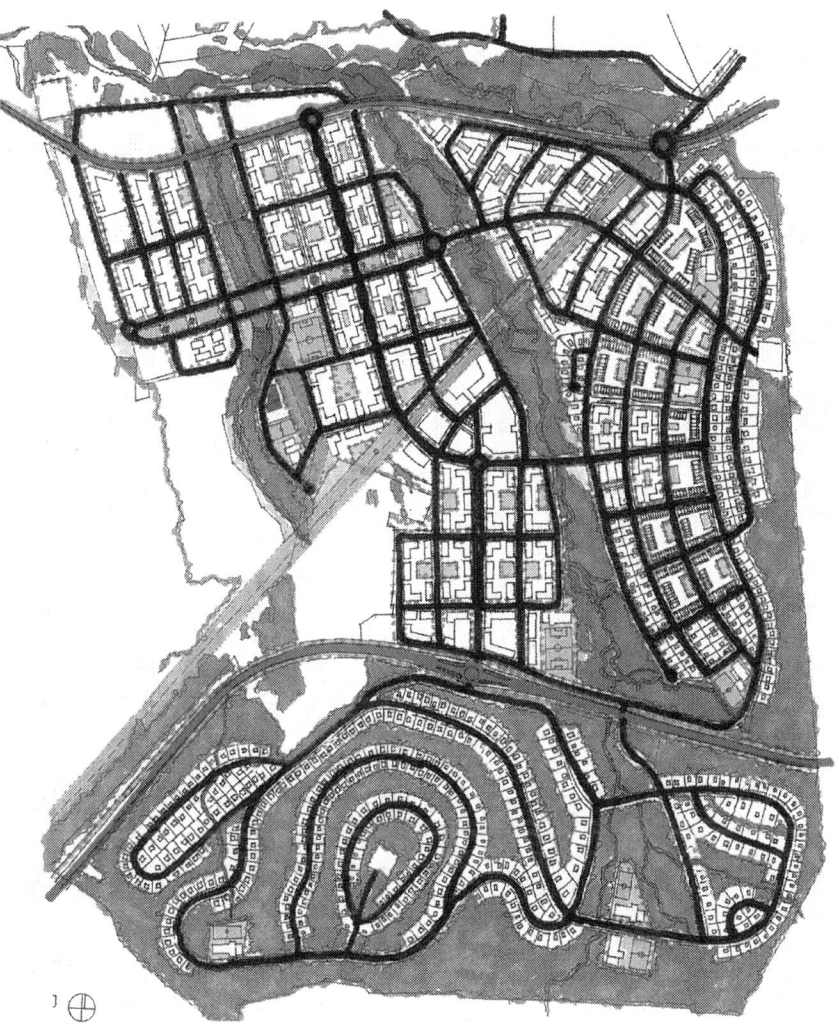

Figure 12.16. Sunnyville street network. A variety of local street types required specific design standards to fit the local Russian context. (Drawings by Don Wuori.)

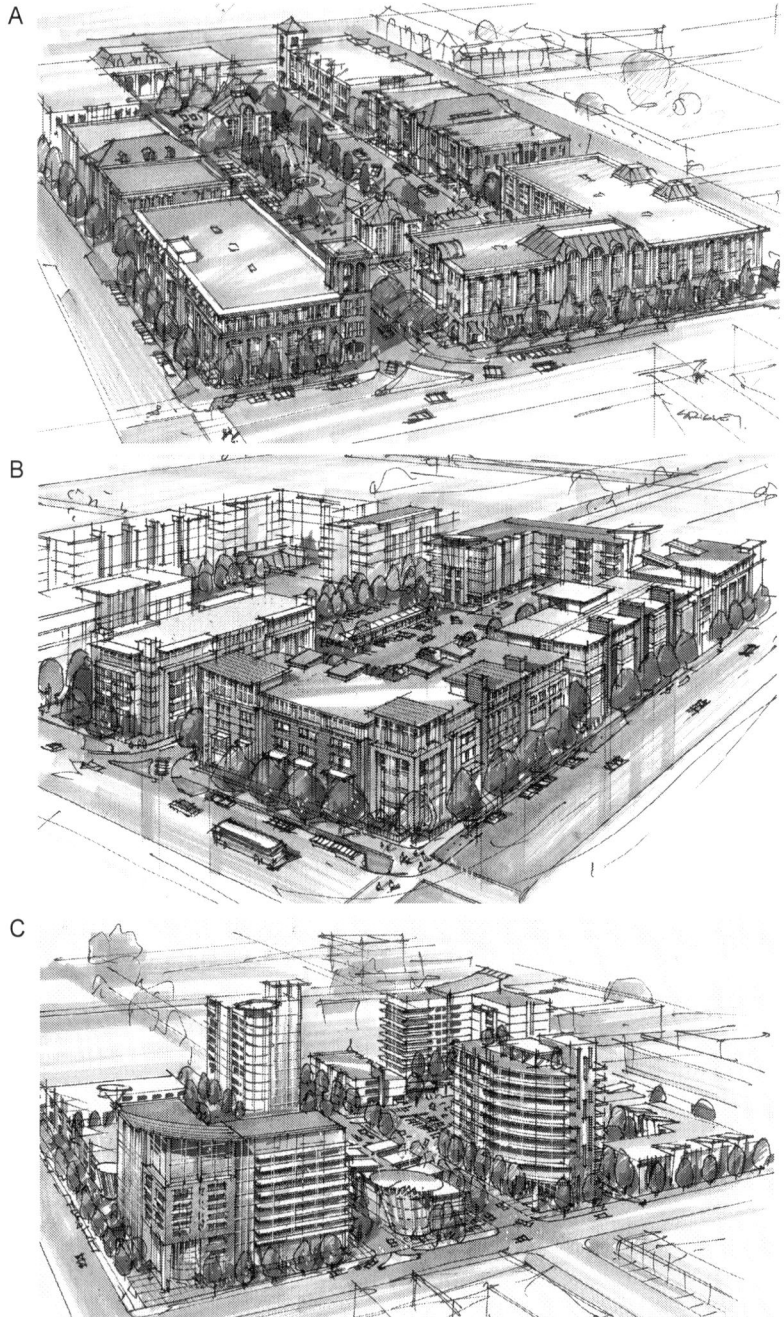

Figure 12.17. Sunnyville super-block architectural options. Three architectural character options are: (A) classic, (B) contemporary, and (C) high-tech. (Drawing by Calum Srigley.)

Figure 12.18. Sunnyville 3-D model. The three-dimensional model shows the form and massing of the proposed new community. (Model by Chris Erickson.)

The intensive design process resulted in the approval of the master plan on October 31, 2011, with an estimated population of 25,000 to 30,000 residents. Any language barriers during the process were bridged by professional translators. The process was exciting and demanding but very satisfying, as ideas evolved quickly into concepts and concept into plans. The translation of the design by Dalta corporation staff and consulting architects to Russian standards was truly amazing. Constant e-mail exchanges provided clarity to a constant stream of questions and challenges.

The final master plan follows the principles of the earlier concept plan, with further refinements and details added. Cooperation and knowledge transfer at the federal, regional, and local government levels resulted in an innovative process and plan with approval in a short time frame. The goals of each level of government were accomplished, and Sunnyville is starting construction in 2012. The MVH team will continue to support the detailed design and implementation of the project to ensure that the original master plan is implemented with the initial intentions (fig. 12.19).

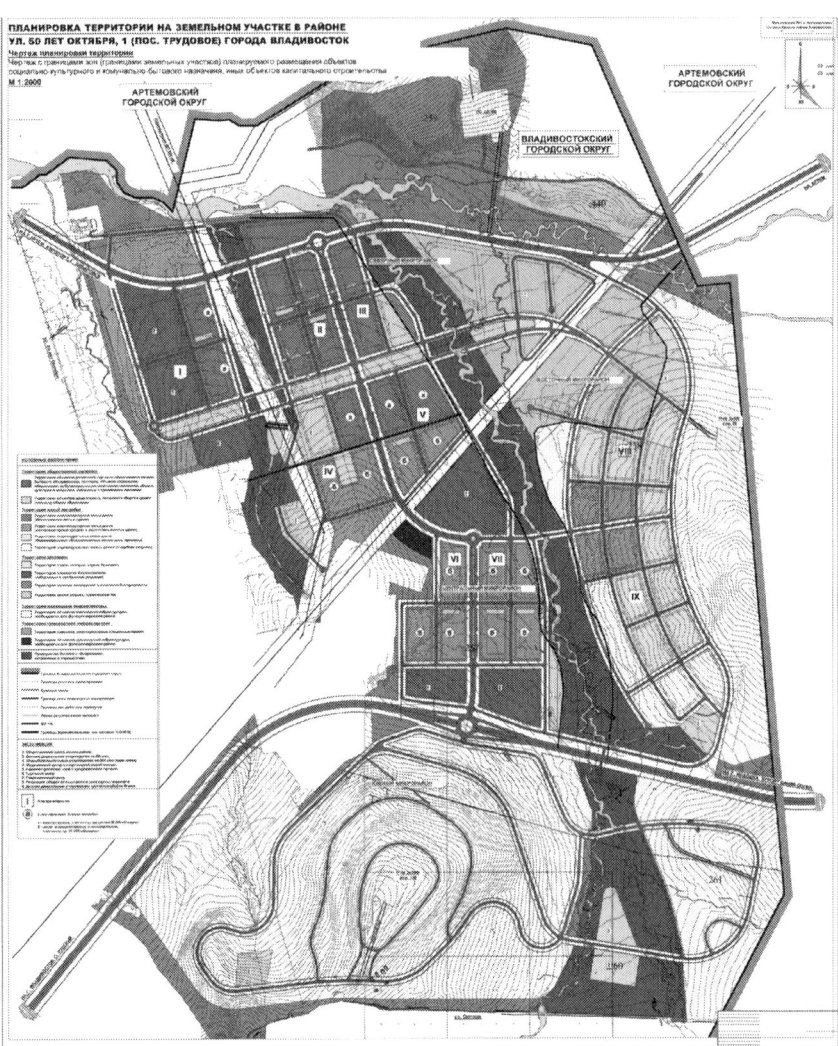

Figure 12.19. Sunnyville final land use plan. The approved land use plan follows very closely the earlier concept plans and is consistent with Russian regulations and policies. (Plan by Dalta Vostok – 1 Corp.)

Case study: Infill and redevelopment, Halifax, Nova Scotia

Fenwick Tower is a thirty-three-story residential building in Halifax, Nova Scotia, Canada. The building and site provide a very interesting case study in a downtown redevelopment in Halifax's South End.[8] Fenwick Tower, completed in 1971, is the highest building east of Montreal, at 321.5 feet (98 m). The property was purchased by Dalhousie University to help serve part of their student housing needs. In 2009, Templeton Properties acquired the property with the intention of improving the residential tower and infilling the balance of the site with other buildings and associated amenities.

A major contributor to the success of the Fenwick Tower redevelopment project was the comprehensive neighborhood participation process that started in September 2009 and culminated in the Halifax Regional Municipality (HRM) council approval in February 2011. The process not only provided valuable input to the form and character of the future redevelopment of the site but contributed valuable ideas for defining neighborhood needs and areas of improvement. The process involved more than ten local groups surrounding Dalhousie University. It is worthwhile to examine not only the content of the plans but the principles, rationale for additional density, community benefits, and sustainability features. This urban design plan is progressive in recognizing the place and context, inviting community input, providing sensitive urban form transitions, and shaping a comprehensive urban design plan that has the potential for significantly improving the surrounding neighborhood. Fenwick Place was renamed Fenwick Tower as a result of community feedback during the development application process.

The following elements informed the application by Templeton Properties to amend the Halifax Municipal Planning Strategy and Halifax Peninsula Land Use Bylaw. They also inform the detailed development agreement that will follow the development application process.

Sustainable and Smart Growth development principles

- *Existing site redevelopment and enhancement.* Development focuses on an existing site in Halifax that has further redevelopment and enhancement potential.

- *Efficient infrastructure and services use.* Development uses existing infrastructure and services that create cost efficiencies for the city, community, and developer.

- *Pedestrian orientation.* Development emphasizes nonmotorized transportation and is located within a five-minute walking distance of basic services.

- *Compact and responsive to local needs.* Development emphasizes compact development form and provides new uses that respond to local needs.

- *Affordability.* Development creates some more affordable units based on CMHC criteria and also creates more affordability through the diversity and choice of housing units provided.

- *Social and cultural improvements.* Improvements to the site include elements that improve the safety, cultural identity, and facilities for the neighborhood (fig. 12.20).

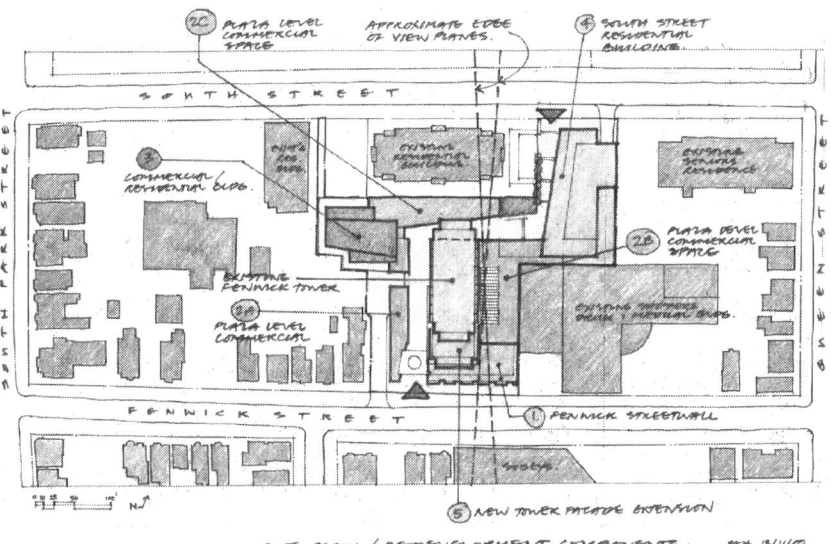

Figure 12.20. Context and site plan, Fenwick Place redevelopment, Halifax, Nova Scotia. The Fenwick Place site is set into one of the historic neighborhoods surrounding Dalhousie University. (Drawings by Al Endall and Calum Srigley.)

Rationale for additional density

The rationale for additional density is based on the community consultation process, a form-based development approach, the efficient use of the site, and additional community amenities.

1. *Community process result.* The additional density emerged from discussions with the community that focused on form, character, and quality of design. The focus was on neighborhood improvements and needs as part of the redevelopment of the site. The development form and associated density evolved out of these discussions.

2. *Form-based approach.* The HRM Downtown Plan is moving toward a richer form-based zoning approach, which emphasizes form and character, as well as neighborhood fit, rather than density limits and land use. The award-winning EcoDensity approach by the city of Vancouver strives to use a similar approach, emphasizing the need to use existing sites more efficiently and consider form-sensitive infill projects to intensify the city where appropriate and feasible. This is the same approach Templeton Properties is taking with the Fenwick site redevelopment.

This sensitive infill building form approach is reflected in

- four-story town houses along Fenwick Street that match the form of Fenwick Street and continue the street wall along the front of the site (fig. 12.21);
- two-story "mews" buildings that line the pedestrian mews through the site—reinforcing and animating the pedestrian scale with inviting commercial retail uses;
- the eight-story West Tower and nine-story South Street Tower, which integrate well with the existing James Place form on South Street (fig. 12.22); and
- enhancements to the main Fenwick Tower that include cladding improvements, internal enhancements, and a slight addition to the front facade to integrate an additional code-compliant stairwell and additional units (fig. 12.23).

The result of this form-based approach is a richer site redevelopment plan that not only emphasizes neighborhood improvements in the form of appropriate building forms but also adds pedestrian connections, public art, community-based businesses, and a meeting place for the community as paramount to measuring its success.

Figure 12.21. Urban design form and principles along Fenwick Street, Fenwick Place redevelopment, Halifax, Nova Scotia. Urban form additions to improve the neighborhood included bringing neighborhood-scale housing to the street front, adding amenities, and improving the streetscape. (Drawings by Al Endall and Calum Srigley.)

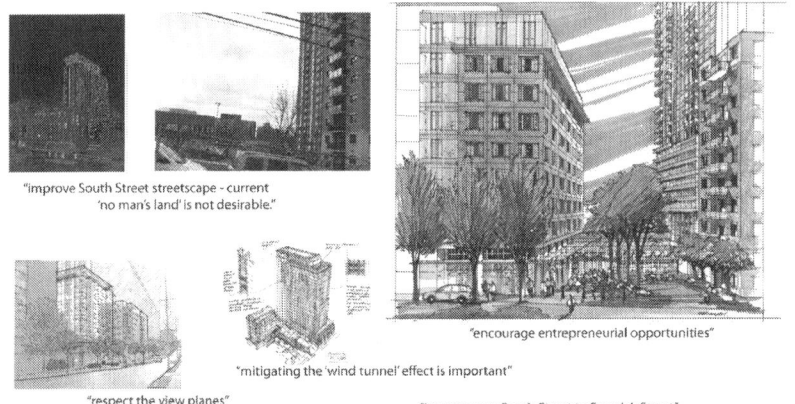

Figure 12.22. Urban design form and principles along South Street, Fenwick Place redevelopment, Halifax, Nova Scotia. Urban design principles set the guiding rules for development. (Drawings by Al Endall and Calum Srigley.)

Figure 12.23. Tower enhancement, Fenwick Place redevelopment, Halifax, Nova Scotia. The tower will be slightly expanded in the front, interiors improved, and the exterior surface redone to enhance its look and function. (Drawing by Calum Srigley.)

3. *Efficient use of site.* The redevelopment plan is currently grossly underutilized, with less than half the site used for development and the balance an eyesore of surface parking or vacant land. The proposal spreads additional density throughout the site with two additional buildings, adding more than half the additional density in a way that fits into the adjacent building fabric and adding neighborhood amenities at the same time. The additional commercial space is primarily lined along the proposed pedestrian mews corridor that is a public access through the site and has a local support service function.

4. *Additional community amenities.* The additional community amenities are a response to the community consultation process, which emphasized the need to improve the neighborhood in terms of streetscape, pedestrian access, and meeting places on and through the site; pedestrian orientation, safety, and security; "greenness" of the site; local retail and office uses; public art and

enhancements; and affordability (benefits further described in the next section; fig. 12.24).

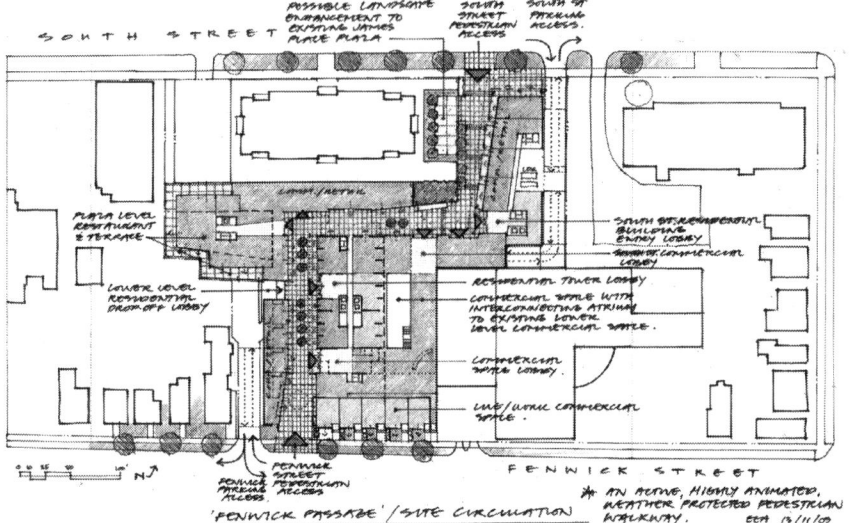

Figure 12.24. Site circulation and pedestrian/vehicular access, Fenwick Place redevelopment, Halifax, Nova Scotia. An interior pedestrian link through the site provides commercial frontage, public art, and rich landscaping for local residents. (Drawing by Al Endall.)

Community benefits

The benefits given to the community through site redevelopment are important in measuring the "net community gain" created by the development. The following is a list of items that evolved as a result of the comprehensive community dialogue.

Choice and diversity of housing

- Ten percent of new units will be "affordable" in accordance with CMHC standards.
- A combination of rental and ownership units will be provided.
- Various unit sizes from bachelor to two bedrooms will be provided.
- The unit orientation and improvements will expand the student emphasis to include young professionals.

Pedestrian-oriented redevelopment

- Fifty underground parking stalls will be dedicated for neighborhood parking use, taking some street parking off the streets in winter and providing a necessary local service.
- Only 10 percent of the existing underground parking stalls are used in the existing Fenwick Tower, and new development parking will be limited, with a pedestrian and bicycle emphasis.
- Bicycle parking will be expanded and provided at various points in the development.
- A car-sharing program will be considered in the redevelopment, with the provision of two car-share stalls, expanding the current nine dedicated locations in Halifax.
- The parking garage will be upgraded and expanded for safety, security, and accessibility, including access to South Street—dispersing the traffic and taking pressure off of Fenwick Street.

Improved streetscape, open space network, and community meeting space

- A through-block pedestrian mews will be provided that connects Fenwick Street and South Street, with appropriate lighting, seating, and a host of locally based retail shops and services focused along the mews for safety and vitality.
- The pedestrian mews and other rooftop spaces will be landscaped to bring plants, flowers, and small trees into the site.
- A number of public art pieces will be placed along the pedestrian mews to animate the space, adding local identity, history, and cultural richness to the experience.
- The streetscape along Fenwick Street will be improved by street trees, a new sidewalk, and six town houses fronting on the street.

Cultural and social neighborhood meeting place

- A community meeting space will be available to neighborhood associations when necessary.

- Retail and office uses will favor local and appropriately scaled businesses (cafés, restaurants, professional offices, and other necessary services).
- The pedestrian mews will be an important "third place" in the neighborhood to hold special gatherings, festivals, and displays.

Sustainability features

The following is a summary of the sustainable features that will be part of site redevelopment and management.

- The Fenwick Tower retrofit is targeting a 50 percent reduction in energy use.
- New buildings will use LEED (Leadership in Energy and Environmental Design) as a reference for building construction and performance.
- The Fenwick Tower will use local materials where possible and appropriate.
- Materials recycling on-site will be carried out during the construction process and following construction.
- Pedestrian and bicycle orientation will continue on-site as part of redevelopment, with expanded car parking being limited, bicycle parking expanded, and fifty local parking stalls being provided to the neighborhood.
- A car-share program for two stalls will be considered on-site.
- Ten percent of new housing units will be affordable based on CMHC criteria.
- New commercial uses will be focused on providing necessary local services and providing for local businesses.
- Landscaping on-site will consider native plants that require less water and are more hardy.
- A number of public art installations will be coordinated to enhance and reflect local identity and culture on-site.
- Roofs will be landscaped, providing amenity space for residents and positive overlooks from adjoining units.

- Site remediation and repair in terms of landscaping and amenity improvement will be embraced in redevelopment.
- Social and public meeting places will be part of the "pedestrian mews" design through the site—encouraging special events, festivals, and community activities throughout the year (fig. 12.25).
- An interior space will be open for neighborhood association meetings to further the idea of community capacity building and stewardship after the project is completed.

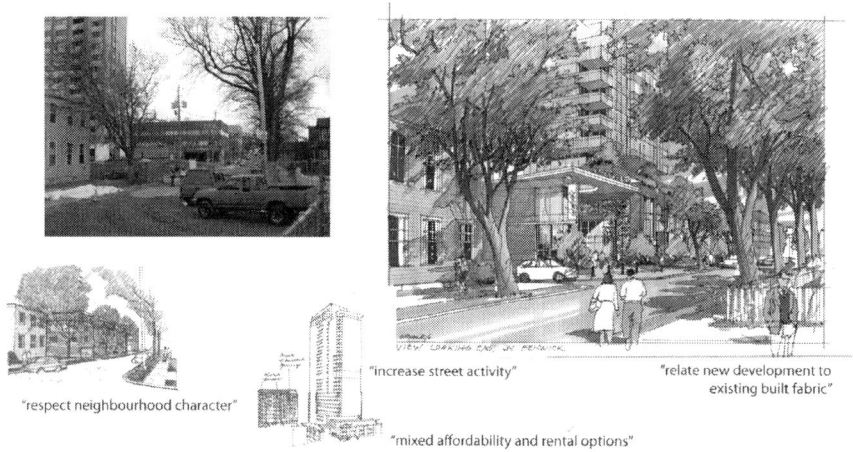

Figure 12.25. Site redevelopment sketch perspective from southwest, Fenwick Place redevelopment, Halifax, Nova Scotia. The redevelopment of the Fenwick Place site results in a revitalization of the street and the community. (Drawings by Al Endall and Calum Srigley.)

The Fenwick Place project represents a significant restoration of a parcel so it better fits into a historic Halifax neighborhood. It also represents a community-based process that brought real and valuable ideas and community needs to the discussion. Initial push-back and guarded comments transformed into supportive comments as the first concepts changed into site plans that reflected the conversations, values, and needs of the local neighborhood. Rather than being an uninvited addition to the Halifax community, the project was unanimously approved by the HRM council.

As we have seen in this chapter, urban core restoration is possible despite the negative trends in many American cities and cities around the world. Valuable lessons of long-term thinking in Chicago and Calgary, harnessed with active neighborhood-based participation as seen in Halifax, and federal/local cooperation in Vladivostok, Russia, can yield breakthrough ideas that bring renewal and spirit to neglected places or places needing redevelopment.

13
THE SUBURBS AND BEYOND

We have clearly institutionalized the art of low-density suburban sprawl. If American policymakers had deliberately set out to construct the most wasteful, inefficient, and land consumptive pattern of development possible, they could hardly have been more successful.

—Randall Arendt, *Rural by Design*

Much of urban design, not surprisingly, focuses on urban examples. Yet, as I have stated, the principles of sustainable urban design apply equally to communities that are not strictly "urban." This chapter looks at two such projects: an example of suburban retrofit in the city of Red Deer in south-central Alberta, Canada, and a rural edge cluster development some 90 miles (145 km) north, in Strathcona County, east of the city of Edmonton. These new suburban edge developments require more compact urban forms, as well as mixed land uses, to overcome the urban sprawl patterns seen everywhere in the world but especially in North America. The case studies in this chapter introduce how to retrofit the suburbs and cluster development to establish the new "urban" in suburbia that more reflects the so-called complete community goals of live, work, and play close by. The results: healthier and more prosperous communities with less reliance on the car and more focus on nonvehicular transport. As we will see, this change certainly is a challenge in these Alberta communities, where, like in Texas, the economy thrives on the oil industries and residents are accustomed to oversized vehicles and long drives.

Suburban retrofit

Suburban retrofit means redeveloping or infilling existing underutilized portions of our suburbs. We have to heal the urban sprawl that took fifty years to create. The traditional suburb is made for sleeping only—single land uses; jobs, commerce, and cultural activities are elsewhere.

What do we want this retrofitted suburb to look and feel like? We want less need for the car and fewer cars. The result is a safer and quieter neighborhood. We want more convenient and comfortable transit—buses and other modes of mass transportation that are on time, close to home, and safe. We want more time to walk and become healthier in a healthier environment. We want more time to get to know our neighbors and enjoy our community. Like the residents in many small towns, we want each person to exchange greetings with everyone they pass on the street. This is a place where a corner store, café, and other basic services are located within a five-minute walk of your house. In essence, we aim to build a community where people care about one another.

The suburbs around our existing cities offer some of the greatest opportunities for redevelopment into complete communities. They have existing built infrastructure of roads, water, sanitary sewers, and services relatively close by. School sites, fire protection services, and police services are already in place. Maybe most importantly, the relatively low densities and aging building stock offer redevelopment potential at higher densities. With our aging population, the need for a more diverse building type and tenure is growing. The single-family house in the suburbs does not match the growing singles population, from younger adults to seniors. These people need more affordable and convenient alternative housing types, including townhomes, row houses, duplexes, and a variety of apartments that offer rental and ownership options.

These higher-density suburban retrofit developments need to be located close to services and transit, which reduces car use and eventually can decrease car ownership completely. Car-share programs eliminate the need for a car or at least the second car. Car-free families are becoming more normal, especially for urban dwellers. Less car ownership has always been the norm in cities like New York and London, where transit is convenient and car ownership is more expensive. The cost of the car, estimated at $8,000 to $10,000 per year, can be used on other, more important things.

With added transit connections in suburban redevelopment, parking requirements can be reduced and parking lots replaced with green space and buildings. This more efficient use of land can reduce service costs per person and decrease the need for tax increases. More community amenities and facilities can come with this retrofit of the suburbs. Increased amenities and services *must* accompany increased density. Otherwise, there is an increased use and demand for services without the corresponding proportionate increase in services.

The word "density" in most neighborhoods is associated with lower residential values, as well as increased traffic, noise, and crime. Community support is difficult to develop for a concept that is perceived as having only negative effects on the local community. There is no easy answer, but if residents are genuinely engaged in the project early in the process, there can be an understanding of what amenities they require in terms of potential community benefits.

Education and information on successful local projects help inform the process. The sustainable urban design plan and the associated policies, guidelines, and regulations are important tools for building trust and support. I have developed a concept called "net community gain," which means that the community is better off after redevelopment than before. The community, along with the local government staff and the developer, can develop a list of benefits (that create community gain, not loss), which can be finalized in the development policies. The list of required community contributions by the developer becomes part of the development agreement to better ensure compliance.

Case study: Increasing density, Red Deer, Alberta

The purpose of this case study is to reexamine an existing underutilized suburban development and retrofit it for higher and more compact densities.[1] These underutilized areas should provide a diversity of housing types and businesses, supply an integrated and rich variety of recreation and mobility opportunities beyond the car, and rebuild complete communities where residents can work, play, and learn within walking distance or a local bus shuttle of their residence. MVH Urban Planning & Design was hired by Red Deer County to work with local landowners, businesses, residents, and developers to create an urban design plan, guidelines, and standards to realize this new development form.

Liberty Crossing represents an outstanding opportunity to build a residential community of up to 8,000 new residents on the edge of a well-established commercial area known as Gasoline Alley (fig. 13.1). The 1,000-acre (405-ha) site is located on the west side of Highway 2 in Red Deer County, on the southwest edge of the city of Red Deer, Alberta. Highway 2 is the main north-to-south highway in Alberta, and Red Deer sits about halfway (78 miles, or 125 km) between the city of Calgary and the city of Edmonton—the two major cities in the province.

Existing uses in Gasoline Alley include a Costco superstore, Staples office supplies store, and a host of other suburban restaurants, offices, car dealerships, and hotels. This development scenario is exactly the opposite of what happens in conventional development. The houses normally come first and the commercial services second, based on demand of the expanding residential population. In this situation, the excellent location on the edge of the city of Red Deer, combined with adjacent expanding employment opportunities and services, makes the site an excellent candidate for suburban retrofit. In other words, Liberty Crossing represents an opportunity to use existing infrastructure and services to upgrade and expand an existing community, versus creating a new community that requires a whole new infrastructure.

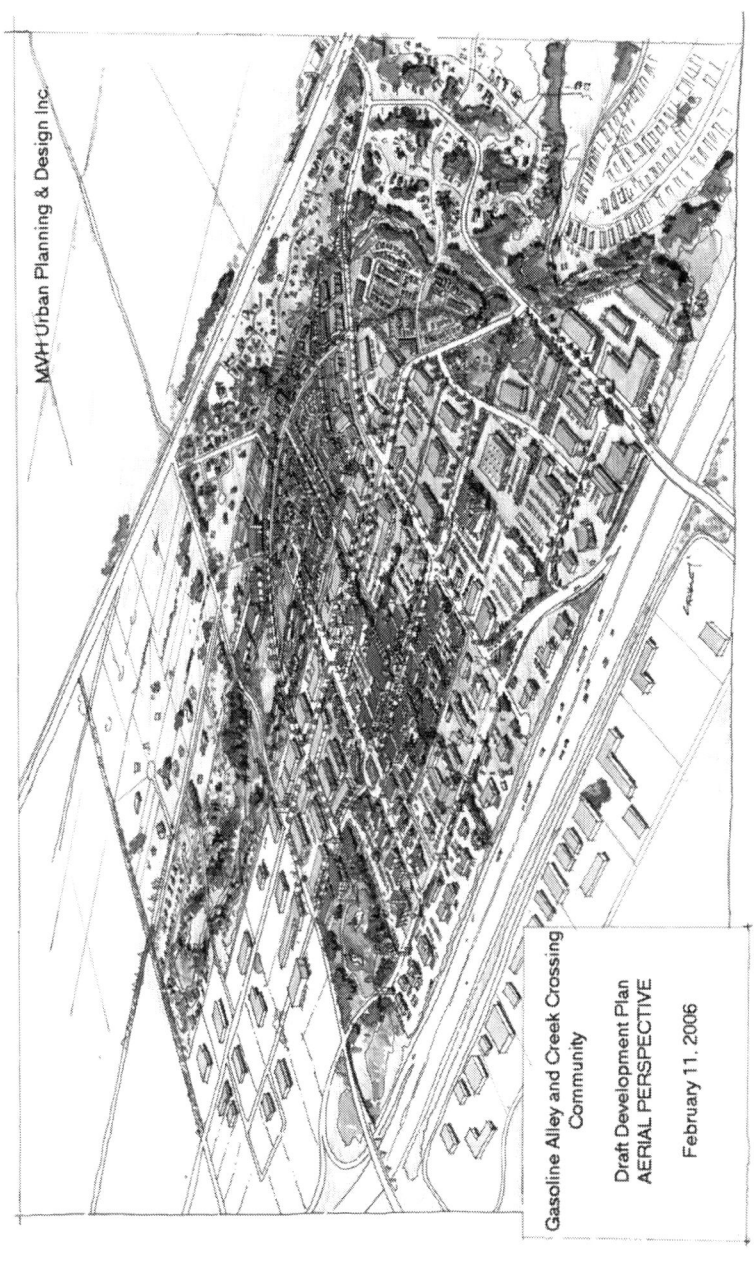

MVH Urban Planning & Design Inc.

Gasoline Alley and Creek Crossing
Community

Draft Development Plan
AERIAL PERSPECTIVE

February 11, 2006

Figure 13.1. Liberty Crossing at Gasoline Alley, Red Deer, Alberta. An aerial perspective sketch of full development potential illustrates existing commercial uses bordering Highway 2 in the foreground and a mix of commercial, light industrial, institutional, recreational, and residential uses extending toward Highway 2A in the background. (Drawing by Calum Srigley.)

Land ownership and land use patterns

Nine landowners control approximately 80 percent of the land at Liberty Crossing (fig. 13.2), which consists of a mix of commercial, industrial, and rural residential properties. Considering the total land area is approximately 1,000 net developable acres (405 ha) without roads, the nine landowners possibly represent up to 800 acres (324 ha). This large area sets the image, tempo, and quality of both development and redevelopment as Liberty Crossing grows.

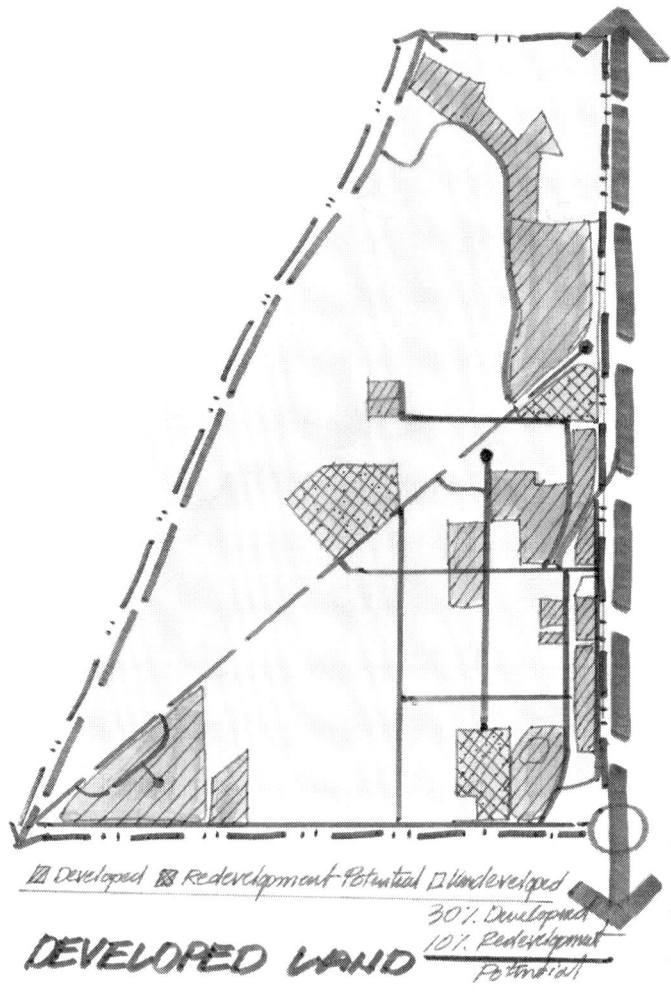

Developed Redevelopment-Potential Undeveloped
30% Developed
10% Redevelopment Potential
DEVELOPED LAND

Figure 13.2. Redevelopment potential, Liberty Crossing at Gasoline Alley, Red Deer, Alberta. Limited owners create significant redevelopment potential.

Development capacity

Determining the development capacity of the site is very important, as this analysis and subsequent planning should balance the market demand for the site with the environmental sensitivities. Gasoline Alley West lands have significant development potential because of their strategic location, readily available developable land, and convenient servicing connections. It is helpful to consider the different types of land, with varying development potential to provide a balance of land uses and opportunities.

Areas with high development potential (no major constraints)
These sites have immediate high development potential, as they are vacant or significantly underutilized, like the site in the southern portion of Gasoline Alley West. At the same time, there are no significant environmental limitations, such as wetlands or the Waskasoo Creek and associated hundred-year floodplain area. Most of these sites have road access and services to the fronts of the properties.

Areas with low to medium development potential (some constraints)
These sites are located adjacent to but outside the Waskasoo Creek hundred-year floodplain and require sensitive cluster development due to the tree canopy and terrain. The section west of the central area also has some wetland sensitivities and therefore could have low to medium development potential pending further investigations. The repair/salvage yard in the northeast corner of Gasoline Alley West is a potential redevelopment site but requires relocation before redevelopment can occur.

Areas with low development potential (major constraints)
These areas are already developed or have high environmental sensitivities, such as the areas in the southwest corner wetland and the southeast Memorial Park, as well as the hundred-year floodplain areas along Waskasoo Creek.

Specific sustainable and smart strategies

This Liberty Crossing plan details strategies that apply the broader-based Municipal Development Plan and Area Structure Plan policies, principles, and goals to the Gasoline Alley West site.

- *Respect existing uses.* Support the retention of existing uses in the transformation so that they can grow and prosper in cooperation with the new residential and support commercial uses (fig. 13.3).

Figure 13.3. Proposed high street, Liberty Crossing at Gasoline Alley, Red Deer, Alberta. The heart of the commercial area is envisioned as having a variety of retail shops and community gathering places. (Drawing by Calum Srigley.)

- *Create a complete neighborhood.* Build a compact and efficient neighborhood where residents and businesses can live, work, shop, and play.

- *Minimize impacts of redevelopment.* Respect the adjoining lands in sensitive redevelopment that contributes green space and amenities while providing appropriate built form.
- *Connect to context.* Encourage a variety of transportation networks with reduced emphasis on the automobile (greenways, bike routes, transit, and facilities), and improve connections to the Waskasoo Trail Network, the city of Red Deer, and adjoining areas.
- *Integrate housing diversity and innovation.* Encourage the provision of a variety of housing units to provide more housing choice, while supporting new types of housing (Creekside Village multiunit residences and home businesses) that expand the possibilities of home ownership, life-cycle housing, and affordability.
- *Retain rural agriculture character.* Develop a strategy that provides for plentiful open space and guidelines that reflect the rural agricultural roots of the area and county.
- *Promote adaptive reuse.* Encourage the adaptive reuse of the Ledcor building as a community asset, and use the structure as a basis for a car museum, view park, and community activities.
- *Maximize environmental sensitivity.* Conserve and expand the local pond and wetland system as part of a natural and local habitat and storm water project; link this green infrastructure network with the Waskasoo Creek trail and environmental system.
- *Increase green space and the quality of the streetscape.* Improve the streetscapes using street furniture and tree/shrub planting, taking care that the planting does not obscure visibility of and access to the adjoining businesses.
- *Provide safe and social public places.* Encourage the development of public places along the street in the Creekside Village area for neighborhood gathering and interaction along with street-oriented residential units to improve the surveillance of these areas.
- *Create enduring value.* Ensure that public and private investment in public infrastructure is well planned to gain maximum value, especially for public safety and amenity in the area.

- *Invite local participation.* Create a sense of local ownership of the plan by inviting participation in the creation of the public spaces and places, including the development of the car museum, the wetland park, the trail greenbelt system, and other public amenities.

The collective potential of Liberty Crossing at Gasoline Alley

"Big ideas" for the redevelopment of Gasoline Alley emerged from the community discussions and the design team. These ideas create a design reference that is authentic to the place and its needs as a functional and prosperous community.

- *Highway strip.* Enhance the highway commercial strip area in its reorientation toward Leva Street.
- *Big-box core.* Conserve and expand the big-box core with other similar and smaller retail establishments.
- *Cruise Street entertainment and education.* Develop a specialty street based on a fifties nostalgic car theme, incorporating neon signs, theaters, specialty car retail, a car museum, and a "show and shine" area as part of a rich tourist and car enthusiast destination program (fig. 13.4).
- *Gasoline Alley West greenbelt.* Create a network of greenways along the north, west, and south part of the site that includes the Waskasoo Creek system, the pond and wetland system on the west and south, and Memorial Park and wetland areas on the southern edge of the site.
- *Creekside residential village.* Develop a residential hamlet/village to create a complete community in the northern section of the site, carefully incorporating compatible existing uses and developing a village core at the corner of Lantern Street and Waskasoo Avenue. The balance of the land surrounding the area will be developed with cluster residential development that will be sensitively located so as to conserve Waskasoo Creek and surrounding treed areas.
- *Support services.* Provide the potential for a secondary school, elementary school, and community center as part of the educational component of the community.

Figure 13.4. Cruise Street, Liberty Crossing at Gasoline Alley, Red Deer, Alberta. This rendering illustrates potential uses and special events, like a car show on this fifties-theme street. (Drawing by Calum Srigley.)

Land use concept

The illustrations and descriptions that follow are meant as preliminary concepts and designations only. Further detailed master planning is required to determine the feasibility of the suggested land uses, transportation network, building forms, and massing, as well as interrelationships with adjoining uses. The intent of the early land use concept is to create rich and diverse land use designations for a stronger overall plan and complete community.

Land use character areas

The accompanying concept diagram (fig. 13.5) illustrates the five major building blocks for the master plan, which can also be described as development areas with unique land use mixes. The subsequent land use character areas and urban design plan refine the ideas into more detailed plans (fig. 13.6).

- The Strip: highway service commercial
- Liberty High Street: mixed-use commercial and residential

- Cruise Street: specialty retail, education, and entertainment
- The village: Creekside residential neighborhood
- Central working core: light industrial and commercial

Figure 13.5. Land use character areas, Liberty Crossing at Gasoline Alley, Red Deer, Alberta. The character areas reflect existing and future uses that together create a more diverse and complete community. (Graphics by Dolores Altin.)

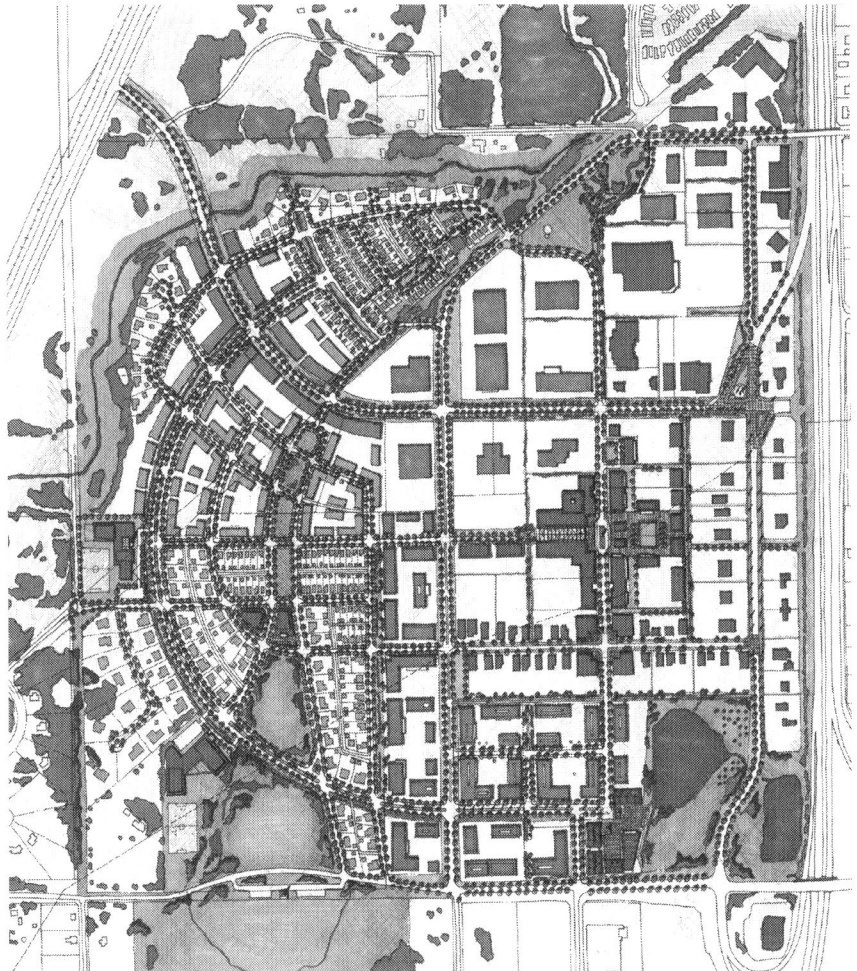

Figure 13.6. Urban design plan, Liberty Crossing at Gasoline Alley, Red Deer, Alberta. The Liberty Crossing plan creates variety of built form and uses, parks on the wetlands and natural streams, schools, a community center, and an elaborate street network. (Drawing by Don Wuori.)

Streets network

The success of the plan for Liberty Crossing will depend on enhancing street access and connections within the community, especially to create a safe hierarchy of arterial, collector, and local streets. These three categories of streets have differing capacity and function within the community:

- Arterial: larger, connecting through streets
- Collector: secondary streets for servicing uses
- Local: smaller service streets principally in residential areas

Further study will lead to the designation and refinement of these streets.

Green network and greenbelt

The green network emphasizes the potential for other pedestrian and bikeway linkages through the green infrastructure system that will combine storm water management with recreation and wetland conservation. This green network collectively defines a greenbelt that is envisioned as ringing the north, west, and south part of the site and linking to the north on the eastern edge of the site through conversion of the service road to a greenway trail.

At the core of this plan is the Waskasoo Creek trail system, which could in turn link to the 16-mile (26-km) Red Deer trail system east of the site. In addition, greenway pathway links in the proposed Creekside Village and along select roadways could provide attractive and safe ways of walking or biking to destinations in the community (fig. 13.7).

Other greenway or blueway (water) features include a series of wetland and storm water management ponds along the southwestern portion of the site and the Memorial Park wetlands. These water features could be part of a more elaborate wetland and storm water system as development unfolds and could possibly be linked as skating ponds in the winter months.

Since the completion of this plan, some development has proceeded, but due to market conditions, much of the new development area remains undeveloped. One developer in particular has proposed a progressive development that incorporates a gross density of 10 units per acre (25 units/ha) and a variety of housing units on 100 acres (40 ha) with infrastructure proceeding, but no housing construction has occurred.

Figure 13.7. Parkway plan, Liberty Crossing at Gasoline Alley, Red Deer, Alberta. The backbone of the Liberty Crossing urban design plan is a comprehensive and generous walking and bikeway network through the community. (Drawing by Calum Srigley.)

Rural edge cluster development

Cluster development (also referred to as conservation design) is a relatively new design strategy that conserves land and transfers the density to a smaller footprint elsewhere on the property. It specifically applies to rural situations where the retention of agricultural land, woodlots, streams, and wildlife areas is important to retaining rural character. These rural values include open space, natural features, views, farmland, and wildlife habit corridors.

Randall Arendt in *Rural by Design* explores various cluster alternatives and compares the visual, physical, social, and economic impacts in the Connecticut River Valley in Western Massachusetts. It is interesting to observe how much of the unspoiled natural scenery, farmland, and historic villages can be conserved. By tucking more compact development into meadows surrounded by trees and set back from the highway, the existing rural character can be retained.[2] In his book *Growing Greener*, Arendt further explores the idea of conservation design by identifying important natural and cultural features using planning tools such as zoning, general plan, and subdivision ordinances to protect these resources and therefore conserve unique values in the community.[3]

These innovative cluster design strategies can be supported by conservation easements that retain the land in its current state. Conservation easements allow the holder to prevent certain uses to protect conservation values. The concept is not new. In fact, conservation easements were written first in the United States in the 1880s to protect parkways designed by Frederick Law Olmsted in the Boston area. Conservation easements cross the United States and Canada. These easements protect American treasures like the Blue Ridge Parkway; preserve farmland and create a greenway along the St. Croix River in Wisconsin; and help to conserve the Olana viewshed in New York's Hudson River Valley.[4]

Transfer of Development Credits (TDC)—called Transfer of Development Rights (TDR) in Canada—is another tool to retain valued land in its current state. It enables the permitted density (units per acre/ha) of the entire parcel of land to be transferred to a smaller portion to conserve farmland, natural features, and wildlife habitat. This tool is often used in cluster development design. In essence, the overall land use density is retained while it is concentrated on a small piece of the site. The remaining land remains in its current state. TDC helps to retain significant natural features, farmland, and wildlife habits while still permitting the landowner the density allocated to his land for development.

The cluster development strategy also relates to historic small-town rural patterns and sizes. The more rural categories of town, hamlet, and village have various historic sizes. The hamlet is normally the smallest and town the biggest, with the village falling in between. The sizes range from 100 to 20,000 residents but normally average 5,000 to 10,000 residents. These small communities normally have human scale, ecological integrity, compactness, mixed uses, a variety of building forms, and connected streets. Their specific setting defines scale, character, and density. From the smallest hamlet of 10 acres (4 ha) to the village of 100 acres (40 ha) and a town of 600 acres (240 ha), each rural urban or suburban edge form requires different land use and servicing requirements. The importance of land conservation and open space is a common theme throughout any rural form of development.[5]

The current method of insensitive suburban and rural design has evolved over the past fifty years and is largely determined by the automobile. The standard engineering design method starts with access and a road network, then fills in land uses and, finally might conserve any remaining "remnant" areas. This method is used to maximize the yield of single-family lots and minimize the cost of infrastructure services, such as streets, water, sanitary sewer, and storm water management. This standard design is a business model, not a community-building model. In fact, it wastes land and is unsustainable. Furthermore, it is a major contributor to urban and rural sprawl.

It is a hard reality that sustainable design is illegal in most municipalities. Zoning, subdivision regulations, and engineering standards do not permit alternatives or sensitive development planning. There is little or no regard for local natural and cultural resources that make a place special. Traffic efficiency takes the front seat, while human ecology and safety take the backseat or, more aptly, the trunk. This design method perpetuates the *Geography of Nowhere* that James Kunstler describes as being isolated, unsafe, and car-driven.[6] But there is another way. This way starts with respecting the natural land features, creating development pockets where appropriate, and finally connecting to a street system that minimizes intrusion onto the site. Let's explore this innovative suburban and rural design approach through a case study in the next section.

A three-step reverse design method

The following case study, on the edge of Sherwood Park, east of Edmonton, Alberta,[7] highlights the importance of three elements that contribute to successful rural and suburban design:

- Shaping the design by first identifying and then retaining the rural character elements, such as natural features, viewsheds, open space, and farmland

- Developing a community design process that actively engages the stakeholders and creates a plan that is broadly supported
- Creating "net community gain" that is not focused on maximizing density of development but rather on creating a design that fits into the surrounding community and contributes to its short- and long-term aspirations and needs

This case study is based on an alternative conservation design process that follows these steps: (1) conserving what is important, (2) developing appropriate uses and densities for what is remaining, and (3) connecting the development to adjacent roads and trails in the most efficient way. I refer to this design method as the reverse method, because it is the reverse sequence from what normally happens. Let's look at the steps in more detail.

The first step starts with identifying what land should be protected based on natural and cultural values. These areas are classified in first and second priority. The difference could be a local, state/provincial, or federal mandatory requirement (first priority) relating to a stream or setback area as compared with a natural feature such as a woodlot that has significant trees (voluntary/second priority). However, the community, developer, or local government staff may highly value the significant stand of trees or a cultural place on the site that is of primary importance but has little or no regulations to protect them. The significant stand of trees and cultural place may still deserve a first-priority designation. A set of specific criteria should be developed for each project that helps in the selection of first- and second-order land protection priorities.

After the identification of land that should be protected, the design process moves on to defining appropriate uses on the development areas. These can be classified as high, medium, and low priority based on location, character, environmental sensitivity, and market factors.

The final step is to determine the road access that connects to the developed areas yet creates the least site disturbance. Development yield (the number of housing units or lots) is not normally negatively affected in cluster design, as the same or more density is transferred to a smaller footprint on the property (the Transfer of Development Credits or Rights, discussed earlier). One of the challenges of cluster development is when the housing market is demanding large lots and the conservation proposal suggests smaller lots or even multifamily housing. This elk ranch case study reveals that the development yield in housing units can far exceed what is permitted in the zoning bylaw.

Case study: Cluster housing, Strathcona County, Alberta

It was a crisp and sunny September day in 2008 when I first set eyes on the property just east of Edmonton, Alberta. I was invited by the landowners to tour the property. The manager of planning for Strathcona County joined the site visit, along with the ranch manager. We shook hands with the owners and then were off to see the site with small four-wheeled all-terrain vehicles (quads, as they are fondly called). The major part of the property was a former elk ranch, and I could immediately see the damage that the elk had done to the property over the years in the grazing areas. Many of the aspen trees had been stripped bare of foliage and had suffered permanent damage. I was looking at remnant aspen tree stands. As we came out into the open meadows after the first stand of aspens, I was struck by how quiet and separated the area was from the surrounding roads and development. The knolls, or small hills, punctuated the terrain and buffered the property from the surrounding noise. I discovered a wonderful place.

Suddenly the stillness was broken by a distant elk call. I gained immediate respect for our tour guide, the ranch manager, as we moved closer to the few remaining elk on the hundred-acre property. Our guide had in-depth knowledge of the property and elk bulls. Only one male bull, the dominant male, was in a separate enclosure with his harem of females. The other males were isolated from this male, as the ranch owner did not want a potential fatal confrontation between the elk bulls. During mating season in the previous year, the manager had found an elk bull dead within the dominant male enclosure, with hundreds of puncture wounds. It is hard to believe that outside mating season the bulls can be timid and docile. We kept our safe distance outside the enclosures as we continued to tour the property. The hilly open meadows and aspen groves had been the elks' home for decades, and now they were being moved due to the encroachment of urban development and growth.

What I observed that day gave me inspiration to develop an innovative cluster design concept for the property. The hills and aspen groves created some dynamic opportunities and challenges for innovative design. The site needed to be reclaimed and healed. It required reforestation. The county definitely wanted something different. Their current cluster lot zoning had simply resulted in large single-family lots isolated to one part of the property. To be fair, the cluster provisions on other development sites resulted in more open space, but so far generally larger and more expensive lots laid out in a modified subdivision configuration.

Engaging the local community

That winter the client sponsored a four-day design charrette (intensive and continuous design discussions and explorations) in liaison with the development partner, county staff, and community. The first evening we traditionally hold a meeting to discuss the issues, challenges, and potential ideas with members of the community. We held this meeting at the local church adjacent to the property. It was a cold winter night and the weather was poor, so we had a limited turnout. In every community meeting, my primary concern is representation of the community so that we hear all points of view. That evening residents from bordering neighborhoods and a representative from the adjoining school attended the meeting. We began with cordial introductions, as is customary in our meetings. I started with the gentlemen to my right. In hindsight I should have been more selective, as the first person you ask for comment can set the tone for the entire community discussion. What happened next I will never forget.

I asked him to introduce himself and his interests. I fondly refer to this gentleman as "Doctor No." He was a medical doctor who lived across the road from the development. As I soon found out, this gentleman had no time for consultants. He stated that we were there not to listen but to get our own way. According to him, the meeting and process was all about what the owners wanted, not about the desires and needs of the community. The rest of the meeting was less confrontational. We worked with the community to define the key issues, opportunities, and ideas that could support a development concept. I knew then that even an innovative cluster design might not win over the entrenched large-lot subdivision advocates in attendance. The majority of attendees lived on large lots, and that was the status quo in the community. They did not know anything else so viewed alternatives as threatening to their lifestyle and community.

Designing for place

Over the next three days our design team worked feverishly to develop a plan that satisfied concerns for traffic, noise, decreased property values, and minimum lot sizes. We created a compelling story of a future community that would be diverse, healthy, and environmentally friendly. We advocated a tree nursery and replanting scheme for the property to reestablish the woodlots and natural landscape. The innovative cluster design resulted in nine types of housing that addressed local needs and the desire to age in the community. These housing units also accommodated younger single people in the community. Larger single-family lots along the edge of the property created a suitable transition to adjacent single-family communities. An extensive trail network connected the housing clusters, adjoining communities, and adjacent school (fig. 13.8).

The extensive open space network—more than 50 percent of the property—served multiple functions, including storm water management, recreation, and visual amenity. It also provided enough space for a potential on-site wastewater management facility. This sensitive approach integrated the street network into the existing lower areas, conserving the unique hilly character, natural drainage, and privacy of the site. The hilly higher points conserved viewing points in the trail network (figs. 13.9 and 13.10). In the end, we did not know how it would be received by the community, staff, or council in the final evening public presentation.

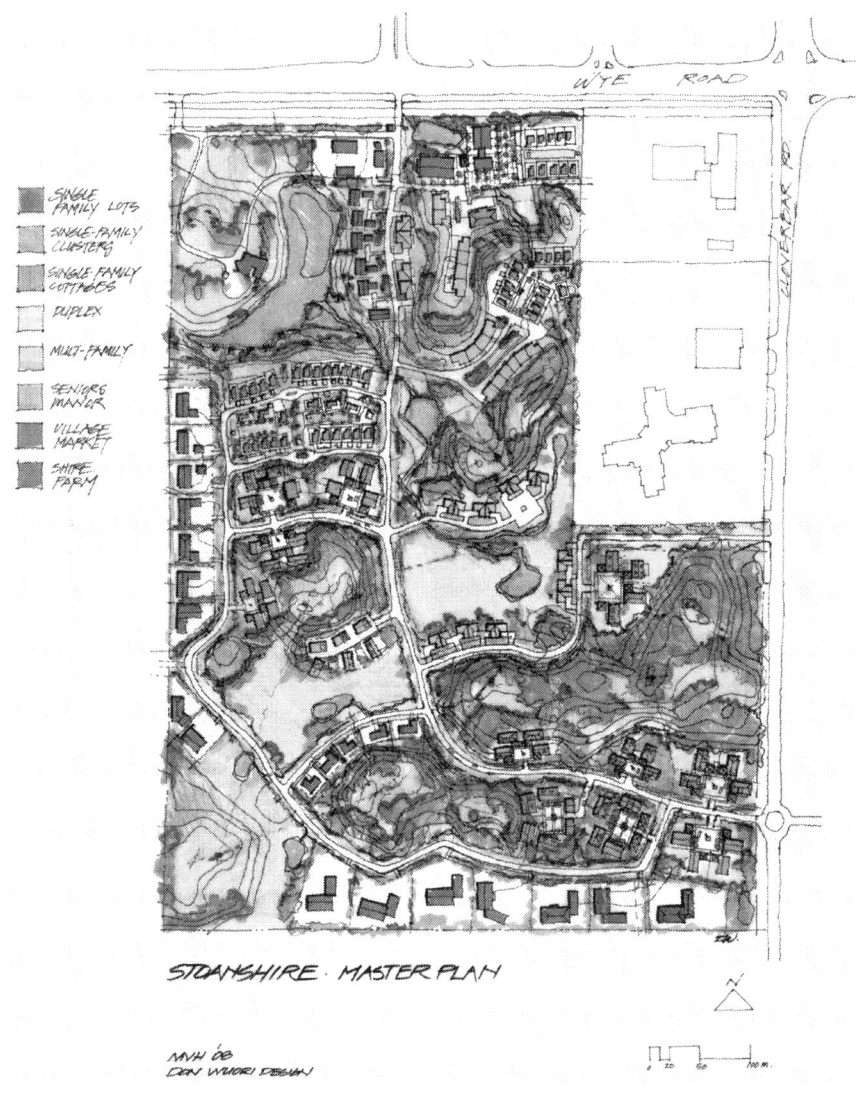

Figure 13.8. Stoanshire master plan, Strathcona County, Alberta.
Nine types of housing, local commercial, natural storm water management, and potential on-site sewage treatment are sustainable development features. (Drawing by Don Wuori.)

Figure 13.9. Single-family housing (left) and single-family housing clusters (right), Strathcona County, Alberta. The plan retains the higher ground as part of site conservation, while increasing density in clustered housing and associated amenities. (Drawing by Calum Srigley.)

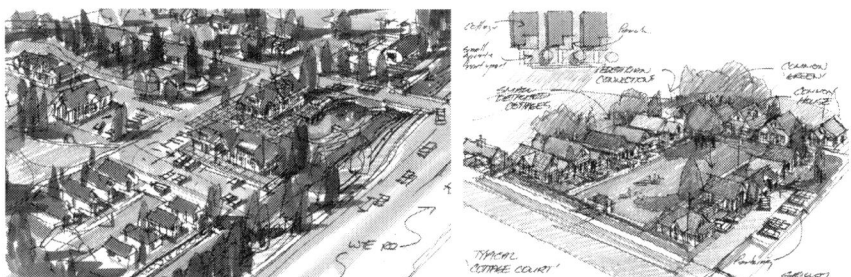

Figure 13.10. The local village center (left) and the cottage court housing cluster (right), Strathcona County, Alberta. The plan provides local services and alternative clustered housing for seniors, singles, and young families. (Drawings by Calum Srigley.)

The verdict

The public slide presentation lasted almost an hour as our team took the audience through our inventory, analysis, and cluster design. We created a compelling story, but the verdict was still out until I asked the audience for comments. "Doctor No" was sitting near the front. His hand shot up, and then came the ultimate surprise. "Doctor No" had been converted to a believer in the project. He stated, "I do not have any questions, and I fully support the project." The farm manager and former police officer then made his way up to the front of the room and shared an emotional story of our process and results that captured the hearts of the audience. He said that when he first showed the design team the beautiful hills on the property, he was convinced that the hills would be gone in the final design. They would fall victim to the standard flat suburban development that left no mark of previous landscape character. The hilly terrain created the magic of the place for him. Now, with emotion in his voice, he was almost overwhelmed that we had conserved the hills and built on the site character. The audience was silent. His short story affirmed our principled process and design. The tide had turned in our favor.

What ensued was a supportive discussion, as community, staff, and council endorsed the plan concept. Further work was needed on water and sanitary sewer servicing of the property, but the conservation scheme worked. Our community process had started out badly because of misperceptions about what new alternative development could do to the community. In realizing the benefits of the cluster design scheme, the community had come to accept the concept. The proposal will provide for positive growth that responds to local needs. The solution contributes value and strength to their community.

Instead of a very limited number of single-family homes on small acreages, this proposal recommended 181 units on approximately 100 acres (40 ha). Both Strathcona County and the surrounding residents supported this concept. The normal solution is more urban sprawl, and that is what the suburban and rural market in many jurisdictions still demands (or so they say). Meanwhile, singles, seniors, and young families are excluded from conventional subdivisions based on cost and little or no alternative housing.

Now we move on to a very important part of the sustainable urban design process that often gets neglected or is ill-conceived. This fourth section of the book describes the framework and provides case studies for getting the sustainable urban design plan implemented. It is amazing how many urban design plans gather dust on a shelf—driven by a wealth of good intentions but with little or no resulting changes in the community. Let's now help solve that challenge.

IV

ACTION BY DESIGN

14
MAKING SUSTAINABLE DESIGN HAPPEN

The difference between what we are doing and what we are capable of doing would solve most of the world's problems.

—Mahatma Gandhi

After all the effort of developing principles, doing analysis, and plan-making (see chapters 4 to 9), we have not created any changes on the ground. We have produced the paperwork for the sustainable urban design, but the project still is not built. This chapter addresses implementation, also referred to here as the action plan—how we actually carry out the intentions of the urban design plan or "family of plans." The implementation of urban design starts with the commitment to build the future. Unfortunately, as I have pointed out already, in many cases, the implementation process in urban design either gets left out completely or is delegated to another party with little or no guidance.

Successful implementation requires six key components:

1. *Vision.* A clear vision must define the results.
2. *Ownership.* Stakeholders must buy into the plan's idea and its execution.
3. *Organization.* The right team must be assembled to get the right jobs done.
4. *Resources.* Partners must commit resources and funding to the project.

5. *Tools.* The right management tools must be in place to get the job done (e.g., zoning, heritage agreements, development agreement, Business Improvement Association, etc.).

6. *Evaluation.* A monitoring program must be approved from the beginning to ensure that the stakeholders receive what is promised in the design plan and associated agreements.

This chapter details the vital elements in successful action plans and also provides a case study of the documentation and evaluation necessary for sustainable urban design projects.

Creating predictable results

The sustainable urban design action plan starts at the beginning of the urban design process with a realistic vision and an integrated process that builds support from the outset. The project consulting team has to start with the end in mind. The team also has to inspire the property developers to help them carry out the project. Responsibility, accountability, and leadership are therefore born as a genuine team effort.

Building support and ownership of the results from the beginning is critical to the success of any project. With the right community and political support, will the director of public works *not* support the project? I very much doubt it. An ancient Chinese proverb says, "Build them a golden bridge." In other words, wisdom says that if you give your stakeholders a proposition that benefits them and has broad support, they will not refuse it. Therefore, the project consulting team has to build the right process from the beginning to get the right results on the ground.

The following discussion of the six action plan elements is structured so that readers can build a customized action plan based on their own situation. Each element begins with a defining statement that sets the context for a series of questions meant to inform the crafting of a strategy to fit the particular situation. These six elements are not numbered in sequence, since some can happen in parallel to one another. Coincidentally, a vision, goals, and principles are the beginning. The evaluation happens at the end or can happen periodically to monitor the project in process.

Vision

Some of the most successful and innovative healthy new communities in North America have one common trait—a clear vision.

- Do we know what we have and value as a community (e.g., community or organizational values)?
- How do we define those values and shape them into a statement about our future development (vision statement)?
- How do we get to that successful vision (goals and principles)?

Ownership

The buy-in by the community, staff, other agencies, and politicians is critical for support and long-term success. Ownership is also a part of motivation to participate and perform. Explicit benefits associated with participation must be described and delivered. The transfer of responsibilities or sharing of responsibilities is the result of project ownership.

- Have we included key stakeholders from the beginning of designing the process? (If they help design it, they normally own it.)
- What benefits do the community, staff, other agencies, and politicians get from this project, and when?
- What risks are associated with the broad ownership, and how we can reduce or eliminate these risks?
- How can we get "official" and "unofficial" ownership so we can be flexible yet spread the burden of the project tasks?
- What early successes can we achieve to bring naysayers on board and to bring visibility to the project for politicians and others? (Success breeds success.)

Organization

An organizational framework needs to be dynamic. Different players may be involved in the process at different times. The evolution of the organization should also recognize the different skills, knowledge, interests, responsibilities, and accountability of the members and how they fit in.

- Who are the key players for getting the job done?
- Who are the workers, and who are the chiefs?
- What incentives are there to get the job done right?
- Does the overall organization hamper getting the work done?
- Do we have clear terms of reference to direct actions and responsibilities?
- Where are the politicians and key leaders involved so the process is proactive and supportive and recognizes the leadership?
- Do we have a leader who can lead and be trusted?
- How does the organization evolve or devolve over time?

Resources

Without people, funding, and other resources, the project will fail. No matter how much goodwill is shown, many projects fizzle out because the proper resources are not realized before the project is initiated.

- What resources do we need to successfully complete the process?
- How can we get the people, funding, and other resources while building support for the project? (Get more, and we obtain more commitment and ownership.)
- What means can we use to tie the initial commitment to an ongoing commitment (e.g., capital plan for a city, incentives program, performance-based contributions)?
- Who will continue to support the longer-term interests of the project (e.g., maintenance costs and other project future costs)?

Tools

There are much more than the "control" and "stick" mechanisms like zoning and regulations to encourage innovation and performance in implementation. Incentives, or "carrots," should be used to encourage ongoing performance and flexibility.

- What *regulatory tools* can we use to encourage performance and innovation (e.g., comprehensive development zones, discretionary zoning, performance zoning, mixed-use districts)?
- What *funding programs* can we use to fund the project properly (e.g., tax abatements, tax credits, in-kind contributions)?
- What *management tools and programs* can we use to create the right framework for multilevel cooperation (e.g., heritage districts, Business Improvement Areas, heritage revitalization agreements, joint venture land agreements, maintenance contracts)?
- What *communication tools* are there to build support and recognize successes along the way (e.g., network tree, e-mail, media)?

Evaluation

Ongoing monitoring is necessary to measure performance. Measuring success can take many forms. Evaluating the project against the original goals (with specific targets) is a first step for achieving consistent results.

- How will we measure performance against our original vision and goals?
- Who and what will be monitored, and when?
- How will the evaluation affect the implementation of the plans?
- How will we change the implementation based on the evaluation results?

Community benefits

The benefits given to the community through site redevelopment are important in measuring the "net community gain" (positive community benefits) created by the development. These benefits can include affordable housing, local parks and recreation space, pathway connections, community-accessible space, nonprofit community organizations space, and public art. A more detailed sample list of community benefit items are included in the Fenwick Place redevelopment case study in chapter 12.

Summary reference chart

Table 14.1 is a reference chart for developing a project implementation strategy. It summarizes the previous six elements in creating a successful action plan. The synergy of the parts makes a more successful overall process and produces better results.

Table 14.1. Summary action plan reference chart		
Element	Subelement	Definitions
VISION: Where do we want to be at the end of the project (5–10 years)?		
	Vision	End view of project
	Goals/Targets	Performance ends
	Principles	Guides to future actions
OWNERSHIP: How do we develop support for the project in the short and long term?		
	Stakeholders	Risks/benefits
	Involvement	Active tasks in project
	Recognition	Political benefits
	Partnerships	Shared responsibilities
ORGANIZATION: How do we organize people and resources to get the job done right?		
	Terms of Reference	Specific tasks, scope, and responsibilities
	Key Players	Decision makers and workers
	Efficient Group Organization	Vertical or horizontal organization chart and interactions
	Connection to Power Sources	Vertical connection to management and political regimes
	Alliances	Interconnected network
RESOURCES: Who and what is available uniquely suited to our strategy, or how do we position ourselves to fit various support structures?		
	People	Supporters
	Funds	Sources of funding
	Partners	Shared responsibilities

Table 14.1. (*continued*)

Element	Subelement	Definitions
TOOLS: What incentives and methods can we use to promote the plan?		
	Regulatory	Zoning and other tools
	Funding	Public and private sources, including in-kind
	Management	Business improvement associations, residents associations, etc.
	Communication	Direct, e-mail network, and media
EVALUATION: How did we do, what do we measure, and when?		
	Vision	Measuring against original vision
	Performance	General performance
	Changes	Amendments to action plan
Long-Term Sustainability: Social, Ecological, and Economic (SEE) Considerations		

Case study: Creating sustainable implementation performance tools, Salisbury Village East, Alberta

Realizing sustainable urban design on the ground has its challenges. For instance, when the development is approved, many of the good sustainable planning principles and ideas are marginalized or eliminated through lack of specific measurement or documentation, or they are simply rationalized as uneconomic, untested, or unfeasible. Such misunderstandings, without support or incentives, often lead to inaction and unacceptable results.

As mentioned earlier, any significant project requires the support and collaboration of many players, including the development group, a consulting group, and the municipality. The recent Salisbury Village East Plan in Strathcona County, just east of Edmonton, Alberta, Canada, provides one example where sustainable performance measures are part of the detailed development approvals. Completed by my firm, MVH Urban Planning & Design Inc., in liaison with other consultants, the plan was approved in March 2011.[1] The project was possible through the continued commitment of the client and client representative, Ross Fraser of Trillium Real Estate Advisors Inc., along with the support of Peter Vana and Susan Maceyovski, to name a few, of Strathcona County. Adjoining developers—ROYOP and their partners (stages 1 and 2, Salisbury Village West)—also played a role and are committed to the plan. The plan is an attempt at connecting sustainable community development with urban design in implementation of the project.

Any new development initiative is always difficult, especially when it requires a change from the norm. This project started out as a typical suburban shopping center proposal, with big-box stores surrounded by a sea of parking. Strathcona County had other ideas. The county had developed a series of twelve sustainability themes that form a basis for measuring sustainable performance in what they referred to as the Sustainable Urban Neighbourhood (SUN) process. These twelve themes formed part of their overall county's Municipal Development Plan and were a requirement as part of any major rezoning applications.

When the application to rezone the property for the suburban shopping center (phase 1) was not approved by council, Peter Vana, then manager of planning for the county, suggested that the developers hire me to facilitate an alternative process. I subsequently facilitated a four-day design charrette using the SUN process. At the end of the design charrette, it was obvious that there was support for innovative sustainable urban design ideas. These included:

- Mixed uses, with retail on the ground floor and office or residential above, along a new main street for shopping
- A variety of housing choices and densities, dispersed parking areas with pedestrian connections, and a network of trails connecting to adjoining neighborhoods
- Community amenities (including an eco-central park learning center and facility)
- The equivalent of LEED-NC (Leadership in Energy and Environmental Design for New Construction)

These early ideas evolved through many discussions and negotiations. What emerged was an improvement to traditional development and a major step forward in sustainable urban design. The process was expensive for the developer and very time-consuming, but good things take time and resources. The significant barriers to sustainable development must be overcome by municipal and regional government leadership. In this case, both were there in evidence, but resistance from developers, retailers, and bankers remains, since these new sustainable urban forms have not been tested in many cases and therefore represent high risk. The consumer is also not willing to pay a significant premium for something that is not normal, especially if they want to resell into a standard market and the market is risk averse to untested new products. And there are additional barriers when it comes to promoting pedestrianism and transit. As I was reminded constantly by one of the county transportation engineers, Strathcona County was still auto-oriented (with an average of 2.8 vehicles per household).

As the project evolved, I became more involved in the next stage of development, adjoining the main site and to the east. This site, Salisbury Village East (Area 3), is the focus of this case study. The Salisbury Village overall area plan has specific goals, principles, and targets associated with each of the twelve aforementioned sustainability themes that aid in measuring sustainable performance when the plan is implemented through individual development applications. These targets also form a framework for specific zoning for the property.

Sustainable plan vision

The challenge is to create a realistic sustainable plan that is practical, achievable, and supported by the community, especially in a suburban context. The Salisbury Village Area Structure Plan provides for necessary compact growth in the county while complementing the municipality's continued growth just east of Edmonton, Alberta. This area structure plan also provides the necessary services that link to adjoining and greater community needs.

The Salisbury Village Area Structure Plan is divided into three subareas—Salisbury Village West (Areas 1 and 2) and Salisbury Village

East (Area 3). Collectively the areas will form a model community that retains the natural flow of the landscape and wetlands, encourages green building technologies, and reduces resource use, energy use, and waste where possible. It will introduce a diverse mix of higher-density multifamily housing to complement an array of commercial uses. The western portion of the Salisbury Village Area Structure Plan will blossom into a compact pedestrian-oriented community centered around a high street, where biking, walking, and local transit provide for the needs of many of its residents and businesses. The eastern portion—Salisbury Village East—will provide a business park focus for offices and some supportive hotel, residential, and retail uses. The result will form a complete community, where residents, businesses, and visitors do not have to go far to have everything they need to live, work, and play in a compact community adjoining a rural setting.

History and special site features

Salisbury Village East (Area 3), the focus of this case study, is a site that has been utilized for various agricultural uses over the years. A farm was located on the land and has since been vacated. The most significant site feature is the wetland in the central area. The rolling landscape is also a special feature, along with a variety of tree stands (native and planted) throughout the site (fig. 14.1).

Figure 14.1. Natural site features, Salisbury Village East, Alberta.
Tree stands, hills, and wetlands create important elements for the site
development plan. (Graphics by Dolores Altin.)

Sustainable Neighbourhood Plan

The Sustainable Neighbourhood Plan for Area 3 uses the twelve themes in the Municipal Development Plan to create a sustainable planning and design approach. The innovative components of the plan include the following:

- *A central wetland area* that could be integrated with an interpretative program for education
- *A comprehensive nature trail network* connecting to the adjoining neighborhoods and land uses
- *A compact mixed-use business campus* complete with a variety of retail uses and hotel/conference facilities, providing local jobs, a residential component, and appropriate support services
- *Reduced parking "footprint" and increased permeable area* by shifting some of the parking below the buildings
- *A nature-oriented storm water management system* that uses surface runoff as a major infrastructure element
- *Greener streets* with additional planting and retained landform where possible (fig. 14.2)

Figure 14.2. Development vision for the Salisbury Village East property. The site development plan presents a sensitive response to the site by conserving the wetland, conserving the hilly landscape as much as possible, and integrating significant tree stands into the plan. (Drawing by Calum Srigley.)

Land use plan and development concept

The land use plan and development concept for the site is an office business park surrounding a natural wetland area and supported by a hotel and retail uses.

- *Business park: office.* The office building forms will start at three stories (two stories above first-level parking) along the east to minimize residential visual impacts. The offices will then transition to a maximum height of five stories (four stories above first-level parking) at the western edge.
- *Mixed business park: hotel, residential, retail.* To complement and support the office uses within the business park, hotel and hotel/residential uses are proposed on the western edge. These hotel and hotel/residential uses will be further supported by retail uses, as well as conference and fitness facilities. The hotel and hotel/residences will have a maximum height of nine stories, including parking (eight stories above first-level parking).
- *Parks/open space.* Greater than 20 percent of the plan area is dedicated to parks, recreation, and conservation (environmental reserve), not including private outdoor amenity space. This comprehensive parks and recreational network consists of substantial wetlands and surrounding tree buffers, the naturalized storm water management ponds/public utility.
- *Public review.* A comprehensive design charrette took place from September 22–25, 2008, which incorporated a workshop and presentation to adjoining landowners and council so that they could review and comment on the strengths and weaknesses of the development concept (figs. 14.3 and 14.4).

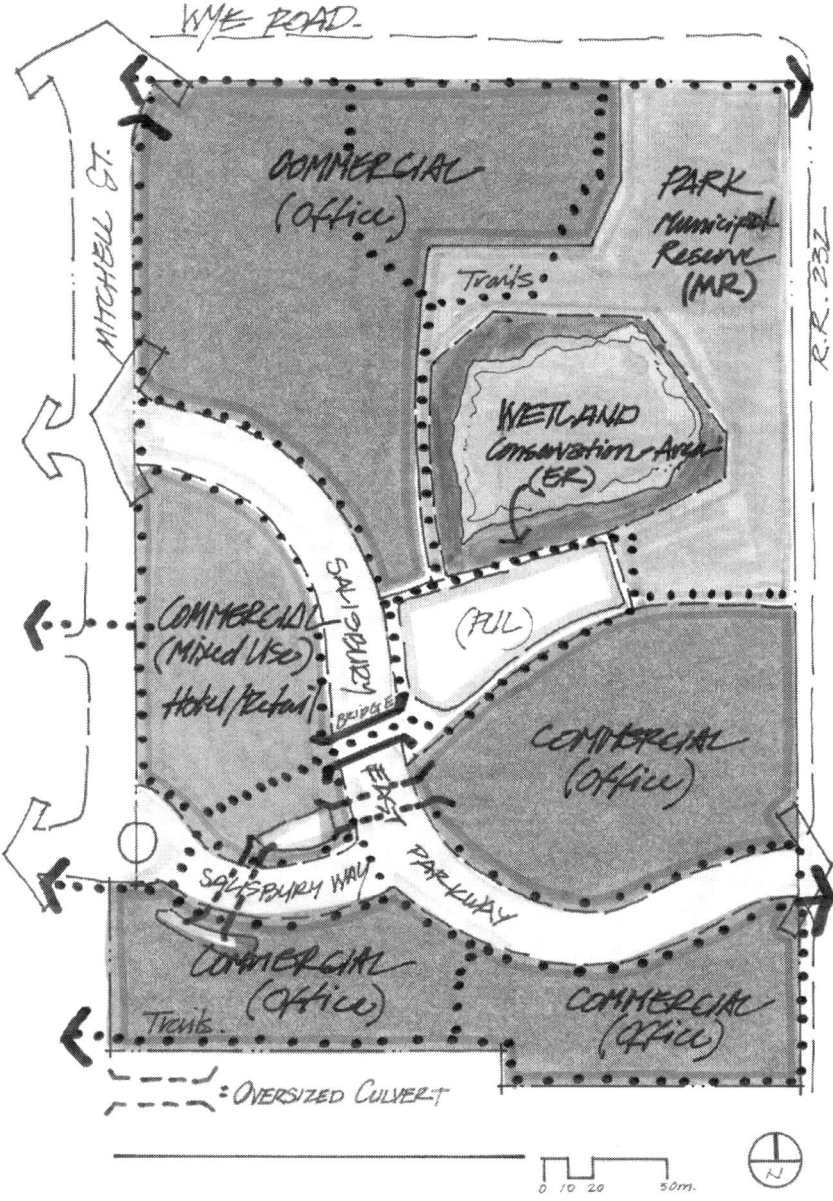

Figure 14.3. Land use plan, Salisbury Village East, Alberta. The land use plan illustrates the conservation of the wetland and the surrounding office and mixed-use commercial uses on the western edge of the site.

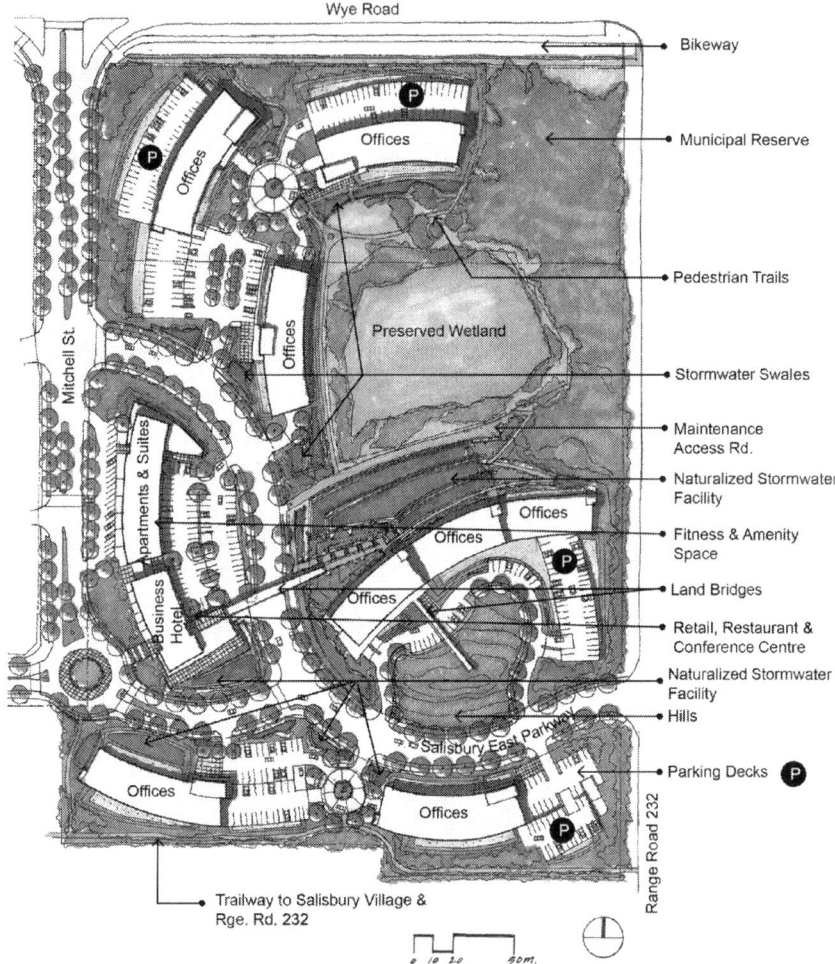

Figure 14.4. Development concept, Salisbury Village East, Alberta.
The development concept shows the detailed site development planning proposals, including building forms, the trail network, storm water management ponds, public amenities, parking, and access.

Regular meetings with a specific Strathcona County staff review group from 2008 through 2011 have informed further detailed studies on the property and refined the development plan to the benefit of the community. A public open house consistent with Strathcona County's policies of public engagement further refined the plan on September 21, 2009. A total of twenty-nine residents registered at the open house, and twenty-six completed the participant comment sheets (table 14.2). The majority of the attendees lived within about a mile (1 to 2 km) of the site.

Table 14.2. Open house results, Salisbury Village East				
Question: Do you strongly or somewhat support the following?	Strongly Support (%)	Somewhat Support (%)	Total Support (%)	Nonsupport (%)
Project Principles	58	27	**85**	15
Open Space and Wetland Amenities	85	11	**96**	4
Land Use	46	46	**92**	8
Transportation Concept	50	31	**81**	19
Overall Master Plan	54	35	**89**	11

Sustainable principles, goals, and targets

The sustainable principles, goals, and targets that follow (tables 14.3 to 14.14) form a reference for implementation, where the actual achievement is compared with the original targets. The format follows in the sequence of the twelve themes of sustainability outlined in Strathcona County's Municipal Development Plan. The intent is to clearly connect the themes with specific principles (guiding rules), goals (end results), and targets (measures) that can be instrumental in implementing the vision of the Salisbury Village Area Structure Plan. Although this case study focuses on Area 3, the following chart applied to all three areas of development for Salisbury Village. The intent in including these detailed tables is to provide a comprehensive list that includes residential, commercial, and recreational uses that can be used as a template for other developments.

Table 14.3. Land theme, Salisbury Village East

GUIDING PRINCIPLES

Respect Natural Features and Landscapes: Retain significant natural features and associated landscapes, where appropriate and possible.

Minimize Impacts of Redevelopment: Respect the adjoining neighborhoods with sensitive development that contributes green space and amenities while providing appropriate built form.

Create a Complete Pedestrian-Oriented Village: Build a compact and efficient mixed-use village of uses that is connected by foot and bicycle to the surrounding community.

Integrate Flexibility and Innovation: Promote a variety of uses, flexibility of phasing, and growth that can respond to market demand and a variety of tenants.

Sustainable Design Goals	Target for Salisbury
Increase the density, innovation, and diversity of housing for all ages	Provide diversity of housing units and types from townhomes to medium and high density, including entry-level housing and senior housing, live/work units, and housing above the retail units.
Maximize public green	Provide greater than 20 percent of site, including all open space.
Create services close to home that are within walking distance	Ensure 100 percent of residents and businesses are within 1,500 feet (450 m) of basic services.
Increase density of pedestrian activity and orientation in community	Provide 40 to 50 percent public part of street for pedestrians by providing a substantial planted boulevard and walking paths or trails on both sides of the street.
Provide jobs close to home	Create a variety of employment opportunities through the provision of commercial retail space, office space, and a business park.
Provide viable transit and an interconnected pedestrian/ bike network	Provide access to transit within 1,300 feet (400 m) of every resident, and provide a comprehensive trail system that reduces car use (see also table 14.7).

Table 14.4. Habitat theme, Salisbury Village East

GUIDING PRINCIPLES

Respect Natural Features and Landscapes: Retain significant natural features and associated landscapes, where appropriate and possible.

Minimize Impacts of Redevelopment: Respect the adjoining neighborhoods with sensitive development that contributes green space and amenities while providing appropriate built form.

Encourage Environmental Stewardship: Promote continued environmental responsibility and lifestyles, including tree stewardship, transit use, waste reduction, energy conservation, and natural water cleansing.

Sustainable Design Goals	Target for Salisbury
Improve wildlife habitat on and through the site	Ensure 50 percent of green space has habitat value.
Conserve habitat in the wetlands	Protect the wetlands areas, as they provide significant habitat value.
Use native vegetation	Use landscaping that incorporates diverse native vegetation species to contribute to habitat value.
Incorporate "naturescaping"	Ensure that public/private interfaces are delineated through landscaping and incorporate "naturescaping" that promotes planting native species that require less watering and maintenance.
Create natural transitions from the built environments	Develop buildings so that they are articulated in response to a natural edge to allow for tree retention or natural vegetation.
Protect the wetlands and edges	Protect 100 percent of the managed and protected wetlands with an average 100-foot (30-m) riparian setback.
Enhance the creek edges	Ensure that the creek area habitats are enhanced.
Naturalize storm water areas	Create a storm water detention pond naturalized for habitat.
Complete trail connections, and retain trees	Ensure that the trail systems are interconnected and trees retained where possible.
Connect on-site and off-site habitat corridors	Connect on-site habitat corridors with off-site corridors.
Retain native vegetation around wetlands	Retain wetland native vegetation bordering the wetland areas.
Retain natural habitat in open space planning	Ensure natural habitat is integrated with open space at many scales throughout Salisbury Village.
Incorporate wildlife habitat into trail network	Integrate wildlife-friendly vegetation into the comprehensive network of trails.
Incorporate wildlife trees into parking lots	Use native vegetation in the commercial parking field to increase the canopy cover and habitat provided for birds and insects.

Table 14.5. Water theme, Salisbury Village East

GUIDING PRINCIPLES

Combine Storm Water Drainage with Natural Flows: Provide an alternative storm water drainage system that combines with the existing stream and wetlands on the property and enhances wildlife habitat while managing on-site water in a responsible manner.

Encourage Environmental Stewardship: Promote continued environmental responsibility and lifestyles, including tree stewardship, transit use, waste reduction, energy conservation, and natural water cleansing.

Sustainable Design Goals	Target for Salisbury
Provide a model for storm water and environmental management	Encourage the natural flow of water and retention of wetland feature areas.
Combine natural flow and rainwater retention features	Retain the natural flow of the stream features where possible, with additional retention features where necessary, to control flows on- and off-site.
Protect wetland areas	Enhance the existing significant wetlands, and protect their natural edges.
Create naturalized water detention features	Create further naturalized water detention features to cleanse water and improve water quality.
Maximize permeable surface by reducing surface parking	Reduce parking standards by efficient underground parking for residences and the business park (Salisbury East), as well as potential shared commercial parking overlaps in off-peak hours.
Reduce off-site impacts of black water and gray water	Create temporary holding capacity on-site to reduce peak loading off-site through enlarged pipes.
Increase water quality and reduce off-site impacts of storm water	Maximize recharge of the groundwater and/or clean surface runoff (more than 50 percent recharge/clean). Minimize impermeable surfaces where possible using .42 gal/acre (4 l/ha) per second standard for maximum runoff.
Maintain the health of aquatic ecosystem	Manage storm water close to where it initially falls, which emulates the natural pattern of storm water penetration and reduces the amount of water that requires municipal treatment or that is being discharged in a deteriorated state. The wetland areas and storm water ponds will help to clean the storm water.
Reduce impacts of storm and sanitary flows off-site	Meet .42 gal/acre (4 l/ha) per second maximum storm water outflow rate. Oversize on-site sewage pipe to minimize off-site capacity requirements.
Reuse water where possible	Adopt a circular approach to water and wastewater resources that reduces the impact on municipal infrastructure, thereby decreasing the long-term costs associated with delivering and treating water.

Table 14.5. (*continued*)

Sustainable Design Goals	Target for Salisbury
Control erosion to reduce negative impacts on water and air quality	Implement an Erosion and Sediment Control Plan for the project sites during construction. Strategies such as silt fencing, sediment traps, and sediment basins will be employed.
Use water-tolerant native plants	Use appropriate landscape types, and design the landscape with indigenous plants to reduce or eliminate irrigation requirements.
Reduce generation of wastewater and potable water demand	Specify high-efficiency plumbing fixtures to reduce wastewater volumes.

Table 14.6. Carbon theme, Salisbury Village East

GUIDING PRINCIPLES

Conserve Energy: Implement a transit-, pedestrian-, and bicycle-oriented community to reduce the use of single occupancy vehicles and the associated carbon footprint. Encourage the consideration of alternative energy sources (district energy and geothermal) to reduce conventional energy use. Design and orient buildings to conserve energy.

Sustainable Design Goals	Target for Salisbury
Reduce storm runoff and fossil fuels, and increase design standards that encourage use of renewable energy sources	Ensure 50 percent of buildings will have good solar orientation.
Reduce use of fossil fuels, and increase use of renewable energy sources	Create energy efficiency in buildings through green building standards.
Design urban form to optimize energy efficiency of buildings and infrastructure	Mitigate energy demand in buildings by designing the building mass to achieve a more efficient ratio of exterior skin area to floor area to reduce heat gains and losses through the building envelope. The higher densities and compact design of Salisbury Village will help minimize energy demand.
Reduce energy demand through tree planting and site planning	Use trees and other landscape features to provide shading from the sun, cooling from the heat, and buffering against wind and cold air. Vegetation can also absorb solar incidence rays, reducing the buildup of temperatures from hard exterior surfaces. The net result is a reduction in the need to mechanically heat or cool interior areas. Locate trees to act as wind breaks and/or shading devices to reduce seasonal heating and cooling needs.
Incorporate renewable energy sources	Design buildings to permit addition of renewable energy technologies in the future. Consider the use of green energy providers.
Provide bike racks and parking	On-site bike racks are conveniently located throughout the site, providing bike parking.
Reduce heat absorption	Roofing specification for all buildings will meet requirements for high reflectivity and high emissivity for a minimum 75 percent of the roof surface.
Optimize building performance	Implement the following fundamental best-practice commissioning procedures. Verify installation, functional performance, training, and operation maintenance documentation.

Table 14.6. (*continued*)

Sustainable Design Goals	Target for Salisbury
Minimize energy use through insulation and mechanical systems design	Design the building to comply with minimum insulated values of R-20 for exterior walls and R-40 for the roof. Design mechanical systems to provide energy-efficient equipment. Include the use of low-energy bulbs and appliances, and consider a "dark sky" policy for areas such as the wetlands.
Encourage the development and use of grid-source renewable energy on a net-zero pollution basis	Determine the energy needs of the building, and investigate opportunities to engage in a green power contract with the local utility. Green power is derived from solar, wind, geothermal, biomass, or low-impact hydro sources.

Table 14.7. Transport theme, Salisbury Village East

GUIDING PRINCIPLES

Improve Mobility: Encourage a variety of transportation networks and universal accessibility with reduced emphasis on the automobile (greenways, walkways, bike routes, and transit) within the site and connecting to the adjoining areas.

Encourage Environmental Stewardship: Promote continued environmental responsibility and lifestyles, including tree stewardship, transit use, waste reduction, energy conservation, and natural water cleansing.

Sustainable Design Goals	Target for Salisbury
Create a transportation and mobility plan	Locate compact residential and commercial uses within walking distance of each other. Reduce residential parking standards (less than 2.6 spaces/unit and shared parking arrangements). Create a bus service to connect to local and regional populations. Provide a comprehensive trail system that encourages walking and biking, including connections to local schools and community facilities, with universal accessibility where possible. Consider a potential car-share program in one or more of the buildings, or a community bus supported by the designated senior housing.
Develop a walkable community	Provide 40 to 50 percent of the public part of the street for pedestrians, allocating appropriate planting boulevards and walkway or trail widths.
Create services close to home that are within walking distance	Ensure that 100 percent of residents are within 1,500 feet (450 m) of basic services.
Increase pedestrian and bikeway connections to adjoining developments	Provide trail and pathway connections to every parcel.
Increase alternative transit, pedestrian, and bicycle network use	Ensure that residents and businesses are within 1,300 feet (400 m) of a transit stop.
Create a safe, clean, and healthy environment that encourages noncar use	Connect greenways and trails to streets, services, and residents.
Reduce the footprint of transportation infrastructure	Keep surface parking and road widths to a minimum, and emphasize pedestrian or community places and spaces. Road widths are kept to a minimum in order to reduce the amount of land that is impermeable and used for cars. Surface parking for the commercial areas will not exceed county standards, and residential parking for the mixed commercial component will be underground. Parking is also designed for visitors and sharing for shopping and recreation.

Table 14.7. (*continued*)

Sustainable Design Goals	Target for Salisbury
Reduce or share parking footprint	Provide 1.5 spaces/residential unit, 4.7 spaces/1,000 square feet (93 m²) of commercial (and shared).
Ensure multiple transportation choices are available	Provide safe and vibrant designated walking and cycling corridors. Prioritize for walking and bicycling, creating affordable, efficient transportation options for everyone. Provide mobility corridors of greenways, narrow roads and laneways, and smaller paths, creating an interconnected network for pedestrians and cyclists that is accessible, safe, and convenient. An internal comprehensive pathway and trail system will be complemented by a pedestrian-friendly street system. Pedestrian and cyclist access through the parking field is humanized through trees and landscape elements.
Ensure the effectiveness of multimodal transportation system	Reduce the distance of residences and employment locations to a range of nonautomobile transportation choices. As land use mix is increased, the proximity between origins and destinations decreases, and transit feasibility increases. Provide a diverse array of residential and commercial land uses in a context of walking, cycling, and transit corridors that entices people out of their cars. Provide transit stops within the development. Implement the north-south and east-west sidewalk and trail network that provides the main pedestrian and cyclist routes through Salisbury Village. Ensure residences are located within a five-minute walk of all community services.
Incorporate a density and mix sufficient to ensure viability of public transit	Increasing the employment density and the jobs-to-housing ratio of Salisbury Village will also increase the viability of public transit, since transit can service both employees and residents in the area. The integrated mix of retail/commercial, residential, live/work, and office employment is located adjacent to the transit streets and the transit stops.
Connect the community with public transit	Provide pedestrian as well as bike trails and sidewalks throughout the site to encourage pedestrian and bicycle usage, and provide connections to the Heritage Trail along the north edge of the site. Bus stops, as discussed with Transportation Department, are provided for and are connected to pedestrian and bike walkway system.

Table 14.8. Food theme, Salisbury Village East

GUIDING PRINCIPLES
Provide for Food Growing, Production, and Distribution Locally: Encourage community gardens and potential distribution of local food goods in the community.

Sustainable Design Goals	Target for Salisbury
Increase local sources of food for sale and consumption	Encourage some produce grown or sold on-site via community gardens. Encourage food stores to buy locally grown produce and products.
Promote community-based food production	Layer visible and accessible food production spaces throughout Salisbury Village. Food-growing opportunities can be integrated into a neighborhood in a layered way, with both public and private spaces used at different levels of intensity. While the central community gardens south of the main wetland park and flex-field offer the most visible and concentrated food growth area, smaller garden plots can be incorporated throughout Salisbury Village, adjoining the residential uses. An east-west and north-south pedestrian/bike trail system provides a linkage to the community gardens, and the central park provides a possible location for a farmers' market on the weekends.

Table 14.9. Materials theme, Salisbury Village East

GUIDING PRINCIPLES

Establish a Comprehensive and Integrated Waste Recycling Program: Embrace reduction in consumption, recycling of waste/materials, and materials reuse as part of the community culture throughout the residential, retail, and office uses.

Encourage Environmental Stewardship: Promote continued environmental responsibility and lifestyles, including tree stewardship, transit use, energy conservation, and natural water cleansing.

Implement Green Building Materials Protocols: Use environmentally sensitive materials and building procedures.

Sustainable Design Goals	Target for Salisbury
Ensure the use of green neighborhood building practices	Design in conformance with standardized green building rating protocols. A range of green building rating protocols are available that effectively address a series of strategies for dealing with materials in Salisbury Village for both commercial and residential buildings. The project has incorporated Canada Green Council, Green Building Code equivalency for the commercial buildings. Twenty-five goals have been identified in which a minimum of at least 75 percent are to be incorporated into the project implementation. Residential units will be built to a Built Green equivalency standard. This includes reducing life-cycle material needs, sourcing materials with low embodied energy, seeking out local and regional suppliers, and incorporating reclaimed and sustainable materials.
Reduce ozone depletion	For new buildings, specify new HVAC equipment that uses no CFC refrigerants.
Facilitate the reduction of waste generated by building occupants that is hauled to and disposed of in landfills	Designate an area for recyclable collection and storage that is appropriately sized and located in a convenient area. Identify local waste handlers and buyers for glass, plastic, office paper, newspaper, cardboard, and organic wastes. Instruct occupants on building recycling procedures.
Divert construction debris from landfill disposal, redirect recyclable recovered resources back to the manufacturing process, and redirect reusable materials to appropriate sites	Adopt a construction waste management plan to divert materials from the landfill. Consider recycling cardboard, metal, brick, concrete, plastic, clean wood, glass, and gypsum wallboard. Designate a specific area on the construction site for recycling. Identify construction haulers and recyclers to handle the designated materials. Note that salvage may include donation of materials to charitable organizations such as Habitat for Humanity.

Table 14.9. (*continued*)

Sustainable Design Goals	Target for Salisbury
Increase demand for building products that incorporate recycled content materials, therefore reducing impacts resulting from extraction and processing of new materials and bypassing energy and greenhouse gas–intensive industrial and manufacturing processes	Specify building products that incorporate recycled materials.
Increase demand for building materials and products that are extracted and manufactured within the region, thereby supporting the use of indigenous resources and reducing the environmental impacts resulting from transportation	Specify regionally sourced products for building construction.
Reduce the use and depletion of finite raw materials and long-cycle renewable materials by replacing them with rapidly renewable materials	Use materials such as bamboo flooring, wool carpets, straw board, linoleum flooring, and others.
Encourage environmentally responsible forest management	Use Forest Stewardship Council (FSC)–certified wood products.
Minimize material use and construction waste over a building's life resulting from premature failure of the building and its constituent parts and assemblies	Minimize premature deterioration of the walls and roof through the use of shading screens, caves, overhangs, scuppers, etc. Use surface materials appropriate to exterior conditions, and continuous air-barrier systems of appropriate strength.
Reduce the quantity of indoor air contaminants that are odorous, potentially irritating, and/or harmful to the comfort and well-being of installers and occupants	Specify low–Volatile Organic Compound (VOC) paints and coatings in construction documents. Specify wood and agrifiber products that contain no added urea-formaldehyde resins. Specify laminating adhesive for field and shop-applied assemblies, including adhesives and veneers that contain no urea-formaldehyde.

Table 14.10. Waste theme, Salisbury Village East

GUIDING PRINCIPLES

Conserve Energy and Reduce Waste: Use innovative building and site-planning methods to conserve energy and reduce waste.

Encourage Environmental Stewardship: Promote continued environmental responsibility and lifestyles, including tree stewardship, transit use, waste reduction, energy conservation, and natural water cleansing.

Sustainable Design Goals	Target for Salisbury
Create sanitary sewer conservation	Reducing the load on the county infrastructure by retaining partial flows on-site through temporary storage through larger pipe sizes.
Reduce energy consumption	Promote energy conservation through green building promotion, including building materials, ventilation, natural lighting, and wind protection. Orient buildings to maximize passive solar orientation.
Reduce, reuse, or recycle waste on-site	Reduce solid waste through a recycling program to be investigated.
Incorporate waste management as a central environmental theme in the community	Design in conformance with standardized green neighborhood and building rating protocols. Implement commercial and residential recycling of paper and cardboard. Recycling continues to be incorporated conveniently within street furniture for visitors, customers, and residents. The central "Eco-center" can be a demonstration area for recycling and responsible management of waste, from glass and plastic to cardboard, paper, and metals.

Table 14.11. Economy theme, Salisbury Village East

GUIDING PRINCIPLES

Encourage Local Employment Diversity: Provide a variety of local jobs and employment opportunities to reduce travel, create local prosperity, and build a sense of complete community.

Stimulate Innovative Opportunities for Home-Based Businesses and Networking: Promote an innovative community where home-based businesses are a lifestyle choice and linked to other service businesses in the community.

Sustainable Design Goals	Target for Salisbury
Provide a balance of retail and office jobs locally	1 foot commercial for every 3 feet of residential Salisbury West Area 1:　　　　　90, 000 square feet (8,362 m²) Area 2　　　　　230,000 square feet (21,368 m²) Salisbury East Area 3:　　　　　395,000 square feet (36,698 m²) (375,000 square feet, or 34,839 m², of office + 20,000 square feet, or 1,859 m², retail—hotel not included) 　　　　Total:　715,000 square feet (66,426 m²)
Distribute a variety of employment and economic opportunities throughout the site to maximize benefits and potential synergies between businesses and residents	Salisbury Village will provide employment for a broad range of workers, from retail sales and restaurant services to professional services, including medical, dental, legal, and accounting, as well as potential corporate head offices in the Salisbury East Business Park.

Table 14.12. Well-being theme, Salisbury Village East

GUIDING PRINCIPLES

Encourage Environmental Stewardship: Promote continued environmental responsibility and healthy lifestyles, including tree stewardship, transit use, waste reduction, energy conservation, and natural water cleansing.

Create Safe and Social Public Spaces: Provide a number of inside and outside public spaces that create opportunities for positive social interaction, universal accessibility, a variety of activities, and special events for all ages.

Follow Healthy Building Standards: Ensure that adequate light and air are provided as part of a healthy buildings package.

Sustainable Design Goals	Target for Salisbury
Provide places to interact, educate, and socialize on-site and connect to other off-site facilities	Build the community "third places" to maximize community interaction, including the eco-center, parks, plazas, water park, and coffee shops.
Create a variety of places for positive and healthy community interaction	Integrate structured and unstructured social gathering places throughout Salisbury Village that have universal accessibility where possible. Areas for social and recreational interaction are distributed throughout Salisbury Village, from the eco-center and wetland feature to various flex-play areas and park spaces. Areas for social interaction and recreational activity are integrated into the pathway corridors and form the essence of the "Main Street" design. The central park provides a possible location for such activities as farmers' markets on the weekends.
Create strong linkages across the community	Provide strong linkages between Salisbury Village and the surrounding neighborhoods. Emphasizing the linkages between different neighborhoods increases the level of social interaction occurring in any one neighborhood. Strong linkages will be provided by the pedestrian/bikeway pathways and bus transit to other parts of the Sherwood Park community.
Ensure Crime Prevention Through Environmental Design (CPTED) is incorporated in the site design	Orient buildings to allow for "eyes on the street." The concept of "eyes on the street" comes from Crime Prevention Through Environmental Design (CPTED), which aims to reduce the crime and the fears associated with crimes through design of the urban environment. Encouraging "eyes on the street" by improving pedestrian activity and watching from business and adjacent residential users creates a sense of ownership of the public realm. A strong street presence is created on "Main Street" by incorporating residential uses above commercial uses. Other residential buildings should have a strong street orientation with individual entries off the street and street-facing townhomes. Individual rear yards and strong street entrances will further advance this goal.

Table 14.12. (*continued*)

Sustainable Design Goals	Target for Salisbury
Eliminate light trespass from the building and site	Site lighting design is to maintain safe light levels while avoiding off-site lighting and night sky pollution. Technologies to be utilized will reduce light pollution and include full cutoff luminaires, low-reflectance surfaces, and low-angle spotlights.
Prevent or minimize exposure of building occupants, indoor surfaces, and systems to environmental tobacco smoke	Prohibit smoking in public buildings and buildings where public have access.
Provide for the effective delivery and mixing of supply air to support the comfort and well-being of building occupants	Design the HVAC system and building envelope to optimize air change effectiveness.
Reduce the quantity of indoor air contaminants that are odorous, potentially irritating, and/or harmful to the comfort and well-being of installers and occupants	Specify low–VOC materials in construction documents.
Provide a thermally comfortable environment that supports the productivity and well-being of building occupants	Design building envelopes to ensure comfort criteria per the standard and HVAC systems to maintain these thermally comfortable environments.

Table 14.13. Equity theme, Salisbury Village East

GUIDING PRINCIPLES
Provide Diversity and Choice: Provide a variety of housing units and tenures, as well as diversity of employment choices.

Sustainable Design Goals	Target for Salisbury
Provide flexibility, universal accessibility, and diversity in housing form and employment opportunities	Design housing and commercial spaces to be adaptable and flexible. Providing residents and building owners with solutions for adapting their homes and offices to suit changing lifestyles enables people to stay in the same neighborhood for a much longer time frame. Designing with this concept in mind means that people do not have to leave the neighborhood because their unit no longer accommodates their needs. The range of permitted uses and the design of the buildings incorporate flexibility into how they are used, in both the present and the future. The range of housing types and tenures will provide "life cycle" housing for young families to seniors.

14.14. Culture theme, Salisbury Village East

GUIDING PRINCIPLES

Provide Safe and Social Public Places: Encourage the development of linked public places for gathering and interaction between the various uses.

Encourage Environmental Stewardship: Promote continued environmental responsibility and lifestyles, including tree stewardship, transit use, waste reduction, energy conservation, and natural water cleansing.

Create Enduring Value: Ensure that public and private investment in public infrastructure is well planned to gain maximum value, especially for public safety and amenity in the area.

Sustainable Design Goals	Target for Salisbury
Create a sense of "special place"	Bring a sense of place to the community. Create a special destination within Sherwood Park for cultural activities and festivals.
Provide places to interact, educate, and socialize on-site and connect to other off-site facilities	Create a variety of places for community interaction, including the eco-center, parks, plazas, water park, and coffee shops.
Provide a wide range of public spaces and places on-site to encourage local activity programming and events	Encourage a wide variety of spaces, plazas, parks, and a main street for residents, visitors, and employees to interact.
Create authentic cultural identification	Reference the natural, cultural, and historic features of the site in urban design, buildings, and public art. Incorporating references to the culture and heritage of Salisbury Village creates a shared sense of pride, ownership, and stewardship, and helps to nourish and sustain a strong character and identity. It provides meaning and diversity to the physical expression of the community and reinforces the emotional connection to Salisbury in the context of Sherwood Park. The wetland areas and the greenway corridors (pathways) incorporate native vegetation and emulate the natural hydrological regime. Street furniture and lighting are designed to incorporate natural and cultural features, including the proposed Heritage Trail along Wye Road. The Salisbury Village "Main Street" can also follow a theme to reflect some of the roots of Sherwood Park.
Bring a pedestrian scale to the buildings, sidewalks, and open space places	Designing identifiable and strongly articulated buildings and other features helps to maintain a sense of place, especially when animation occurs at a pedestrian scale. Ensuring that spaces throughout the neighborhood are appropriately scaled and characteristically different based on their exposure, accessibility, and location also helps to reinforce a sense of community identity.

The Salisbury Village East Neighborhood Plan provides a comprehensive checklist (chart) of requirements for implementation that are specific for the site and follow twelve themes of sustainability. The six required components of the successful action plan introduced at the beginning of the chapter— vision, ownership, organization, resources, tools, and evaluation—create the overall framework necessary for successful implementation of the sustainable urban design plan.

The next two chapters profile the Metro Vancouver region and the city of Vancouver. These two case studies take implementation further— analyzing the performance of sustainable regions and cities on the ground. To be a sustainable city, the city has to be part of a sustainable region.

15
METRO VANCOUVER: SUSTAINABLE REGIONALISM

The protection of the region's livability must be supplemented by a transition to sustainability.

—Michael Harcourt and Ken Cameron, *City Making in Paradise*

This chapter examines the Vancouver region, set on the west coast of Canada and home to the 2010 Winter Olympics. It looks at the regional planning framework and associated decisions that created the policy context for sustainable regional planning and design on the ground. It summarizes the process, products, and associated decisions that shaped the Vancouver region and set precedents for the future not only for this region but also for evolving urban regions around the world. This discussion also sets the regional context for the city of Vancouver sustainable urbanism chapter that follows.

In 1792, Captain George Vancouver recognized the scenic potential of what was to become Metro Vancouver, British Columbia. "To describe the beauty of this region will, on some occasion, be a very grateful task for the pen," he wrote.[1] This coastal area is the most temperate region in Canada and the gateway to the Pacific Ocean.

Over the next forty years, Metro Vancouver is expected to grow from 2.3 to 3.4 million people as the third-largest metropolitan area in Canada, adding an estimated 600,000 jobs and 550,000 homes.[2] Factors such as an aging population, smaller households, smart transportation, and higher environmental priorities will be important economic and social drivers that will further change the face of the region. Maintaining a critical balance among managing growth, retaining neighborhood character, and establishing new neighborhoods through insightful urban design will be central to the quality of the emerging region and the cities within it.

The Vancouver region's form is shifting to higher intensification of land uses. The president of one of the region's largest housing development companies recently commented, "We don't build single-family housing anymore," referring to the radical transformation of building type and consumer demand that has evolved over the past twenty years in the Greater Vancouver area (now known as Metro Vancouver). Limited land, escalation in prices, and quality design are some of the factors making higher density "cool" in the region. The massive influx of immigrants from Asian countries, among others, over the past twenty-five years has especially fed the high-rise markets in the region as the original office boom transitioned to the creative economy and a tourism emphasis.

Major transformations are happening. Transit use is on the rise, with a target of 50 percent of all regional travel to be made by sustainable modes (walking, cycling, and transit) by 2040.[3] Compared with the cities of Portland and Seattle, Vancouver is making critical advances in sustainable forms of urbanism, especially increasing housing densities.[4] This information comes from the Sightline Institute, a nonprofit organization that creates a "scorecard" each year of the Cascadia megaregion from Vancouver to Portland—a geographical region shaped by physical form, location, and planning traditions.

Region by design
Without a regional planning and design structure, the growth of cities is largely uncontrolled and is ruled predominantly by land economics. The result, as we have seen in many North American cities, is urban sprawl—a never-ending conglomeration of sameness and single uses. Cars dominate. The consequences in the long run are costly, environmentally irresponsible, and inefficient. It takes regional policy structure, cooperation, and priorities to determine a long-term framework that makes more sense and is governed by the collective benefits of sound planning. The Vancouver region is much more

than suburbia, and a successful regional model extends far beyond downtown Vancouver. This regional model of development was not an accident but the result of fifty years of strategic processes and plans, culminating in critical decisions that shape the region today and into the future.

First, the Vancouver region has to be placed in a geographic and demographic context to understand the unique and dynamic nature of the area. For this first regional discussion, Vancouver will be referred to as the organic city that extends well beyond its political boundaries to the physical geography that cradles and contains its growth and future potential. The Vancouver region, now officially named Metro Vancouver, consists of twenty-two municipalities and one electoral area. The region has experienced nearly 60 percent population growth, from 1.2 million in 1981 to over 2 million in 2006. At the same time, only approximately 50 percent of the region is developable because of the establishment of the Green Zone (agricultural lands, parks, forested lands, wetlands, protected watersheds, and lands too steep to develop). No wonder Vancouver is very thoughtful about the land it has remaining for expansion. Developable land is a very scarce resource. Careful urban design matters.

Those planning Vancouver made some key decisions over the past fifty years that have helped shape the destiny of the city and region. The following is a brief historical summary that focuses on urban design and the associated planning policies that created the foundation for desirable sustainable urban form and densities.

1. Saying no to urban renewal and the freeway through downtown

The city of Vancouver is one of the only cities in North America that does not have a freeway running through its downtown. Most cities are trying to dismantle their downtown freeways to regain access to the city's heart or to valued waterfronts that have been barricaded for decades. Vancouver's farsighted decision is the result of an active community saying no to an urban renewal push in the 1950s and 1960s, coupled with a freeway proposal to alleviate traffic challenges (fig. 15.1).

It took the heroic and persistent efforts of community activists, such as Shirley Chan and Darlene Marzari, to stop the "slum clearance" initiative that would have eradicated a good portion of the Strathcona neighborhood. The January 1968 council meeting marked the death of the freeway proposal that would have scarred Chinatown and Strathcona indefinitely.[5] At stake were the rich histories and traditions of these established communities. Chinatown and Strathcona were thought to be somewhat alterable, if not disposable, in the name of "urban renewal" that destroyed the historic fabric and cultural roots of many core areas in North America at that time.[6]

The victory in saving the neighborhoods and saying no to the freeway proposal created a number of other benefits and spin-offs that affected future planning and design in Vancouver, including the following:

- definitively changing the way the city and the region view transportation and methods to move people, not cars, through the region and city
- creating a new public participation movement in planning and design that swayed political will
- establishing the worth of all neighborhoods and their intrinsic historic and cultural values
- providing a gateway for heritage conservation efforts to consider the retention of buildings, neighborhoods, and landscapes

Figure 15.1. Highway to destruction, Vancouver, British Columbia. The view from Comox and Thurlow Streets of the proposed "Big Trench" freeway in 1960 shows minibridges on Robson, Haro, Alberni, and Georgia Streets (sketch, left). The architectural rendering (right) shows the proposed two hundred residential and office towers along the Gastown waterfront in 1966 and the waterfront freeway. (Source: *Vancouver Sun.*)

2. *Creating the Agricultural Land Reserve and the green zones*

Ken Cameron was one of the true architects of the Livable Region Strategic Plan, serving as a member of the planning team and then for twenty-six years as manager of planning for the Greater Vancouver Regional District (now Metro Vancouver). According to him, one of the key form-makers for the region was the creation of the Agricultural Land Reserve (ALR) in 1973, which became the foundation for the Green Zone established in the Livable Region Strategic Plan in 1996.

Only 5 percent of British Columbia's land is suitable for agriculture, and only 1 percent is classified as Class One.[7] Much of this Class One land is located in Metro Vancouver. Like the "Golden Horseshoe" area in Southern Ontario that runs from Toronto to Niagara Falls, the most fertile lands around the city of Vancouver have been under pressure for urban development for decades. By 1973, an estimated 20 percent of all arable land in British Columbia had been consumed by urban development.[8] There was an urgent need to protect farmland. The formation of the Agricultural Land Reserve through the provincial Land Commission Act in 1973 signaled the preservation of land suitable for farming and the associated production of food, especially for the Greater Vancouver area. The ALR has continued to be the main device for agricultural land retention over the past few decades. It and the associated Agricultural Land Commission were reinforced by the subsequent Green Zone policy of the Greater Vancouver Regional District, which required cooperation from the member municipalities to create a green superstructure for the region (fig. 15.2).

The move to limit development on valuable agricultural land had a number of important impacts on urban design and planning, including the following:

- limiting the amount of development land in the region and therefore encouraging higher densities and compact development
- creating a stable commitment to agricultural land and production as a local necessity for sustainable local food systems

- through the Green Zone initiative, developing a formidable green working landscape for the region as its "lungs"—all adding to the region's livability

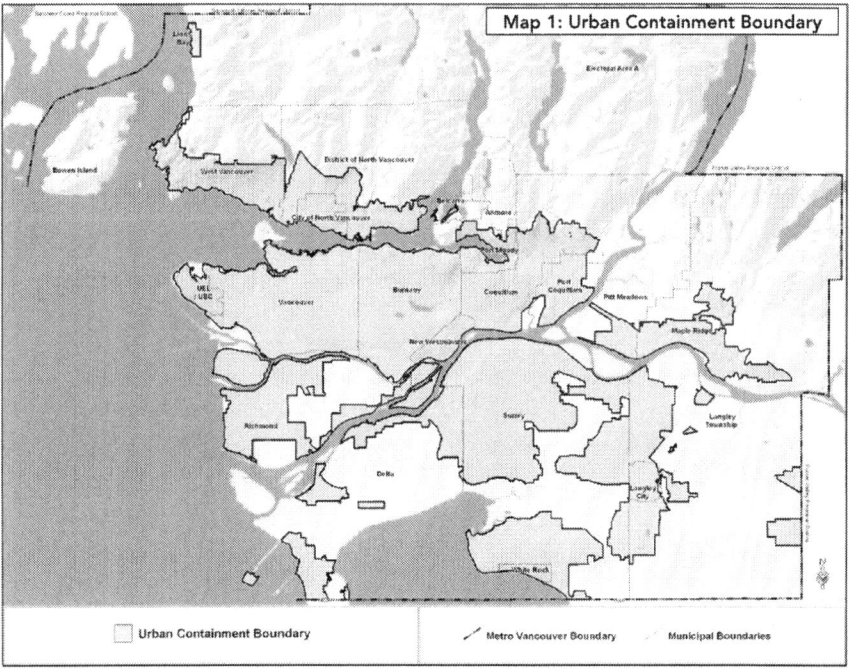

Figure 15.2. Urban containment boundary, Metro Vancouver, British Columbia (2009). This map illustrates the importance of containing and concentrating growth while retaining agricultural land, green zone for recreation, and other conservation areas. (Source: *Metro Vancouver Draft Regional Growth Strategy*, 2009.)

3. *Committing to a transportation framework and regional town center concept*

As a regional planning agency, Metro Vancouver provides the infrastructure to each of its member municipalities. This authority has created a more cooperative planning approach, as much by civil necessity as by healthy evolution and cooperation. The emergence of TransLink, the South Coast British Columbia Transportation Authority, added muscle to regional transportation—in both its conceptual development and its implementation. Originally conceived as an implementation tool for the

Livable Region Strategic Plan and its associated regional transportation plans, TransLink was the first transportation authority in North America that was responsible for not only the planning, finance, and management of all public transit but also the system of major roads and bridges, cycling infrastructure, and transportation demand management.

TransLink's original governance and legislative structure featured policy direction from a board of local elected representatives and a legislative mandate to adhere to the region's growth management strategy and economic and air quality objectives. However, conflicting views in the region as to where and what kinds of transportation improvements should be made and the associated financial commitments were a challenge to decision making from the outset. As a result, the province of British Columbia amended the legislation in 2007 to replace the board of elected representatives with a "business" board and to sever the connection to regional policies and plans. TransLink is now essentially a provincial organization to implement the province's farsighted transportation concepts in a comprehensive and integrated manner within a financial framework that can support little more than existing facilities and services.

Oddly enough, Metro Vancouver does not have an overall land use plan that regulates land uses across the region. Instead, its planning directions were shaped by the Livable Region proposals originating in 1975. These ideas were amplified and formalized in the Livable Region Strategic Plan as a regional growth strategy in 1996, which was an overall vision implemented by its member municipalities through their specific land use plans and zoning. This vision championed the idea of a series of regional town centers connected to each other and to the heart of downtown Vancouver by a light rapid transit system. The town centers and transit system defined the major structural elements for the plan (fig. 15.3). The Green Zone formed the next layer, reflecting the original regional planning concept of "cities in a sea of green."

These regional planning policies created the growth framework and set the basis for an investment of billions of dollars in Burnaby Town Centre (Metrotown) and Surrey City Centre—major residential and retail centers in the region. Metrotown is an established retail and residential center in the region, while Surrey City Centre is now emerging as the powerhouse south of the Fraser River, anchored by Simon Fraser University and a new civic center. Notwithstanding all these efforts and successes, continued regional suburban growth, dispersion of employment into auto-dependent business parks, limited financial resources, and the continued reliance on the single-occupant vehicle continue to challenge the region's sustainable growth goals.

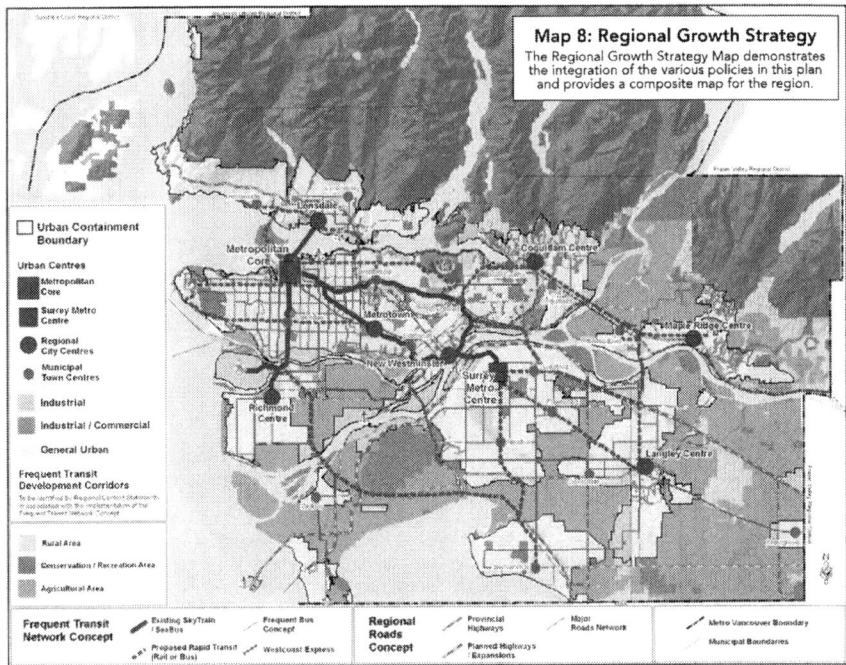

Figure 15.3. Regional growth strategy, Metro Vancouver, British Columbia (2009). This map illustrates the regional town center concept linked by a rapid transit system. (Source: *Metro Vancouver Draft Regional Growth Strategy*, 2009.)

Municipalities working cooperatively

The overall growth management structure for the region provides significant lessons and creates the framework for each municipality to work together in designing and planning their edges. The structure also informs a number of enlightened policy directions for other metropolitan regions to follow, including the following:

- concentrating commercial and job growth in a few priority growth centers in the municipalities that also contain key public facilities (libraries, schools)
- linking these centers with fast, efficient transit and creating multi-modal link opportunities to buses and other modes of transportation
- intensifying the town centers with high-density residential uses to support the commercial uses throughout the day and evening
- planning for regional growth management and transportation in an integrated, iterative way so that transportation reinforces growth management and vice versa
- planning infrastructure and servicing based on a more concentrated model for efficiency and conserving the valuable green zones for recreation, as well as environmental and agricultural protection
- creating a spirit of collaboration and cooperation among member municipalities and other public authorities that translates into the collective power of shaping an outstanding region
- bringing planning, financing, and operations for transit, roads, transportation demand management, and cycling together under one agency financed primarily with revenues from transportation users (i.e., fares, fuel taxes, parking levies, etc.)

In the past thirty years, the region has continued its transformation from primarily single-family housing sprawl to a variety of more compact housing forms and regional centers. The proportion of new homes that were single detached was 56 percent in 1980; by 2010 it had dropped to 30 percent. This dramatic change can be illustrated through a strategic planning and urban design project in the township of Langley, 28 miles (45 km) east of Vancouver, linked by the Trans-Canada Highway. The township of Langley has a growing population of 106,000 people (in 2012) within an area of 119 square miles (307 km²) and is expected to double in population over the next thirty years. The township of Langley is dominated by 75 percent Agricultural Land Reserve (ALR), so the remaining 25 percent requires a more compact development approach. This project presents a series of progressive planning policies that resulted in a much improved and supported plan. Continuing interest by the township of Langley in more compact development is encouraging a move toward community sustainability.

In 2005, MVH Urban Planning & Design facilitated a conversation between the township of Langley and developers that essentially will double the density in the newly proposed Willoughby Town Centre area (part of the Yorkson Neighbourhood Plan).[9] The Yorkson Neighbourhood Plan proposes 80 percent multiple-family units and an overall density of fifteen units per acre (thirty-seven units/ha)—a high density relative to other suburban locations. The Willoughby Town Centre plan proposed—for example, within the mixed residential designation—that on a 5-acre (2-ha) block, 50 percent would be single-family housing and 50 percent multiple-family housing units. This strategy will create a mixed-density neighborhood and will not permit strata developments with separate driveway entrances. The plan doubles the density in the Willoughby Town Centre plan area and was supported by the developers involved in the area, particularly as land prices rose above $1 million per acre ($2.5 million/ha).

The proposed intensification translated into a diversity of housing types combined with a rich community amenity package—always crucial when increasing density. The township of Langley project represents a cooperative effort to define and solve complex intensification challenges by offering mutual benefits to all parties through quality urban design, while retaining neighborhood character, social equity, and economic efficiencies.

The rise of the Vancouver region and critical decisions for contained growth, green zones, and regional town centers continues to require foresight and courage by all the regional municipalities. The Metro Vancouver board gave a second reading to the Greater Vancouver Regional District Growth Strategy in January 2011 as a step toward implementing Metro Vancouver's Sustainable Region Framework, adopted by the regional board in 2008. The most recent plan introduces climate change as an integral part of the growth strategy, along with protecting agriculture, recreation, and conservation lands; and supporting the regional economy by protecting industrial land uses, identifying places for jobs, connecting transit in a regional network, and building complete and healthy communities. Metro

Vancouver is taking a leadership role in translating sustainable concepts into regional policies and strategies that are implementable through local programs and initiatives.

The next chapter will shift our focus from the region (Metro Vancouver) to the city of Vancouver and carefully define the historic evolution, urban design terms, and policies that are now widely known as the "Vancouver model."

16
CITY OF VANCOUVER: SUSTAINABLE URBANISM

> Vancouver has achieved an urban renaissance more comprehensive than any other city in North America.
>
> —John Punter, *The Vancouver Achievement*

Vancouver is a city framed by dramatic mountains on the edge of the Pacific Ocean, brimming with natural resources from rivers and rain forests (fig. 16.1). Up to the late 1960s, Vancouver was frequently referred to as "a setting in search of a city," but the past fifty years set the foundation for its current recognition as one of the top cities in the world.

This chapter examines the city of Vancouver and its aspirations to become the greenest city in the world. It not only summarizes the innovative processes and policy frameworks but examines the detailed design elements that collectively shape the unique nature of Vancouver's urban design. The objective of this discussion is to enrich our understanding of the importance of local design leadership, detailed design directions, and a collaborative relationship with the real estate development community in shaping sustainable urbanism.

Top-of-the-world city

In 2011, Vancouver was selected as the third most livable city in the world out of 140 cities surveyed by the Economist Intelligence Unit, a market research department of *The Economist* magazine. Vancouver placed

411

first in 2010. Only Melbourne, Australia, and Vienna, Austria, exceeded Vancouver as the place where people prefer to live if they could choose anywhere in the world.

Today, Vancouver is a city of almost 650,000 people in a region of over 2.3 million people. Residents from a mix of cultures speak more than seventy different languages in this city that embraces cultural diversity. With a major influx of Asian immigrants to Vancouver in the 1990s, more than 50 percent of the residents speak English as their second language. At 13,817.6 people per square mile (5,335 per km^2) in 2006, downtown Vancouver is the fourth most densely populated incorporated city with a population above 500,000 in North America, after New York City, San Francisco, and Mexico City.[1]

The city of Vancouver downtown urban design is also on the world stage. The "Vancouver model," "Vancouverism," and other terms have been coined to describe the outstanding results (and weaknesses, although few) of farsighted public and private leadership in visioning and actualizing the future city. "Vancouverism" is used to describe the philosophies and approaches that have resulted in multiple uses and high-density core areas; a transit-focused and auto-restrained transportation system; exquisite urban design in form and function to echo a spectacular natural setting; and a diverse multicultural population.[2]

The city's existing form, urban design, and focus on "livability," also known as the "Vancouver model," refer to the tower and podium combination that creates a livable street and block interface, as well as a high-quality streetscape and public amenity component. This model comes from a number of processes and the evolution of policies and guidelines that collectively created the armature for progressive and "well-mannered" urban design.[3] The results of the "Living First" strategies[4] and the attendant design and planning policies helped double the residential population downtown from 1990 to 2012. Other performance measures are also formidable. More than 50 percent of people living downtown walk to work, and the patterns of transit use and bike use are changing significantly as the city's urban design evolves.

The city continues to attract planners, politicians, and architects from around the world to discover the magic potion that makes Vancouver outstanding. The story of Vancouver's downtown renaissance contrasts

Figure 16.1. Downtown peninsula and context, Vancouver, British Columbia. This photo shows Granville Island in the foreground under the Granville Street Bridge, False Creek in the middle ground, and Stanley Park in the background (upper left). (Photo credit: globalairphotos.com.)

with so many cities across North America that have abandoned their downtowns for suburbia. This phenomenon is most vividly illustrated by the abandoned houses and blocks of cities such as downtown Detroit. Lack of supportive policy, complex issues, and economic forces still favor the suburbs over downtowns for residential living in the majority of cities across North America.

Setting, historical decisions, and city policy framework

In addition to the role of recent policy initiatives, it is important to understand the natural setting and early decisions that shaped Vancouver's destiny as a world city. The city's setting, planning process, and major projects collectively help to define Vancouver today.

Natural edges and connections

A major part of Vancouver's green legacy was created early in its development. In 1888, one the greatest city parks was opened in the name of Lord Stanley of Preston, the governor-general of Canada at the time. Stanley Park, a magnificent urban forest, is situated on the western edge of the downtown peninsula, bordered on the north by Burrard Inlet and on the south by False Creek, another saltwater inlet. An estimated 80,000 trees cover most of the 1,000 acres (400 ha) of land—a singular city-center park unmatched on the North American continent and a remnant of a vast west coast rain forest that once covered the city. This natural recreational oasis sits on the doorstep of 40,000 people who live in the city's residential West End and counterbalances the urban concentration in the downtown. It is visited by an estimated 2.5 million pedestrians, cyclists, and in-line skaters every year. A famous 5.5-mile (8.8-km) seawall encircles the park, which is crisscrossed by approximately 120 miles (200 km) of trails and roads. Stanley Park is ranked the sixteenth best park in the world and sixth in North America by Project for Public Spaces of New York City.

The vision of the 1929 Bartholomew Plan for Vancouver helped extend the green of Stanley Park along English Bay to False Creek in a grand promenade that forms the backbone of an extensive 14-mile (22.5-km) seawall walkway and bikeway system. We tend to underestimate the impact of parks like Stanley Park on the physical and cultural health of urban centers today. In Vancouver, the 1,800-acre (729-ha) Pacific Spirit Park, bordering the city's west side, provides another great natural oasis, as does the waterfront that wraps itself around much of the city. This juxtaposition of nature and city adds to the dynamic theater of the cityscape and makes Vancouver that much more sensational to see and experience.

Over 100,000 people live in downtown Vancouver today, and another 20,000 residents will join them in another ten to twenty years. The areas of Granville Slopes (fig. 16.2), North False Creek, Downtown South, Coal Harbour, and Southeast False Creek have brought new life to previous industrial areas.

In addition to the downtown core area, the other real heart of Vancouver is its long-established residential neighborhoods and the rich contrasts that they bring to the city. The design signature of landscape architect Frederick Todd in the late 1800s can be readily seen in the sweeping boulevards, grand tree canopies, and street parks of Shaughnessy. The rural pastoral character of Southlands seems a world away from the hustle and bustle of downtown. The more central, tightly knit urban fabric of Kitsilano contrasts with the suburban cluster development of Champlain Heights in the southeastern corner of the city.

Figure 16.2. Built form of Granville Slopes, Vancouver, British Columbia. Located west of North False Creek and east of the West End, this neighborhood was developed in the 1980s and reveals some of the classic "Vancouver model" elements—mixed-use buildings, a continuous waterfront walkway, and the extension of streets and street-end views.

Classic street grid and the emergence of the streetcar city

Cities are sculpted in large part too by human hands in the form of streets, blocks, and transportation corridors. Vancouver is no exception. Since the 1800s, when the first surveys of the city began, the design of Vancouver followed the classic street grid that shaped blocks for development. The size of those blocks and their natural interconnectedness provided multiple opportunities for access and mobility throughout the city. Until 1945,

Vancouver evolved as a streetcar city—walkable and transit accessible. The streetcar arterials remain the social hubs of the adjoining neighborhoods, within a five-minute walk of every household and brimming with convenient neighborhood services, such as cafés, professional offices, and grocery stores. Downtown is no exception, as Granville, Robson, Davie, and Denman Streets are overflowing with life. The emerging block pattern (264 by 396 feet, or 81 by 121 m) provided not only for single-family housing but also, in frequent cases, for the eventual high-rise intensification that consumes much of the downtown today.[5] After 1945, the suburban boom was on; the streetcar was eliminated as the popular mode of transport, replaced first by trolley and then by diesel buses. However, this smart and sustainable urban streetcar framework is still in place, a basis for adaptable future urban form that capitalizes on its efficiencies and conveniences.

Three citywide plans that shape Vancouver

How did the city of Vancouver help develop and lead the shaping of the communities just discussed? How did the city respond to continuing growth pressures and help direct development through progressive policies? The city had a choice to either sit back and respond to crisis on a project-by-project basis or adopt a proactive posture. The tradition of aggressive community participation made the proactive approach the only real option for the city. In order to find enduring and enlightened compatible solutions, they needed to lead, not follow.

Mounting pressure for redevelopment showed up in a variety of major project proposals and surging property values in the single-family residential areas. With average house prices skyrocketing in excess of $650,000 in the early 1990s, character homes were being demolished to make way for "monster" homes with little or no sympathy for neighborhood character. New owners were removing large trees from private property to install paved lawns, and longtime residents had had enough of wholesale exploitation of their established neighborhoods. At the same time, young and old residents wanted to stay in their community, but the necessary housing choices and affordability did not exist. These reasons, among others, motivated the city of Vancouver to embark on a number of initiatives intended to set a structure to manage growth in the city. Three specific plans resulted: CityPlan (1995), the Greenways Plan (1995), and the Transportation Plan (1997), which collectively set a citywide policy framework for the future.

These plans alone do not hold the power of form-makers in the city. It is in their implementation that we see the transformation of the city, as we know it. Growth or no growth is not an option. It is the way growth is managed; therein lies the solution. A new vocabulary emerged as a result of these initiatives, and embedded in this new vocabulary was a new way of viewing the city and of setting priorities in the city's capital allocations. These plans were developed with a high level of public involvement, and each established a set of priorities and action plans based on public feedback. In this way, the major directives that developed received broad-based public support.

Within these city plans, three major forces fundamentally affected the future form and function of Vancouver—land use intensification and mixed use; greenfrastructure (moving people, not cars); and the rise of the public realm and community partnerships—all three of which are discussed in more detail below.

Land use intensification and mixed use

One of the major directions of CityPlan is to concentrate growth in the existing neighborhood centers. Part of this policy is to increase density in these areas and the mix of uses so that jobs and services are closer to home. The function will not only be to provide more of what is there but to diversify the housing stock in each area and provide for a more pedestrian-oriented community. Numerous projects in Kitsilano and Mount Pleasant have disproved the perception that increased density decreases property values, safety, and neighborhood character. Instead, under carefully articulated design guidance, these infill projects can revitalize areas and bring further investment in the public infrastructure, elevating the quality and character of the whole area. This transition to higher densities will not necessarily be an easy one, but if amenities and service improvements complement these proposals within a sensitive urban design guideline framework, then public concerns will transform into public support.

Greenfrastructure: Move people, not cars

As mentioned earlier in the regional discussion, Vancouver city council made a major decision in the 1960s that would affect the direction of transportation in the city. Council determined that no freeways would be built through the city, thus giving it the distinction of making it the only major city in Canada without freeways through its core. Meanwhile, the region's reliance on the automobile continues to exert pressure on Vancouver.

The 1997 Transportation Plan reasserted this priority, but other earlier initiatives set the groundwork for moving Vancouver into the greening mode, because the people of Vancouver wanted it and declared it as one of their top priorities. These priorities reversed the traditional order, placing pedestrians, cyclists, transit, and servicing trips ahead of the single-occupant vehicle. This resetting of priorities radically changed the way the city approached transportation planning. In 1994, a CityPlan survey of Vancouver residents ranked public places, safety, and environment as the most important priorities for the city. The priority for greening the city was further reinforced by a convincing 1996 survey of one thousand city residents that showed 73 percent felt increased regulation was needed to preserve more trees.

The Vancouver Greenways Plan (1997) formalizes the idea of providing a whole network of pedestrian and bicycle pathways throughout the city (fig. 16.3). A total of 85 miles (210 km) of pathways are planned, with a major portion completed as a result of earlier initiatives such as the seawall walkway around Stanley Park and English Bay and fifteen years of implementation. A distinguishing characteristic of the Vancouver Greenways Plan is that more than 50 percent of the greenways will be on city streets (fig. 16.4). The goal is to have a city greenway within a fifteen-minute walk or a ten-minute bike ride of every Vancouver resident. These city greenways will be supplemented by neighborhood greenways that will create a finer network at the local level.

Related city initiatives, such as street gardening, public art, the Tree Trust, and blueways (improving water access and use in the city), are empowering neighborhoods to take control of their destinies with the

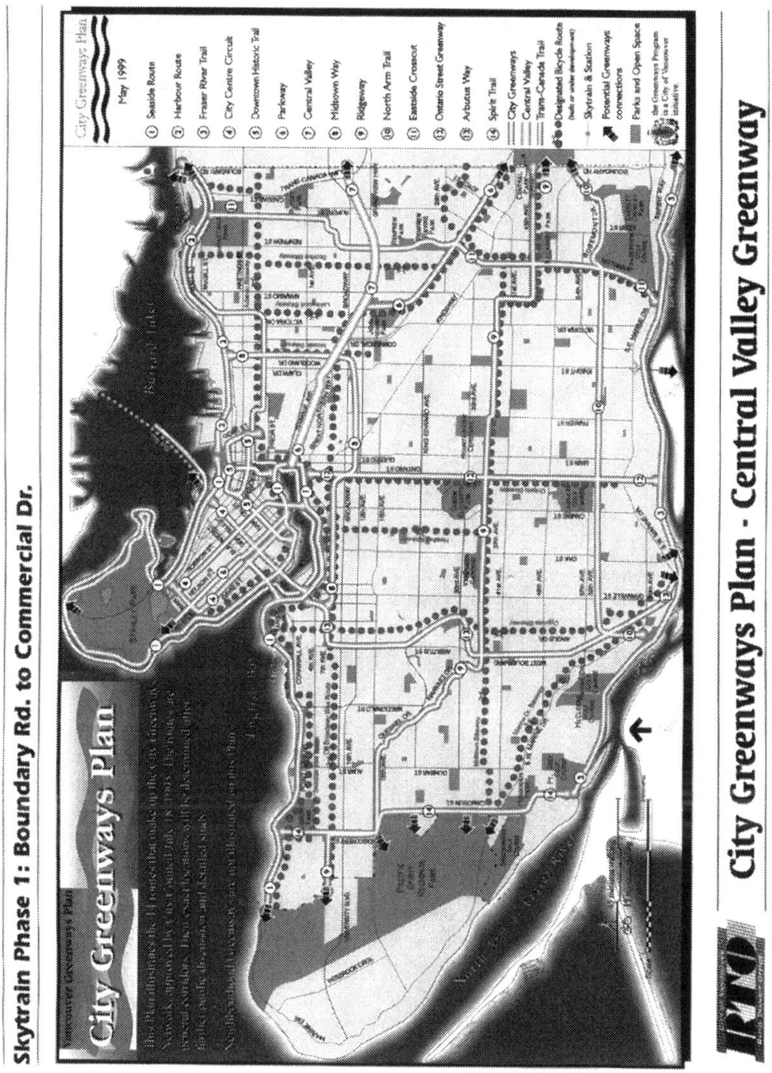

Figure 16.3. Greenways Plan, Vancouver, British Columbia. This plan sets out an interconnected network of pathways for pedestrians and cyclists to move through the city in an accessible, safe, and convenient manner. (Source: City of Vancouver.)

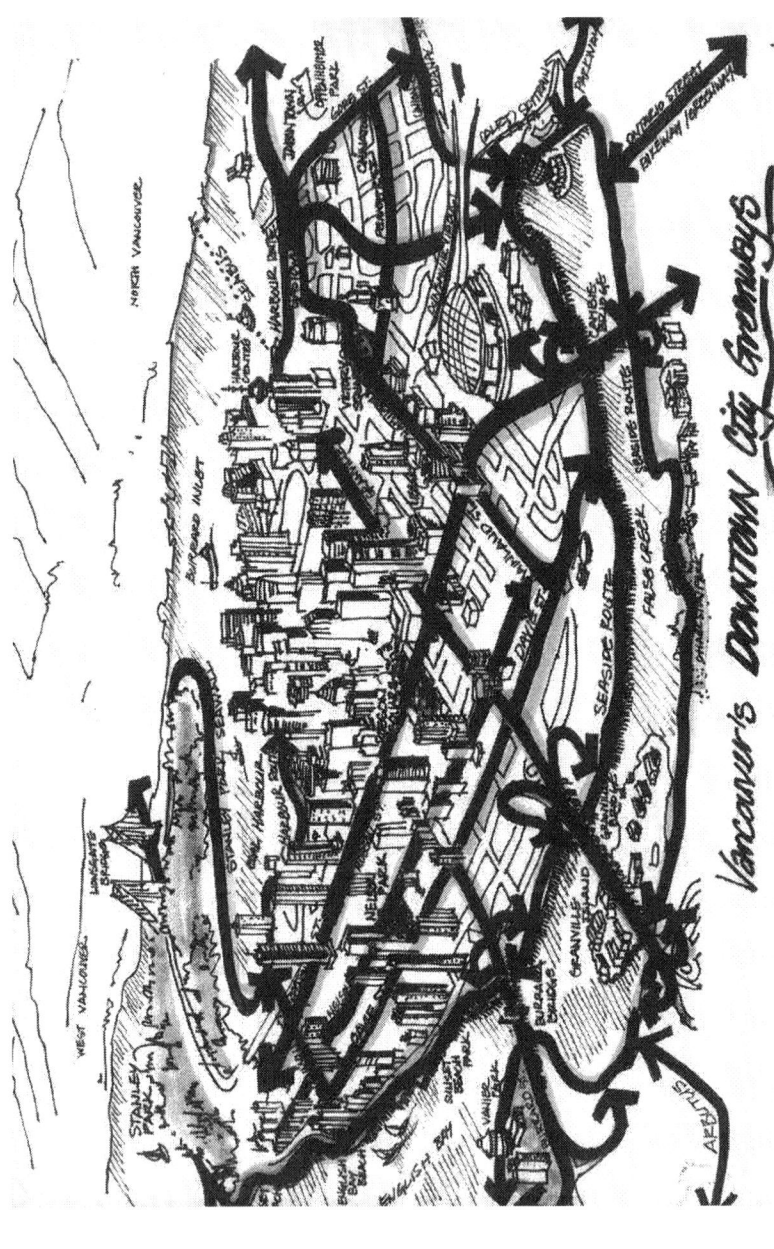

Figure 16.4. Downtown greenways, Vancouver, British Columbia. This early sketch by the author shows the comprehensive network of "public ways," pathways, and trails existing and proposed in and around downtown Vancouver. (Source: City of Vancouver.)

support of the city. Other initiatives that have brought residents in closer touch with nature and conservation include increasing permeable surfaces to reduce flooding and runoff; initiating the rain barrel program to conserve water; and daylighting streams. Between 1995 and 1997 alone, Vancouver added 14,000 trees to the city as a result of various tree-planting programs. This represents an estimated 5 to 7 percent addition to Vancouver's urban forest in just two years.

Rise of the public realm and community partnerships
Streets cover 30 percent of Vancouver. Safe, attractive, and vibrant streets underpin a transformation of the downtown and surrounding neighborhoods. The city has introduced design guidelines for a number of downtown streets. Successful examples of combining the design of private and public property can be seen in Granville Slopes, Triangle West, and Georgia Street. In Downtown South, developers are required to set the building back 12 feet (3.7 m), thereby providing approximately 22 feet (6.7 m) of space between the building wall and the curb. This area allows for a double row of trees and an enhanced definition of the residential or commercial front doors (figs. 16.5 and 16.6). Elevated entries, low walls, grass borders, layered planting, subtle railings, and street furnishings articulate the sense of private, semiprivate, and public space. All these elements bring a sense of continuity, pedestrian scale, and necessary pedestrian function to these streets. "Eyes on the street" and the design of spaces between the buildings, as well as human-scaled and transparent street definition, are paramount.[6]

This partnership between the city and landowners is also exemplified in initiatives such as the citywide Green Streets[7] and Neighbourhood Greenways programs in neighborhoods outside downtown. These programs include planting corner bulges and traffic circles associated with traffic-calming measures; adopting the ongoing maintenance of these areas; as well as adding seating, public art, and pedestrian lighting to provide inviting and safe pathways through the local community. These streets can become a promenade that feels safe and inviting. The streets also contribute to a sense of community, which is sorely lacking in many cities.

Figure 16.5. Downtown South streetscape, Vancouver, British Columbia. Early conceptual sketches illustrate a single and double row of street trees—the first outside row is in the city of Vancouver street right-of-way while the second row of street trees is located in the required setback from the private property line.

Figure 16.6. Downtown South streetscape, Vancouver, British Columbia. This photo shows early stages of implementation with immature trees.

"Vancouver model" principles, process, and design innovations

Behind the successful urban design results in Vancouver are a whole series of innovations in process and design frameworks that shape the projects on the ground but remain behind the scenes, without specific publicity. Excellent cooperation on process and detailed design,[8] supported by direct Vancouver Planning Department policy and guideline documents, provide insights into the conscious structure behind the design and planning innovations.

Policy framework: The family of plans

The city of Vancouver, under the liberation of its city charter, did not have (and still does not have) a prescriptive overall land use plan (or Official Community Plan) that other municipalities in British Columbia are mandated to have. Instead, the city developed an overall general directions plan (CityPlan), approved in 1995 and implemented by individual "visions" for neighborhoods. Other plans—for example, the Transportation Plan and Greenways Plan—provide more specific guidelines on special topics throughout the city. The downtown and major development sites are also governed by specific plans and policies (Official Development Plans) that describe comprehensive development policy for each area. These areas include the megaprojects of North False Creek, Coal Harbour, Southeast False Creek, Downtown South, Arbutus Neighborhood, Collingwood Village, and East Fraser Lands.

Discretionary zoning

The zoning in Vancouver provides a basis for innovation and incentives. It is essentially a negotiated process that requires community amenities and other considerations in return for additional floor space (normally residential). Within downtown neighborhoods the floor space ratio (FSR) ranges from 4.0 to 5.0, which translates into high-rise towers and sufficient density to compensate for increased amenities. This discretion provides a portal to attain an expansive and customized public realm and amenity package for each neighborhood as it expands and additional services are required.

Differences in the city's flexibility and responsiveness in terms of negotiating design alternatives and public amenities in rezonings are important to highlight. In some situations (e.g., Downtown South), the projects already had a street structure in place and involved multiple developers on relatively small parcels. This situation contrasted with the new megaprojects, such as North False Creek, that involved one developer, included a large piece of land, and required a new street and block structure. These megaprojects, having large land holdings and a single developer, allowed more flexibility in negotiating and exploring innovations in urban form, as well as amenities.

Design guidelines, special policies, and principles

The city of Vancouver continues to play a key leadership role in setting the policy framework for development. Vancouver has developed a series of design guidelines that are customized to different locations and are framed by overarching principles and policies. These principles, policies, and guidelines collectively translate to different design treatments that create variety yet fit each location within the city.

The following "Living First" principles[9] set the guiding rules that shaped residential emphasis in downtown Vancouver.

- Limit commuter access into the downtown.
- Prioritize walking, cycling, and transit.
- Integrate new development by extending and connecting with existing patterns.
- Develop complete neighborhood units with supportive commercial services, including community amenities and schools.
- Provide a diversity of housing types, including both market and nonmarket housing (20 percent target for nonmarket and 25 percent suitable for families), mixed incomes, family and nonfamily households, special needs housing, and unique housing choices (floating homes and lofts).
- Encourage fine-grained mixed use and proximity of live, work, play, and learn both vertically and horizontally.
- Expand sidewalks as outdoor rooms and "third places" for social activity and interaction, supported by special design guidelines and unique treatments in different areas.
- Create park and greenway connections to extend and include developments in the Metro Vancouver mobility and recreation network.

Specific design guidelines help shape the physical distinctiveness of the "Vancouver model." These start at the context level and progress through the block to the building and street level. The following list represents signature elements and is not meant to be all-inclusive. (Specific guidelines and policies for each area or neighborhood outline further nuances in adaptation and application; see figs. 16.7 and 16.8.)

- View corridors are retained specific to the downtown skyline and views to the mountains.
- Building orientation, access, and entries are identified.

- Maximum building height and massing are specified, with smaller floor plates and slimmer building profiles.
- Transparent and "lighter" building materials are required for a more integrated building massing and a brighter complexion.
- Continuous weather protection is mandatory at ground level at entries and along commercial storefronts (varies in some parts).
- Each design area has rich streetscape requirements for the private and public realm.
- All ground-floor dwelling units have individual entries.
- Parking garages are hidden or completely underground.
- Buildings have maximum and minimum heights along street frontages.
- Terraces or gardens are located at ground-floor dwelling unit entries.
- Building facades are articulated so that the individual townhomes are distinguished from one another.
- Specific design elements are specified within the setback areas at the ground elevation.
- Individual dwelling entries are raised at least 3.3 feet (1 m) above ground elevation.
- Retail and other on-street uses are separated to manage noise and bring housing to street level.
- Blank walls are not acceptable, so wrapping windows around corners or detailed stoops, or street animation is necessary.
- Bland plazas are avoided in favor of more usable park space built into each building cluster.
- Vehicular access and curb cuts are minimized by providing access through rear entrances off lanes.
- Above- and below-ground walkways are not permitted, as they take energy and activity from the street.
- Sun and shade are delicately handled, with required studies and design attention.
- Private and semiprivate green roofs and programmed spaces are maximized to green the overlooks and to provide active and passive space for residents, as well as businesses.

Figure 16.7. False Creek North (Concord Pacific Place), Vancouver, British Columbia. This photograph reveals a multitude of successful urban design elements, including an active mixed-use ground floor that wraps around the corner, a unified two-story street wall for pedestrian scale, extension of the city's street grid to the waterfront with street-end views, a central boulevard on the access street to calm traffic, slim towers with light materials to reduce visual impact and visual permeability, and reuse of the roundhouse historical building as a community center.

Figure 16.8. Public park and public realm, Downtown South, Vancouver, British Columbia. The addition of public park space and intricate street design treatment—including bike racks, seating, boulevard shrub and tree planting, as well as stepped transitions—are making this neighborhood attractive, safe, active, and vibrant.

Review and approval processes for major projects

Overall, major projects in Vancouver require a special process that involves the developers, public, and politicians in liaison with assigned staff. The project is scrutinized through a number of filters. The process allows for consensus building on large-scale conceptual issues at the beginning and for detailed design at the end.

The design development and approval process consists of the following distinct steps:

- Development of policy broadsheet (Official Development Plan) by staff and developers while engaging in a series of public workshops and council reviews
- Building of the development framework plan by staff and developer, refined through public workshops and council hearings
- Development of detailed design guidelines within each block of the neighborhood, with consulting architects and landscape architects consulting with local stakeholders and with feedback from city council
- Submission of rezoning application based on development plan and design guidelines with formal staff review and the Urban Design Panel (an independent council-appointed group of design experts) and review by the Development Permit Board
- Final public hearing by city council

Vancouver pays attention to details in implementation. Whether it be building or landscape inspections supported by consulting architects, landscape architects, and engineers, the design drawings are carefully implemented on-site. This conscientious attention to detail in implementation through the monitoring and inspections defines the difference between excellence and unacceptable performance. Building materials application, omissions of details, and material quality are all variables that need constant due diligence in implementation. Otherwise, many of the good intentions can be lost at the hands of a contractor. Requiring a high standard in construction is critical to success, especially in complex projects where multiple steps are occurring at the same time or in close succession.

Emerging building types

It is interesting to observe actual urban design results. The design guidelines and policies have resulted in three new building types:

- Point towers above two to three town house bases
- Point towers rising from six- to eight-story apartment blocks containing ground-floor "cityhomes"
- Four- to twelve-story apartment blocks containing ground-floor cityhomes

Cityhomes are distinguished from townhomes in that they contain two-story ground-floor units with an additional two to six floors above them, accessed by a common street-level lobby. They also have a common garage-level lobby, common elevators, and common internal corridors. These building types can be categorized in typologies, as has been done here, but actual observation of the constructed buildings reveals a healthy variation in design details. These buildings feature diversity in building window treatments, color palette and highlights, tree-planting and walkways treatments, lighting, terrace details, roof use and articulation, cornice and parapet expressions, as well as a mix of ground-floor uses.

Financing growth

The city of Vancouver requires that the developers pay for growth associated with development so that the taxpayer does not shoulder this burden. A recent exception has been the Southeast False Creek project (also known as the Olympic Village), a situation that was not anticipated but which was a result of various unforeseen factors (2008 financial crisis and others). The overriding principle is that all developers should pay their fair share of public utilities and facilities.

Developers are responsible for the site improvements and streetscape improvements adjoining the site. Either they build the street improvements, or the city completes them on their behalf. The balance of off-site improvements related to development are normally part of development cost levies that are paid by the developer to cover parks, day care, replacement housing, and basic infrastructure. Community Amenity Contributions pay for additional public amenities such as community centers and social housing. Public amenity contributions in major projects differ in that they can cover libraries, schools, public art, and specialty items required by the project. These contributions help ensure, along with quality implementation monitoring, that the project is not only implemented properly but that the community benefits as a whole as it grows.

Next step: The greenest city in the world challenge

We are the greenest city in North America and want to be the greenest city in the world by 2020.

—Gregor Robertson, mayor of Vancouver, June 2010

The city of Vancouver is not resting on its laurels. The next level is the "sustainable" city concept, advanced through initiatives such as "EcoDensity" and now through the "Greenest City in the World" initiative. Building neighborhood networks and celebrating culture are core to this initiative. This is a lofty initiative, but it is well under way, with ten clear goals and an action plan delivered in early 2011, as part of an extensive community support network (see www.talkgreenvancouver.ca).

The city of Vancouver faces significant ongoing obstacles in transforming the suburban landscape outside its urban core. In fact, nearly 70 percent of the city of Vancouver is zoned single-family housing. So outside the downtown core (the peninsula), and not unlike other cities, Vancouver planners face opposition in neighborhood intensification, reflected in the ongoing neighborhood visioning processes and the recent EcoDensity initiative.[10] In Vancouver's core area, the city still faces the challenges of dealing with homelessness, combating drug-related crime, and balancing office and residential development to achieve a complete and inclusive community downtown.

The excellent quality of life in Vancouver is partially recognized by a number of international organizations who have called it one of the most livable cities in the world. Still, these are merely superficial indicators. The real proof is on the ground and in the continuing community-building processes that retain that quality of life in physical, social, and economic terms.

Success factors

Much of Vancouver's future development will take place in its established neighborhoods. One hopes that the negative results of the wholesale destruction of entire sections of North American cities in the fifties and sixties under the guise of urban renewal have convinced city planners of the primary importance of retaining the social and historical fabric of the city. Vancouver's current EcoDensity program, with the addition of laneway housing and various other small infill opportunities, does not radically change the look and feel of neighborhoods. The "soft touch" in urban design therefore becomes paramount, with preference for smaller, incremental steps rather than large swaths of development.

Numerous examples of successful and sensitive site development should guide the city's future urban form decisions. The best urban design frequently weaves itself into the surrounding cityscape without the contrasting qualities that normally mark award-winning designs. In order to reach this goal of an enduring and thriving city, the city must respect the word of the local residents and the underlying land patterns. Restoration, rejuvenation, and revitalization then also become genuine design directives, engrained in the sustainable urban design process, not cosmetic and fashionable. Unearthing hidden streams, planting small remnant woodlands, expanding the grass and nature in the city, and shrinking street pavement for increased pedestrian use also then become major form-makers that may start with small incremental steps but together form an extensive addition to our public and private realm. Such initiatives will bring renewed life to city streets everywhere, help make our communities safer, and create an intricate web of pathways and places.

To reflect on Vancouver's achievements is to recognize the key leaders and activists who protected what was necessary, the processes that brought rigor to urban design review, and the collaborative partnerships that brought community, developer, and the city together to actualize design intent on the ground. A commitment to excellence in sustainable urbanism created a focus on exemplary site design. It is not simple—but attainable with passion, commitment, and tenacity within a discretionary regulatory framework that creates additional incentive for design performance.

The conclusion of this book reflects on the need for sustainable urbanism and outlines a series of steps forward to guide the next stage of great world cities, towns, and villages.

17
CONCLUSION

We need a new image of order, which shall include the organic and the personal, and eventually embrace all the offices and functions of man. Only if we can project that image shall we be able to find a new form for the City.

—Lewis Mumford, *The City in History*

Our sustainable urban design journey is now complete, yet it has only just begun. The world is at the edge—of disaster or a renaissance. I believe the future will be largely determined by our choices. The emerging sustainability revolution is both a response to our current challenges and a catalyst for positive transformation. Yet sustainable planning in itself is not enough, for it is simply theory. The integration of sustainable community development with urban design is a means to link theory with practice.

This is the intent of this book: to link the theory of sustainability with urban design practice to create a new model—"dynamic urban design." The model uses a framework (place, process, and plans), components (social, ecological, and economic), and measurement (elements, principles, and targets) to define the full potential of this sustainable urban design approach. The model is somewhat complex but, when reduced to components and steps, is not only clear but attainable on the ground around the world. The vision is a city, town, or village that is compact, healthy, and self-sustaining. The case study illustrations in this book prove that this integrated process is starting to work even though challenges remain.

Barriers to change

A great divide remains between what is viewed as acceptable development in the urban environment versus the suburban and rural design context. Further, urban design professionals' views often conflict with community views. The vision of a compact, transit-oriented community directly conflicts with the traditional view of dispersed, auto-dependent suburban or rural development. Also, the word "density," often associated with sustainable community development, has a certain social stigma. Noise, overcrowding, traffic jams, and crime are often the community fears voiced against this new sustainable dream for our communities.

The North American dream of a single house on a large lot with at least two cars in the garage is still held by many as the cultural reference for the epitome of success. This has been the norm for over fifty years. Unfortunately, this vision is increasingly held by people in other countries. The single home represents status, freedom, privacy, and free will to many. In contrast, the image of the city as the dark, overcrowded den of crime is still foremost in many suburbanites' minds. This urban decay is still the case in some inner-city neighborhoods in the United States, never mind slums of the developing world cities. The media perpetuates especially the negative aspects of the city.

Different interests drive how people see city form in the short and long term. Political, development, or private self-interest can often be masked as community interest. Political interest is shaped by short-term, voter-driven motivations. Development interest is driven primarily by business. Private interests are principally driven by the individual rights and freedoms associated with property rights. These interests are often veiled as community interests. From a short-term perspective, self-interest makes sense. However, from a longer-term, sustainable community development perspective, such self-interest is shortsighted. How do we overcome or change this short-term view of the world?

Change agents

Three fundamental changes are required to create a sustainable urban design. The first is to change people's attitudes. The second is to change the process itself. The third requires a change in results.

To change people's attitudes toward sustainable urban design, we need to elevate participant views from self-interest to community interest. Defining common interest is at the core. Less time driving, more time relaxing, reduced crime, increased quality of life, lower housing costs, more housing choice, and improved health changes people's views. Converting sustainable urban design concepts to community benefits can change attitudes or at least cause a shift toward project support. Personal benefits outweigh the alternative of increased commuting time, increased crime, excessive tax increases, and decreased personal health. An engineer colleague refers to this attitude as "enlightened self-interest."

So *are* attitudes shifting? How do people view living downtown now compared with five to ten years ago? The quality of life, convenience, activity, proximity, and lifestyle certainly can trump the isolated suburban existence. I tested this thesis with my students first a few years ago. Their ages ranged from twenty-five to fifty, and the genders split equally between male and female. There were approximately forty people in the class. I carefully described the choices—a 2,500-square-foot (250-m²) new suburban home and an 800-square-foot (80-m²) downtown apartment in Vancouver. What I found out was predictable but showed a promising trend—about half said they would like to live downtown, and the other half said they would rather live in suburbia. I put the same question to a different class in 2011, a graduate urban studies class. The age and gender split was similar to the first class, but the number of students was fifteen instead of forty. The shift in view surprised me. All the students chose downtown Vancouver.

This result shows promise for changing attitudes. Although mine is not a scientific survey, it reveals that, depending on the city, living downtown in a highly urban environment is a viable alternative. Balancing a desirable lifestyle with jobs and housing, as downtown Vancouver has done over the past two decades, can create compelling attraction factors for residential growth. More than 100,000 people live in Vancouver's downtown, and more than 50 percent walk to work every day. Bringing these features of urban living to our suburban environments and our rural urban designs, at a smaller scale, is both feasible and necessary.

The second required change deals with process. Even if you do not adopt the whole process proposed in this book, you can customize parts of it for other projects. The process has to be visionary and include all interests at the discussion table at the beginning of and throughout the process. Identifying common ground—such as increasing street safety, real estate values, community facilities, transit access, and housing diversity— must be done at the outset. From the initial stages of vision formation through analysis and plan-making, the best process builds trust and understanding in the community. Otherwise, the best sustainable urban design solution will not receive approval, let alone be built. Partnerships and collaboration also start at the onset of the process to build vested interest and commitment.

The third required change improves sustainable urban design results. We are seeing a shift to new urban forms that reconsider over fifty years of expensive overdesign and underperformance, especially in suburban areas. Past suburban development might be viewed as having an attractive physical form but require measurement in economic, social, and ecological benefits. The results should prove that good sustainable urban design makes more common sense and satisfies not only self-interests but the greater community interests. Sustainable urban design produces economic benefits that save money, time, and resources, as well as creates more local jobs. It has distinct social benefits that include greater housing choice, more diverse places to meet, and a sense of more connectedness to neighbors. It creates and protects the sense of place. It makes the community safer yet more accessible and healthier. Sustainable urban design also has significant ecological or environmental benefits. These benefits include improved health, greater conservation of natural elements, and more responsible use of natural systems, resources, and processes.

Combining change agents for greater strength

How do we combine these three necessary changes of converting attitudes, creating an effective process, and proving success by results? When combined, the strength of these three change agents can be most effective. I want to share with you two experiences that combine these three components. The first experience involves the redesign of a section of Abbott Street in Kelowna, British Columbia, Canada. Through the process, a wide roadway dominated by speeding traffic was transformed into a pedestrian-oriented local street.[1] The second experience involves the design of a new community called Cambrian Crossing, east of Edmonton, Alberta, Canada.

The design process was not easy at the beginning in the city of Kelowna. There were historical disagreements between the community and the city's engineering department. Trust needed to be rebuilt between the two parties. Our design team designed a process that included meetings and workshops that openly discussed issues, challenges, and alternatives. Attitudes changed through the process. Over time, the street redesign evolved to a recreation corridor with an emphasis on people rather than cars. The engineering department actually reclassified the street to a recreational corridor. As the barriers came down, the local community actively engaged in the redesign of this street. In the end, the community's design was built with minor technical adjustments by the engineering department. The city has since developed a policy on traffic calming that applies elsewhere. Once trust is established, political support and funding follow. Construction started a few months later, and the first phase was complete that year.

How do we measure the results of this process? For me, one of the most satisfying ways is to go to the site and observe the changes after the design is built. The obvious results are physical: reduced traffic speed and volume, expanded treed boulevards, separated bicycle and pedestrian pathways, improved lighting, increased meeting places, and improved historical recognition of place through public art installations. Economic benefits of these improvements will no doubt lead to increased property values in time. Most satisfying for me are the observed social changes to the street. There is notably more pedestrian and bicycle activity during the day and night. There is a whole change in feel, experience, and priority for the street. It is truly a recreation corridor for the community with a pedestrian and bicycle priority, yet it accommodates the automobile as a visitor to the community, not the dominator it once was.

My observations are capped by a conversation I had with local residents. Two middle-aged women were walking along the sidewalk as I was observing and taking photos of the physical results (fig. 17.1). They were friendly and engaged me as they passed. "Did you have anything to do with this design?" they asked. I responded, "Yes, I helped redesign the street." Without hesitation, they enthusiastically said, "You did an amazing job! We walk here every day and love the place." A feeling of satisfaction came over me as the women walked off into the distance. These statements solidify the results; not only are there measurable ecological and economic benefits, but the social sense of place is improved. The roadway for cars that once split the neighborhood is now a street where the community meets. Sustainable urban design comes home on Abbott Street. It is reflected in the Abbott Street Heritage District's slogan, "Where community and heritage live together."

Figure 17.1. Abbott Street, Kelowna, British Columbia. The transformed Abbott Street after construction shows the separate pedestrian and bicycle recreation pathways, new landscaping including pedestrian-scaled lighting, and narrow car lanes.

The Kelowna example illustrates redesigning a section of an existing urban neighborhood. The Cambrian Crossing example illustrates the design process for an entire new sustainable community in a suburban location.[2] The Cambrian Crossing project is located on a 785-acre (318-ha) site north of Highway 16 and west of Highway 21 in Strathcona County, Alberta, Canada. Old Man Creek bisects the property of rolling farmers' fields. A small established suburban neighborhood is located to the north, while industrial land uses dominate the western border of the property.

Through a Joint Planning Initiative structure, the developer worked closely with the county to develop a sustainable community plan and associated design for the land. The developer already was well along in the process of approving an industrial development when the county approached them with an alternative. The county realized that they would run out of servable residential land within an estimated three to five years, and the Cambrian parcel was the last large parcel within the Urban Service Boundary. In exchange for a reduced review and approvals process, as well as staff support, the county wanted to alter the plan to combine residential, commercial, and recreational uses with a variety of industrial uses. The initiative embraced the concept for a complete and sustainable local community where residents could live, work, and play.

I joined the consulting team to help facilitate the process, build common sustainable interests, and design the plan. As part of this process, tasks and timelines were agreed to, with the county helping to manage and expedite the process (referred to locally as the Sustainable Urban Neighborhood process, or SUN process). Different attitudes toward development were soon replaced by principles of sustainability that had compelling economic, ecological, and social grounding. Both parties developed a vision and set of principles that became the foundation of the plan.

Adjoining landowners were skeptical at first of the process and potential results. Why would the area be anything but industrial, because that was the major land use pattern west of the site? What would the mix of uses bring to the area? Over the course of workshops and a four-day design charrette, the community came to support the proposal. The proposal would provide numerous benefits to the community, including increased real estate values, convenient services, recreation, jobs, and improvements to the road network.

Eight different neighborhoods shape Cambrian Crossing, each with its own identity and mix of uses. The proposal presents a community that will house up to 7,200 residents in 2,600 units. Jobs will be close to home. Approximately 1.7 jobs per household are provided within the community. A supportive eco-industrial network intends to reduce waste and increase the efficient production, exchange, and use of resources. The county and the developer are considering district energy options that will harness energy from waste. Two schools and two places of worship will provide the educational and spiritual needs of the community. A commercial service district will serve the industrial portion, while two local neighborhood service centers and a more major central town center will serve the balance of the residents. Basic services will be located within a five-minute walk of most residents. Schools are also within a five-minute walk, supported by an interconnected network of trails and pathways along the Old Man Creek corridor and throughout the neighborhoods. A bus transit network will further help movement patterns throughout the community and to other destinations (figs. 17.2 and 17.3).

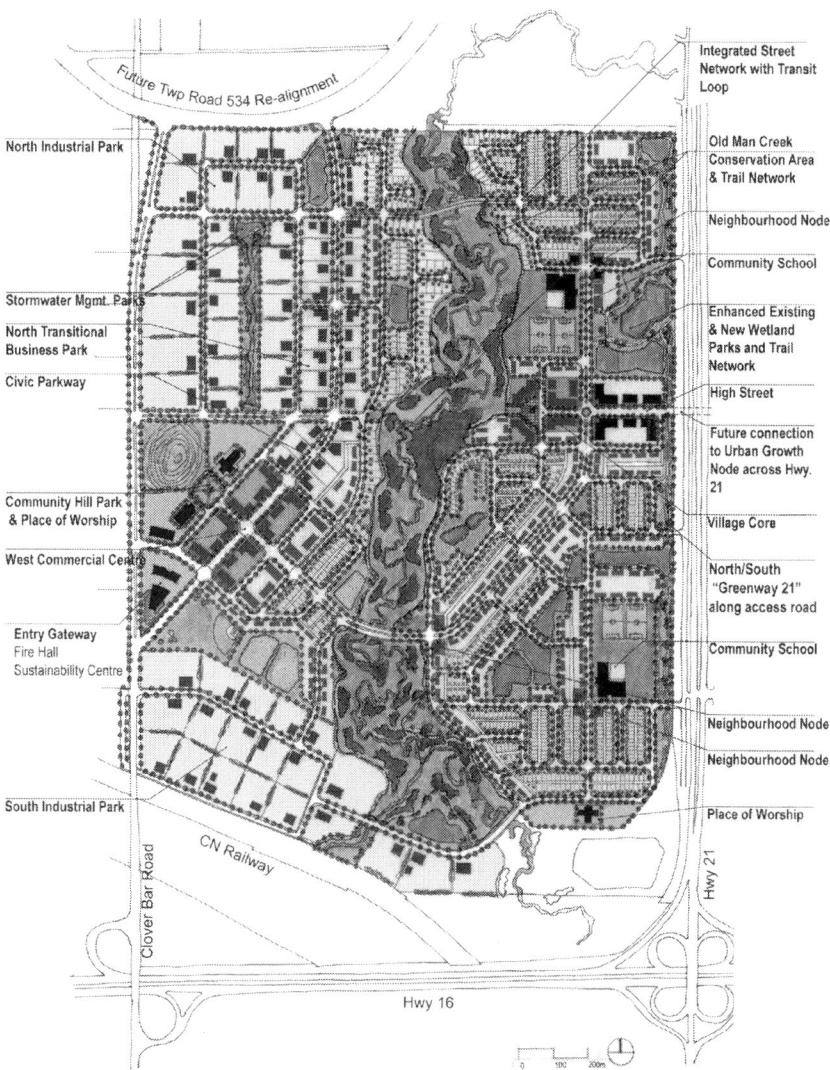

Figure 17.2. Master plan, Cambrian Crossing, Alberta. This illustrative master plan details the sustainable design features. (Drawing by Don Wuori.)

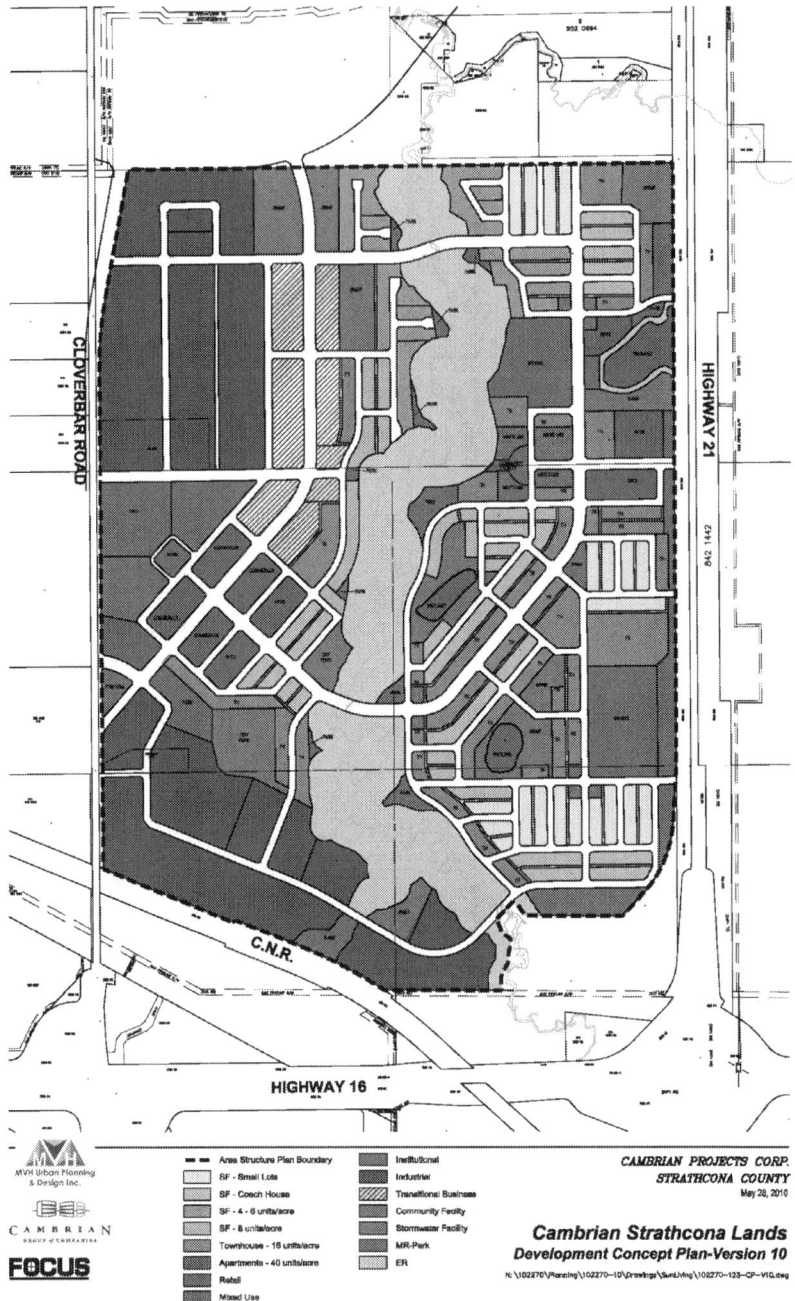

Figure 17.3. Land use plan, Cambrian Crossing, Alberta. This plan shows the variety of land uses that provide for a complete community where residents can live, work, and play. (Plan by FOCUS Corp.)

A variety of single-family and multifamily options invites single to elderly people into the community, with higher densities closest to the neighborhood centers for convenience and supportive activities. The diversity of housing includes single houses, single houses with coach houses, row houses, town houses, and three- to four-story apartments (fig. 17.4). An average density of fifteen units per acre (thirty-eight units/net residential ha) provides for compact living that is mainly ground-oriented, important especially in suburban locations. Open space and recreation are close by, and water features have multiple functions as environmental features, storm water ponds, and recreation amenities. The resulting plan is designed as a complete sustainable community. The developer is pleased, as the market demand shifted to residential. County staff brought the proposal forward to council, and Cambrian was approved within twelve months of initiation. Like any project of this size, Cambrian Crossing continues to face challenges, especially in servicing this property and associated road improvements. The framework remains in place for a sustainable new community design (figs. 17.5 and 17.6).

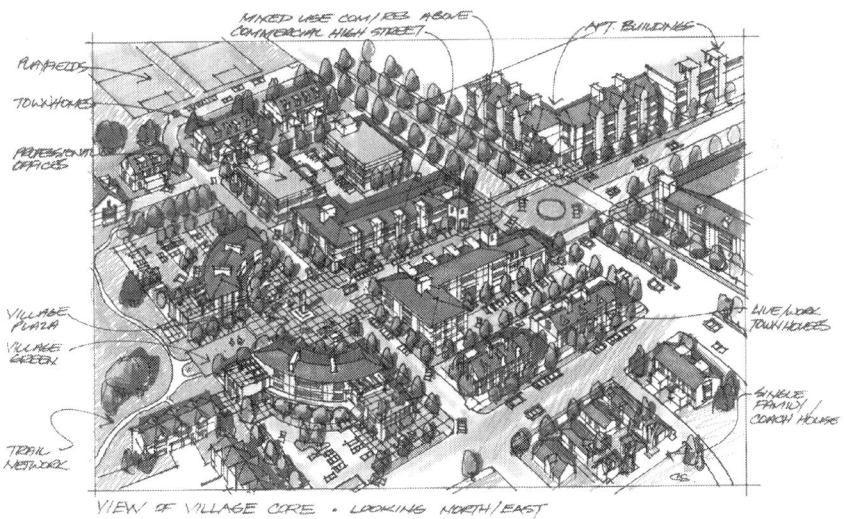

Figure 17.4. Diversity of housing types, Cambrian Crossing, Alberta. This illustration describes the many housing types included in the Cambrian Plan to provide housing choice and invite all age groups to live there. (Drawing by Calum Srigley.)

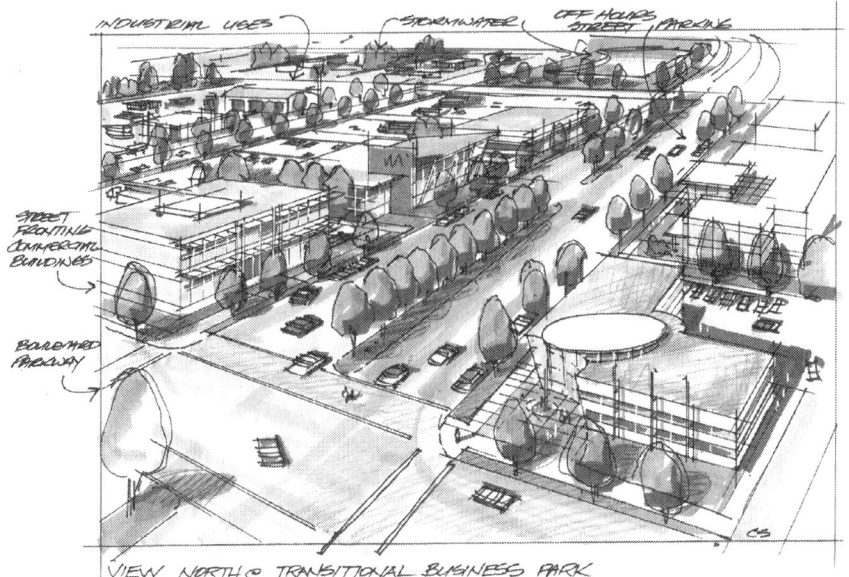

Figure 17.5. Business/industrial uses, Cambrian Crossing, Alberta.
The business and industrial uses provide the majority of the local jobs in
the Cambrian community. (Drawing by Calum Srigley.)

Figure 17.6. Village nodes, Cambrian Crossing, Alberta. These local
mixed-use centers provide basic services close to home and important
gathering areas in the community. (Drawing by Calum Srigley.)

These two case studies illustrate the benefits of considering the collective power of attitude, process, and results as important change agents that will advance sustainable urban design. Our future choices depend on their use and effectiveness in changing urban and suburban form.

Change starts with us

This book has explored the meaning of sustainable urban design—the importance of place, people, customized processes, and the family of plans. To be more effective as urban designers or active citizens in developing urban forms, we must find innovative ways to improve our knowledge, skills, abilities, and processes. At the core of creating positive outcomes is our ability to uncover the beauty of our cities, towns, and villages. We will catalyze positive change if we bring more nature into our cities and if we improve the balance among commercialism, livability, and creativity.

It is a fact that we are a product of our education and training. Once we have received the degree and the professional seals, we carry on tradition—telling our clients what is good for them rather than listening to them to articulate their needs and aspirations. A balanced combination of listening to community members and sharing our professional wisdom can uncover the magic elements of each place and lead to a visionary plan. While engaged in this process, we build on the past, act in the present, and script the future by harnessing the ecological integrity, economic potential, and robust cultural vitality of a place. We are *all* part of the solution.

I leave you with this guidance to help you hone your talents in urban design:

Discover observation and meditation in place.
- Consider the site as precious.
- Spend time experiencing the site at different times by carefully observing what is happening socially, ecologically, and economically.
- Sketch different aspects of the site, and photograph it to see the site through multiple lenses.

Develop active listening skills.
- Elicit ideas by asking questions and getting community members to tell stories.
- Walk the site with community members to discover unique features of a place.
- Record these ideas by drawing and expressing the information in different ways (e.g., create a legacy book of ideas completed with the help of the community members).

Create a story of the community's future.
- Organize your thoughts into a logical and inspirational story that builds on the place, creates direct community benefits, and improves the community surrounding the site.
- Use your imagination to discover new ideas and incorporate them into sustainable urban design elements that inspire action.
- Finally, build passion for your work, express your uniqueness, and be satisfied only with excellence. Present with enthusiasm, and lead with insights. This approach creates the necessary momentum for major transformations in our cities, towns, and villages.

The world needs a dynamic new vision for sustainable urban design to satisfy the needs of its communities. The task is waiting for you! So now is the time to act. I hope this book has inspired you to take a journey of discovery, innovation, and service.

APPENDICES

APPENDIX A: ECONOMICS CHECKLIST

Purpose: This list of economic questions and measurements helps build the program and form for sustainable urban planning, design, and development. The checklist differs from conventional land economic analysis in that it measures value for *private interests*, *local government*, and the *local community* (hence referred to as three-dimensional analysis).

Questions to be answered include the following:

1. **Demographic profile**
   a. What are the demographic trends (population growth and characteristics) past, present, and future of the region and the locality?
   b. How do these trends apply to the immediate site area, and what is the current demographic profile that lives in the area?

2. **Market characteristics**
   a. What are the characteristics of the market *supply* (inventory and type of land use/unit, land costs and sale patterns, size of market, and draw for commercial/industrial, etc.)?
   b. What are the characteristics of market *demand* (absorption patterns, price patterns, projected growth, and associated assumptions for the site)?
   c. Where are new and emerging markets (niche housing, coach houses, lock-off suites, lane housing, live/work units, etc.)?

3. **Development program**

   a. How do these patterns apply to the development of form and types of land uses (commercial, residential, industrial, institutional, etc.)?

   b. What comparable projects are there in the vicinity of the site that prove viability and/or competition?

   c. Can the site sell or lease the units projected, and over what period of time?

   d. How would you phase the development in segments and uses?

   e. What public amenities (e.g., parks, open spaces, washrooms, transit stop) and facilities (e.g., school, community center, arts and culture center) are expected by the local government and/or the community in order to obtain approval?

   f. What other nonmarket housing (seniors, co-op, or other) is required by the local government?

4. **Revenue, cost, value analysis**

   a. What is the value of the land based on existing and potential land uses?

   b. What is the revenue potential of the property uses (sell/lease and hold—commercial versus residential and other mixes)?

   c. What are the hard costs in the area of land, materials, and servicing of the project?

   d. What are the costs for off-site improvements, as well as amenities and facilities required by the local government and/or community?

   e. What are the soft costs (nonconstruction costs), such as consulting services and funding costs?

   f. What is the payback period for sustainable features, such as ground-source heating or solar energy?

   g. What is the "full cost" accounting of the social, economic, and ecological changes proposed in the development?

   h. What is the short-term return on investment?

   i. What is the phasing for the development?

j. What is the long-term potential value (over 10 to 20 years) and return on investment, including inflation factor and escalation of costs/revenues?

k. Who could partner to fund the project (e.g., other developer, local government, provincial/state government, federal government, or other nongovernment organization)?

5. **Overall risk/value analysis**
    a. What are the risks and benefits of proceeding with the development to the developer, local government, and community?
    b. What is the overall net community gain when adding up all the advantages and disadvantages?

Table A.1 provides a simple framework for analysis of the private, municipal, and community goals, strategies, and potential risks/rewards in a sustainable urban design project. Without this multiple-stakeholder analysis, the various interests are either not adequately addressed or left out altogether. The strategies and risk/reward columns should be filled in based on the specific project.

Table A.1. 3-D checklist (private, municipal, and community)				
3-D Analysis	Goals	Strategies	Measures	Risk/Reward
Private	Short-term, medium-term, and long-term profit, as well as corporate image		Timing of approvals, costs, revenues, return on investment, and net present value	
Municipal	Services, cost/revenue, land values, taxes, affordability, and equity		Value/spin-offs, taxes, quantity of development, and community support	
Community	Services (amenities/facilities), taxes, safety and security, traffic, environment, noise, and real estate values		Community improvements: services, taxes, safety and security, traffic, environment, noise, and real estate values	

APPENDIX B: SUSTAINABILITY SCORECARD

Table B.1 provides a tool for evaluating sustainable urban design projects. Four categories or themes provide a basis to measure project performance (Your Project Green) against nineteen elements of sustainability. Baseline comparisons are provided (Super Green and Business as Usual measurements) as a basis to determine the level of green commitment in the project. Specific project variations of location, land use, and other factors are not considered in this analysis. For a more comprehensive application, see the Salisbury Village East case study in chapter 14, along with tables 14.3 to 14.14.

Table B.1. Sustainable urban design project performance measurement

Category/Themes	Complete Community Sustainable Design Goals	Performance Comparisons (Super Green)	Targets (Business as Usual)	Your Project Green
1. Carbon, Transport, Land Use	**Live, Work, and Play in Close Proximity**			
Compact mixed use	Create services close to home that are within walking distance	100 percent of residents within 1,500 feet (450 m) of basic services	50 percent or fewer residents within 1,500 feet (450 m) of basic services	
Walkable	Increase density of pedestrian activity and orientation in community	50 percent public part of street for pedestrians	40 percent public part of street for pedestrians	
Connected to surrounding land uses and services	Increase pedestrian and bikeway connections to adjoining facilities and developments	Comprehensive trail and pathway connections	Few trail and pathway connections	
Jobs/housing balance	Increase on-site jobs to reduce off-site commuting and increase local community identity	350 square feet (32.5 m²) per job; 1,500 jobs; portion of housing units should be live/work	No jobs locally; no housing units live/work except home businesses	
Reduced car dependency	Increase alternative transit, pedestrian and bicycle network use	1,300 feet (400 m) to transit stop	2,625 feet (800 m) to transit stop	
Green streets	Create a safe, clean, and healthy environment that encourages noncar use	Greenways and trails connected to streets	Separate trails or greenways and walkways	
Parking	Reduce or share parking footprint	1 space per residential unit; 4.5 spaces per 1,000 square feet (93 m²) commercial (shared)	2 spaces per residential unit; 4.5 spaces per 1,000 square feet (93 m²) commercial	

454

Table B.1. (*continued*)

Category/Themes	Complete Community Sustainable Design Goals	Performance Comparisons (Super Green)	Targets (Business as Usual)	Your Project Green
2. Materials, Waste, Energy	**No Waste and Increase Energy Efficiency**			
Alternative energy	Reduce use of fossil fuels, and increase use of renewable energy sources	10 percent of the energy produced on-site; 90 percent of energy from renewable energy (includes hydroelectric)	0 percent alternative energy produced on-site; 50 percent from renewable energy	
Green building standard	Reduce use of fossil fuels and storm runoff, and increase design standards that encourage use of renewable energy sources	75 percent of buildings have good solar orientation; plants on 25 percent of roof area	50% of buildings have good solar orientation; plants on 0 percent of roof area	
Sanitary process	Reduce off-site impacts of black water and gray water	25 percent of sewage treated on-site	No sewage treated on-site	
Solid waste management	Reduce, reuse, or recycle waste on-site	Reduce solid waste by 44 lb (200 kg) per person per year	Some solid waste recycling	
3. Water, Food, Natural Habitat	**Protect and Improve Natural Ecosystems**			
Storm water management	Increase water quality and reduce off-site impacts of storm water	100 percent recharge/clean; no more than 50 percent impermeable	Less than 50 percent recharge/clean; no more than 80 percent impermeable	
Habitat enhancement	Improve wildlife habitat on and through the site	60 percent of green space has habitat value	10 percent of green space has habitat value	
Community gardens	Increase local sources of food for sale and consumption	12.5 percent of produce grown on-site	No produce grown on-site	

455

Table B.1. (continued)

Category/Themes	Complete Community Sustainable Design Goals	Performance Comparisons (Super Green)	Targets (Business as Usual)	Your Project Green
Maximize public green	Expand natural open space and parks in every part of the site	2.75 acres (1.1 ha) of sustaining space per 1,000 population	Variable environmental reserve and 10 percent municipal reserve	
4. Well-Being, Equity, Culture	**Create a Healthy, Inclusive, Diverse, and Culturally Rich Community**			
Housing choice	Increase the diversity of housing for all ages	Diversity of housing, including seniors, entry level, and nonmarket housing that is more affordable	Single-family housing as the dominant housing form with some multifamily units	
Commercial development	Provide a balance of retail and office jobs locally	1 square foot (0.093 m^2) of commercial for every 15 square feet (1.4 m^2) of residential	Commercial and residential development separate and not connected	
Community facilities	Provide places to interact, educate, and socialize on-site and connect to other off-site facilities	30,000-square-foot (2,787 m^2) community center; day care facilities	10,000- to 20,000-square-foot (929 to 1,858 m^2) community center	
Strong sense of place/ culture	Provide a wide range of public spaces and places on-site to encourage local activity, programming, and events	Wide variety of spaces, plazas, and places to interact	Limited spaces and places	
Long-Term Sustainability Goal: Social, Ecological, and Economic Balance, Net Gain, and Efficiency for the Next Generation				

456

NOTES

Introduction

Epigraph on page 1 is from David W. Orr, *The Last Refuge: Patriotism, Politics, and the Environment in the Age of Terror* (Washington, DC: Island Press, 2004), 60.

1. McKinsey Global Institute, *Urban World: Cities and the Rise of the Consumer Class* (New York: McKinsey & Co., 2012), 3, 4.
2. *LEED 2009: Neighborhood Development* (Washington, DC: US Green Building Council, 2011), n.p.
3. Ibid.
4. Andrés Edwards, *The Sustainability Revolution: Portrait of a Paradigm Shift* (Gabriola Island, BC: New Society Publishers, 2005).
5. Andrés Duany, Jeff Speck, and Mike Lydon, *The Smart Growth Manual* (New York: McGraw-Hill, 2010), sec. 1.15.
6. Haya El Nasser and Paul Overberg, "Large Cities Got Larger During Slump," *USA Today*, June 28, 2012, p. 3A.
7. Edward Glaeser, *Triumph of the City: How Our Greatest Invention Makes Us Richer, Smarter, Greener, Healthier, and Happier* (New York: Penguin Books, 2011), 6.
8. The Prince's Foundation for Building Community, www.princes-foundation.org.

Chapter 1

Epigraph on page 11 is from Richard Marshall, "The Elusiveness of Urban Design: The Perpetual Problems of Definition and Role," *Harvard Design*

Magazine (Spring/Summer 2006), 32. Quote on page 16 is from Judy and Michael Corbett, *Designing Sustainable Communities: Learning from Village Homes* (Washington, DC: Island Press, 2000), 7.

1. Jonathan Barnett, *Urban Design as Public Policy: Practical Methods for Improving Cities* (New York: Architectural Record, 1974).
2. Mark Roseland, *Toward Sustainable Communities: Resources for Citizens and Their Governments* (Gabriola Island, BC: New Society Publishers, 2005), n.p.
3. World Wildlife Fund et al., *Living Planet Report* (Gland, Switzerland: World Wildlife Fund, United Nations Environment Program, and Global Footprint Network, 2004).
4. Sustainable development also includes qualitative as well as quantitative improvements in our well-being, such as community peace and safety, vitality, sense of belonging, social network, identity, distribution of employment, and shelter. Roseland, *Toward Sustainable Communities.*
5. Ibid.
6. Rocky Mountain Institute et al., *Green Development: Integrating Ecology and Real Estate* (New York: John Wiley & Sons, 1998).
7. See US Green Building Council (USGBC), www.usgbc.org.
8. Congress of the New Urbanism, *Charter for the New Urbanism* (New York: McGraw-Hill, 1999), v (Preamble).
9. Timothy Beatley and Kristy Manning, *The Ecology of Place: Planning for Environment, Economy and Community* (Washington, DC: Island Press, 1997).
10. Douglas Farr, *Sustainable Urbanism: Urban Design with Nature* (Hoboken, NJ: Wiley & Sons, 2007).
11. John Lang, *Urban Design: The American Experience* (New York: John Wiley & Sons, 1994).

Chapter 2
Epigraph on page 27 is from David Macaulay, *City: A Story of Roman Planning and Construction* (Boston: Houghton, Mifflin, 1974), 8. Quote

on page 37 is from Daniel Burnham and Edward Bennett, *The Plan for Chicago* (Chicago: Commercial Club of Chicago, 1909), 1.

1. Kevin Lynch, *Good City Form* (Cambridge, MA: MIT Press, 1981).
2. Witold Rybczynski, *City Life* (Toronto: HarperCollins, 1995).
3. A. E. J. Morris, *History of Urban Form* (New York: John Wiley, 1979).
4. Lewis Mumford, *The City in History: Its Origins, Its Transformations, and Its Prospects* (New York: Harcourt, Brace & World, 1961).
5. Erik Larson, *The Devil in the White City* (New York: Vintage Books, 2003).
6. Ibid., 49.

Chapter 3

Epigraph on page 45 is from James Howard Kunstler, *The Geography of Nowhere: The Rise and Decline in America's Man-Made Landscape* (New York: Touchstone Books, 1993), 113.

1. Douglas Kelbaugh, *Common Place: Toward Neighborhood and Regional Design* (Seattle, WA: University of Washington Press, 1997); Peter Calthorpe, *The Next American Metropolis: Ecology, Community and the American Dream* (New York: Princeton Architectural Press, 1993).
2. TransCanada Trail, http://tctrail.ca.
3. Andrés Duany, Elizabeth Plater-Zyberk, and Jeff Speck, *Suburban Nation: The Rise of Sprawl and the Decline of the American Dream* (New York: North Point Press, 2000).
4. Jane Jacobs, *The Death and Life of Great American Cities* (New York: Random House, 1961).
5. Kevin Lynch, *Image of the City* (Cambridge, MA: MIT Press, 1960).
6. Ian McHarg, *Design with Nature* (Garden City, NY: Natural City Press, 1969); William Whyte, *Cluster Development* (New York: American Conservation Association, 1964), and *The Last Landscape* (Garden City, NY: Anchor Books, 1968).
7. Anne Whiston Spirn, *The Granite Garden: Urban Nature and Human Design* (New York: Basic Books, 1984); Michael Hough, *City Form and*

Natural Process (London: Routledge, 1984), and *Out of Place: Restoring Identity to the Regional Landscape* (Hartford, CT: Yale University Press, 1990).

8. William Whyte, *City: Rediscovering the Center* (New York: Doubleday, 1988).

9. Jan Gehl and Lars Gemzoe, *New City Spaces* (Copenhagen: Danish Architectural Press. Copenhagen, 2001), 56 and 58.

10. Allan B. Jacobs, Elizabeth MacDonald, and Yodan Rofé, *The Boulevard Book: History, Evolution, Design of Multiway Boulevards* (Cambridge, MA: MIT Press, 2002).

11. Allan B. Jacobs, *Great Streets.* (Cambridge, MA: MIT Press, 1993), 8 and 9.

12. Christopher Alexander, Sara Ishikawa, and Murray Silverstein, *A Pattern Language: Towns, Buildings, Construction* (Oxford: Oxford University Press, 1977).

13. Kevin Lynch, *Good City Form* (Cambridge, MA: MIT Press, 1981).

14. Oscar Newman, *Defensible Space: Crime Prevention through Urban Design* (New York: Macmillan, 1973).

15. Calthorpe, Peter, *Next American Metropolis: Ecology, Community and the American Dream* (New York: Princeton Architectural Press, 1993).

16. Andrés Duany, Elizabeth Plater-Zyberk, and Robert Alminana, *The New Civic Art: Elements of Town Planning* (New York: Rizzoli International, 2003).

17. David O'Neill, *The Smart Growth Tool Kit: Community Profiles and Case Studies to Advance Smart Growth Practices* (Washington, DC: Urban Land Institute, 2000).

18. Alexander Garvin, *The American City: What Works, What Doesn't* (2nd ed.) (New York: McGraw-Hill, 2002), 338.

19. Congress of the New Urbanism, *Charter.*

20. Randall Arendt, *Rural by Design* (Chicago: American Planning Association, 1994).

21. Farr, *Sustainable Urbanism.*

22. Patrick Condon, *Seven Rules for Sustainable Communities: Design Strategies for the Post-Carbon World* (Washington, DC: Island Press, 2010).

23. Lang, *Urban Design*, esp. pp. 135–145.

24. Jacobs, *Death and Life*; also *The Economy of Cities* (New York: Random House, 1969), and *Cities and the Wealth of Nations* (New York: Random House, 1984).

25. See *Value in Urban Design* (London: Commission for Architecture and the Built Environment; Department of Environment, Transport and the Regions, 2001).

Chapter 4

Epigraph on page 71 is from Witold Rybczynski, *City Life* (Toronto: HarperCollins, 1995), 232. Quote on page 85 is from Andrés Duany, Elizabeth Plater-Zyberk, and Jeff Speck, *Suburban Nation: The Rise of Sprawl and the Decline of the American Dream* (New York: North Point Press, 2000), 183.

1. See also Michael A. von Hausen, *100 Timeless Urban Design Principles* (Vancouver, BC: Simon Fraser University, 2008).

2. Lynch, *Good City Form*.

3. Ibid. See also Commission for Architecture and the Built Environment, *By Design: Urban Design in the Planning System* (London: Thomas Telford Publishing, 2000), 36–39.

Chapter 5

Epigraph on page 95 is from Christopher Alexander, Hajo Neis, Artemis Anninou, and Ingrid King, *A New Theory of Urban Design* (New York: Oxford University Press, 1987), 15.

1. Sylvia Holland and Michael von Hausen, *Public Process Playbook* (Vancouver, BC: Simon Fraser University, 2007).

2. Ibid., 6.

Chapter 6

Epigraph on page 121 is from Edmund N. Bacon, *Design of Cities,* rev. ed. (New York: Penguin Books, 1976), 33. The quote on page 122 is from

Douglas Kelbaugh, *Common Place: Toward Neighborhood and Regional Design* (Seattle, WA: University of Washington Press, 1997), 7.

1. Malcolm Gladwell, *The Tipping Point: How Little Things Make a Difference* (New York: Little, Brown & Company, 2000), and *Blink: The Power of Thinking Without Thinking* (New York: Little, Brown & Company, 2005).
2. Credits: The New Elita Project was completed by MVH Urban Planning & Design Inc. in 2008 in association with P. Turje and Associates, Don Wuori Design Consultant, Calum Srigley Design Consultant, and Take Out Design Graphics+.

Chapter 7
Epigraph on page 153 is from Alan AtKisson, *The ISIS Agreement: How Sustainability Can Improve Organizational Performance and Transform the World* (London: Earthscan, 2008), 228.

1. Credits: Lower Twelfth Street Area Plan, City of New Westminster, British Columbia. MVH Urban Planning & Design Inc. (lead consultant) completed this work in 2004 with the Hulbert Group International Inc., Don Wuori Design, Calum Srigley Design Consultant, Paul Rollo and Associates Ltd., Take Out Graphics+, and in association with the City of New Westminster. This project was recognized by the Planning Institute of British Columbia with an Award of Excellence in 2005.
2. Credits: Weyerhaeuser Lands Master Plan, Ucluelet, British Columbia. This Weyerhaeuser Lands work was completed by MVH Urban Planning & Design Inc. in 2005 in association with Shine On Consulting, Wayne Wenstob, and Take Out Design Graphics+, under the direction of Weyerhaeuser in association with the District of Ucluelet. This project was recognized with an Award of Excellence (Honourable Mention) from the Planning Institute of British Columbia for Comprehensive Policy Plans and an Award of Excellence for Leadership and Innovation from the Union of British Columbia Municipalities in 2006.

Chapter 8

Epigraph on page 183 is from Jonathan Barnett, *Urban Design as Public Policy: Practical Methods for Improving Cities* (New York: Architectural Record, 1974), 31.

1. Parking pockets are clusters of street parking spaces divided by extended landscaped areas with trees and shrubs in mid block or just low landscaping at intersections.

Chapter 9

Epigraph on page 219 is from Richard Hedman with Andrew Jaszewski, *Fundamentals of Urban Design* (Chicago: American Planning Association, 1984), 136.

1. Credits: City of Langley Downtown Master Plan, Langley, British Columbia. These policies, guidelines, and regulations are generalized for these purposes, but much of the work was completed in affiliation with the City of Langley Downtown Plan 2009 under the guidance of the City of Langley. The Downtown Master Plan received an Award of Excellence from the Planning Institute of British Columbia in 2010. The consulting team members consisted of MVH Urban Planning & Design Inc. as prime consultant along with Don Wuori Design, Calum Srigley Design Consultant, Colliers International, and Take Out Design Graphics+.

2. Credits: City of Medicine Hat Flats Design Guidelines, Medicine Hat, Alberta. These guidelines and regulations are generalized for these purposes, but much of the work was completed in affiliation with the City of Medicine Hat Flats Area Redevelopment Plan in 2009. The consulting team members consisted of MVH Urban Planning & Design Inc. as prime consultant with Don Wuori Design, Calum Srigley Design Consultant, and in association with the City of Medicine Hat.

Chapter 10

Epigraph on page 253 is from Douglas Farr, *Sustainable Urbanism: Urban Design with Nature* (Hoboken, NJ: John Wiley & Sons, 2007), 64.

Chapter 11

Epigraph on page 265 is from *New Urban News*, July/August 2002. Quote on page 277 from Mark McCullough. Quote on page 298 is from the *Globe and Mail*, March 12, 2011, S6.

1. "LEED for Neighborhood Development," US Green Building Council, 2011. http://www.usgbc.org/DisplayPage.aspx?CMSPageID=148.
2. Congress for the New Urbanism [website]. http://www.cnu.org.
3. For more information about the Canada Lands Company, go to http://www.clc.ca.
4. Credits: Garrison Crossing. Developer: Canada Lands Company; MVH Urban Planning & Design Inc.; Ankenman Architects Associates Inc.; Omega & Associates Engineering Ltd.; Bunt & Associates Engineering Ltd.; Buzan Electrical Consultants Limited; R. Kim Perry & Associates Inc.; and Arbortech Consulting Ltd.

Chapter 12

Epigraph on page 301 is from City of Chicago, *The Chicago Central Area Plan: Preparing the Central City for the 21st Century* (Chicago: City of Chicago, 2003), introductory letter.

1. City of Chicago, *The Chicago Central Area Plan: Preparing the Central City for the 21st Century* (Chicago: City of Chicago, 2003), 3.
2. Daniel Burnham and Edward Bennett, *Plan of Chicago* (New York: Princeton Architectural Press, 1993).
3. City of Chicago, *Chicago Central Area Plan*, v.
4. Credits: Calgary Midtown Project. This case study was adopted from an article in *Plan Canada* (Spring 2005) by Michael von Hausen, the lead consultant on the project, in collaboration with Thom Mahler and Larry Pollock, both of the City of Calgary's Downtown and Inner City Planning Section. The City of Calgary retained Team ICE (Interactive Collaborative Experience) in 2004 to prepare this ambitious vision that resulted in *Midtown: An Urban Design Strategy For Midtown Calgary*. Team ICE consists of Michael von Hausen of MVH Urban

Planning & Design Inc. (lead consultant), Rick Hulbert and Alfonso Tejada of the Hulbert Group International Inc., and Don Wuori of Don Wuori Design. Team ICE was assisted by Blake Hudema of Hudema Consulting, Glen Pardoe of Bunt and Associates Engineering Ltd., Calum Srigley Design Consultant, Frank Ducote, Urban Design Consultant, and Dolores Altin of Take Out Graphics+.

5. International Centre for Sustainable Cities, http://sustainablecities .net/.

6. *Midtown: An Urban Design Strategy for Midtown Calgary.* von Hausen, Michael. MVH Urban Planning & Design Inc., Surrey, British Columbia, 2004.

7. Credits: Sunnyville New Community. Developer: Dalta-Vostok-1 Corp., Oleg Drozdov, President; Russian Housing Development Foundation (RHDF); Canada Mortgage and Housing Corporation; MVH Planning and Design Inc. (lead consultant); P. Turje and Associates; Don Wuori Design; Calum Srigley Design Consultant; and Endall Elliot Associates Architects, 2011.

8. Credits: Fenwick Place, Halifax, Nova Scotia. This project involved MVH Urban Planning Design Inc., Endall Elliot Associates Architects, Calum Srigley Design Consultant, and Michael Napier Architects, under the guidance of Templeton Properties of Halifax in 2009 and 2010.

Chapter 13

Epigraph on page 337 is from Randall Arendt, *Rural by Design: Maintaining Small Town Character* (Chicago: American Planning Association, 1994), 19.

1. Credits: Liberty Crossing at Gasoline Alley, Red Deer County, Alberta. This work was completed in 2006 by MVH Urban Planning & Design Inc. in association with Don Wuori Design, Calum Srigley Design Consultant, Take Out Graphics+, and Hudema Consulting under the direction of Harry Harker, community planning director of Red Deer County. The project was awarded the 2007 Award of Excellence by the Alberta Institute of Planners.

2. Randall Arendt, *Rural by Design: Maintaining Small Town Character* (Chicago: American Planning Association, 1994).

3. Randall Arendt, *Growing Greener: Putting Local Conservation into Local Plans and Ordinances* (Washington, DC: Island Press, 1999).

4. Julie Anne Gustanski and Roderick Squires, *Protecting the Land: Conservation Easements Past, Present, and Future* (Washington, DC: Island Press, 2000).

5. Anton C. Nelessen, *Visions for a New American Dream: Process, Principles, and an Ordinance to Plan and Design Small Communities* (Chicago: American Planning Association, 1994).

6. James Howard Kunstler, *The Geography of Nowhere: The Rise and Decline in America's Man-Made Landscape* (New York: Touchstone, 1993).

7. Credits: Stoanshire Development, Strathcona County, Alberta. This project was completed by MVH Urban Planning & Design Inc. in association with Don Wuori Design, Calum Srigley Design Consultant, and Take Out Design Graphics+ in 2008.

Chapter 14
Epigraph on page 365 is from Mahatma Gandhi.

1. Credits: Salisbury Village East, Strathcona County, Alberta. This project was completed by MVH Urban Planning & Design Inc. in association with Endall Elliot Associates Architects, Don Wuori Design, Calum Srigley Design Consultant, and Take Out Design Graphics+ from 2008 to 2011.

Chapter 15
Epigraph on page 399 is from Michael Harcourt and Ken Cameron*, City Making in Paradise: Nine Decisions that Saved Vancouver* (Vancouver, BC: Douglas & McIntyre, 2007), 10.

1. Mike Harcourt and Ken Cameron, *City Making in Paradise: Nine Decisions that Saved Vancouver* (Vancouver, BC: Douglas & McIntyre, 2007), 2.

2. Metro Vancouver, *Metro Vancouver Draft Regional Growth Strategy* (Burnaby, BC, 2009).

3. TransLink, *Metro Vancouver TransLink Management Plan* (2010).

4. "Cascadia Scorecard," Sightline Institute (2010), http://www.sightline.org/pubtype/scorecard/2010.

5. Harcourt and Cameron, *City Making*.

6. Jacobs, *Death and Life*.

7. Harcourt and Cameron, *City Making*, 60.

8. Ibid.

9. Credits: Township of Langley, Yorkson Neighbourhood Plan, Bylaw No. 4030, Schedule W-2 Willoughby Community Plan, adopted by Council July 16, 2001, with amendments to October 3, 2011.

Chapter 16

Epigraph on page 411 is from John Punter, *The Vancouver Achievement: Urban Planning and Design* (Vancouver, BC: UBC Press, 2003), 3. Quote on page 430 is from opening remarks, Green City opening event, by Gregor Robertson, mayor of Vancouver, June 2010.

1. Patrick Condon and Jackie Teed, eds., *Sustainability by Design: A Vision for a Region of 4 Million People* (Vancouver, BC: Design Centre for Sustainability, University of British Columbia, 2006); also Condon, *Seven Rules*.

2. Harcourt and Cameron, *City Making*.

3. John Punter, *The Vancouver Achievement: Urban Planning and Design* (Vancouver, BC: UBC Press, 2003); Lance Berelowitz, *Dream City: Vancouver and the Global Imagination* (Vancouver, BC: Douglas & McIntyre, 2005).

4. Larry Beasley, "'Living First' in Downtown Vancouver," *Zoning News* (American Planning Association), April 2000. Available at http://vancouver.ca/commsvcs/currentplanning/living.htm.

5. Berelowitz, *Dream City*.

6. "Eyes on the street" is a phrase coined by Jane Jacobs, *The Death and Life of Great American Cities*, 1961; Jan Gehl wrote of designing

the spaces between buildings in *Life Between Buildings: Using Public Space* (New York: Van Nostrand Reinhold, 1987); street definition is addressed in Allan B. Jacobs, *Great Streets*.

7. Green Streets program, https:Vancouver.ca/engsvcs/streets/green streets/.

8. For insights into process, see Beasley, "'Living First' in Downtown Vancouver," and Punter, *Vancouver Achievement*. On design, see Elizabeth Macdonald, "Street-Facing Dwelling Units and Livability: The Impacts of Emerging Building Types in Vancouver's New High-Density Residential Neighborhoods," *Journal of Urban Design* 10, no. 1 (February 2005): 13–38.

9. Larry Beasley, "'Living First' in Downtown Vancouver," *Zoning News* (American Planning Association), April 2000. Available at http://vancouver.ca/commsvcs/currentplanning/living.htm.

10. City of Vancouver, *EcoDensity: Vancouver EcoDensity Charter* and *EcoDensity: Initial Actions*, adopted June 10, 2008. Both documents available at http://vancouver.ca/commsvcs/ecocity/.

Chapter 17: Conclusion

Quote on page 433 is from Lewis Mumford, *The City in History: Its Origins, Its Transformations, and Its Prospects* (New York: Harcourt, Brace & World, 1961), 4.

1. Credits: Abbott Street, Kelowna, BC. This project was completed by Stantec Corporation and MVH Urban Planning & Design Inc. in association with the City of Kelowna in 2002.

2. Credits: Cambrian Crossing, Strathcona County, Alberta. This project was completed in 2011 by MVH Urban Planning & Design Inc. with the Focus Corporaton, Endall Elliot Associates Architects, Don Wuori Design, Calum Srigley Design Consultant, Take Out Design Graphics+, and in association with the Cambrian Group of Companies and Strathcona County.

BIBLIOGRAPHY AND FURTHER READING

Alexander, Christopher, Sara Ishikawa, and Murray Silverstein. *A Pattern Language: Towns, Buildings, Construction*. Oxford: Oxford University Press, 1977.

Alexander, Christopher, Hajo Neis, Artemis Anninou, and Ingrid King. *A New Theory of Urban Design*. New York: Oxford University Press, 1987.

Antonelli, Paola. "The World in 2036." *The Economist: The World in 2011* (January 2011), 113.

Arendt, Randall. *Rural by Design: Maintaining Small Town Character*. Chicago: American Planning Association, 1994.

―――. *Growing Greener: Putting Local Conservation into Local Plans and Ordinances*. Washington, DC: Island Press, 1999.

Arnold, Henry. *Trees in Urban Design*. New York: Van Nostrand Reinhold, 1993.

AtKisson, Alan. *The ISIS Agreement: How Sustainability Can Improve Organizational Performance and Transform the World*. London: Earthscan, 2008.

Bacon, Edmond. *Design of Cities*. Rev. ed. New York: Penguin Books, 1976.

Barnett, Jonathan. *Urban Design as Public Policy: Practical Methods for Improving Cities*. New York: Architectural Record, 1974.

Bartholomew, Harland, and Associates. *A Plan for the City of Vancouver, British Columbia*. Vancouver, BC: City of Vancouver, 1929.

Bartsch, C., E. Collaton, A. E. Goode, et al. *Strategies for Successful Infill Development*. Washington, DC: Northeast-Midwest Institute and the Congress for the New Urbanism, 2001.

Beasley, Larry. "'Living First' in Downtown Vancouver." *Zoning News* (American Planning Association), April 2000. Available at http://vancouver.ca/commsvcs/currentplanning/living.htm.

Beatley, Timothy, and Kristy Manning. *The Ecology of Place: Planning for Environment, Economy and Community.* Washington, DC: Island Press, 1997.

Berelowitz, Lance. *Dream City: Vancouver and the Global Imagination.* Vancouver, BC: Douglas & McIntyre, 2005.

Burnham, Daniel, and Edward Bennett. *The Plan for Chicago.* Chicago: Commercial Club of Chicago, 1909.

――――. *Plan of Chicago.* New York: Princeton Architectural Press, 1993.

Calthorpe, Peter. *The Next American Metropolis: Ecology, Community and the American Dream.* New York: Princeton Architectural Press, 1993.

Calthorpe, Peter, and William Fulton. *The Regional City: Planning for the End of Sprawl.* Washington, DC: Island Press, 2001.

Calthorpe, Peter, and Sim Van der Ryn. *Sustainable Communities: A New Synthesis for Cities, Suburbs and Towns.* San Francisco: Sierra Club Books, 1986.

Campbell, Elisa, and Jackie Teed. "Getting to Minus 80: Urban Form Strategies for Measurably Achieving Greenhouse Gas Emissions Reduction Targets." *Plan Canada* 50, no. 4 (Winter 2010): 18–21.

Campbell, Scott. "Green Cities, Growing Cities, Just Cities? Urban Planning and the Contradictions of Sustainable Development." *Journal of American Planning Literature* 62, no. 3 (Summer 1996): 296–310.

Carmona, Matthew, and Steve Tiesdell, eds. *Urban Design Reader.* Oxford: Architectural Press, 2007.

"Cascadia Scorecard." Sightline Institute, 2010. http://www.sightline.org/pubtype/scorecard/2010.

City of Chicago. *The Chicago Central Area Plan: Preparing the Central City for the 21st Century.* Chicago: City of Chicago, 2003.

City of Vancouver. *Vancouver's Urban Design: A Decade of Achievement.* Vancouver, BC: City of Vancouver, 1999.

_____. *Vancouver's New Neighborhoods: Achievements in Planning and Urban Design*. Vancouver, BC: City of Vancouver, 2003.

_____. *EcoDensity: Vancouver EcoDensity Charter* and *EcoDensity: Initial Actions*, adopted June 10, 2008. Both documents available at http://vancouver.ca/commsvcs/ecocity/.

Collins, George R., and Christine C. Collins. *Camillo Sitte: The Birth of Modern City Planning*. New York: Rizzoli International, 1986.

Commission for Architecture and the Built Environment. *By Design: Urban Design in the Planning System*. London: Thomas Telford Publishing, 2000.

_____. *The Value of Urban Design*. London: Thomas Telford Publishing, 2001.

Condon, Patrick. *Design Charrettes for Sustainable Communities*. Washington, DC: Island Press, 2008.

_____. *Seven Rules for Sustainable Communities: Design Strategies for the Post-Carbon World*. Washington, DC: Island Press, 2010.

Condon, Patrick, and Joanne Proft, eds. *Sustainable Urban Landscapes: The Surrey Design Charrette*. Vancouver, BC: James Taylor Chair in Landscape and Liveable Environments, University of British Columbia, 1996.

_____. *Sustainable Urban Landscapes: The Brentwood Design Charrette*. Vancouver, BC: James Taylor Chair in Landscape and Liveable Environments, University of British Columbia, 1999.

Condon, Patrick, and Jackie Teed, eds. *Sustainability by Design: A Vision for a Region of 4 Million People*. Vancouver, BC: Design Centre for Sustainability, University of British Columbia, 2006.

Congress for the New Urbanism. *Charter of the New Urbanism*. New York: McGraw-Hill, 1999.

Corbett, Judy and Michael Corbett. *Designing Sustainable Communities: Learning from Village Homes*. Washington, DC: Island Press, 2000.

Covey, Stephen R. *The Seven Habits of Highly Effective People: Restoring the Character Ethic*. New York: Fireside, 1989.

_____. *The Eighth Habit: From Effectiveness to Greatness*. New York: Simon & Schuster, 2005.

Cullen, Gordon. *The Concise Townscape.* London: Architectural Press, 1961.

Dittmar, Hank. *Transport and Neighborhoods.* Edge Futures 4. London: Black Dog, 2008.

Dittmar, Hank, G. Mayhew, J. Hulme, and C. Smallwood. *Valuing Sustainable Urbanism: A Report Measuring and Valuing New Approaches to Residentially Led Mixed Use Growth.* London: The Prince's Foundation, 2007.

Duany, Andrés, Elizabeth Plater-Zyberk, and Robert Alminana. *The New Civic Art: Elements of Town Planning.* New York: Rizzoli International, 2003.

Duany, Andrés, Elizabeth Plater-Zyberk, and Jeff Speck. *Suburban Nation: The Rise of Sprawl and the Decline of the American Dream.* New York: North Point Press, 2000.

Duany, Andrés, Jeff Speck, and Mike Lydon. *The Smart Growth Manual.* New York: McGraw-Hill, 2010.

Edwards, Andrés. *The Sustainability Revolution: Portrait of a Paradigm Shift.* Gabriola Island, BC: New Society Publishers, 2005.

El Nasser, Haya, and Paul Overberg. "Large Cities Got Larger During Slump." *USA Today,* June 28, 2012, p. 3A.

Energy Information Administration. *Greenhouse Gases, Climate Change, and Energy.* Washington, DC, 2008.

Engwicht, David. *Reclaiming Our Cities and Towns: Better Living with Less Traffic.* Philadelphia, PA: New Society Publishers, 1993.

Eronn, Robert. *Ecological Living in Sweden: Ideas and Practical Experience.* The Swedish Institute, May 1991.

Ewing, Reid, Keith Bartholomew, Steve Winkelman, Jerry Walters, and Don Chen. *Growing Cooler: The Evidence on Urban Development and Climate Change.* Washington, DC: Urban Land Institute, 2008.

Fader, S. *Density by Design: New Directions in Real Estate Development* (2nd ed.). Washington, DC: Urban Land Institute, 2001.

Farr, Douglas. *Sustainable Urbanism: Urban Design with Nature.* Hoboken, NJ: John Wiley & Sons, 2007.

Fink, Charles A., and Robert Searns. *Greenways: A Guide to Planning, Design and Development.* Washington, DC: Island Press, 1993.

Fisher, Roger, and William Ury. *Getting to Yes: Negotiating Agreement Without Giving In.* New York: Penguin Books, 1983.

Florida, Richard. *Who's Your City? How the Creative Economy Is Making Where You Live the Most Important Decision of Your Life.* Toronto: Random House Canada, 2008.

Foot, David. *Boom, Bust and Echo: How to Profit from the Coming Demographic Shift.* Toronto: Macfarlane Walter & Ross, 1996.

Garnham, Harry Launce. *Maintaining the Spirit of Place: A Process for the Preservation of Town Character.* Mesa, AZ: PDA Publishers, 1985.

Garvin, Alexander. *The American City: What Works, What Doesn't* (2nd ed.). New York: McGraw-Hill, 2002.

Gatje, Robert F. *Great Public Squares: An Architect's Selection.* New York: Norton & Co., 2010.

Gehl, Jan. *Life Between Buildings: Using Public Space.* New York: Van Nostrand Reinhold, 1987.

Gehl, Jan, and Lars Gemzoe. *New City Spaces.* Copenhagen: Danish Architectural Press, 2001.

Gladwell, Malcolm. *The Tipping Point: How Little Things Make a Difference.* New York: Little, Brown & Company, 2000.

———. *Blink: The Power of Thinking Without Thinking.* New York: Little, Brown & Company, 2005.

Glaeser, Edward. *Triumph of the City: How Our Greatest Invention Makes Us Richer, Smarter, Greener, Healthier, and Happier.* New York: Penguin Books, 2011.

Gustanski, Julie Ann, and Roderick Squires. *Protecting the Land: Conservation Easements Past, Present, and Future.* Washington, DC: Island Press, 2000.

Hall, Peter. *Cities of Tomorrow.* Cambridge, MA: Basil Blackwell, 1988.

Harcourt, Mike, and Ken Cameron. *City Making in Paradise: Nine Decisions that Saved Vancouver.* Vancouver, BC: Douglas & McIntyre, 2007.

Hart, Maureen. *A Guide to Sustainable Community Indicators.* Montreal, QC: QLF/Atlantic Center for the Environment, 1995.

Hawken, Paul. *The Ecology of Commerce: A Declaration of Sustainability.* New York: Harper Collins, 1993.

Hedman, Richard, with Andrew Jaszewski. *Fundamentals of Urban Design*. Chicago: American Planning Association, 1984.

Hegemann, Werner, and Elbert Peets. *The American Vitruvius: An Architects' Handbook of Civic Art*. New York: Architectural Book Publishing, 1922.

Hodge, Gerald. *Planning Canadian Communities: An Introduction to the Principles, Practices and Participants* (2nd ed.). Toronto: Nelson Canada, 1991.

Holland, Sylvia, and Michael von Hausen. *Public Process Playbook*. Vancouver, BC: Simon Fraser University, 2007.

Hough, Michael. *City Form and Natural Process.* London: Routledge, 1984.

_____. *Out of Place: Restoring Identity to the Regional Landscape.* Hartford, CT: Yale University Press, 1990.

Hygeia Consulting Services and REIC Ltd. *Changing Values, Changing Communities: A Guide to the Development of Healthy, Sustainable Communities.* Report for Canada Mortgage and Housing Corporation. Ottawa, 1995.

Integrating Stormwater Management into the Urban Fabric. Conference proceedings, American Society of Landscape Architects, Portland, OR, November 7–8, 1996.

Jacobs, Allan B. *Great Streets.* Cambridge, MA: MIT Press, 1993.

Jacobs, Allan B., Elizabeth Macdonald, and Yodan Rofé. *The Boulevard Book: History, Evolution, Design of Multiway Boulevards.* Cambridge, MA: MIT Press, 2002.

Jacobs, Jane. *The Death and Life of Great American Cities.* New York: Random House, 1961.

_____. *The Economy of Cities.* New York: Random House, 1969.

_____. *Cities and the Wealth of Nations.* New York: Random House, 1984.

_____. *Dark Age Ahead.* New York: Random House, 2004.

Jarvis, Frederick. *Site Planning and Community Design for Great Neighborhoods.* Washington, DC: Home Builder Press, 1993.

Kalinsky, Leah. *Smart Growth for Neighborhoods: Affordable Housing and Regional Vision.* Washington, DC: National Neighborhood Coalition, 2001.

Kelbaugh, Douglas. *Common Place: Toward Neighborhood and Regional Design.* Seattle, WA: University of Washington Press, 1997.

Klassen, Ina T. *Knowledge-Based Design: Developing Urban and Regional Design into a Science.* Netherlands: University of Delft, 2004.

Knox, Paul L. "Creating Ordinary Places: Slow Cities in a Fast World." *Journal of Urban Design* 10, no. 1 (February 2005): 1–11.

Kostof, Spiro. *The City Assembled: The Elements of Urban Form Through History.* Boston: Little, Brown, 1992.

Kunstler, James Howard. *The Geography of Nowhere: The Rise and Decline in America's Man-Made Landscape.* New York: Touchstone Books, 1993.

Lang, Jon. *Urban Design: The American Experience.* New York: John Wiley & Sons, 1994.

Larice, Michael, and Elizabeth Macdonald, eds. *The Urban Design Reader.* London: Routledge, 2007.

Larson, Erik. *The Devil in the White City.* New York: Vintage Books, 2003.

"LEED for Neighborhood Development." US Green Building Council, 2011. http://www.usgbc.org/DisplayPage.aspx?CMSPageID=148.

LEED 2009: Neighborhood Development. Washington, DC: US Green Building Council, 2011.

Lennertz, Bill, Aarin Lutzenhiser, and Andrés Duany. *The Charrette Handbook.* Washington, DC: American Planning Association, 2006.

Leung, Hok Lin. *Land Use Planning Made Plain.* Kingston, ON: Ronald Frye & Co., 1989.

Lozano, Eduardo. *Community Design and the Culture of Cities.* Cambridge: Cambridge University Press, 1990.

Lynch, Kevin. *The Image of the City.* Cambridge, MA: MIT Press, 1960.

———. *Managing the Sense of a Region.* Cambridge, MA: MIT Press, 1976.

———. *Good City Form.* Cambridge, MA: MIT Press, 1981.

Macaulay, David. *City: A Story of Roman Planning and Construction.* Boston: Houghton, Mifflin, 1974.

Macdonald, Elizabeth. "Street-Facing Dwelling Units and Livability: The Impacts of Emerging Building Types in Vancouver's New High-

Density Residential Neighborhoods." *Journal of Urban Design* 10, no. 1 (February 2005): 13–38.

Marshall, Richard. "The Elusiveness of Urban Design: The Perpetual Problems of Definition and Role," *Harvard Design Magazine* (Spring/Summer 2006): 21–32.

Mawson, Thomas H. *Calgary: A Preliminary Scheme for Controlling the Economic Growth of the City Confidential Appendix to the Report on the Preliminary Town Planning Scheme for Calgary*. City of Calgary, 1914.

Mays, John Bentley. "Imagine." *International Architecture and Design*, Winter 2011, 40–42.

McHarg, Ian. *Design with Nature*. Garden City, NY: Natural City Press, 1969.

Metro Vancouver. *Metro Vancouver Draft Regional Growth Strategy*. Burnaby, BC, 2009.

Morris, A. E. J. *History of Urban Form*. New York: John Wiley, 1979.

Mumford, Lewis. *The City in History: Its Origins, Its Transformations, and Its Prospects*. New York: Harcourt, Brace & World, 1961.

Nelessen, Anton C. *Visions for a New American Dream: Process, Principles, and an Ordinance to Plan and Design Small Communities*. Chicago: American Planning Association, 1994.

Newman, Oscar. *Defensible Space: Crime Prevention through Urban Design*. New York: Macmillan, 1973.

Newman, Peter, and Jefferey Kenworthy. *Sustainability and Cities: Overcoming Automobile Dependence*. Washington, DC: Island Press, 1999.

O'Neill, David. *The Smart Growth Tool Kit: Community Profiles and Case Studies to Advance Smart Growth Practices*. Washington, DC: Urban Land Institute, 2000.

Orr, David W. *The Last Refuge: Patriotism, Politics, and the Environment in the Age of Terror*. Washington, DC: Island Press, 2004.

Petit, Jack, Debra Bassert, and Cheryl Kollin. *Building Greener Neighborhoods: Trees as Part of the Plan*. Washington, DC: Home Builder Press, 1995.

Punter, John. *The Vancouver Achievement: Urban Planning and Design.* Vancouver, BC: UBC Press, 2003.

Rees, William, and Mark Roseland. "Sustainable Communities: Planning for the 21st Century." In *Sustainable Development and the Future of Cities*, edited by Bernd Hamm and Pandurang K. Muttagi, UNESCO-Most Publication. Oxford & IBH Publishing.

Rees, William, and Mathis Wackernagel. *Our Ecological Footprint.* Gabriola Island, BC: New Society Publishers, 1996.

Rocky Mountain Institute. *Green Development: Integrating Ecology and Real Estate.* New York: John Wiley & Sons, 1998.

Roseland, Mark. *Toward Sustainable Communities: Resources for Citizens and Their Governments.* Gabriola Island, BC: New Society Publishers, 2005.

Rowe, Colin, and Fred Koetter. *Collage City.* Cambridge, MA: MIT Press, 1980.

Rudofsky, Bernard. *Streets for People: A Primer for Americans.* New York: Van Nostrand Reinhold, 1982.

Rybczynski, Witold. *City Life.* Toronto: HarperCollins, 1995.

———. *Last Harvest: How a Cornfield Became New Daleville.* New York: Scribner, 2007.

Rypkema, Donovan D. *The Economics of Historic Preservation: A Community Leader's Guide.* Washington, DC: National Trust for Historic Preservation, 1994.

Schumacher, E. F. *Small Is Beautiful.* London: Sphere Books, 1974.

Shirvani, Hamid. *The Urban Design Process.* New York: Van Nostrand Reinhold, 1985.

Sitte, Camillo. *City Planning According to Artistic Principles.* Vienna: Verlag Carl Graeser, 1889. Complete translation in G. R. Collins, C. C. Collins, and Camillo Sitte, *The Birth of Modern City Planning* (New York: Rizolli International Publications, 1986).

Soja, Edward W. "Designing the Postmetropolis." *Harvard Design Magazine* (Harvard University Graduate School of Design), Fall 2006/Winter 2007, 43–49.

Spirn, Anne Whiston. *The Granite Garden: Urban Nature and Human Design.* New York: Basic Books, 1984.

Stokes, Samuel. *Saving America's Countryside: A Guide to Rural Conservation*. Baltimore, MD: Johns Hopkins University Press, 1989.

Trancik, Roger. *Finding Lost Space: Theories of Urban Design*. New York: Van Nostrand Reinhold, 1986.

TransLink. *Metro Vancouver TransLink Management Plan*. 2010.

Unwin, Raymond. *Town Planning in Practice*. London: T. Fisher Unwin, 1909. Reissued by Princeton Architectural Press, 1994.

Urban Design Associates. *The Urban Design Handbook: Techniques and Working Methods*. New York: W. W. Norton & Company, 2003.

Urban Landscape Task Force. *Greenways—Publicways*. Vancouver, BC: City of Vancouver, 1991.

Value in Urban Design. London: Commission for Architecture and the Built Environment; Department of Environment, Transport and the Regions, 2001.

Vitruvius. *The Ten Books of Architecture*. Cambridge, MA: Harvard University Press, 1914.

Von Hausen, Michael A. *Midtown: An Urban Design Strategy for Midtown Calgary*. Calgary: City of Calgary, 2004.

Von Hausen, Michael A. *Real Estate Economics in Urban Design: The Role of Civic Economics in Place-Making*. Vancouver, BC: Simon Fraser University, 2004.

———. *100 Timeless Urban Design Principles*. Vancouver, BC: Simon Fraser University, 2008.

Whyte, William. *Cluster Development*. New York: American Conservation Association, 1964.

———. *The Last Landscape*. Garden City, NY: Anchor Books, 1968.

———. *City: Rediscovering the Center*. New York: Doubleday, 1988.

World Commission on Environment and Development (WCED). *Our Common Future*. New York: Oxford University Press, 1987.

Wynn, Graeme, and Timothy Oke. *Vancouver and Its Region*. Vancouver, BC: UBC Press, 1992.

ONLINE RESOURCES

Canada Lands Company
www.clc.ca

Congress for the New Urbanism
www.cnu.org

Green Streets program, Vancouver, British Columbia
https://vancouver.ca/engsvcs/streets/greenstreets/

International Centre for Sustainable Cities
http://sustainablecities.net/

National Gallery of Canada
www.gallery.ca

Ocean West
www.oceanwest.com

Prince's Foundation for Building Community
www.princes-foundation.org

Project for Public Spaces
www.pps.org

Russian Housing Development Foundation
http://www.fondrgs.ru/en/

Sightline Institute
www.sightline.org

Talk Green Vancouver
www.talkgreenvancouver.ca

Trans Canada Trail
http://tctrail.ca

US Green Building Council
www.usgbc.org

GLOSSARY

Affordable housing. Accessible, adequate housing available at a cost that does not compromise the attainment and satisfaction of an individual's other basic needs. Occupant needs can be cost-effectively met by quality design if identified early in the process. Affordable housing in a general sense can be partially satisfied by providing a diversity of housing types and tenures. In the strict sense of the word, affordable housing can be defined as not exceeding 30 percent of the household income (Canada Mortgage and Housing Corporation).

Area Redevelopment Plan (ARP). An Area Redevelopment Plan in Alberta is a planning document, adopted as a bylaw by city council, that sets out comprehensive land use policies and other proposals that help guide the future of communities or a designated area. An ARP supplements the Land Use Bylaw by giving a local policy context and specific land use and development guidelines on which the development authority can base its judgments when rendering decisions on land use and development applications.

Built form. Buildings and structures that represent the three-dimensional man-made components of urban design.

Classicism. Classicists believe the grandeur of urban design is understood through monumental architectural expression as placement of objects in space and their formal interrelationships (e.g., Pope Sixtus V in the 1500s, who emphasized the importance of landmark obelisks and building positions).

Cluster development. A rural development concept that groups houses or buildings together to conserve open space and natural resources.

Coach house. A self-contained dwelling unit located by the back lane, normally above a garage or carport and not to exceed 645 square feet (60 m²).

Community. A group of people living in a particular locality who share government and often have a common cultural and historical heritage. Normally, a community can consist of several smaller neighborhoods and represent a sector of the city or larger community.

Concept. A general notion or idea that creates the basis for further detailed design.

Connections. The linkages within the community that bring together and move pedestrians, bicycles, vehicles, etc., from one area to another.

Council. The governing body of the city or municipality.

Density. The number of dwelling units on a site expressed in dwelling units per acre or units per hectare. Density can also be expressed by floor area ratio (FAR) or in some jurisdictions floor space ratio (FSR). FAR means the quotient of the gross floor area of a building divided by the gross site area. FAR is one of the ways to control the size or density of a building in relation to the size of the parcel of land it occupies. See the examples below. The building may also be regulated by building setbacks (i.e., front yard, side yard, and rear yard), building height, site or lot coverage or landscaping, parking, etc., depending on different land use districts. *See also Floor area ratio.*

FAR demonstration: A lot area of 100 by 100 feet has a gross site area of 10,000 square feet (100 x 100). Development potential based on FAR:

FAR 1 = 10,000 sq. ft x 1 = 10,000 sq. ft of gross floor area

FAR 2 = 10,000 sq. ft x 2 = 20,000 sq. ft of gross floor area

FAR 3 = 10,000 sq. ft x 3 = 30,000 sq. ft of gross floor area

Design charrette. An intensive series of meetings, workshops, and presentations with multiple stakeholders and experts to advance innovative ideas.

Development authority. The development officer or other body who approves development applications.

Development officer. An officer of the municipality who is charged with the responsibility of administering the Land Use Bylaw and deciding upon applications for development permits.

Development permit. A document authorizing a development, issued by a development officer pursuant to the Land Use Bylaw (Zoning Bylaw) or any previous bylaw or other legislation authorizing development within the city, and which includes the plans and conditions of approval.

Direct control or comprehensive development zone (CDZ). A land use area that requires additional consideration and sensitivity to the future use and development of land or buildings within this area.

District. An area identified by a distinguishing feature such as land use, heritage, cultural, and/or any other significant characteristic.

Ecological empiricism. Ecological empiricists emphasize the importance of human behavior and its interaction with the architectural and natural world in the form of functional descriptions, explained in terms of understanding as a measured response (e.g., Frederick Law Olmsted, in his classic Central Park design in New York City and Chicago World Exposition-site planning, created a setting for interaction of humans with nature).

Enhancement. The augmentation of an area, street, or open space in quality, value, beauty, or effectiveness.

Floor area ratio (FAR) or floor space ratio (FSR). The quotient of the gross floor area of a building divided by the gross site area. FAR is the ratio of the building to the lot area. For example, if the building areas cover 100 percent of the site with one floor, that equals 1.0 FAR. Alternatively, if the building area covers half the site with two floors, it is still 1.0 FAR. The calculation is total square feet (m²) of building (area of building) divided by the area of the site. In some jurisdictions FAR is referred to as floor space ratio (FSR). *See also Density.*

Gateway. An urban design feature or area that provides visual identification, access, direction, and/or celebration of the community for those entering.

Greenfrastructure. A description of infrastructure elements that can be designed where possible to mimic natural systems such as rainwater, natural planting, waste water, and potable water systems.

Heritage Overlay District. The Downtown Heritage Overlay District is intended to create a specific area that recognizes the importance of significant buildings and landscapes that should be further considered for conservation, enhancement, and recognition within an area. The extent of conservation, enhancement, and recognition will be determined by further regulations and design guidelines with a specific plan, as well as further work in identifying the specific significance of individual buildings and landscapes.

Landmark. A building or structure, such as a bridge, memorial, or public art, and/or landscape that has a special historical, architectural, or cultural significance.

Landscaping (soft and hard). The modification and enhancement of a site through the use of any or all of the following elements: vegetation such as trees, shrubs, hedges, grass, and ground cover (soft landscaping); nonvegetative material such as brick, stone, concrete, tile, wood, or other material (hard landscaping); architectural elements consisting of sculptures and the like.

Land Use Bylaw (Zoning Bylaw). This bylaw establishes procedures to process and decide upon land use amendment and development applications and divides the city into land use districts or zones. It sets out the rules that affect how each piece of land in the city may be used and developed. It also includes the actual zoning maps.

Land Use District (Zone). An area of the city designated for particular uses contained in the Land Use Bylaw. For example, C-4 is the primary Land Use District in an area that has an emphasis on commercial uses.

Legal suite. A self-contained unit in a single dwelling that has a separate entrance and parking in the back lane only.

Mass/massing. The arrangement of the bulk of a building on a site and its visual impact in relation to adjacent buildings.

Mixed-use development. The development of land, a building, or a structure with two or more different uses in a compact form, such as residential, office, and retail.

Mode. A method of travel. Examples include walking, cycling, transit, and vehicular.

Modernist rationalism. Modern rationalists view the world from simply a technocratic and object base, extending that (rational) thinking into architectural form. Its meaning can be open to interpretation based on context (e.g., Le Corbusier, 1920s—the city as a tool).

Multidwelling (family) residential. These land use areas are intended to serve the community by providing intensification of residential to increase populations that support amenities and transportation modes. Multidwelling areas shall be sensitively integrated and designed. Where policy directs, multidwelling residential may be designed in conjunction with other uses, such as commercial.

Neighborhood. An area that is primarily residential and/or primarily residential or mixed use. Each neighborhood is planned to be primarily residential with considerations for supporting land uses, movement systems, public realm and design, and amenities that would achieve complete and integrated neighborhoods.

Neighborhood node. A place within a neighborhood at which an activity or complex of activities takes place to meet local needs and foster a "sense of place" or unique identity for the neighborhood. Components of the neighborhood node may include the basic needs of open spaces, grocery stores, health and community association facilities, childcare and seniors amenities, and transit.

Net community gain. The community or neighborhood is better off after development than before development. This difference should be measured by the increase in community services, safety, traffic, noise, real estate values, and other values that can determine the extent of the improvements to the quality of life.

New Urbanism. A movement that promotes the restoration of existing urban centers and towns within coherent metropolitan regions, the reconfiguration of sprawling suburbs into communities of real neighborhoods and diverse districts, the conservation of natural resources, and the preservation of our built legacy. The movement is based on traditional neighborhood design of the early twentieth century.

Open space. An area or place that is open and accessible to all citizens, regardless of gender, race, ethnicity, age, or socioeconomic level. Also refers to the public realm (streets, sidewalks, etc.), parks, urban plazas, and so on.

Pedestrian-oriented or pedestrian-friendly. An environment designed to make movement (on foot or by wheelchair) attractive and comfortable for various ages and abilities (i.e., visually and hearing-impaired, mobility-impaired, developmentally challenged, situationally impaired). Considerations include separation of pedestrian and vehicular circulation, building scale and street walls, street furniture, clear directional and informational signage, safety, visibility, shade, lighting, surface materials, trees, sidewalk width, prevailing wind direction (canopies), intersection treatment, curb cuts, ramps, and landscaping.

Parking courts. A variation of a parking lot that is divided into smaller units, well landscaped, and designed to be pedestrian-friendly with walkways, sitting areas, lighting, and shelter.

Pedestrian scale/human scale. The scale (height or proportions) and comfort level that the street level and lower stories of a building provide for the pedestrian as they walk alongside the building(s).

Phenomenological contextualism. Phenomenological contextualists carefully observe and interpret what is in the urban environment, which in turn translates to drawings, illustrations, and descriptions of objects within a context of other objects. In essence, this is a thoughtful reflection on observations (e.g., Gordon Cullen, 1961—drawings of townscape in England).

Promenade. A formally designed wide pedestrian-priority walkway that includes urban features (e.g., benches, garbage receptacles, pedestrian-scale lighting)

Public realm. The area of space in the urban environment that is between the built form. The public realm consists of three different domains: public domain (all publicly owned streets, sidewalks, rights-of-way, parks, and other publicly accessible open spaces, and public and civic buildings and facilities); semiprivate domain (the space between a building facade and a public sidewalk, as well as any private spaces that may be accessible to the public, such as enclosed atriums or gallerias, etc.; semiprivate space ties together the public realm connections— streets, sidewalks, etc.—and built form in a comprehensive and connected public realm); and private domain (private space or buildings that are visually incorporated into the public realm and allow(s) for limited or no physical access to the public).

Quality. Character with respect to fineness or grade of excellence.

Redevelopment. Rebuilding of an urban residential, commercial, or other land use area that is in decline or in need of a new vision and policy direction.

Setback. An area measured as a distance from a public right-of-way or private lot line, restricting building development in this area.

Shall. Where "shall" is used in a policy, the policy is considered mandatory. However, where actual quantities or numerical standards are contained within a mandatory policy (for example, density policies), the quantities and standards may be deviated from provided that the deviation is necessary to address unique circumstances that will otherwise render compliance impractical or impossible, and the intent of the policy is still achieved.

Should. Where "should" is used in a policy, the intent is that the policy is to be complied with. However, the policy may be deviated from in a specific situation where the deviation is necessary to address unique circumstances that will otherwise render compliance impractical or impossible or to allow an acceptable alternative means to achieve the intent of the policy.

Sidewalk. Walkway principally used for pedestrians and located to the side of a thoroughfare within a road right-of-way.

Single-dwelling residential. Primarily single-dwelling areas. These areas are intended to serve the traditional single-family dwelling needs of the community and city while providing an opportunity for sensitively integrated infill development. It is the intent of these areas to support intensification for the purposes of enhancing the single-dwelling areas while not impacting the quality of a primarily single-dwelling residential area.

Smart Growth. Land use, development practices, and the efficient use of tax dollars to enhance the quality of life, preserve the natural environment, save money over time by limiting costly urban sprawl, and create more livable and vibrant neighborhoods.

Social utopianism. Social utopians explore ideal living environments from a social organization perspective, seeking a better quality of life for all. This movement was particularly evident in the United Kingdom during the industrialized 1800s, when living conditions created health and social problems (e.g., Ebenezer Howard, Garden City movement, Welwyn Garden City and Letchworth, United Kingdom, 1898 to 1908).

Streetscape. All the elements that make up the physical environment of a street and define its character, including paving, trees, lighting, building type and style, setbacks, pedestrian amenities, and street furniture.

Suburban retrofit. An emerging trend in urban design that redevelops existing suburban development that is aging, can infill additional density, and incorporate various other land uses.

Sustainable development. Land development that aims to meet human needs while conserving the environment so that these needs can be met not only in the present but also in the future. The three areas of sustainable development are environmental sustainability, economic sustainability, and social sustainability, together representing a more holistic approach.

Traffic calming. The combination of mainly physical measures that reduce the negative effects of motor vehicle use, alter driver behavior, and improve conditions for nonmotorized street users. Typical devices include street narrowing, traffic circles, curb extensions (bulges), diverters, and speed bumps.

Trails. Pathways and sidewalks designated for pedestrian and bicyclists that are generally for recreation purposes.

Transfer of Development Credits (TDC). A tool to retain valued land in its current state that enables the permitted density (units per acre/ha) of the entire parcel to be transferred to a smaller portion to conserve farmland, natural features, and wildlife habitat. Called Transfer of Development Rights (TDR) in Canada.

Transit. All components of providing transit to residents, workers, and tourists (i.e., type of transit, routes, schedules, etc.).

Transit oriented development (TOD). A classification of higher-density mixed used development that is located within walking distance of high volume rapid transit stops.

Typological empiricism. Typological empiricists classify building forms, open space, parks, and streets into a series of types based on uniform characteristics (e.g., formal geometry, elements, and measurement, reflected in the work of Christopher Alexander from 1975 to 1990—pattern language—and more literally that of Andrés Duany et al.—New Urbanism).

Urban design. The process by which cities, towns, and villages are planned, designed, and built.

Urban edges. Areas that have the potential for urban development versus a natural state. Such development might be promenades, plazas, commercial uses, etc.

Wayfaring. Traveling, especially by foot, and the graphic information that provides direction, orientation, and interpretation of place for such a journey.

Yard. That portion of a site that is not covered by a building.

DEVELOPMENT PLANNING AND URBAN DESIGN SERIES

Other publications available in this series by Michael von Hausen include the following:

Eco-Plan: Community Ecological Planning and Sustainable Design. Simon Fraser University, Vancouver, 2011.

100 Timeless Urban Design Principles. Simon Fraser University, Vancouver, 2008.

Public Process Playbook (coauthored with Sylvia Holland). Simon Fraser University, Vancouver, 2007.

Real Estate Economics in Urban Design: The Role of Civic Economics in Place-Making. Simon Fraser University, Vancouver, 2004.

Urban Design and Planning Graphics Resource Book: Effective Visual Communications for Informed Decision-Making. Simon Fraser University, Vancouver, 2004.

Leading Edges: Alternative Development Standards in British Columbia Municipalities. Real Estate Foundation of British Columbia, Vancouver, 2002.

These publications are available through

Michael A. von Hausen MCIP, CSLA, MLAUD, LEED'AP
President, MVH Urban Planning & Design Inc.
Telephone: (604) 536-3990; Fax: (604) 536-3995
E-mail: vhausen@telus.net / Website: www.mvhinc.com

The goal of these publications is to provide timely, affordable, and accessible information to advance sustainable and smart urban design, as well as sensitive and efficient land development planning.

ABOUT THE AUTHOR

Michael von Hausen is president of MVH Urban Planning & Design Inc., an international consulting firm that has received numerous local, national, and international awards for innovative planning and design work. The firm practices urban design and development planning in Canada, the United States, Russia, China, and Mexico. Michael has represented Canada on behalf of the Canada Mortgage and Housing Corporation on missions to China and Russia, providing expertise in sustainable urban development. He is a registered professional planner, landscape architect, and LEED-accredited professional. He completed his undergraduate degree at the University of Guelph in landscape architecture (honors) and his master's degree in urban design at Harvard University with a specialty in real estate development.

Michael is adjunct professor in the Urban Studies Program at Simon Fraser University. He is also chief instructor and curriculum coordinator for the award-winning Urban Design Certificate Program in the City Program at Simon Fraser University. He teaches across Canada in Vancouver, Calgary, Edmonton, and Ottawa. Michael has also taught at the University of British Columbia and University of Colorado. In addition, he facilitates the four courses of the School of Development for the Urban Development Institute in Vancouver, British Columbia. He was recognized as an honored member of the Heritage Register of Who's Who for Executives and Professionals in 2012.

He can be reached at vhausen@telus.net, or view his website at www.mvhinc.com.

SUBJECT INDEX

C

US Green Building Council (USGBC), 20, 265
Utilities, 101

V

Vana, Peter, 372
Vancouver, British Columbia, 212–13, 215
   challenge of sustainability in, 430–31
   CityPlan, 423–24
   citywide plans for, 416–22
   design guidelines, special policies, and principles in, 424–27
   emergence of the streetcar city, 415–16
   financial growth in, 429–30
   green legacy of, 413–15
   as livable city, 411–13
   municipalities in, 406–9
   success of development, 431–32
   sustainable regionalism in, 399–409
   sustainable urbanism in, 411–32
   zoning in, 424
Vancouver, Captain George, 399
Vancouver Greenways Plan (1997), 418–21
"Vancouverism," 412, 423
Vegetation, 101

W

Walking, 84
   paths, 291
Washington, DC, 36–37
Waste, reduction of, 208
Water, sustainability strategies for, 207
Wayfaring, 487
Weyerhaeuser Lands, Ucluelet, British Columbia, case study, 164–81
"White City," 38
Whyte, William H., 51, 55, 68
Wildlife, 84, 101
Willoughby Town Centre, 408
World Bank, 17
Wright, Frank Lloyd, 45, 67

Y

Yard, 487
Yorkson Neighbourhood Plan, 408

Z

Zero-energy housing, 266
Zones, 483
   land reserve and green, 403–4
Zoning
   CD-10, 298
   comprehensive development, 171
   single-use large-lot, 49
   in Vancouver, British Columbia, 424
Zoning Bylaws, 63, 126, 483

INDEX TO FIGURES AND TABLES

H

I

K

L

508

T

Z

22585249R00313

Printed in Great Britain
by Amazon